Dave Taylor

Sams **Teach Yourself**

Unix

in **24**
Hours

FIFTH EDITION

800 East 96th Street, Indianapolis, Indiana, 46240 USA

Sams Teach Yourself Unix in 24 Hours, Fifth Edtion

ISBN-13: 978-0-672-33730-7

ISBN-10: 0-672-33730-4

Library of Congress Control Number: 2015913255

Printed in the United States of America

First Printing October 2015

Trademarks

All terms mentioned in this book that are known to be trademarks or service marks have been appropriately capitalized. Sams Publishing cannot attest to the accuracy of this information. Use of a term in this book should not be regarded as affecting the validity of any trademark or service mark.

Warning and Disclaimer

Every effort has been made to make this book as complete and as accurate as possible, but no warranty or fitness is implied. The information provided is on an "as is" basis. The author and the publisher shall have neither liability nor responsibility to any person or entity with respect to any loss or damages arising from the information contained in this book.

Special Sales

For information about buying this title in bulk quantities, or for special sales opportunities (which may include electronic versions; custom cover designs; and content particular to your business, training goals, marketing focus, or branding interests), please contact our corporate sales department at corpsales@pearsoned.com or (800) 382-3419.

For government sales inquiries, please contact governmentsales@pearsoned.com.

For questions about sales outside the U.S., please contact international@pearsoned.com.

Acquisitions Editor
Mark Taber

Managing Editor
Sandra Schroeder

Senior Project Editor
Tonya Simpson

Copy Editor
Kitty Wilson

Indexer
WordWise Publishing Services, LLC

Proofreader
Laura Hernandez

Technical Editors
Siddhartha Singh
Brian Tiemann

Editorial Assistant
Vanessa Evans

Cover Designer
Mark Shirar

Compositor
codeMantra

Contents at a Glance

Table of Contents

About the Author

Dave Taylor is president of Intuitive Systems, LLC, a consulting firm focused on online communications and marketing strategies. Founder of four Internet startups, he has been involved with Unix and the Internet since 1980, having created the popular Elm Mail System and Embot mail autoresponder. A prolific author, he has been published more than 1,000 times, and his most recent books include the best-selling *Wicked Cool Shell Scripts* and *Learning Unix for Mac OS X*.

A popular columnist for *Linux Journal*, he also writes a tech Q&A column for the *Boulder Colorado Daily Camera* newspaper. Previously, he was a research scientist at HP Palo Alto Laboratories. He has contributed software to the 4.4 release of Berkeley Unix (BSD), and his programs are found in all versions of Linux and other popular Unix variants.

Dave has a bachelor's degree in computer science (University of California at San Diego), a master's degree in educational computing (Purdue University), and an MBA (University of Baltimore), and he is a top-rated public speaker who frequently offers workshops on online marketing, blogging, and various technical topics. His official home page on the Web is http://www.DaveTaylorOnline.com, and his email address is d1taylor@gmail.com.

Dave also maintains three weblogs online, Ask Dave Taylor (at www.askdavetaylor.com), where he fields questions from readers on a wide variety of topics; GoFatherhood (at www.GoFatherhood.com), where he talks about the challenges and joys of parenting; and Dave On Film (www.DaveOnFilm.com), where he shares his reviews of the latest movies. You're invited to get involved at all three!

Dedication

To the lights of my life: Ashley, Gareth, and Kiana.

Acknowledgments

However you slice it, you can't write a book locked in a cave (even if there's a high-speed Internet connection and fancy computer therein), and this book has evolved over many, many years, starting its life as an *Interactive Unix* tutorial I was writing for Sun Microsystems. In the interim, a number of people have added their spices to the stew, most notably my co-author for the first and second editions of *Teach Yourself Unix in 24 Hours*, James C. Armstrong, Jr.

In this new fifth edition, I've been delighted by the cooperative and talented team at Sams Publishing, again, and would like to specifically thank Mark Taber and Tonya Simpson, and my tech editors Brian Tiemann and Siddhartha Singh for all their ideas and commentary on how to make this book really superb. Any technical errors remaining are my own responsibility.

Finally, I would like to acknowledge and thank my kids for letting me focus on updating this book, chapter by chapter, even when there were games and other activities that could have proven more fun. I wouldn't trade them in, even for a 1THz PC! :-)

We Want to Hear from You!

As the reader of this book, *you* are our most important critic and commentator. We value your opinion and want to know what we're doing right, what we could do better, what areas you'd like to see us publish in, and any other words of wisdom you're willing to pass our way.

We welcome your comments. You can email or write to let us know what you did or didn't like about this book—as well as what we can do to make our books better.

Please note that we cannot help you with technical problems related to the topic of this book.

When you write, please be sure to include this book's title and author as well as your name and email address. We will carefully review your comments and share them with the author and editors who worked on the book.

Email: feedback@sampublishing.com

Mail: Sams Publishing
800 East 96th Street
Indianapolis, IN 46240 USA

Reader Services

Visit our website and register this book at informit.com/register for convenient access to any updates, downloads, or errata that might be available for this book.

Introduction

Welcome to the fifth edition of *Sams Teach Yourself Unix in 24 Hours!* This book has been designed to be helpful as a guide as well as a tutorial for both beginning users and those with previous Unix or Linux experience. The reader of this book is assumed to be intelligent, but no familiarity with Unix is expected or required.

Does Each Chapter Take an Hour?

You can learn the concepts in each of the 24 lessons in one hour. If you want to experiment with what you learn in each lesson, you might take longer than an hour. However, all the concepts presented here are straightforward. If you are familiar with Windows applications or the Macintosh, you will be able to progress more quickly through the lessons.

What if I Take Longer Than 24 Hours?

Since the publication of the first edition of this book, I've received a considerable amount of praise and positive feedback, but the one message that has always been a surprise is "I finished your book, but it took me a lot longer than 24 hours." Now you can read here, directly from the author: That's okay! Take your time and make sure you try everything as you go along. Learning and remembering are more important than speed. And if you do finish it all in 24 hours, let me know!

How to Use This Book

This book is designed to teach you topics in one-hour lessons. All the books in the *Sams Teach Yourself* series enable you to start working and become productive with a topic as quickly as possible. This book will do that for you!

Each hour, or lesson, starts with an overview of the topic to inform you of what to expect in that lesson. The overview helps you determine the nature of the lesson and whether the lesson is relevant to your needs.

Main Section

Each lesson has a main section that discusses the lesson topic in a clear, concise manner by breaking the topic down into logical components and explaining each component clearly.

Interspersed throughout each lesson are special elements, called tips, notes, and cautions, which provide additional information.

NOTE

Notes are designed to clarify the concept that is being discussed or elaborate on the subject. If you are comfortable with your understanding of the subject, you can bypass them without danger.

TIP

Tips inform you of tricks or elements that are easily missed by most computer users. You can skip them, but often tips show you an easier way to do a task.

CAUTION

A caution deserves at least as much attention as a tip because cautions point out problematic elements of the topic being discussed. Ignoring the information contained in a caution could have adverse effects on the task at hand. These are the most important special elements in this book.

Tasks

This book offers another special element called tasks. These step-by-step exercises are designed to walk you quickly through the most important skills you can learn in Unix.

Workshops

The Workshop section at the end of each lesson provides lists of key terms and exercises that reinforce concepts you learned in the lesson and help you apply them in new situations. You can skip the Workshop section, but we recommend that you go through the exercises to see how the concepts can be applied to other common tasks. The key terms are also compiled in one alphabetized list in the Glossary at the end of the book.

Goals for This Hour

In the first hour, you will learn

▶ The history of Unix
▶ Why it's called Unix
▶ What multiuser systems are all about
▶ The difference between Unix and other operating systems
▶ About command-line interpreters and how users interact with Unix
▶ How to use man pages, Unix's online reference material
▶ Other ways to find help in Unix

Welcome to *Sams Teach Yourself Unix in 24 Hours*, Fifth Edition! This hour starts you toward becoming a Unix (or, shhh, Linux) expert. Our goal for the first hour is to introduce you to some history of the operating system and teach you where to find help online.

What Is Unix?

Unix is a computer operating system, a control program that works with users to run programs, manage resources, and communicate with other computer systems. Several people can use a Unix computer at the same time; hence Unix is called a *multiuser system*. Any of these users can also run multiple programs at the same time; hence Unix is called *multitasking*. Because Unix is such a pastiche—a patchwork of development—it's a lot more than just an operating system. Unix has more than 500 individual commands. These range from simple utilities for viewing or copying files to the quite complex: those used in high-speed networking, file-revision management, and software development.

Most notably, Unix is a multichoice system. As an example, Unix has three different primary command-line user interfaces (in Unix, the command-line user interface is called a *shell*): the Bash shell, the C shell, and the Korn shell. In addition, a number of graphical interfaces exist, too, including KDE, Unity, and Gnome. Often, soon after you learn to accomplish a task with a particular command, you discover a second or third way to do that task. This is simultaneously the greatest strength of Unix and a source of frustration for both new and longtime users.

Why are all these choices such a big deal? Think about why Microsoft Windows and Apple Macintosh interfaces are so easy to use: Both are designed to give the user *less* power. Both have dramatically fewer commands and precious little overlap in commands: You can't click a button and find out how many of your Windows files are over a certain size, and you can't drag a Mac file icon around to duplicate it in its own directory. The advantage to these interfaces is that, in either system, you can learn the one-and-only way to do a task and be confident that you're as sophisticated in doing that task as the next person is. It's easy. It's quick to learn. It's exactly how the experts do it, too.

Unix, by contrast, is much more like a spoken language, with commands acting as verbs, command options (which you'll learn about later in this lesson) acting as adjectives, file and directory names as nouns, and the more complex command sequences acting akin to sentences. How you do a specific task can, therefore, be completely different from how your Unix-expert friend does the same task. Worse, some specific commands in Unix have many different versions, partly because of the variations from different Unix vendors. (You've heard of these variations and vendors, I'll bet: Linux from Red Hat [and many others], Solaris from Oracle, System V Release 4 [pronounce that "system five release four" or, to sound like an ace, "ess-vee-are-four"], BSD [pronounced "bee-ess-dee"] Unix from the University of California at Berkeley, HP-UX from Hewlett-Packard, and AIX from International Business Machines, are some of the primary players. Each is a little different from the others.) Another contributor to the sprawl of modern Unix is the energy of the Unix programming community; a Unix user can decide to write a new version of a command to solve slightly different problems, thus many users spawn many versions of a command.

And then there's the complicated world of Linux. Originally, Linux was developed as a license-free alternative to Unix, but it has since very much taken on a life of its own across the inter-vening years and now accounts for most of the servers on the Internet, many of the systems developers use, and in some cases a splendid alternative operating system for laptop users. Fortunately for you, Linux has retained its Unix soul, and this book will also get you up to speed and comfortable with the command-line interface on Linux systems, too.

Given the multichoice nature of the Unix OS, I promise to teach you the most popular commands, and, if alternatives exist, I will teach you about those, too. The goal of this book is for you to learn Unix and to be able to work alongside longtime Unix folk as a peer, sharing your expertise with them and continuing to learn about the system and its commands from them and from other sources.

NOTE

I must admit that I too am guilty of re-creating various Unix commands, including those for an electronic mail system, a simple line-oriented editor, a text formatter, a programming language inter-preter, a calendar manager, and even slightly different versions of the file-listing command ls and the remove-files command rm. As a programmer, I found that trying to duplicate the functionality of a particular command or utility was a wonderful way to learn more about both Unix and programming.

A Brief History of Unix

To understand why the Unix operating system has so many commands and why it's still one of the premier multiuser, multitasking operating systems available, but also the most successful and the most powerful multichoice system for computers, you'll have to travel back in time. You'll need to learn where Unix was designed, the goals of the original programmers, and what has happened to Unix in the subsequent decades.

Unlike DOS, Windows, OS/2, Mac OS X, Linux, NT, VMS, and just about any other operating system, Unix was created by a couple of programmers as a fun project. It evolved through the efforts of hundreds of programmers, each of whom was exploring unique ideas of particular aspects of OS design and user interaction. In this regard, Unix is not like other operating systems, needless to say!

It all started back in the late 1960s, in a dark and stormy laboratory, deep in the recesses of the American Telephone and Telegraph (AT&T) corporate facility in New Jersey. Working with the Massachusetts Institute of Technology, AT&T Bell Labs was co-developing a massive, monolithic operating system called Multics. On the Bell Labs team were Ken Thompson, Dennis Ritchie, Brian Kernighan, and other members of the Computer Science Research Group who would prove to be key contributors to the new Unix operating system.

When 1969 rolled around, Bell Labs was becoming increasingly disillusioned with Multics, an overly slow and expensive system that ran on General Electric mainframe computers that themselves were expensive to run and rapidly becoming obsolete. The problem was that Thompson and the group really liked the capabilities that Multics offered, particularly the individual-user environment implemented within a multiple-user system.

In that same year, Thompson wrote a computer game called Space Travel, first on Multics and then on the GECOS (GE computer operating system). The game was a simulation of the movement of the major bodies of the solar system, with the player guiding a ship, observing the scenery, and attempting to land on the various planets and moons. The game wasn't much fun on the GE computer, however, because performance was jerky and irregular, and, more importantly, it cost almost $100 in computing time for each game.

In his quest to improve the game, Thompson found a little-used Digital Equipment Corporation PDP-7, and with some help from colleague Dennis Ritchie, he rewrote the game for the PDP-7. Development was done on the GE mainframe and hand-carried to the PDP-7 on paper tape.

After he'd explored some of the capabilities of the PDP-7, Thompson couldn't resist building onto the game, creating an underlying development and computing environment. This started with an implementation of an earlier file system he'd designed and then grew as Thompson added processes, simple file utilities (cp, mv), and a command interpreter that he called a *shell*. It wasn't until the following year that the newly created system acquired its name, Unix, which Brian Kernighan suggested as a pun on Multics.

The Thompson file system was built around the low-level concept of *i-nodes*, linked blocks of information that together compose the contents of a file or program. These i-nodes were kept in a list called the *i-list*, subdirectories, and special types of files that described devices and acted as the actual device driver for user interaction. What was missing in this earliest form of Unix were *pathnames*. No slash (/) was present, and subdirectories were referenced through a confusing combination of file links that proved too complex, causing users to stop using subdirectories. Another limitation in this early version was that directories couldn't be added while the system was running but had to be added to the preload configuration.

In 1970, Thompson's group requested and received a Digital PDP-11 system for the purpose of creating a system for editing and formatting text. It was such an early unit that the first disk did not arrive at Bell Labs until four months after the CPU showed up. The first important program on Unix was the text-formatting program roff, which—stay with me now—was inspired by Doug McIlroy's BCPL program on Multics, which in turn had been inspired by an earlier program called runoff on the CTSS operating system.

The initial customer was the Patent Department inside Bell Labs, a group that needed a system for preparing patent applications. The new "Unix" system was a dramatic success, and it didn't take long for other folks inside Bell Labs to begin clamoring for their own Unix computer systems.

The C Programming Language

Now that you've learned some Unix history, let's talk a bit about the C programming language, the programming language that is integral to the Unix system.

In 1969, the original Unix had a very low-level assembly language compiler available for writing programs; all the PDP-7 work was done in this primitive language. Just before the PDP-11 arrived, McIlroy ported a language called TMG to the PDP-7, which Thompson then tried to use to write a FORTRAN compiler. That didn't work, and instead he produced a language called B. Two years later, in 1971, Ritchie created the first version of a new programming language based on B, a language he called C. By 1973, the entire Unix system had been rewritten in C for portability and speed.

Today C continues to be a popular programming language, available for just about any computer (and just about any handheld device, game system, or telephone) you can name. Variations of C known as C++ and C# (pronounced "c-plus-plus" and "c-sharp," respectively) power much of the modern Windows and Mac OS X systems environments, too.

Unix Becomes Popular

In the 1970s, AT&T hadn't yet been split up into the many regional operating companies known today, and the company was prohibited from selling the new Unix system. Hoping for the best,

Bell Labs distributed Unix to colleges and universities for a nominal charge. These institutions also were happily buying the inexpensive and powerful PDP-11 computer systems—a perfect match. Before long, Unix was the research and software-development operating system of choice.

The Unix of today is not, however, the product of a couple of inspired programmers at Bell Labs. Many other organizations and institutions contributed significant additions to the system as it evolved from its early beginnings and grew into the monster it is today. Most important were the C shell, TCP/IP networking, vi editor, Berkeley Fast File System, and sendmail electronic mail–routing software from the Computer Science Research Group of the University of California at Berkeley. Also important were the early versions of UUCP and Usenet from the University of Maryland, University of Delaware, and Duke University. After dropping Multics development completely, MIT didn't come into the Unix picture until the early 1980s, when it developed the X Window System as part of its successful Athena project. Fifteen years and five releases later, X (more formally, X11R6) is the predominant windowing system standard on all Unix systems, and it is the basis of Gnome, KDE, Unity, and Open Desktop.

Gradually, large corporations have become directly involved with the evolutionary process, notably Hewlett-Packard, Sun Microsystems, and IBM. Smaller companies have started to get into the action, too, with Unix available from Apple for the Macintosh (it's the underpinning of Mac OS X) and Linux systems built upon the concepts of Unix from Red Hat, Debian, and many other vendors for PCs.

Today, Unix runs on all sizes of computers, from humble PC laptops to powerful desktop-visualization workstations, and even to supercomputers that require special cooling fluids to prevent them from burning up while working. It's a long way from Space Travel, a game that, sadly, isn't part of Unix anymore.

What's All This About Multiuser Systems?

Among the many *multi* words you learned earlier was one that directly concerns how you interact with the computer: multiuser. The goal of a multiuser system is for all users to feel as though they've been given their own personal computer, their own individual Unix system, although they actually are working within a large system. To accomplish this, each user is given an *account*—usually based on the person's last name or initials or another unique naming scheme—and a home directory, the default place where the user's files are saved. This leads to a bit of a puzzle: When you're working on the system, how does the system know that you're you? What's to stop someone else from masquerading as you, going into your files, prying into private letters, altering memos, or worse?

In the early days, anyone could walk up to your Macintosh or PC when you weren't around, flip the power switch, and pry, and you couldn't do much about it. For a computer sitting on your desk in your office, that's okay; the system is not a shared multiuser system, so verifying who you are when you turn on the computer isn't critical.

But Unix is designed for multiple users, so it is very important that the system can confirm your identity in a manner that precludes others from masquerading as you. As a result, all accounts have passwords associated with them—as with a PIN for a bank card, keep it a secret!—and when you use your password in combination with your account, the computer can be pretty sure that you are who you're claiming to be. For obvious reasons, when you're finished using the computer, you should always remember to exit your session, or, in effect, to turn off your virtual personal computer when you're done.

Next hour, you'll learn your first Unix commands. At the top of the list are commands to log in to the system, enter your password, and change your password to be memorable and highly secure.

Cracking Open the Shell

Another unusual feature of Unix systems, especially for those of you who come from either the Macintosh or Windows environments, is that Unix is primarily designed to be a command-line–based system rather than a more graphically based system. That's a mixed blessing. It makes Unix harder to learn, but the system is considerably more powerful than one that asks you to fiddle with a mouse to drag little pictures about on the screen. In Unix parlance, a command-line interpreter is called a shell, and you'll see that various shells are available, differing in both syntax and capabilities.

Graphical interfaces to Unix are built within the X Window System environment. Notable ones are KDE, OpenWindows, Gnome, and Unity. Even with the best of these, however, the command-line heart of Unix still shines through, and in my experience, it's impossible to use all the power that Unix offers without turning to a shell.

If you're used to writing letters to your friends and family or even just producing simple grocery lists, you won't have any problem with a command-line interface: It's a command program that you tell what to do. When you type specific instructions and press the Return key, the computer leaps into action and immediately performs whatever command you've specified, even if it's dangerous, such as the command sequence that requests the system to "remove all my files."

NOTE

Throughout this book, I refer to pressing the Return key, but your keyboard might have this key labeled as "Enter" or marked with a left-pointing, specially shaped arrow. These all mean the same thing.

In Windows, you might move a file from one folder to another by opening the folder, opening the destination folder, fiddling around for a while to be sure that you can see both folders onscreen at the same time, and then clicking and dragging the specific file from one place to the other. In Unix it's much easier: Typing the following simple command does the trick:

    mv folder1/file folder2

This command automatically also ensures that the file has the same name in the destination directory.

This might not seem like much of a boon, but imagine that you want to move all files with names that start with the word project or end with the suffix .c (C program files). This task could be quite tricky and could take a lot of patience with a graphical interface. Unix, however, makes it easy:

```
mv project* *.c folder2
```

Soon you will not only understand this command but also be able to compose your own examples!

Getting Help

Throughout this book, the focus is on the most important and valuable flags and options for the commands covered. That's all well and good, but how do you find out about the other alternatives that might actually work better for your use? That's where the Unix *man pages* come in. You will learn how to browse them to find the information desired.

Task 1.1: Man Pages, Unix Online Reference

It's not news to you that Unix is a very complex operating system, with hundreds of commands that can be combined to execute thousands of possible actions. Most commands have a considerable number of options, and all seem to have some subtlety or other that it's important to know. But how do you figure all this out? You need to look up commands in the Unix online documentation set. Containing purely reference materials, the Unix *man pages* (*man* is short for *manual*) cover every command available.

To search for a man page, enter man followed by the name of the command about which you seek additional information. Many sites also have a table of contents for the man pages (it's called a whatis database, for obscure historical reasons). You can use the all-important -k flag for keyword searches to find the name of a command if you know what it should do but you just can't remember what it's called. The -k option will give you a list of manual pages that refer to the keyword you specify.

A *flag* or *switch* is a command-line option, an option that changes the behavior of the command you're using. In this instance, man displays the man page for the specified command, but if you modify its behavior with the -k flag, it instead searches the command documentation database to identify which subsets relate to the keyword you've specified.

NOTE

A command performs a basic task, which can be modified by adding flags to the end of the command when you enter it on the command line. These flags are described in the man pages. For example, to use the -k flag for man, enter this:

    % man -k

NOTE

The command apropos is available on most Unix systems and is often just an alias to man -k. If it's not on your system, you can create it by adding the line alias apropos='man -k \!' to your .profile file.

The Unix man pages are organized into nine sections, as shown in Table 1.1. This table is organized for System V, but it generally holds true for Linux and Berkeley systems, too, with these few changes: BSD has I/O and special files in Section 4, administrative files in Section 5, and miscellaneous files in Section 7. Some BSD systems also split user commands into further categories: Section 1C for intersystem communications and Section 1G for commands used primarily for graphics and computer-aided design. Solaris, too, has its own unique layout, such as sections 9E, 9F, and 9S, which deal with device drivers, and a complete lack of Section 6 (games). On any Unix system, the command man man (get it? The manual for the manual) will give you the complete synopsis.

Man pages in different sections might have the same name, so you might need to specify in which section to find the page. In addition, sometimes you'll be looking for a user-level command and find a match in Section 2 or 3. Those aren't what you seek; they're specifically for Unix programmers, as you can see in the table.

TABLE 1.1   System V Unix Man Page Organization

Section	Category
1	User commands
1M	System maintenance commands
2	System calls
3	Library routines
4	Administrative files
5	Miscellaneous
6	Games
7	I/O and special files
8	Administrative commands

1. The `mkdir` man page is succinct and exemplary. Here's what you'll see when you enter the `man mkdir` command:

% man mkdir

```
MKDIR(1)                  FreeBSD General Commands Manual               MKDIR(1)

NAME
     mkdir - make directories

SYNOPSIS
     mkdir [-p] [-m mode] directory_name ...

DESCRIPTION
     Mkdir creates the directories named as operands, in the order specified,
     using mode rwxrwxrwx (0777) as modified by the current umask(2).

     The options are as follows:

     -m      Set the file permission bits of the final created directory to
             the specified mode.  The mode argument can be in any of the
             formats specified to the chmod(1) command.  If a symbolic mode is
             specified, the operation characters ``+'' and ``-'' are
             interpreted relative to an initial mode of ``a=rwx''.

     -p      Create intermediate directories as required.  If this option is
             not specified, the full path prefix of each operand must already
             exist.  Intermediate directories are created with permission bits
             of rwxrwxrwx (0777) as modified by the current umask, plus write
             and search permission for the owner.

     The user must have write permission in the parent directory.

DIAGNOSTICS
     The mkdir utility exits 0 on success, and >0 if an error occurs.

SEE ALSO
     rmdir(1)

STANDARDS
     The mkdir utility is expected to be IEEE Std1003.2 (``POSIX.2'')
     compatible.

HISTORY
     A mkdir command appeared in Version 1 AT&T UNIX.

BSD                                                                           1
%
```

NOTE

Notice in the example that in the first line, the command itself is in boldface type, but everything else is not bold. Throughout this book, whenever an example contains both user input and Unix output, the user input is bold so that you can easily spot what you are supposed to enter.

The very first line of the output tells me that it's found the `mkdir` command in Section 1 (user commands) of the man pages, with the middle phrase, `FreeBSD General Commands Manual`, indicating that I'm running on a version of Unix called FreeBSD. The `NAME` section always details the name of the command and a one-line summary of what it does. `SYNOPSIS` explains how to use the command, including all possible command flags and options.

`DESCRIPTION` is where all the meaningful information is, and it can run on for dozens of pages, explaining how complex commands such as `csh` or `vi` work. `SEE ALSO` suggests other commands that are related in some way. The Revision line at the bottom is different on each version of `man`, and it indicates the last time, presumably, that this document was revised.

2. The same man page from an Oracle Solaris workstation is quite different, as shown in Figure 1.1.

3. Not sure of a specific command? That's where `man -k` or its alias `apropos` comes in handy:

```
% man -k date | head -18
1. date(1) /usr/share/man/man1/date.1
date - write the date and time

2. gdate(1) /usr/share/man/man1/gdate.1
date - print or set the system date and time

3. strptime(3c) /usr/share/man/man3c/strptime.3c
strptime - date and time conversion

4. ftime(3c) /usr/share/man/man3c/ftime.3c
ftime - get date and time

5. clock(1t) /usr/share/man/man1t/clock.1t
clock - Obtain and manipulate dates and times

6. stime(2) /usr/share/man/man2/stime.2
stime - set system time and date
%
```

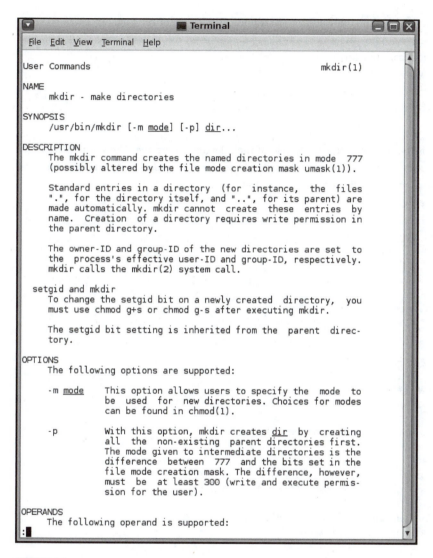

FIGURE 1.1
mkdir man page on an Oracle Solaris system.

See that | head -18? That limits the output of the man command to just the first 18 lines. Omit that, and you'll get a lot more information scrolling across your screen. We'll go far deeper into these multicommand sequences called *pipes* as we travel through the book!

4. To learn a succinct snippet of information about a Unix command, you can check to see whether your system has the whatis utility. You can even ask it to describe itself (a bit of a philosophical conundrum):

```
% whatis
whatis(1)  NAME  /usr/share/man/man1/whatis.1
whatis - display a one-line summary about a keyword
%
```

In fact, this is the line from the NAME field of the relevant man page. The whatis command is different from the apropos command because it considers only command names rather than all words in the command description line:

```
% whatis cd
No LSB modules are available.
Distributor ID:    Ubuntu
Description:      Ubuntu 15.04
Release:    15.04
Codename:    vivid
```

Now see what apropos does:

```
% apropos cd
1. cd(1t) /usr/share/man/man1t/cd.1t
cd - Change working directory

2. cd(1) /usr/share/man/man1/cd.1
cd, chdir, pushd, popd, dirs - change working directory

3. cdrw(1) /usr/share/man/man1/cdrw.1
cdrw - CD read and write

4. sound-juicer(1) /usr/share/man/man1/sound-juicer.1
sound-juicer, gnome-cd - GNOME CD ripper and player

5. cdio(7i) /usr/share/man/man7i/cdio.7i
cdio - CD-ROM control operations

6. eject(1) /usr/share/man/man1/eject.1
eject - eject media such as CD-ROM from drive

7. cdrecord(1) /usr/share/man/man1/cdrecord.1
cdrecord - record audio or data CD, DVD or BluRay

8. hsfs(7fs) /usr/share/man/man7fs/hsfs.7fs
hsfs - High Sierra & ISO 9660 CD-ROM file system

9. sd(7d) /usr/share/man/man7d/sd.7d
sd - SCSI disk and ATAPI/SCSI CD-ROM device driver
```

```
10. cdda2wav(1) /usr/share/man/man1/cdda2wav.1
cdda2wav - dumps CD audio data into sound files with extra data verification

11. brasero(1) /usr/share/man/man1/brasero.1
brasero - Simple and easy to use CD/DVD burning application for the Gnome
Desktop

12. rmmount(1m) /usr/share/man/man1m/rmmount.1m
rmmount - removable media mounter for CD-ROM, Jaz drive, and others
others %
```

5. One problem with man is that it really isn't too sophisticated. As you can see in the example in step 4, apropos (which, recall, is man -k) lists everything it encounters, whether it's intended for a programmer or a user. I don't care much about file formats, games, or miscellaneous commands when I'm looking for a command. I'll try this:

```
% alias apropos="man -k \!* | uniq | grep 1"
% apropos cd
1. cd(1t) /usr/share/man/man1t/cd.1t
2. cd(1) /usr/share/man/man1/cd.1
3. cdrw(1) /usr/share/man/man1/cdrw.1
4. sound-juicer(1) /usr/share/man/man1/sound-juicer.1
6. eject(1) /usr/share/man/man1/eject.1
7. cdrecord(1) /usr/share/man/man1/cdrecord.1
10. cdda2wav(1) /usr/share/man/man1/cdda2wav.1
11. brasero(1) /usr/share/man/man1/brasero.1
12. rmmount(1m) /usr/share/man/man1m/rmmount.1m
%
```

That's much better.

6. I'd like to look up one more command—sort—before I'm done here:

```
% man sort

SORT(1)                                                      SORT(1)


NAME
       sort - sort lines of text files

SYNOPSIS
       sort   [-cmus] [-t separator] [-o output-file] [-T tempdir]
       [-bdfiMnr] [+POS1 [-POS2]] [-k POS1[,POS2]] [file...]
       sort {--help,--version}

DESCRIPTION
       This manual page documents the GNU version of sort.   sort
       sorts,  merges,  or  compares all the lines from the given
       files, or the standard input if no  files  are  given.   A
```

```
file  name  of  `-' means standard input.  By default, sort
writes the results to the standard output.

sort has three modes of  operation:  sort  (the  default),
merge,  and  check  for sortedness.  The following options
change the operation mode:

-c    Check whether the given files are  already  sorted:
      if  they are not all sorted, print an error message
      and exit with a status of 1.

-m    Merge the given files by sorting them as  a  group.
      Each  input  file  should  already  be  individually
      sorted.  It always works to sort instead of  merge;
      merging  is  provided  because it is faster, in the
      case where it works.

A pair of lines is compared as follows: if any key  fields
have been specified, sort compares each pair of fields, in
the order specified on the command line, according to  the
associated  ordering  options, until a difference is found
or no fields are left.
--More--
```

On almost every system, the man command feeds output through a so-called pager program so that information won't scroll by faster than you can read it. You also can save the output of a man command to a file if you'd like to study the information in detail: man mkdir > mkdir.manpage. We'll talk more about file redirection a bit later in the book.

Notice in the sort man page that many options exist for the sort command (certainly more than discussed in this book). As you learn Unix, if you find areas about which you'd like more information, or if you need a capability that doesn't seem to be available, check the man pages. There just might be a flag for what you seek.

NOTE

You can obtain lots of valuable information by reading the introduction to each section of the man pages. Use man 1 intro to read the introduction to Section 1, for example.

If your version of man doesn't stop at the bottom of each page, you can remedy the situation by using alias man='man \!* | more'.

Unix was one of the very first operating systems to include online documentation. The man pages are an invaluable reference. Most of them are poorly written, unfortunately, and precious few include examples of actual usage. However, for quick reminders of flags and options, or as an easy way to find out the capabilities of a command, man is great. I encourage you to explore the man pages and perhaps even read the man page on the man command itself.

Task 1.2: Other Ways to Find Help in Unix

Reading the man pages is really the best way to learn about what's going on with Unix commands, but some alternatives also can prove helpful. Some systems have a `help` command. Many Unix utilities make information available with the `` `h ``, `-help`, or `-?` flag, too. Finally, one trick you can try is to feed a set of gibberish flags to a command, which sometimes generates an error and a helpful message reminding you of what possible options the command accepts.

1. At the University Tech Computing Center, the support team has installed a `help` command:

```
% help
Look in a printed manual, if you can, for general help. You should
➡ have someone show you some things and then read one of the tutorial papers
(e.g., UNIX for Beginners or An Introduction to the C Shell) to get
started. Printed manuals covering all aspects of Unix are on sale at the
bookstore.

Most of the material in the printed manuals is also available online
via "man" and similar commands; for instance:

apropos keyword - lists commands relevant to keyword
whatis filename - lists commands involving filename
man command - prints out the manual entry for a command
help command - prints out the pocket guide entry for a command
➡ are helpful; other basic commands are:
cat - display a file on the screen
date - print the date and time
du - summarize disk space usage
edit - text editor (beginner)
ex - text editor (intermediate)
finger - user information lookup program
learn - interactive self-paced tutorial on Unix
--More(40%)--
```

Your system might have something similar. However, be careful if you're running on an HP-UX system, as its `help` command isn't intended to enlighten shell users but to do something else entirely. Type `man help` to find out more.

2. Some versions of commands offer helpful output if you specify the `-h` flag:

```
% ls -h
usage: ls [ -acdfgilqrstu1ACLFR ] name ...
%
```

Then again, others don't:

```
% ls -h
Global.Software    Mail/      Src/      history.usenet.Z
Interactive.Unix   News/      bin/      testme
%
```

In that case, try `--help` and keep your fingers crossed.

A few commands offer lots of output when you use the `-h` flag:

```
% elm -h
Possible Starting Arguments for ELM program:
arg     Meaning
-a      Arrow - use the arrow pointer regardless
-c      Checkalias - check the given aliases only
-dn     Debug - set debug level to 'n'
-fx      Folder - read folder 'x' rather than incoming mailbox
-h      Help - give this list of options
-k      Keypad - enable HP 2622 terminal keyboard
-K      Keypad&softkeys - enable use of softkeys + "-k"
-m      Menu - Turn off menu, using more of the screen
-sx      Subject 'x' - for batchmailing
-V      Enable sendmail voyeur mode.
-v      Print out ELM version information.
-w      Supress warning messages...
-z      Zero - don't enter ELM if no mail is pending
%
```

Unfortunately, there isn't a command flag common to all Unix utilities that lists the possible command flags.

3. Sometimes you can obtain help from a program by incurring its wrath. You can specify a set of flags that are impossible, unavailable, or just plain puzzling. I always use `-xyz` because they're uncommon flags:

```
%  man -xyz
usage:      man [-] [-adFlprt] [-M path] [-T macro-package ] [ -s section ]
name ...
    man [-M path] [-s section] -k keyword ...
    man [-M path] -f file ...
    man [-M path] [-s section] -K keyword ...
$
```

For every command that does something marginally helpful, there are a half-dozen commands that give useless, and amusingly different, output for these flags:

```
$ bc -xyz
bc: illegal option -- x
usage: bc [ -c ] [ -l ] [ file ... ]
$ file -xyz
file: illegal option -- x
file: illegal option -- y
file: illegal option -- z
```

```
usage: file [-dh] [-M mfile] [-m mfile] [-f ffile] file ...
       file [-dh] [-M mfile] [-m mfile] -f ffile
       file -i [-h] [-f ffile] file ...
       file -i [-h] -f ffile
       file -c [-d] [-M mfile] [-m mfile]
$ grep -xyz
grep: illegal option -- x
grep: illegal option -- z
Usage: grep [-c|-l|-q] -bhinsvw pattern file . . .
$
%
```

You can't rely on programs being helpful about them, but you can rely on the man page being available for just about everything on the system.

As much as I'd like to tell you that a wide variety of useful and interesting information is available within Unix on the commands therein, in reality, Unix has man pages but precious little else. Furthermore, some commands installed locally might not even have man page entries, which leaves you to puzzle out how they work. If you encounter commands that are undocumented, I recommend that you ask your system administrator or vendor what's going on and why there's no further information on the program.

Summary

In this first hour, the goal was for you to learn a bit about Unix, where it came from, and how it differs from other operating systems that you might have used in the past. You also learned about the need for security on a multiuser system and how a password helps maintain that security, so that your files aren't easily read, altered, or removed by anyone but you.

You also learned what a command shell, or command-line interpreter, is all about, how it differs from graphically oriented interface systems such as Macintosh and Windows, and how it's not only easy to use but considerably more powerful than systems that have you drag and drop little pictures.

Finally, you learned about getting help on Unix. Although there aren't many options, you do have the manual pages available, as well as the command-line arguments and apropos.

Workshop

The Workshop summarizes the key terms you've learned and poses some questions about the topics presented in this lesson. It also provides you with a preview of what you will learn in the next hour.

Key Terms

account   This is the official one-word name by which the Unix system knows you. Mine is `taylor`.

arguments   Not any type of domestic dispute, arguments are the set of options, parameters, and filenames specified to Unix commands. When you use a command such as `vi test.c`, all words other than the command name itself (`vi`) are arguments to the program.

command   Each program in Unix is also known as a command: The two words are interchangeable.

i-node   The Unix file system is like a huge notebook full of sheets of information. Each file is like an index tab, indicating where the file starts in the notebook and how many sheets are used. The tabs are called i-nodes.

man page   Each standard Unix command comes with some basic online documentation that describes its function. This online documentation for a command is called a man page. Usually, the man page lists the command-line flags and some error conditions.

multitasking   A multitasking computer is one that can run more than one program, or task, at a time.

multiuser   Computers intended to have more than a single person working on them simultaneously are designed to support multiple users, hence the term *multiuser*. By contrast, personal computers are almost always single-user because someone else can't be running a program or editing a file while you are using the computer for your own work.

pathname   Unix is split into a wide variety of different directories and subdirectories, often across multiple hard disks and even multiple computers. So that the system needn't search laboriously through the entire mess each time you request a program, the directories you reference are stored as your search path, and the location of any specific command is known as its *pathname*.

shell   To interact with Unix, you type in commands to the command-line interpreter, which is known in Unix as the *shell*, or *command shell*. It's the underlying environment in which you work with the Unix system.

Exercises

Each hour concludes with a set of questions for you to contemplate. Here's a warning up front: Not every question has a definitive answer. After all, you are learning about a multichoice operating system!

   1. Name the three *multi* concepts that are at the heart of Unix's power.

2. Is Unix more like a grid of streets, letting you pick your route from point A to point B, or more like a directed highway with only one option? How does this compare with other systems you've used?

3. Systems that support multiple users always ask you to say who you are when you begin using the system. What's the most important thing to remember when you're finished using the system?

4. If you're used to graphical interfaces, try to think of a few tasks that you feel are more easily accomplished by moving icons than by typing commands. Write those tasks on a separate piece of paper, and in a few days, pull that paper out and see whether you still feel that way.

5. Think of a few instances in which you needed to give a person written instructions. Was that easier than giving spoken instructions or drawing a picture? Was it harder?

Preview of the Next Hour

In the next hour, you'll learn how to log in to the system at the login prompt and how to log out of the system. You'll learn how to use the `passwd` command to change your password, how to use the `id` command to find out who the computer thinks you are, and lots more!

Getting onto the System and Using the Command Line

Goals for This Hour

In this hour, you will learn

▶ How to log in to and log out of the system

▶ How to change your password with the `passwd` command

▶ About choosing a memorable and secure password

▶ How to find out who the computer thinks you are

▶ How to find out who else is on the system

▶ How to find out what everyone is doing on the system

▶ About checking the current date and time

In this second Unix lesson, it's time for you to log in to the system and try some commands. This hour focuses on learning the basics of interacting with your Unix machine.

This hour introduces many commands, so it's very important that you have a Unix system available on which you can work through all the examples. Most examples have been taken from a PC running Solaris 11, a variant of Unix System V Release 4, and have been double-checked on both a BSD-based system and a Mac OS X command line. Any variance between the three is noted. If you have a Unix system available, odds are good that it's based on either AT&T System V or Berkeley Unix.

Beginning Your Session

Before you can start interacting with the Unix command shell of your choice, you need to learn how to log in to your account. The good news is that it's easy! Let's have a look.

Task 2.1: Logging In to and Out of the System

Because Unix is a multiuser system, user authentication is always enforced: You always need to provide credentials (generally a username and a password) to the system so that it knows who you are. Some modern user-friendly flavors of Unix (such as Mac OS X) allow you to bypass this requirement by always booting into a single user's desktop session, but this is just a convenience feature; under the hood, all Unix flavors are the same, and all require that you authenticate yourself at some stage of the process.

Old-school hardware terminals do still exist, or you might choose to boot a Linux or FreeBSD box directly to the textual console; but if you're new to Unix, you'll most likely need an application known as a terminal to access the command line. Most graphical operating systems include one. I use the Terminal app included with Mac OS X (in the Utilities folder) whether I'm accessing my local system or just opening an environment in which to connect to a remote system via `ssh`.

TIP

Most Linux flavors have a prominently available terminal program for your use; on a Windows PC, your best bet is the freeware program PuTTY, available at http://www.putty.org.

If you need to actually log in, the first thing you'll see on the screen will look something like this:

```
GNU/Linux ado.aplonis.net 5:38pm on Tue, 8 Jul 2014
login:
```

The first line of this challenge prompt indicates what variant of Unix the system is running (GNU/Linux in this case), the hostname of the computer system, and the current time and date. The second line asks for your login, also known as your username or account name.

NOTE

If you connect to a Unix server via the network, using either `telnet` or `ssh`, you'll see the same login prompt, though I strongly recommend that you always use `ssh` for security reasons. If you use a terminal program within a graphical environment, you won't need to log in because you've already logged in to your GUI session.

1. Know your account name. It would be nice if computers could keep track of users by simply using full names so that I could enter `Dave Taylor` at the login prompt. Alas, like the Internal Revenue Service, the Department of Motor Vehicles, and many other agencies, Unix does not use names but instead assigns each user a unique identifier. This identifier, called an *account name*, has eight characters or fewer and is usually based on the user's first or last name, although it can be any combination of letters and numbers. I have two account names, or logins, on the systems I use: `taylor` and, on another machine where someone already had that account name, `d1taylor`.

2. Know your password. Perhaps your account name is on a piece of paper with your initial password, both assigned by the Unix system administrator. If you do not have this information, you need to track it down before you can go further. Some accounts might not have an initial password; in that case, you won't have to enter one the first time you log in

to the system. If that's the case, *create a password* for your own security. In a few minutes, you will learn how you can give yourself the password of your choice by using the Unix command `passwd`.

Note that a lot of systems are accessible only through the `ssh` function, and so a common way to connect to a modern system is to open up a local terminal app on your Mac or PC and type in something like:

```
$ ssh taylor@intuitive.com
```

where `taylor` is the account name and `intuitive.com` is the name of the remote host. If that's how you need to access your Unix system remotely, it's actually easier than using the login/password sequence; you just need to make extra sure that you type in everything exactly as prompted.

3. At the login prompt, enter your account name if needed:

```
login: taylor
Password:
```

Be particularly careful to use exactly what your administrator tells you to use (for example, the accounts `taylor`, `Taylor`, and `TAYLOR` are all different to Unix). After you've entered your account name, the system moves the cursor to the next line and prompts you for your password. If you're using the `ssh` sequence, then the prompt will include your account name, as shown here:

```
taylor@intuitive.com's password:
```

Either way, when you enter your password, the system won't echo it (that is, won't display it) on the screen. That's okay. Lack of an echo doesn't mean anything is broken; instead, this is a security measure to ensure that even if people are looking over your shoulder, they can't learn your secret password by watching your screen. Be certain to type your password correctly because you won't see what you've typed and have a chance to correct it.

NOTE

If you enter either your login or your password incorrectly, the system complains with an error message:

```
login: taylor
Password:
Login incorrect
login:
```

Most systems give you three or four attempts to get both your login and password correct, so try again. Don't forget to enter your account name at the login prompt each time, as required. Be careful, though: Too many failed login attempts, and you might lock out your account and have to contact the administrator for help.

4. After you've successfully entered your account name and password, you are shown some information about the system, some news for users, perhaps a fortune, and an indication of whether you have electronic mail. The specifics will vary, but here's an example of what I see when I log in to my account:

```
login: taylor
Password:
Last login: Thu Jul 7 17:00:23 on ttyAe
You have mail.
$
```

NOTE

The dollar sign prompt is Unix's way of telling you that it's ready for you to enter some commands. It is the equivalent of a soldier saluting and saying, "Ready for duty!" or an employee saying, "What shall I do now, boss?"

Your system might be configured so that you have a slightly different prompt here. The possibilities include a % for the C shell, your current location in the file system, the current time, the command-index number (which you'll learn about when you learn how to teach the Unix command-line interpreter to adapt to your work style rather than vice versa), and the name of the computer system itself. Here are some examples:

```
[/users/taylor] :
(mentor) 33 :
taylor@mentor %
```

Your prompt might not look exactly like any of these, but you know you're looking at a prompt because it's at the beginning of the line on which your cursor sits, and it reappears each time you've completed working with any Unix program. That's how you know the program has completed its task.

5. At this point, you're ready to enter your first Unix command, exit, to sign off from the computer system. Try it. On my system, entering exit shuts down all my programs and quits the terminal app. On other systems, it returns you to the login prompt. Many Unix systems offer a pithy quote as you leave, too.

```
% exit
He who hesitates is lost.
login:
```

NOTE

You might be able to end your session by pressing Ctrl-D. Some shells will catch this and prompt you to determine whether you want to end your session; others will exit. Ctrl-D is actually an end-of-file character; it may be different on your system.

---

6. If you have a direct connection to the computer because you're using a shared system in a computer center, library, or similar, odds are very good that logging out causes the system to prompt for another account name, enabling the next person to use the system. If you manually connected to the system via the Internet, you probably will see something more like the following example. After being disconnected from the remote system, you'll then be able to safely shut down your local computer:

```
% exit
Did you lose your keys again?

Connection to 154.23.11.140 closed.
```

NOTE

Unix is *case sensitive*, so the `exit` command is not the same as `EXIT`. If you enter a command all in uppercase, the system won't find any such program or command and instead will respond with the complaint `command not found`. Get in the habit of using all lowercase for commands and Unix input. Lowercase is the natural Unix style.

At this point, you've stepped through the toughest parts of getting started with Unix. You have an account, know the password, have logged in to the system, and have entered a simple command telling the computer what you want to do, and the computer has done it!

Task 2.2: Changing Passwords with `passwd`

Having logged in to a Unix system, you can clearly see that many differences exist between Unix and a PC or Macintosh personal computer. Certainly the style of interaction is different. With Unix command lines, the keyboard becomes the exclusive method of instructing the computer what to do, and the mouse sits idle. One of the greatest differences is that Unix is a multiuser system, as you learned in the preceding hour. As you learn more about Unix, you'll find that this characteristic has an impact on various tasks and commands. The next Unix command you'll learn about is one that exists because of the multiuser nature of Unix: `passwd`.

With the `passwd` command, you can change the password associated with your individual account name. As with your personal identification number (PIN) for automated-teller machines, the value of your password is directly related to how secret it remains.

NOTE

Unix is careful about the whole process of changing passwords. It requires you to enter your current password to prove you're really you. Imagine that you are at a computer center and have to leave the room to make a quick phone call. Without much effort, a prankster could lean over and quickly change your environment or even delete some critical files! That's why you should log out if you're not going to be near your system, and that's also why passwords are never echoed in Unix.

---

1. Consider what happens when I use the `passwd` command to change the password associated with my account:

```
% passwd
Changing password for taylor.
Old password:
New passwd:
Retype new passwd:
%
```

2. Notice that I never received any visual confirmation that the password I actually entered was the same as the password I thought I entered. This is not as dangerous as it seems, though, because if I had made any typographical errors, the password I entered the second time (when the system said `Retype new passwd:`) wouldn't have matched the first. In a no-match situation, the system would have warned me that the information I supplied was inconsistent:

```
% passwd
Changing password for taylor.
Old password:
New passwd:
Retype new passwd:
Mismatch - password unchanged.
%
```

3. Smart systems will complain if you pick a really bad password or one that's just obviously too short. I tried `cat` on my Oracle Solaris system, and the `passwd` command complained:

```
passwd: Password too short - must be at least 6 characters.
```

Oops. In the next section you'll learn about how to pick good, hard-to-guess but easy-to-remember passwords.

After you change the password, don't forget it. Resetting it to a known value if you don't know the current password requires the assistance of a system administrator or other operator. Using a trick to remember your password can be a Catch-22, though: You don't want to write down the password because that reduces its secrecy and you don't want to make it too easy to remember because someone else can then guess it, but you don't want to forget it, because that can be all sorts of hassle. You want to be sure that you pick a good password, too, as described in Task 2.3.

Task 2.3: Picking a Secure Password

If you're an aficionado of old movies, you are familiar with the thrillers in which the hoods break into an office and spin the dial on the safe a few times, snicker a bit about how the boss shouldn't have chosen his daughter's birthday as the combination, and crank open the safe. (If you're really familiar with the genre, you recall films in which the criminals rifle the desk drawers and find the combination of the safe taped to the underside of a drawer as a fail-safe, or a failed safe, as the case may be. Hitchcock's great film *Marnie* has just such a scene.) The moral is that even the best secret password is useful only if you keep it secret.

For computers, security is tougher because a fast computer system can test all the words in an English dictionary against your account password faster than you can say "don't hack me, bro." If your password is *kitten* or, worse yet, your account name, any semicompetent bad guy could be in your account and messing with your files in no time. This is called a *dictionary attack*.

Most modern Unix systems have some *heuristics*, or smarts, built in to the `passwd` command; the heuristics check to determine whether what you've entered is reasonably secure.

The tests performed typically answer these questions:

▶ Is the proposed password at least six characters long? (A longer password is more secure.)

▶ Does it have both digits and letters? (A mix of both is best.)

▶ Does it mix upper- and lowercase letters? (A mix is best.)

▶ Does it include at least one punctuation character? (adding a %, !, @, or even . is best)

▶ Is it in the online dictionary? (You should avoid common words.)

▶ Is it a name or word associated with the account? (`Dave` would be a bad password for my account `taylor` because my full name on the system is Dave Taylor).

Some versions of the `passwd` program are more sophisticated, and some less, but generally the following are good guidelines for picking a secure password:

1. An easy way to choose memorable and secure passwords is to think of them as small sentences rather than as a single word with some characters surrounding it. If you're a fan of Alexander Dumas and *The Three Musketeers*, then "All for one and one for all!" is a familiar cry, but it's also the basis for a couple of great passwords. Easily remembered derivations might be the punnish `aw14ONE?` or `a41&14A!`.

2. If you've been in the service, you might have the old U.S. Army jingle stuck in your head: "Be All You Can Be." Try thinking of that phrase as a series of abbreviations and letters: `ballucanb`. Turn that into a good password with a few additional tweaks: `4ballu@canb`. You might have a self-referential password: `account4me` or `MySekrit` would work. If you're ex-Vice President Dan Quayle, `1Potatoe` could be a memorable choice. (`potatoe` by itself wouldn't be particularly secure because it lacks digits and lacks uppercase letters and because it's a simple variation on a word in the online dictionary.)

3. Another way to choose passwords is to find acronyms that have special meaning to you. Don't choose simple ones. Remember, short ones aren't going to be secure. But if you have always heard that "Real programmers don't eat quiche!" then `Rpdeq!` could be a complex password that you'll easily remember.

4. Many systems you use every day require numeric passwords to verify your identity, including the automated-teller machine (with its PIN), government agencies (with the Social Security number), and the Department of Motor Vehicles (your driver's license number or vehicle license). Each of these actually is a poor Unix password because it's too easy for someone to find out your license number or Social Security number. And a series of nothing but numbers is a terrible password anyway!

NOTE

The important thing is to come up with a strategy of your own for choosing a password that is both memorable and secure. Then keep the password in your head rather than write it down.

Why be so paranoid? For a small Unix system that will sit on your desk and won't have any other users, a high level of concern for security is, to be honest, unnecessary. As with driving a car, though, it's never too early to learn good habits. Any system that has Internet access means that it's probably accessible *from* the Internet, too, and that means it's at risk of hackers trying to break in, a target for delinquents who relish the intellectual challenge of breaking into an account and then altering and destroying files and programs purely for amusement.

The best way to avoid trouble is to develop good security habits now, when you're first learning about Unix. Learn how to recognize what makes a good, secure password, pick one for your account, and keep it a secret. Don't write it down, or, if you must, keep that note secure too and notify your admin if it gets lost. A little prevention can be a lot easier than mopping up after a security breech.

With that in mind, log in again to your Unix system and try changing your password. First, change it to easy and see whether the program warns you that easy is too short or otherwise a poor choice. Then try entering two different secret passwords to see whether the program notices the difference. Finally, pick a good password, using the preceding guidelines and suggestions, and change your account password to be more secure.

Seeing What's Going On Around You

You're logged in, looking at the command prompt, and ready to delve into this Unix thing. Great! Let's have a look.

Task 2.4: Who Are You?

While you're logged in to the system, you can learn a few more Unix commands, including a couple that can answer a philosophical conundrum that has bothered men and women of thought for thousands of years: Who am I?

1. The easiest way to find out "who you are" is to enter the `whoami` command:

```
% whoami
taylor
%
```

Try it on your system. The command lists the account name associated with the current login.

2. Ninety-nine percent of the commands you type with Unix have a single specific spelling and will fail if you get creative. With `whoami`, however, adding spaces to transform the statement into proper English—that is, entering `who am I`—dramatically changes the result. On my system, I get the following results:

```
% who am i
taylor      pts/2        Oct 27 10:11     (:0.0)
%
```

On a Mac system, it doesn't show (:0.0) otherwise things work well.

This tells me quite a bit about my identity on the computer, including my account name and where and when I logged in. Try the command on your system to see what results you get.

In this example, my account name is `taylor`. The `pts/2` is the current communication line I'm using to access the system, and you can see that I logged in at 10:11 using a regular communications socket. (The :0.0 is relevant under the X Window System, something we won't cover for quite a while in this book.)

NOTE

Unix is full of oddities that are based on historical precedent. One is `tty` or `pty` to describe a computer or terminal line. This comes from the earliest Unix systems, in which Digital Equipment Corporation teletypewriters were hooked up as interactive devices. The teletypewriters quickly received the nickname tty, and all these years later, when people wouldn't dream of hooking up a teletypewriter, the line is still known as a `tty` (or `pty`, for "pseudo terminal") line.

---

3. One of the most dramatic influences Unix systems have had on the computing community is the propensity for users to work together on a network, hooked up by telephone lines and modems (the predominant method until the middle to late 1980s) or by high-speed network connections to the Internet (a more common type of connection today). Regardless of the connection, however, you can see that each computer needs a unique identifier to distinguish it from others on the network. In the early days of Unix, systems had unique hostnames, but as hundreds of systems have grown into millions, this has proved to be an unworkable solution.

4. The alternative was what's called a domain-based naming scheme, where systems are assigned unique names within specific subsets of the overall network. Here's an example:

`mentor.utech.edu`

The computer I use is within the `.edu` domain (read the hostname and domain—`mentor.utech.edu`—from right to left), meaning that the computer is located at an educational institution. Then, within the educational institution subset of the network, `utech` is a unique descriptor, and, therefore, if other UTech universities existed, they couldn't use the same top-level domain name. Finally, `mentor` is the name of the computer itself.

5. As with learning to read addresses on envelopes, learning to read domain names can unlock much information about a computer and its location. For example, `lib.stanford.edu` is the library computer at Stanford University, and `ccgate.infoworld.com` tells you that the computer is at InfoWorld, a commercial computer site, and that its hostname is `ccgate`. You'll learn more about this later when you learn how to use electronic mail to communicate with people throughout the Internet.

6. Another way to find out who you are in Unix is to use the `id` command. The purpose of this command is to tell you what group or groups you're in and the numeric identifier for your account name (known as your *user ID number* or *user ID*). Enter `id` and see what you get. I get the following result:

```
% id
uid=100(taylor) gid=10(staff)
%
```

NOTE

If you enter `id` and the computer returns a different result or indicates that you need to specify a filename, don't panic. On many Berkeley-derived systems, the `id` command is used to obtain low-level information about files.

---

7. In this example, you can see that my account name is `taylor` and that the numeric equivalent, the user ID, is `100`. (Here it's abbreviated as `uid`—pronounce it "you-eye-dee" to sound like a Unix expert). Just as the account name is unique on a system, so also is the user ID. Fortunately, you rarely, if ever, need to know these numbers since they're used by the OS internally, so focus on the account name and group name.

8. Next, you can see that my group ID (or `gid`) is `10` and that group number `10` is known as the `staff` group. It's the only group to which I belong.

On another system, I am a member of two different groups:

```
% id
uid=103(taylor) gid=10(staff) groups=10(staff),44(ftp)
%
```

Although I have the same account name on this system (`taylor`), you can see that my user ID and group ID are both different from those in the earlier example. Note also that I'm a member of two groups: the `staff` group, with a group ID of `10`, and the `ftp` group, with a group ID of `44`.

You've now learned a couple different ways to have Unix give you some information about your account. Later, you'll learn how to set protection modes on your files so that people in your group can read your files but so those not in your group are barred from access.

Task 2.5: Finding Out What Other Users Are Logged In to the System

The next philosophical puzzle that you can solve with Unix is "Who else is there?" The answer, however, is rather restricted, limited to only those people currently logged in to the same computer at the same time. Three commands are available to get you this information, and the one you choose depends on how much you'd like to learn about the other users: `users`, `who`, and `w`.

1. The simplest of the commands is the `users` command, which lists the account names of all people using the system:

```
% users
david mark taylor
%
```

In this example, `david` and `mark` are also logged in to the system with me. Try this on your computer and see what other users—if any—are logged in to your computer system.

2. A command that you've encountered earlier in this hour can be used to find out who is logged on to the system, what line they're on, and how long they've been logged in. That command is `who`:

```
% who
taylor    vt/7       Oct 27 14:10    (:0)
david     pts/1      Dec 27 15:54    (:0.0)
mark      pts/2      Oct 27 11:51    (:0.0)
%
```

Here, you can see that three people are logged in: `taylor` (me), `david`, and `mark`. Furthermore, you can now see that `david` is logged in by connection `pts/1` and has been connected since December 27 at 3:54 p.m. You can see that `mark` has been connected since just before noon on October 27 on line `pts/2`. Note that I have been logged in since 14:10, which is 24-hour time for 2:10 p.m. Unix doesn't always indicate a.m. or p.m.

The `user` and `who` commands can tell you who is using the system at any particular moment, but how do you find out what they're doing?

Task 2.6: What Is Everyone Doing on the Computer?

To find out what everyone else is doing, there's a third command, w, that serves as a combination of "Who are they?" and "What are they doing?"

1. Consider the following output from the w command:

```
% w
2:12pm  up 7 days,  5:28,  3 users, load average: 0.33, 0.33, 0.02
User    tty          login@  idle   JCPU  PCPU  what
taylor  vt/7         27Oct14         2:35  2:07  python2.6 /usr/lib/
                                                 ➥ system-config
david   pts/1        3:54pm  2:04    15    33    bash
mark    pts/2        27Oct14  43                 -csh
%
```

This is a much more complex command than users or who, and it offers more information. Notice that the output is broken into different areas. The first line summarizes the status of the system and, rather cryptically, the number of programs that the computer is running at one time. Finally, for each user, the output indicates the username, the tty, when the user logged in to the system, how long it's been since the user has done anything (in minutes and seconds), the combined CPU time of all jobs the user has run, and the amount of CPU time taken by the current job. The last field tells you what you wanted to know in the first place: What are the users doing?

In this example, the current time is 2:12 p.m., and the system has been up for 7 days, 5 hours, and 28 minutes. Currently three users are logged in, and the system is very quiet, with an average of 0.33 jobs submitted (or programs started) in the last minute; 0.33 jobs, on average, in the last 5 minutes; and 0.02 jobs in the last 15 minutes.

taylor is the only user actively using the computer (that is, who has no idle time) and is using the python command. User david is sitting in the bash shell, which has gone for quite awhile without any input from the user (2 hours and 11 minutes of idle time). The program already has used 15 seconds of CPU time and, overall, david has used 33 seconds of CPU time. User mark has a C shell running, as indicated by -csh. (The leading dash indicates that this is the program that the computer launched automatically when mark logged in. This is akin to how the system automatically launches the Finder on a Macintosh.) User mark hasn't actually done anything yet: Notice that there is no accumulated computer time for that account.

2. Now it's your turn. Try the w command on your system and see what kind of output you get. Try to interpret all the information based on the explanation here. One thing is certain: Your account should have the w command listed as what you're doing.

On a multiuser Unix system, the w command gives you a quick and easy way to see what's going on.

Task 2.7: Checking the Current Date and Time

You've learned how to orient yourself on a Unix system, and you are now able to figure out who you are, who else is on the system, and what everyone is doing. What about the current time and date?

1. Logic suggests that time shows the current time and date the current date; but this is Unix, and logic doesn't always apply. In fact, consider what happens when I enter time on my system:

    ```
    % time

    real    0m0.000s
    user    0m0.000s
    sys     0m0.000s
    %
    ```

    The output is cryptic to the extreme and definitely not what you're interested in finding out. The program is showing how much user time, system time, and CPU time has been used by the command interpreter itself, broken down by input/output operations and more. (The time command is more useful than it looks, particularly if you're a programmer.)

    On other Unixes, you might find time to be a missing command, a built-in shell function, or something completely different. In all cases, it won't tell you the current time.

2. Well, time didn't work, so what about date?

    ```
    % date
    Sat Jun  617:05:32 MST 2015
    %
    ```

    That's more like it!

    Try the date command on your computer and see whether the output agrees with your watch.

How do you think date keeps track of the time and date when you've turned off the computer? Does the computer know the correct time if you unplug it for a few hours? (I hope so. Almost all computers today have little batteries inside for just this situation.)

Summary

This hour focuses on giving you the skills required to log in to a Unix system, figure out who you are and what groups you're in, change your password, and log out again. You also learned how to list the other users of the system, find out what Unix commands they're using, and check the date and time.

Workshop

The Workshop summarizes the key terms you've learned and poses some questions about the topics presented in this lesson. It also provides you with a preview of what you will learn in the next hour.

Key Terms

account name   This is the official one-word name by which the Unix system knows you; mine is `taylor`. (*See also* **account** in Hour 1, "What Is This Unix Stuff?")

domain name   Unix systems on the Internet, or any other network, are assigned a domain within which they exist. This is typically the company (for example, `microsoft.com` for Microsoft Corporation) or institution (for example, `lsu.edu` for Louisiana State University). The domain name is always the entire host address, except the hostname itself. (*See also* **hostname**.)

heuristic   An approach or a procedure for accomplishing a specific task, not guaranteed of success but widely accepted as providing good results for relatively little effort. Think "rule of thumb."

hostname   Unix computers all have unique names assigned by the local administration team. The computers I use are `limbo`, `well`, `netcom`, and `mentor`, for example. Enter `hostname` to see what your system is called.

login   A synonym for account name, this also can be a verb (when it's two words: log in) that refers to the process of connecting to the Unix system and entering your account name and password for your account.

user ID (uid)   This is the numeric equivalent of the account name, which the system uses for internal bookkeeping.

Exercises

1. Why can't you have the same account name as another user? How about user ID? Can you have the same `uid` as someone else on the system?

2. Which of the following are good passwords, based on the guidelines you've learned in this hour?

```
foobar     4myMUM     Blk&Blu
234334     Laurie     Hi!
2cool.     rolyat     j j kim
```

3. Are the results of the two commands `who am i` and `whoami` different? If so, explain how. Which do you think you'd rather use when you're on a new computer?

4. List the three Unix commands for finding out who is logged in to the system. Describe about the differences between the commands.

5. One of the commands in the answer to question 4 indicates how long the system has been running. (In the example, it had been running for seven days.) What value do you think there is for keeping track of this information?

6. If you can figure out what other people are doing on the computer, they can figure out what you're doing, too. Does that bother you? Why or why not?

Preview of the Next Hour

The next hour focuses on the Unix hierarchical file system. You'll learn about how the system is organized, how it differs from Windows and Macintosh hierarchical file systems, the difference between relative and absolute filenames, and the mysterious . and .. directories. You'll also learn about the `env`, `pwd`, and `cd` commands, as well as the HOME and PATH environment variables.

HOUR 3
Moving About the File System

Goals for This Hour

In this hour, you will learn

▸ What a hierarchical file system is all about

▸ How the Unix file system is organized

▸ How Mac and PC file systems differ from Unix

▸ The difference between relative and absolute filenames

▸ About hidden files in Unix

▸ About the special directories . and ..

▸ About the `env` command

▸ About the user environment variables PATH and HOME

▸ How to find where you are with `pwd`

▸ How to move to another location with `cd`

This third hour focuses on the Unix hierarchical file system. You'll learn how the system is organized, how it differs from the Macintosh and Windows hierarchical file systems, the difference between relative and absolute filenames, and the mysterious . and .. directories. You'll also learn about the env, pwd, and cd commands and the HOME and PATH environment variables.

The preceding hour introduced many Unix commands, but this hour takes a more theoretical approach, focusing on the Unix file system, how it's organized, and how you can navigate it. This hour focuses on the environment that tags along with you as you move about, particularly the HOME and PATH variables. After that is explained, you'll learn about using the env command as an easy way to show environment variables, and you'll learn how to use the pwd and cd pair of commands for moving about directly.

What a Hierarchical File System Is All About

In a nutshell, a hierarchy is a system organized by graded categorization. A familiar example is the organizational structure of a company, where workers report to supervisors and supervisors report to middle managers. Middle managers, in turn, report to senior managers, and senior managers report to vice-presidents, who report to the president of the company. Graphically, this hierarchy looks as shown in Figure 3.1.

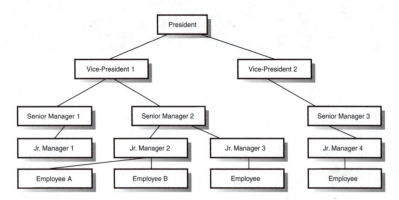

FIGURE 3.1
A typical organizational hierarchy.

You've doubtless seen this type of illustration before, and you know that a higher position indicates more control. Each position is controlled by the next highest position or row. The president is top dog in the organization, but each subsequent manager is also in control of his or her own small fiefdom.

A file system is similar to an organizational chart. Imagine each of the managers in the illustration as a file folder and each of the employees as a piece of paper, filed in a particular folder. Open any file cabinet, and you probably see things organized this way: Filed papers are placed in labeled folders, and often these folders are filed in groups under specific topics. The drawer might then have a specific label to distinguish it from other drawers in the cabinet, and so on.

That's exactly what a hierarchical file system is all about. You want to have your files located in the most appropriate place in the file system, whether at the very top, in a folder, or in a nested series of folders. With careful use, a hierarchical file system can contain thousands of files and still allow users to find any individual file quickly.

On my computer, the lessons of this book are organized in a hierarchical fashion, as shown in Figure 3.2.

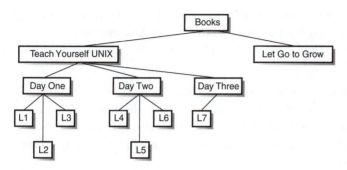

FIGURE 3.2
File organization for the lessons of *Sams Teach Yourself Unix in 24 Hours, Fifth Edition*.

Task 3.1: The Unix File System Organization

A key reason the Unix hierarchical file system is so effective is that anything that is not a folder is a file. Programs are files in Unix, device drivers are files, documents and spreadsheets are files, your keyboard is represented as a file, your display is a file, and even your `tty` line and mouse are files. This is one of the chief factors in the flexibility of Unix and what has made it such a popular tool for programmers, who tend to seek well-understood, consistent access to system resources rather than having to use different tools for every situation.

The top level of the Unix file structure (/) is known as the root directory or slash directory, and it always has a certain set of subdirectories, including `bin`, `dev`, `etc`, `lib`, `mnt`, `tmp`, and `usr`. There can be a lot more, however.

You can obtain a listing of the files and directories in your own top-level directory by using the `ls -F /` command. (You'll learn all about the `ls` command in the next hour. For now, just be sure that you enter exactly what's shown in the example.)

On a different computer system, here's what I see when I enter that command:

```
% ls -F /
Mail/          export/        public/
News/          home/          reviews/
add_swap/      kadb*          sbin/
apps/          layout         sys@
archives/      lib@           tftpboot/
bin@           lost+found/    tmp/
boot           mnt/           usr/
cdrom/         net/           utilities/
chess/         news/          var/
dev/           nntpserver     vmunix*
etc/           pcfs/
```

In this example, any filename that ends with a slash (/) is a folder (Unix calls these *directories*). Any filename that ends with an asterisk (*) is a program. Anything ending with the at sign (@) is a *symbolic link* (a pointer to another file or directory elsewhere in the file system), and everything else is a normal, plain file.

As you can see from this example, and as you'll immediately find when you try the command yourself, there is much variation in how different Unix systems organize the top-level directory. There are some directories and files in common, and once you start examining the contents of specific directories, you'll find that hundreds of programs and files always show up in the same place from one Unix to another.

It's as if you're a new file clerk at a law firm. Although this firm might have a specific approach to filing information, the approach may be similar to the filing system of other firms where you have worked in the past. If you know the underlying organization, you can quickly pick up the specifics of a particular organization.

Try the command `ls -F /` on your computer system and try to identify, as previously explained, each of the directories in the listing you get.

The output of the previous `ls` command shows the files and directories in the top level of your system. Next, you'll learn about the commonly found directories.

The `bin` Directory

In Unix parlance, programs are considered *executables* because users can execute them. (In this case, *execute* is a synonym for *run*, not an indication that you get to wander about murdering innocent applications!) When the program has been compiled, it is translated from source code—what a programmer might write in C++ or Java—into what's called a *binary* format. Add the two together, and you have a common Unix description for an application—an executable binary.

It's no surprise that the original Unix developers decided to have a directory labeled `binaries` to store all the executable programs on the system. Remember the primitive teletypewriter discussed earlier? Having a slow system to talk with the computer had many ramifications you might not expect. The single most obvious one was that everything became quite concise. There were no lengthy words like `binaries` or `listfiles`, but rather there were succinct abbreviations; `bin` and `ls` are, respectively, the Unix equivalents.

The `bin` directory (pronounce it to rhyme with "tin") is where all the executable binaries were kept in early Unix. Over time, as more and more executables were added to Unix, having all the executables in one place proved unmanageable, and the `bin` directory split into multiple parts with different purposes (/bin, /sbin, /usr/bin).

The `dev` Directory

Among the most important portions of any computer are its device drivers. Without them, you wouldn't have any information on your screen (because the information arrives courtesy of the display device driver), you wouldn't be able to enter information (because the information is read and given to the system by the keyboard device driver), and you wouldn't be able to use your hard drive (which is managed by the disk device driver).

Remember, everything in Unix is a file. Every component of the system, from the keyboard driver to the hard disk, is a file.

Earlier, you learned how almost anything in Unix is considered a file in the file system, and the `dev` directory is an example. All device drivers—often numbering into the hundreds—are stored as separate files in the standard Unix `dev` (devices) directory. Pronounce this directory name "dev," not "dee-ee-vee."

The `etc` Directory

Unix administration can be quite complex, involving management of user accounts, the file system, security, device drivers, hardware configurations, and more. To help, Unix designates the `etc` directory as the storage place for all administrative files and information.

Pronounce the directory name "ee-tea-sea," "et-sea," or "etcetera." All three pronunciations are common.

The `lib` Directory

Like your own community, Unix has a central storage place for function and procedural libraries. These specific executables are included with specific programs and allow programs to offer features and capabilities that are otherwise unavailable. The idea is that if programs want to include certain features, they can reference only the shared copy in the Unix library rather than having a new, unique copy.

Pronounce the directory name "libe" or "lib" (to rhyme with the word *bib*).

The `lost+found` Directory

With multiple users running many different programs simultaneously, it's been a challenge over the years to develop a file system that can remain synchronized with the activity of the computer. Various parts of the Unix *kernel*—the brains of the system—help with this problem. When files are recovered after any sort of problem or failure, they are placed here, in the `lost+found` directory, if the kernel cannot ascertain the proper location in the file system. This directory should be empty almost all the time.

This directory is commonly pronounced "lost and found" rather than "lost plus found."

The `mnt` and `sys` Directories

The `mnt` (pronounced "em-en-tea") and `sys` (pronounced "sis") directories are safely ignored by everyday Unix users. The `mnt` directory is intended to be a common place to mount external media—hard disks, removable cartridge drives, and so on—in Unix. On many systems, though not all, `sys` contains files indicating the system configuration.

The `tmp` Directory

A directory that you can't ignore, the `tmp` directory (pronounced "temp") is used by many of the programs in Unix as a temporary file-storage space. If you're editing a file, for example, the editor makes a copy of the file, saves it in `tmp`, and you work directly with that, saving the new file back to your original only when you've completed your work.

On most systems, `tmp` ends up littered with various files and executables left by programs that don't remove their own temporary files. On one system I use, it's not uncommon to find 10–30 megabytes of files wasting space.

Even so, if you're manipulating files or working with copies of files, `tmp` is the best place to keep the temporary copies. Indeed, on some Unix workstations, `tmp` actually can be the fastest device on the computer, allowing for dramatic performance improvements over working with files directly in your home directory.

The `usr` Directory

The last of the standard directories at the top level of the Unix file system hierarchy is the `usr`—pronounced "user"—directory. Originally, this directory was intended to be the central storage place for all user-related commands and data—the stuff directly relevant to users, as opposed to the system. After decades of evolution, however, `/usr` has come to encompass everything from Python libraries to system-wide applications, just because its boundaries have always been ill defined. Many companies have their own interpretations of what should go here, and there's no telling what you'll find in this directory anymore.

Other Miscellaneous Stuff at the Top Level

In addition to all the directories previously listed, various other directories and files commonly occur in Unix systems. Some files might have slight variations in name on your computer, so when you compare your listing to the following files and directories, be alert for possible alternative spellings.

A file you must have in order for Unix to exist at all is one usually called `unix` or `vmunix`, or named after the specific version of Unix on the computer. The file contains the actual Unix operating system. The file must have a specific name and must be found at the top level of the file system. Hand-in-hand with the operating system is another file called `boot`, which helps during initial startup of the hardware.

Notice in some of the output earlier in this lesson that the Linux-specific files `boot` and `vmunix` appear. By comparison, a listing from a Solaris workstation shows `boot` and `zvboot` as the two relevant files (plus a kernel directory containing plugin modules). Mac OS X, by contrast, hides its boot files and kernel much deeper in the system than the root level.

The home directory, `/home` (or, on Mac OS X, `/Users`), is a central place for organizing all files owned by specific users. Listing this directory is usually an easy way to find out what accounts are on the system, too, because by convention each individual account directory is named after the user's account name. On one system I use, my account is `taylor`, and my individual account directory is also called `taylor`. Home directories are always created by the system administrator.

The `net` directory, if set up correctly, is a handy shortcut for accessing other computers on your network.

The `tftpboot` directory is a relatively new feature of Unix. The letters stand for "Trivial File Transfer Protocol boot." Don't let the name confuse you, though; this directory contains versions of the kernel suitable for X Window System–based terminals and diskless workstations to run Unix. The upshot is that it's what allows your computer to boot off an operating system that's hosted somewhere else in the network, without even being installed locally.

Some Unix systems have directories named for specific types of peripherals that can be attached. On a Solaris workstation, you can see an examples with the directory `cdrom`, which is used for CD-ROMs and other optical discs.

Another Solaris feature is the `opt` directory, which stores add-on programs and components from Oracle and from third parties (and can also be used in much the same way as `var` is used in Linux—to store data such as Web content). The `opt` directory doesn't generally exist in Linux or FreeBSD, but whereas Linux tends to use both `var` and `usr` for vague and sometimes overlapping purposes, FreeBSD attempts to enforce a strict conceptual division between variable files (that is, files that change naturally with the system's operation, such as mailboxes, log files, and database contents) and static, permanently installed fixtures of direct relevance to users. As you can tell, the philosophical distinctions that separate the many flavors of Unix continue to contribute to their widely varying characters to the present day.

Many more directories are present in Unix, but this lesson gives you an idea of how things are organized.

Directory Separator Characters

If you look at the organizational chart presented earlier in this hour (refer to Figure 3.1), you see that employees are identified simply as "employee" where possible. Because each has a unique path upward to the president, each has a unique identifier if all components of the path upward are specified.

For example, the rightmost of the four employees could be described as "Employee managed by Jr. Manager 4, managed by Senior Manager 3, managed by Vice-President 2, managed by the President." Using a single character, instead of "managed by," can considerably shorten the description: Employee/Jr. Manager 4/Senior Manager 3/Vice-President 2/President. Now consider the same path specified from the very top of the organization downward: President/Vice-President 2/Senior Manager 3/Jr. Manager 4/Employee.

Because only one person is at the top, that person can be safely dropped from the path without losing the uniqueness of the descriptor: /Vice-President 2/Senior Manager 3/Jr. Manager 4/Employee.

In this example, the / (pronounce it "slash") is serving as a *directory separator character*, a convenient shorthand to indicate different directories in a path.

The idea of using a single character to separate hierarchical levels isn't unique to Unix, but using the forward slash is historically unusual. On the classic Macintosh, the system uses a colon to separate directories in a pathname. (Next time you're on a Mac, try saving a file called `test:file` and see what happens.) DOS uses a backslash; for example, `\DOS` indicates the DOS directory at the top level. The characters `/tmp` indicate the tmp directory at the top level of the Unix file system, and `:Apps` is a folder called `Apps` at the top of an old-school Macintosh file system.

NOTE

Ever since Mac OS X came onto the scene, the conventions of the classic Mac OS have gradually been phased out, including the use of colons as directory separators. As a true Unix, Mac OS X uses forward slashes pervasively, and has contributed greatly (along with the standard URL format now made ubiquitous by the Web) to making the slash the de facto standard across all operating systems. However, one vestige of the old Mac OS remains: Unlike in any other Unix, you're allowed to use slashes in filenames, but you can't use colons (the idea being that you're probably more likely to want to use a slash than a colon in a typical filename). But look again: This is only for show at the GUI level. Try creating a file in TextEdit called `test/file.txt`, and then look at it in Terminal with the `ls` command. You'll see that the file you created is actually called `test:file.txt`. Tricky, huh?

On the Macintosh, you rarely encounter the directory separator because almost all users live in the graphical interface and don't even know that there's a Unix system—and command-line interface—lurking beneath the GUI environment. Windows also offers a similar level of freedom from having to worry about much of this complexity, although you'll still need to remember whether A: is your floppy disk (if you even have one in this day and age) or hard disk drive.

The Difference Between Relative and Absolute Filenames

Specifying the exact location of a file in a hierarchy to ensure that the filename is unique is known in Unix parlance as specifying its *absolute filename* (or *absolute pathname*). That is, regardless of where you are within the file system, the absolute filename always specifies a particular file. By contrast, relative filenames are not unique descriptors and can refer to many different files, depending on where you are when you refer to the file.

To understand this, consider the files shown in Figure 3.3.

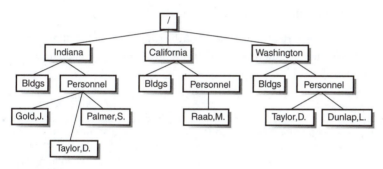

FIGURE 3.3
A simple hierarchy of files.

If you are currently looking at the information in the Indiana directory, Bldgs uniquely describes one file: the Bldgs file in the Indiana directory. That same name, however, refers to a different file if you are in the California directory or the Washington directory. Similarly, the directory Personnel leaves you with three possible choices until you also specify which state you're interested in.

As a possible scenario, imagine that you're reading through the Bldgs file for Washington and some people come into your office and interrupt your work. After a few minutes of talk, they comment about an entry in the Bldgs file in California. You turn to your Unix system and bring up the Bldgs file, and it's the wrong file. Why? You're still in the Washington directory.

These problems arise because of the lack of specificity of *relative filenames*. Relative filenames describe files that are referenced relative to an assumed position in the file system. In Figure 3.3, even Personnel/Taylor,D. isn't unique because it can be found in both Indiana and Washington.

To avoid these problems, you can apply the technique you learned earlier: specifying all elements of the directory path from the top down. To look at the Bldgs file for California, you could simply specify /California/Bldgs. To check the Taylor,D. employee in Indiana, you'd use `/Indiana/Personnel/Taylor,D.`, which is different, you'll notice, from `/Washington/Personnel/Taylor,D.`.

Learning the difference between these two notations is crucial to surviving the complexity of the hierarchical file system in Unix. Without it, you'll spend half your time verifying that you are where you think you are or, worse, not moving about at all and not taking advantage of the organizational capabilities.

If you're ever in doubt as to where you are or what file you're working with in Unix, simply specify its absolute filename. You always can differentiate between relative and absolute filenames by looking at the very first character: If it's a slash, you've got an absolute filename (because the filename is rooted to the very top level of the file system). If you don't have a slash as the first character, the filename's a relative filename.

Earlier I told you that in the `/home` directory at the top level of Unix, I have a home directory called `taylor`. In absolute filename terms, I'd properly say that I have `/home/taylor` as a unique directory.

NOTE

To add to the confusion, most Unix people don't pronounce the slashes, particularly if the first component of the filename is a well-known directory. I would pronounce `/home/taylor` as "home taylor," but I would usually pronounce `/newt/awk/test` as "slash newt awk test." When in doubt, pronounce the slash.

As you learn more about Unix, particularly about how to navigate the file system, you'll find that having a clear understanding of the difference between relative and absolute filenames proves invaluable. Remember that the rule of thumb is that if a filename begins with /, it's absolute.

Task 3.2: Hidden Files in Unix

One of the best aspects of living in an area for a long time, frequenting the same shops, and visiting the same restaurants, is that the people who work at each place learn your name and preferences. Many Unix applications can perform the same trick, remembering your preferred style of interaction, what files you last worked with, which lines you've edited, and more, through *preference files*.

On the Macintosh, there's a folder within each user's home directory called `Library`. Within that there's another folder called `Preferences`, which is a central storage place for preference files, organized by application. On my Macintosh, for example, I have about 75 different preference files in this directory, so I can have all my programs remember the defaults I prefer.

Unix must support many users at once, so Unix preference files can't be stored in a central spot in the file system. Otherwise, how would the system distinguish between your preferences and those of your colleagues? To avoid this problem, all Unix applications store their preference files in your home directory.

Programs want to be able to keep their own internal preferences and status stored in your directory, but these aren't for you to work with or alter. If you use DOS, you're probably familiar with how Windows solves this problem: Certain files are hidden and do not show up when you use DIR, in DOS, or in the File Manager to list files in a directory.

Macintosh people don't realize it, but the Macintosh also has lots of hidden files. On the topmost level of the Macintosh file system, for example, the following files are present, albeit hidden from normal display: .DS_Store, Desktop DB, .VolumeIcon.icns, NavMac8000QSFile, and my personal favorite, .symSchedScanLockxz. Displaying hidden files on the Macintosh is very difficult, as it is with Windows.

Fortunately, the Unix rule for hiding files is much easier than that for either the Mac or PC. No secret status flag reminds the system not to display the file when listing directories. Instead, the rule is simple: Any filename that starts with a dot (.) is a *hidden file*.

NOTE

A *hidden file* is any file with a dot as the first character of the filename.

If the filename or directory name begins with a dot, it won't show up in normal listings of that directory. If the filename or directory name has any other character as the first character of the name, it lists normally.

1. Turn to your computer and enter the `ls` command to list all the files and directories in your home directory:

```
% ls -F
Archives/       Mail/         RUMORS.18Sept  mailing.lists
InfoWorld/      News/         bin/           newlists
LISTS           OWL/          iecc.list      src/
%
```

You can see that I have 12 items in my own directory, 7 directories (the directory names have a slash as the last character because of the -F, remember), and 5 files. Files have minimal rules for naming, too. Avoid slashes, spaces, and tabs, and you'll be fine.

2. Without an explicit direction to the contrary, Unix is going to let the hidden files remain hidden. To add the hidden files to the listing, you just need to add a -a flag to the

command. Turn to your computer and try the `ls  -aF` command to see what hidden files are present in your directory. These are my results:

```
% ls -aF
./              .gopherrc       .oldnewsrc      .sig            RUMORS.18Sep
../             .history*       .plan           Archives/       bin/
.Agenda         .info           .pnewsexpert    InfoWorld/      iecc.list
.aconfigrc      .letter         .report         LISTS           mail.lists
.article        .login          .rm-timestamp   Mail/           newlists
.cshrc          .mailrc         .rnlast         News/           src/
.elm/           .newsrc         .rnsoft         OWL/
%
```

Many dot files tend to follow the format of a dot, followed by the name of the program that owns the file, with `rc` as the suffix. In my directory, you can see six dot files that follow this convention: `.aconfigrc`, `.cshrc`, `.gopherrc`, `.mailrc`, `.newsrc`, and `.oldnewsrc`.

Because of the particular rules of hidden files in Unix, they are often called *dot files*, and you can see that I have 23 dot files and directories in my directory.

NOTE

The `rc` suffix (meaning "resource config") tells you that this file is a configuration file for a particular utility. For instance, `.cshrc` is the configuration file for the C shell and is executed every time the C shell (`/bin/csh`) is executed. You can define aliases for C shell commands and a special search path, for example.

NOTE

Because it's important to convey the specific filename of a dot file, pronunciation is a little different from elsewhere in Unix. The name `.lynxrc` would be spoken as "dot-lynx-are-sea," and `.mailrc` would be "dot mail are sea." If you can't pronounce the program name, odds are good that no one else can either, so `.cshrc` is "dot-sea-ess-aitch-are-sea."

Other programs create many different dot files and try to retain a consistent naming scheme. You can see that `.rnlast` and `.rnsoft` are both from the `rn` program, but it's difficult to know simply from the filenames that `.article`, `.letter`, `.newsrc`, `.oldnewsrc`, and `.pnewsexpert` are all also referenced by the `rn` program. Recognizing this problem, some application authors designed their applications to create a dot directory, with all preference files neatly tucked into that one spot. The `elm` program does that with its `.elm` hidden directory.

Some files are directly named after the programs that use them: The `.Agenda` file is used by the agenda program, and `.info` is used by the `info` program. Those almost have a rule of their own, but it's impossible to distinguish them from `.login`, from the `sh` program; `.plan` for the `finger` program; `.rm-timestamp` from a custom program of my own; and I frankly have no idea what program created the `.report` file!

This should give you an idea of the various ways that Unix programs name and use hidden files. As an exercise, list all the dot files in your home directory and try to figure out which program created each file. Check by looking in the index of this book to see whether a program by that name exists, if it's a `.xxx` file. If you can't figure out which programs created which files, you're not alone. Keep the list handy; refer to it as you learn more about Unix while exploring this book, and by the time you're done, you'll know exactly how to find out which programs created which dot files.

Task 3.3: The Special Directories . and ..

I haven't mentioned two dot directories, although they show up in my listing and most certainly show up in your listing, too. They are dot and dot-dot (`.` and `..`), and they're shorthand directory names that can be terrifically convenient.

The *dot* directory is shorthand for the current location in the directory hierarchy; the *dot-dot* directory moves you up one level, to the parent directory.

Consider again the list of files shown in Figure 3.3. If you were looking at the files in the `California Personnel` directory (best specified as `/California/Personnel`) and wanted to check quickly an entry in the `Bldgs` file for `California`, either you'd have to use the absolute filename and enter the lengthy `ls /California/Bldgs`, or, with the new shorthand directories, you could enter `ls ../Bldgs`.

As directories move ever deeper into the directory hierarchy, the dot-dot notation can save you much typing time. For example, what if the different states and related files were all located in my home directory `/home/taylor`, in a new directory called `business`? In that case, the absolute filename for employee `Raab,M.` in California would be `/home/taylor/business/California/Personnel/Raab,M.`, which is unwieldy and a great deal to type if you want to hop up one level and check on the `buildings` database in `Indiana`!

You can use more than one dot-dot notation in a filename, too, so if you're looking at the `Raab,M.` file and want to check on `Dunlap,L.`, you could save typing in the full filename by instead using `../../../Washington/Personnel/Dunlap,L.`. Look at Figure 3.3 to see how that would work; trace back one level for each dot-dot in the filename.

So you know why the dot-dot shorthand is helpful, but what about the single-dot notation that simply specifies the current directory?

I haven't stated it explicitly yet, but you've probably figured out that one ramification of the Unix file system organization, with its capability to place applications anywhere in the file system, is that the system needs some way to know where to look for particular applications. Just as if you were looking for something in a public library, in Unix, having an understanding of its organization and a strategy for searching is imperative for success and speed.

Unix uses an ordered list of directories called a *search path* for this purpose. The search path typically lists five or six different directories on the system where the computer checks for any application you request.

The question that arises is, "What happens if your own personal copy of an application has the same name as a standard system application?" The answer is that the system always finds the standard application first, if its directory is listed earlier in the search path.

To avoid this pitfall, use the dot notation, which forces the system to look in the current directory rather than search for the application. If you wanted your own version of the `ls` command, for example, you'd need to be in the same directory as the command and enter `./ls` to ensure that Unix would use your version rather than the standard version.

1. Enter `./ls` on your computer and watch what happens.

2. Enter `ls` without the dot notation, and you'll instantly see how the computer searches through various directories in the search path, finds the `ls` program, and executes it—automatically.

When you learn about `cd` (change directory) later in this hour, you also will learn other uses of the dot-dot directory, but the greatest value of the dot directory is that you can use it to force the system to look in the current directory and nowhere else for any file specified.

Task 3.4: The `env` Command

You've learned much about the foundations of the Unix file system and how applications remember your preferences through hidden dot files. There's another way, however, that the system remembers specifics about you, and that's through your user environment. The *user environment* is a collection of specially named variables (mnemonically named values) that have specific values.

1. To view your environment, you can use the `env` command. Here's what I see when I enter the `env` command on my system:

```
% env
HOME=/home/taylor
SHELL=/bin/csh
TERM=vt100
PATH=/home/taylor/bin:/bin:/usr/bin:/usr/ucb:/usr/local/bin:
➥/usr/unsup/bin:.
MAIL=/usr/spool/mail/taylor
LOGNAME=taylor
TZ=EST5
%
```

2. Try it yourself and compare your values with mine. You might find that you have more defined in your environment than I do because your Unix system uses your environment to keep track of more information.

The output of the `env` command shows some of the standard environment variables. Table 3.1 describes what they do.

TABLE 3.1   Common Shell Environment Variables and What They Do

Variable	Description
HOME	The directory where you log in and store all your personal files
SHELL	The program you run as your command-line interpreter
TERM	The type of terminal emulation you need to provide cursor graphics
PATH	A list of directories searched when you enter a command
MAIL	The file where your incoming mail is stored
LOGNAME	Your login name (account name)

NOTE

Many Unix systems offer the `printenv` command instead of `env`. If you enter `env` and the system complains that it can't find the `env` command, try using `printenv` instead. All examples here work with either `env` or `printenv`.

Task 3.5: PATH and HOME

The two most important values in your environment are the name of your home directory (HOME) and your search path (PATH). Your home directory (as it's known) is the name of the directory in which you always begin your Unix session.

The PATH environment variable lists the set of directories, in left-to-right order, that the system searches to find commands and applications you request. You can see from the example that my search path tells the computer to start looking in the `/home/taylor/bin` directory, and then sequentially try `/bin`, `/usr/bin`, `/usr/ucb`, `/usr/local/bin`, `/usr/unsup/bin`, and `.` before concluding that it can't find the requested command. Without a PATH, the shell wouldn't be able to find any of the many, many Unix commands. At a minimum, you always should have `/bin` and `/usr/bin`.

1. You can use the `echo` command to list specific environment variables, too. Enter `echo $PATH` and `echo $HOME`. If you forget the $, then the shell doesn't know you are

specifying that you want to know the value of the named variable. Try it; you'll see what I mean.

When I enter the two echo statements as shown above, I get the following results:

```
% echo $PATH
/home/taylor/bin:/bin:/usr/bin:/usr/ucb:/usr/local/bin:/usr/unsup/
➥ bin:.
% echo $HOME
/home/taylor
%
```

2. Your PATH value is probably similar, although certainly not identical, to mine, and your HOME is /home/accountname or something similar (where accountname is your account name).

Try it for yourself. Any surprises in your PATH?

Task 3.6: Find Where You Are with pwd

So far you've learned a lot about how the file system works but not much about how to move around in the file system. With any trip, the first and most important step is to find out your current location—that is, the directory in which you are currently working. In Unix, the command pwd tells you the *present working directory*.

1. Enter pwd:

```
% echo $HOME
/home/taylor
% pwd
/home/taylor
%
```

The output should be identical to the output you saw when you entered env HOME because you're still in your home directory.

Think of pwd as a compass that's always capable of telling you where you are. It also tells you the names of all directories above you because it always lists your current location as an absolute directory name.

Task 3.7: Moving to Another Location with cd

The other half of the dynamic duo is the cd command, which is used to change directories. The format of this command is simple, too: cd new-directory (where new-directory is the name of the new directory you want).

1. Try moving to the very top level of the file system and entering `pwd` to see whether the computer agrees that you've moved:

```
% cd /
% pwd
/
%
```

2. Notice that `cd` doesn't produce any output. Many Unix commands operate silently like this, unless an error is encountered. The system then indicates the problem. You can see what an error looks like by trying to change your location to a nonexistent directory. Try the `/taylor` directory to see what happens:

```
% cd /taylor
/taylor: No such file or directory
%
```

3. Enter `cd` without specifying a directory. What happens? I get the following result:

```
% cd
% pwd
/home/taylor
%
```

4. Here's where the HOME environment variable comes into play. Without any directory specified, `cd` moves you back to your home directory automatically. If you get lost, it's a fast shorthand way to move to a known location without fuss.

   Remember the dot-dot notation for moving up a level in the directory hierarchy? Here's where it also proves exceptionally useful. Use the `cd` command without any arguments to move to your home directory, and then use `pwd` to ensure that's where you've ended up.

5. Now, move up one level by using `cd ..` and check the results with `pwd`:

```
% cd
% pwd
/home/taylor
% cd ..
% pwd
/home
%
```

6. Use the `ls -C -F` command to list all the directories contained at this point in the file system:

```
% ls -C -F
armstrong/   christine/   guest/    laura/   matthewm/  shane/
bruce/       david/       higgins/  mac/     rank/      taylor/
cedric/      green/       kane/     mark/    shalini/   vicki/
%
```

Beware, though; on large systems, this directory could easily have hundreds of different directories. On one system I use, almost 550 different directories are on one level above my home directory in the file system!

Try using a combination of `cd` and `pwd` to move about your file system. Remember that without any arguments, `cd` always zips you right back to your home directory.

Summary

This hour focused on the Unix hierarchical file system. You've learned the organization of a hierarchical file system, how Unix differs from traditional Macintosh and DOS systems, and how Unix remembers preferences with its hidden dot files. This hour also explained the difference between relative and absolute filenames, and you've learned about the . and .. directories. You've learned four new commands: `env` to list your current environment, `echo` to show a particular value, `cd` to change directories, and `pwd` to find your present working directory location.

Workshop

The Workshop summarizes the key terms you've learned and poses some questions about the topics presented in this lesson. It also provides you with a preview of what you will learn in the next hour.

Key Terms

absolute filename   Any filename that begins with a leading slash (/); it uniquely describes a single file in the file system.

binary   A binary is a file format that is intended for the computer to work with directly rather than for humans to peruse. *See also* **executable**.

device driver   All peripherals attached to the computer are called *devices* in Unix, and each has a control program always associated with it, called a *device driver*. Examples are the device drivers for the display, keyboard, mouse, and all hard disks.

directory   This type of Unix file is used to group other files, equivalent to a folder. Files and directories can be placed inside other directories, to build a hierarchical system.

directory separator character   On a hierarchical file system, there must be some way to specify which parts of a full filename are directories and which part is the actual filename. This is particularly important when you're working with absolute filenames. In Unix, the directory separator character is the slash (/), so a filename like `/tmp/testme` is easily interpreted as a file called `testme` in a directory called `tmp`.

dot   This is shorthand notation for the current directory.

dot-dot   This is shorthand notation for the directory one level higher up in the hierarchical file system from the current location.

dot file   A dot file is a configuration file used by one or more programs. These files are called dot files because the first letter of the filename is a dot, as in .profile or .login. By default, the ls command doesn't list dot files, making them also hidden files in Unix. *See also* **hidden file.**

executable   An executable is a file that has been set up so that Unix can run it as a program. This is also shorthand for a binary file. You also sometimes see the phrase *binary executable*, which is the same thing. *See also* **binary.**

hidden file   By default, the Unix file-listing command ls shows only files whose first letter isn't a dot (that is, files that aren't dot files). All dot files, therefore, are hidden files, and you can safely ignore them without any problems. *See also* **dot file.**

home directory   This is your private directory and is also where you start out when you log in to the system.

kernel   The kernel is the underlying core of the Unix operating system itself. This is akin to the concrete foundation under a modern skyscraper.

preference file   These are what dot files (hidden files) really are: They contain your individual preferences for many of the Unix commands you use.

relative filename   Any filename that does not begin with a slash (/) is a relative filename, a filename whose exact meaning depends on where you are in the file system. For example, the file test might exist in both your home directory and the root directory: /test is an absolute filename and leaves no question about which version is being used, but test could refer to either copy, depending on your current directory.

root directory   The directory at the very top of the file system hierarchy is known as the root, or slash, directory.

search path   A search path is a list of directories used to find a command. When a user enters the command ls, the shell looks in each directory in the search path to find a file ls, either until it is found or until the list is exhausted.

slash   The directory at the very top of the file system hierarchy is known as the root, or slash, directory.

symbolic link   A file that contains a pointer to another file rather than contents of its own. This can also be a directory that points to another directory rather than having files of its own. It is a useful way to have multiple names for a single program or to allow multiple people to share a single copy of a file.

user environment   This is a set of values that describe the user's current location and modify the behavior of commands.

working directory   This is the directory where the user is working.

Exercises

1. Can you think of information you work with daily that's organized in a hierarchical fashion? Is a public library organized hierarchically?

2. Which of the following files are hidden files and directories, according to Unix?

   ```
   .test    hide-me    ,test    .cshrc
   ../      .dot.      dot      .HiMom
   ```

3. What programs most likely created the following dot files and dot directories?

   ```
   .cshrc     .rnsoft    .exrc      .print
   .tmp334    .excel/    .letter    .vi-expert
   ```

4. In the following list, identify the items that are absolute filenames:

   ```
   /Personnel/Taylor,D.
   /home/taylor/business/California
   ../..
   Recipe:Gazpacho
   ```

5. Remember the list of directories found on all Unix systems (/bin, /dev, /etc, /lib, /lost+found, /mnt, /sys, /tmp, /usr)? Use cd and pwd to double-check that they are all present on your own Unix machine.

Preview of the Next Hour

In the next hour, you'll learn all about the ls command that you've been using, including an extensive discussion of command flags. The command touch enables you to create your own files, and du and df help you learn how much disk space is used and how much is available, respectively. You'll also learn how to use the valuable gzip command, which helps you minimize your disk-space usage.

HOUR 4

Listing Files and Managing Disk Usage

Goals for This Hour

In this hour, you will learn

- ▶ All about the `ls` command
- ▶ About special `ls` command flags
- ▶ How to create files with `touch`
- ▶ How to check disk space usage with `du`
- ▶ How to check available disk space with `df`
- ▶ How to shrink big files with `gzip`

This hour introduces you to the `ls` command, one of the most commonly used commands in Unix. The discussion includes more than a dozen different command options, or flags. You'll also learn how to use the `touch` command to create files, how to use the `du` command to see how much disk space you're using, and how to use the `df` command to see how much disk space is available. Finally, you'll learn how the `gzip` command can help you minimize your disk space usage, particularly on files you do not use very often.

This first hours focused on some basic Unix commands, particularly those for interacting with the system to accomplish common tasks. In this hour, you'll expand you knowledge by analyzing characteristics of the system you're using, and you'll learn a raft of commands for creating your own Unix workspace. You'll also learn more about the Unix file system and how Unix interprets command lines. In addition to the `cd` and `pwd` commands that you learned about in the preceding hour, here you'll learn how to use `ls` to wander in the file system and see what files are kept where.

Unlike with the Windows and Macintosh operating systems, information about the Unix system itself is often difficult to obtain. In this hour, you'll learn easy ways to ascertain how much disk space you're using with the `du` command. You'll also learn how to interpret the oft-confusing output of the `df` command, which enables you to see instantly how much total disk space is available on your Unix system.

This hour concludes with a discussion of the `gzip` command, which enables you to shrink the size of any file or set of files. You'll see that modern Unixes actually include four different compression programs, and you'll learn how they compare.

The `ls` Command

This section introduces you to the `ls` command, which enables you to examine the file system and see what files are kept where.

Task 4.1: All About the `ls` Command

From the examples in the preceding hour, you've already figured out that the command used to list files and directories in Unix is the `ls` command.

All operating systems have a similar command, a way to see what's in the current location. If you used the ancient precursor to Windows, DOS, for example, you would be familiar with the `DIR` command. DOS also has command flags, which are denoted by a leading slash before the specific option. For example, `DIR /W` produces a directory listing in wide-display format. The `DIR` command has quite a few other options and capabilities.

Listing the files in a directory is a pretty simple task, so why all the different options? You've already seen some examples, including `ls -a`, which lists hidden dot files. The answer is that there are many different ways to look at files and directories, as you will learn.

1. The best way to learn what `ls` can do is to go ahead and use it. Turn to your computer, log in to your account or bring up your Terminal application, and try each command as it's explained.

2. The most basic use of `ls` is to list files. The command `ls` lists all the files and directories in the present working directory (recall that you can check what directory you're in with the `pwd` command at any time):

```
% ls
Archives      Mail        RUMORS.18Sept   mailing.lists
InfoWorld     News        bin             newels
LISTS         OWL         iecc.list       src
```

Notice that the files are sorted alphabetically from top to bottom, left to right. This is the default, known as *column-first order* because it sorts downward, then across. You should also note how things are sorted in Unix: The system differentiates between uppercase and lowercase letters, unlike Windows. (The Macintosh remembers whether you use uppercase or lowercase letters for naming files, but it doesn't distinguish between them internally. Try it. The next time you use a Macintosh, name one file `TEST` and then try creating another file called `test`.)

NOTE

Some of the Unix and Linux versions available for the PC have an ls that behaves slightly differently and can list all files in a single column rather than in multiple columns. If your PC does this, use the -C flag to ls to force multiple columns.

It's important that you always remember to type Unix commands in lowercase letters, unless you know that the particular command is actually uppercase; remember that Unix treats Archives and archives as different filenames, so it should be no surprise that it also treats LS and ls as different commands. Also, avoid entering your account name in uppercase when you log in. Unix has some old compatibility features that make using the system much more difficult if you use an all-uppercase login. If you ever accidentally log in with all uppercase, log out and try again in lowercase.

Task 4.2: Having ls Tell You More

Without options, the ls command offers relatively little information. Questions you might still have about your directory include these: How big are the files? Which are files, and which are directories? How old are they? What hidden files do you have?

1. Enter ls -s to find out file sizes:

```
% ls -s
total 563
    1 Archives     1 Mail      5 RUMORS.18Sept   280 mailing.lists
    1 InfoWorld    1 News      1 bin              2 newels
  261 LISTS        1 OWL       4 iecc.list        1 src
```

2. To ascertain the size of each file or directory listed, you can use the -s flag with ls. The size indicated is the number of kilobytes, rounded upward, for each file. The first line of the output also indicates the total amount of disk space used, in kilobytes, for the contents of this directory (563 in this case). The summary number does not, however, include the contents of any subdirectories, so it's deceptively small.

NOTE

A kilobyte is 1,024 bytes of information, and a byte is a single character. The preceding paragraph, for example, contains slightly more than 400 characters. Unix works in units of a *block* of information, which, depending on which version of Unix you're using, is either 1 kilobyte or 512 bytes. (Solaris, for example, uses 512-byte blocks.) Most Unix systems work with a 1-kilobyte block, however. When you use the -s flag, you're shown how many of these blocks each file contains.

3. Here is a further definition of what occurs when you use the -s flag: ls -s indicates the number of blocks each file or directory occupies. You then can use simple calculations to convert blocks into bytes. For example, the ls command indicates that the LISTS file

in my home directory occupies 261 blocks. A quick calculation of block size × number of blocks reveals that the maximum file size of LISTS is 133,632 bytes.

You can always estimate size by multiplying the number of blocks by 1,000. Be aware, however, that in large files, the difference between 1,000 and 1,024 is significant enough to introduce an error into your calculation. As an example, bigfile is more than 3 megabytes in size (a megabyte is 1,024 kilobytes, which is 1,024 bytes, so a megabyte is 1,024×1,024, or 1,048,576 bytes):

```
% ls -s bigfile
3648 bigfile
```

4. The file actually occupies 3,727,360 bytes. If I estimated its size by multiplying the number of blocks (3,648, as seen in the output of the preceding command) by 1,000 (which equals 3,648,000 bytes), I'd have underestimated its size by 79,360 bytes. (Remember, blocks × 1,000 is simply an easy estimate!)

NOTE
_____

The preceding example reveals something else about the ls command: You can specify individual files or directories you're interested in viewing and avoid having to see all files and directories in your current location.

_____

NOTE
_____

Depending on what shell you're using and what version of Unix you have, you might be able to press the Tab key while typing in a filename and have it automatically completed if it's unambiguous. Try it; if you have this shortcut, it's great!

_____

5. You can specify as many files or directories as you like, and you separate them with spaces:

```
% ls -s LISTS iecc.list newels
261 LISTS        4 iecc.list      2 newels
```

In the preceding hour, you learned that Unix identifies each file that begins with a dot (.) as a hidden file. Your home directory is probably littered with dot files, which retain preferences, status information, and other data. To list these hidden files, use the -a flag to ls:

```
% ls -a
.              gopherrc      .oldnewsrc     .sig         RUMORS.18Sept
..             .history      .plan          Archives     bin
.Agenda        .info         .pnewsexpert   InfoWorld    iecc.list
.aconfigrc     .letter       .report        LISTS        mailing.lists
.article       .login        .rm-timestamp  Mail         newels
.cshrc         .mailrc       .rnlast        News         src
.elm           .newsrc       .rnsoft        OWL
```

You can see that this directory contains more dot files than regular files and directories. This is not uncommon in a Unix home directory. However, it's rare to find any dot files other than the standard dot and dot-dot directories (which are in every directory in the entire file system) in directories other than your home directory. (These dot files are typically created by applications you use, and they should be edited only with care.)

6. You used another flag to the `ls` command—the `-F` flag—in the preceding hour. Do you remember what it does?

```
% ls -F
Archives/      Mail/           RUMORS.18Sept  mailing.lists
InfoWorld@     News/           bin/           newels
LISTS          OWL/            iecc.list      src/
```

Adding the `-F` flag to `ls` appends suffixes to certain filenames so that you can ascertain more easily what types of files they are. Three different suffixes can be added, as shown in Table 4.1.

TABLE 4.1   Filename Suffixes Appended by `ls  -F`

Suffix	Example	Meaning
/	`Mail/`	`Mail` is a directory.
*	`prog*`	`prog` is an executable program.
@	`bin@`	`bin` is a symbolic link to another file or directory.

7. Mac and Windows users can both create aliases, separate files that do not contain information but act instead as pointers to the actual target files. Aliases can exist either for specific files or for folders. Windows folk might also know such a file as a "shortcut" file.

Unix has offered a similar feature forever, which in Unix jargon is called a *symbolic link*. A symbolic link, such as `bin` in Table 4.1, contains the name of another file or directory rather than any contents of its own. If you could peek inside, it might look like `bin = @/usr/bin`. Every time someone tries to look at `bin`, the system shows the contents of `/usr/bin` instead.

You'll learn more about symbolic links and how they help you organize your files in Hour 6, "Creating, Moving, Renaming, and Deleting Files and Directories." For now, just remember that if you see an `@` after a filename, it's a link to another spot in the file system.

8. A useful flag for `ls` (one that might not be available in your version of Unix) is the `-m` flag. This flag outputs the files as a comma-separated list. If there are many files, using `-m` can be a quick and easy way to see what's available:

```
% ls -m
Archives, InfoWorld, LISTS, Mail, News, OWL, RUMORS.18Sept,
bin, iecc.list, mailing.lists, newels, src
```

Sometimes you might want to list each of your files on a separate line, perhaps for a printout you want to annotate. You've learned that the -C flag forces recalcitrant versions of ls to output in multiple columns. Unfortunately, the opposite behavior isn't obtained by use of a lowercase c. (Unix should be so consistent!) Instead, use the -1 flag to indicate that you want one column of output. Try it.

Task 4.3: Combining Flags

The different flags you've learned so far are summarized in Table 4.2.

TABLE 4.2   Some Useful Flags to ls

Flag	Meaning
-a	List all files, including any dot files.
-F	Indicate file types: / = directory and * = executable.
-m	Show files as a comma-separated list.
-s	Show size of files, in blocks (typically, 1 block = 1,024 bytes).
-C	Force multiple-column output on listings.
-1	Force single-column output on listings.
-l	Show long-listing format, including permissions, ownership, size, and date.

What if you want a list, generated with the -F conventions, that simultaneously shows you all files and indicates their types?

1. Combining flags in Unix is easy. All you have to do is run them together in a sequence of characters and prefix the whole thing with a dash:

```
% ls -aF
./              .gopherrc       .oldnewsrc      .sig
../             .history*       .plan           Archives/
.Agenda         .info           .pnewsexpert    InfoWorld/
.aconfigrc      .letter         .report         LISTS
.article        .login          .rm-timestamp   Mail/
.cshrc          .mailrc         .rnlast         News/
.elm/           .newsrc         .rnsoft         OWL/
```

2. Sometimes it's more convenient to keep all the flags separate. This is fine, as long as each flag is prefixed by its own dash:

```
% ls -s -F
total 403
    1 Archives/      1 Mail/       5 RUMORS.18Sept   280 mailing.lists
    1 InfoWorld/     1 News/       1 bin/              2 newels
  261 LISTS          1 OWL/        4 iecc.list         1 src/
```

3. Try some of these combinations on your own computer. Also try to list a flag more than once (for example, `ls -sss -s`) or list flags in different orders.

Very few Unix commands care about the order in which flags are listed. Because it's the presence or absence of a flag that's important, listing a flag more than once also doesn't make any difference.

Task 4.4: Listing Other Directories Without Changing Location

Every time I try to do any research in the library, I find myself spending hours and hours there, but it seems to me that I do less research than I think I should. That's because most of my time is for the tasks between the specifics of my research: finding the location of the next book and finding the book itself.

If `ls` constrained you to listing only the directory you were in, it would hobble you in a similar way. Using only `ls` would slow you down dramatically and force you to use `cd` to move around each time.

Instead, just as you can specify certain files by using `ls`, you can specify certain directories you're interested in viewing.

1. List `/usr` on your system:

```
% ls -F /usr
5bin/          diag/          lddrv/         share/         ucbinclude@
5include/      dict/          lib/           source/        ucblib@
5lib/          etc/           local/         spool@         xpg2bin/
acc/           export/        lost+found/    src@           xpg2include/
acctlog*       games/         man@           stand@         xpg2lib/
adm@           hack/          mdec@          sys@
bin/           hosts/         old/           system/
boot@          include/       pub@           tmp@
demo/          kvm/           sccs/          ucb/
```

Try this yourself. You probably have different files and directories listed in your own `/usr` directory. Remember, @ files are symbolic links in the listing, too.

2. You can also specify more than one directory:

```
% ls /usr/local /home/taylor
/home/taylor:
Global.Software    Mail/              Src/                history.usenet.Z
Interactive.Unix   News/              bin/
/usr/local/:
T/                 emacs/             ftp/               lists/             motd~
admin/             emacs-18.59/       gnubin/            lost+found/        netcom/
```

```
bin/          etc/          include/      man/          policy/
cat/          faq/          info/         menu/         src/
doc/          forms/        lib/          motd          tmp/
```

In this example, the `ls` command also sorted the directories before listing them. I specified that I wanted to see `/usr/local` and then `/home/taylor`, but it presented the directories in opposite order.

NOTE

I've never been able to figure out how `ls` sorts directories when you ask for more than one to be listed; it's not an alphabetical listing. Consider it a mystery. Remember that if you must have the output in a specific order, you can use the `ls` command twice in a row.

---

3. Here's where the dot-dot shorthand for the parent directory can come in handy. Try it yourself:

```
% ls -m ..
ashley, bruce, cedric, christine, david, gareth,
guest, higgins, james, kiana, linda, mac, mark,
rank, shalini, shane, taylor, Vicki
```

If you were down one branch of the file system and wanted to look at some files down another branch, you could easily find yourself using the command `ls ../Indiana/ Personnel` or `ls -s ../../source`.

4. There's a problem here, however. You've seen that you can specify filenames to look at those files and directory names to look at the contents of those directories, but what if you're interested in a directory itself, not in its contents? You might want to list just two directories—not the contents, just the directory names themselves, as shown here:

```
% ls -F
Archives/      Mail/          RUMORS.18Sept  mailing.lists
InfoWorld/     News/          bin/           newlists
LISTS          OWL/           iecc.list      src/
% ls -s LISTS Mail newlists
  261 LISTS          2 newlists
Mail:
total 705
  8 cennamo      27 ean_houts     4 kcs      21 mark      7 sartin
 28 dan_sommer    2 gordon_haight 34 lehman   5 raf       3 shelf
 14 decc         48 harrism      64 mac       7 rock      20 steve
  3 druby        14 james        92 mailbox   5 rustle   18 tai
```

5. The problem is that `ls` doesn't know that you want to look at `Mail` unless you tell it not to look inside the directories specified. The command flag needed is `-d`, which forces `ls` to list directories rather than their contents. The same ls command, but with the -d flag, has dramatically different output:

```
% ls -sd LISTS Mail newlists
  261 LISTS          1 Mail/          2 newlists
```

Try some of these flags on your own system and watch how they work together.

To list a file or directory, you can specify it to ls. Directories, however, reveal their contents unless you also include the -d flag.

Special ls Command Flags

It should be clear to you that Unix is the Swiss Army knife of operating systems. Even the simplest commands have dozens of different options. On Mac OS X, for example, ls has more than 33 different flags. Like nearly any other command in Unix, it's a tool with a million uses—most of which come from your own creativity and personal taste, and its real power comes from how it's used in conjunction with other tools and commands, as you will see later.

Task 4.5: Changing the Sort Order in ls

What if you wanted to look at files but wanted them to show up in a directory sorting order different from the default (such as column-first order)? How could you change the sort order in ls?

1. The -x flag sorts across, listing the output in columns, or row-first order (where entries are sorted across, then down):

```
% ls -a
.                    .elm              .plan            Global.Software
..                   .forward          .pnewsexpert     Interactive.Unix
.Pnews.header        .ircmotd          .rnlast          Mail
.accinfo             .login            .rnlock          News
.article             .logout           .rnsoft          Src
.cshrc               .newsrc           .sig             bin
.delgroups           .oldnewsrc        .tin             history.usenet.Z
% ls -x -a
.                    ..                .Pnews.header    .accinfo
.article             .cshrc            .delgroups       .elm
.forward             .ircmotd          .login           .logout
.newsrc              .oldnewsrc        .plan            .pnewsexpert
.rnlast              .rnlock           .rnsoft          .sig
.tin                 Global.Software   Interactive.Unix Mail
News                 Src               bin              history.usenet.Z
```

2. Even more ways exist to sort files in `ls`. If you want to sort by most recently accessed to least recently accessed, you use the `-t` flag:

```
% ls -a -t
./                 ../                .rnlock            .cshrc
.newsrc            News/              .rnlast            .sig
.oldnewsrc         .tin/              .rnsoft            .plan
.article           .ircmotd           Interactive.Unix   Mail/
.elm/              .delgroups         .accinfo*          .Pnews.header*
.forward           .login             Src/               .pnewsexpert
history.usenet.Z   bin/               Global.Software    .logout
```

From this output, you can see that the most recently accessed files are `.newsrc` and `.oldnewsrc` and that it's been quite a while since `.logout` was touched. Try using the `-t` flag on your system to see which files you've been accessing and which you haven't.

3. So far, you know three different approaches to sorting files within the `ls` command: column-first order, row-first order, and most recently accessed-first order. But more options exist in `ls` than just these three. For example, the `-r` flag reverses any sorting order:

```
% ls
Global.Software    Mail/              Src/               history.usenet.Z
Interactive.Unix   News/              bin/
% ls -r
history.usenet.Z   Src/               Mail/              Global.Software
bin/               News/              Interactive.Unix
```

4. Things can become confusing when you combine some of these flags. Try to list the contents of the directory that is one level above the current directory, sorted so the most recently accessed file is last in the list. At the same time, you want to know which items are directories and the size of each file. Use this:

```
% ls -r -t -F -s ..
total 150
   2 bruce/      2 rank/        2 kiana/       14 higgins/
   2 linda/      2 christine/   2 shane/        6 mac/
   2 cedric      2 peggy/       4 paul/        10 mark/
   2 james@      4 taylor/      4 gareth/       6 ashley/
   2 vicki/      2 guest/       6 shalini/      4 david/
```

A better and easier way to type the preceding command would be to bundle flags into the single argument `ls -rtFs ..`, which would work just as well, and you'd look like an expert!

Task 4.6: Listing Directory Trees Recursively in `ls`

In case things aren't yet complicated enough with `ls`, two more important valuable flags are available. One is the `-R` flag, which causes `ls` to recursively list directories below the current or specified directory. (If you are familiar with DOS, you can think of using the -R flag with ls as equivalent to the DOS tree command.) If you think of listing files as a numbered set of steps, recursion is simply adding a step—if this file is a directory, list its contents too—to the list.

1. When I use the -R flag, here's what I see:

```
% ls -R
Global.Software    Mail/      Src/      history.usenet.Z
Interactive.Unix   News/      bin/
Mail:
Folders/  Netnews/
Mail/Folders:
mail.sent  mailbox    steinman   tucker
Mail/Netnews:
postings
News:
uptodate   volts
Src:
sum-up.c
bin:
Pnews*    punt*    submit*
```

2. Try it yourself. Notice that ls lists the current directory and then alphabetically lists the contents of all subdirectories. Notice also that the Mail directory has two directories within it and that those are also listed here.

Viewing all files and directories below a certain point in the file system can be a valuable way to look for files (although you'll soon learn better tools for finding files). If you aren't careful, though, you can get hundreds or thousands of lines of information streaming across your screen. Do not enter a command such as ls -R / unless you have time to sit and watch a *lot* of information fly past.

TIP

You can usually interrupt a long-running command by pressing Ctrl-C.

If you try to list the contents of a directory when you don't have permission to access the information, ls warns you with an error message:

```
% ls ../marv
../marv unreadable
```

Now ask for a recursive listing, with indications of file type and size, of the directory /etc, and see what's there. The listing will include many files and subdirectories, but they should be easy to wade through due to all the notations ls uses to indicate files and directories.

Task 4.7: Long Listing Format in `ls`

You've seen how to estimate the size of a file by using the `-s` flag to find the number of blocks it occupies. To find the exact size of a file in bytes, use the `-l` flag. (Use a lowercase letter L. The numeral 1 produces single-column output, as you've already learned.)

1. The first long listing shows information for the `LISTS` file:

```
% ls -l LISTS
-rw------- 1 taylor     106020 Oct  8 15:17 LISTS
```

The output is explained in Figure 4.1.

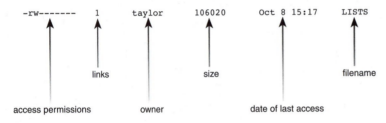

FIGURE 4.1
The meaning of the `-l` output for a file.

For each file and directory in the Unix file system, the owner, size, name, number of other files pointing to it (links), and access permissions are recorded. The creation, modification, and access times and dates are also recorded for each file. The modification time is the default time used for the `-t` sorting option and listed by the `ls` long format.

Permissions Strings

Interpreting permissions strings is a complex issue because Unix has a sophisticated security model. Security revolves around three different types of user: the owner of the file, the group of which that the file is a part, and everyone else.

The first character of the permissions string, identified in Figure 4.1 as *access permissions*, indicates the kind of file. The two most common values are d for directories and - for regular files. Be aware that there are many other file types that you'll rarely, if ever, see.

The following nine characters in the permissions string indicate what type of access is allowed for different users. From left to right, these characters show what access is allowed for the owner of the file, the group that owns the file, and everyone else.

Figure 4.2 shows how to break down the permissions string for the `LISTS` file into individual components.

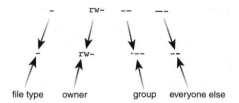

FIGURE 4.2
Reading access permissions for `LISTS`.

Each permissions string is identically composed of three components—permission for reading, writing, and execution—as shown in Figure 4.3.

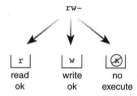

FIGURE 4.3
Elements of a permissions string.

Armed with this information—specifically, knowing that a - character means that the specific permission is denied—you can see that `ls` shows that the owner of the file, `taylor`, as illustrated in Figure 4.1, has read and write permission. Nobody else either in `taylor`'s group or in any other group has permission to view, edit, or run the file. There's lots more on this subject in the next hour!

Earlier you learned that just about everything in Unix ends up as a file in the file system, whether it's an application, a device driver, or a directory. The system keeps track of whether a file is executable because that's one way it knows whether `LISTS` is the name of a file or the name of an application.

Task 4.8: Long Listing Format for Directories in `ls`

The long form of a directory listing is almost identical to a file listing, but the permissions string is interpreted in a very different manner.

1. Here is an example of a long directory listing:

```
% ls -l -d Example
drwxr-x---   2 taylor        1024 Sep 30 10:50 Example/
```

Remember that you must have both read and execute permissions for a directory. If you have either read or execute permission but not both, the directory will not be usable (as though you had neither permission). Write permission, of course, enables the user to alter the contents of the directory or add new files to the directory.

2. The `Example` directory can be interpreted as shown in Figure 4.4.

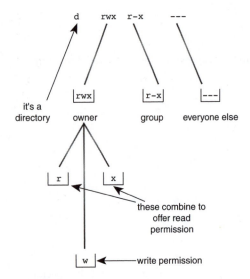

FIGURE 4.4
Elements of directory permissions.

I've never understood the nuances of a directory with read but not execute permission, or vice versa, and explanations from other people have never proven to be correct. It's okay, though, because I've never seen a directory on a Unix system that was anything other than `---`, `r-x`, `rw-`, or `rwx`.

3. Now try using the `-l` flag yourself. Move to your home directory and enter `ls -l` as shown here:

```
% ls -l
total 403
drwx------  2 taylor        512 Sep 30 10:38 Archives/
drwx------  3 taylor        512 Oct  1 08:23 InfoWorld/
-rw-------  1 taylor      46901 Oct  8 15:17 LISTS
drwx------  2 taylor       1024 Sep 30 10:50 Mail/
```

```
drwx------   2 taylor        512 Oct   6 09:36 News/
drwx------   2 taylor        512 Sep  30 10:51 OWL/
-rw-------   1 taylor       4643 Sep  20 10:49 RUMORS.18Sept
drwx------   2 taylor        512 Oct   1 09:53 bin/
-rw-------   1 taylor       3843 Oct   6 18:02 iecc.list
-rw-rw----   1 taylor     280232 Oct   6 09:57 mailing.lists
-rw-rw----   1 taylor       1031 Oct   7 15:44 newlists
drwx------   2 taylor        512 Sep  14 22:14 src/
```

The size of a directory is usually in increments of 512 bytes, though some Unixes show exactly how big the *directory of filenames therein* is. (Unix doesn't indicate how big the files in a directory are, just the sum size of all the filenames themselves.) The second field, the "link," is an interesting and little-known value when a directory is being listed. Instead of counting up the number of other files that point to the file (that is, the number of files that have a link to the current file), the second field indicates the number of directories that are contained in that specific directory. Remember that all directories have dot and dot-dot, so the minimum value is always 2.

4. Consider the following example of a directory listing:

```
% ls -Fa
./              .gopherrc       .oldnewsrc      .sig            OWL/
../             .history*       .plan           Archives/       RUMORS.18Sept
.Agenda         .info           .pnewsexpert    Cancelled.mail  bin/
.aconfigrc      .letter         .report         InfoWorld/      iecc.list
.article        .login          .rm-timestamp   LISTS           mailing.lists
.cshrc          .mailrc         .rnlast         Mail/           newlists
.elm/           .newsrc         .rnsoft         News/           src/
% ls -ld .
drwx------  10 taylor       1024 Oct  10 16:00 ./
```

5. Try entering ls -ld . and see whether it correctly identifies the number of directories in your home directory. Move to other directories and see whether the listing agrees with your own count of directories.

The output from the ls -l command is unquestionably complex and packed with information. Interpretation of permissions strings is an important part of understanding and being able to use Unix, and more explanation is offered in subsequent hours.

Table 4.3 summarizes the many different command flags for ls that you have learned in this hour.

TABLE 4.3 Summary of Command Flags for `ls`

Flag	Meaning
-1	Force single-column output on listings.
-a	List all files, including any dot files.
-C	Force multiple-column output on listings.
-d	List directories rather than their contents.
-F	Indicate file types: / = directory and * = executable.
-l	Generate a long listing of files and directories.
-m	Show files as a comma-separated list.
-r	Reverse the order of any file sorting.
-R	Recursively show directories and their contents.
-s	Show size of files, in blocks (typically 1 block = 1,024 bytes).
-t	Sort output in most-recently modified order.
-x	Sort output in row-first order.

Without a doubt, `ls` is one of the most powerful and, therefore, confusing commands in Unix. The best way for you to learn how all the flags work together is to experiment with different combinations.

Task 4.9: Creating Files with the `touch` Command

At this point, you know about various Unix tools that help you move through the file system and learn about specific files. Now it's time to use the `touch` command, which helps you create new files on the system, independent of any program other than the shell itself. This can prove very helpful for organizing a new collection of files, for example.

The main reason that `touch` is used in Unix is to force the last-modified time of a file to be updated, as the following example demonstrates:

```
% ls -l iecc.list
-rw-------   1 taylor        3843 Oct  6 18:02 iecc.list
% touch iecc.list
% ls -l iecc.list
-rw-------   1 taylor        3843 Oct 10 16:22 iecc.list
```

Because the `touch` command changes modification times of files, anything that sorts files based on modification time will, of course, alter the position of that file when the file is altered by `touch`.

1. Consider the following output:

```
% ls -t
mailing.lists    LISTS             News/            OWL/             src/
Cancelled.mail   newlists          bin/             Mail/
RUMORS.18Sept    iecc.list         InfoWorld/       Archives/
% touch iecc.list
% ls -t
iecc.list        RUMORS.18Sept     News/            OWL/             src/
mailing.lists    LISTS             bin/             Mail/
Cancelled.mail   newlists          InfoWorld/       Archives/
```

You probably will not use touch for this purpose very often.

2. If you try to use the touch command on a file that doesn't exist, the program creates the file:

```
% ls
Archives/        LISTS             OWL/             iecc.list        src/
Cancelled.mail   Mail/             RUMORS.18Sept    mailing.lists
InfoWorld/       News/             bin/             newlists
% touch new.file
% ls
Archives/        LISTS             OWL/             iecc.list        newlists
Cancelled.mail   Mail/             RUMORS.18Sept    mailing.lists    src/
InfoWorld/       News/             bin/             new.file
% ls -l new.file
-rw-rw----   1 taylor            0 Oct 10 16:28 new.file
```

The new file has zero bytes, as can be seen in the ls -l output. Notice that by default the files are created with read and write permission for the user and anyone in the user's group. You'll learn in the next hour how to specify, by using the umask command, your own default permission for files.

You won't need touch very often, but it's valuable to know.

Task 4.10: Checking Disk Space Usage with du

One advantage that Windows and Macintosh systems have over Unix is that they make it easy to find out how much disk space you're using and how much remains available. On a Mac, viewing folders by size shows disk space used, and the bottom of any Finder window shows available space.

Like a close-mouthed police informant, Unix never volunteers any information, so you need to learn two new commands. The du (disk usage) command is used to find out how much disk space is used; the df (disk free) command is used to find out how much space is available.

1. The du command lists the size, in kilobytes, of all directories at or below the current point in the file system.

```
% du
11        ./OWL
38        ./.elm
20        ./Archives
14        ./InfoWorld/PIMS
28        ./InfoWorld
710       ./Mail
191       ./News
25        ./bin
35        ./src
1627      .
```

Notice that du goes two levels deep to find the InfoWorld/PIMS subdirectory, adding its size to the size indicated for the InfoWorld directory. At the very end, it lists 1,627 kilobytes as the size of the dot directory—the current directory. As you know, 1,024 kilobytes is a megabyte. Through division, you'll find that this directory is taking up 1.5MB of disk space.

NOTE

As with ls, Solaris uses its default block size of 512 bytes to indicate file sizes, so you'll need to divide by 2 to get kilobyte-based sizes. Alternatively, use the -h option to display the sizes in human-readable format, with K and M suffixes. This option is available in all modern Unix flavors.

---

2. If you are interested in only the grand total, you can use the -s flag to output just a summary of the information.

```
% du -s
1627      .
```

Of course, you can look anywhere on the file system, but the more subdirectories there are, the longer it takes.

3. It is possible to get error messages with du:

```
% du -s /etc
/etc/shadow: Permission denied
307932    /etc
```

In this example, one of the directories within the /etc directory has a permissions set that denies access:

```
% ls -ld /etc/shadow
-r--------  2 root           683 Oct 10 16:34 /etc/shadow/
```

The du command summarizes disk usage only for the files and directories it can read, so regardless of the size of the shadow file, I'd still have the same size indicated.

4. Although by default du lists only the sizes of directories, it also computes the size of all files. If you're interested in that information, you can, by adding the -a flag, have the program list it for all files:

```
% cd InfoWorld
% du -a
9        ./PIM.review.Z
5        ./Expert.opinion.Z
4        ./PIMS/proposal.txt.Z
1        ./PIMS/task1.txt.Z
2        ./PIMS/task2.txt.Z
2        ./PIMS/task3.txt.Z
2        ./PIMS/task4.txt.Z
2        ./PIMS/task5.txt.Z
2        ./PIMS/task6.txt.Z
1        ./PIMS/contact.info.Z
14       ./PIMS
28       .
```

The problems of the -a flag for du are similar to those for the -R flag for ls. That is, there might be more files in a directory than you care to view.

Task 4.11: Checking Available Disk Space with df

Disks in Unix are typically partitioned into several volumes, each with its own purpose and segregated from the rest of the system. Even on a personal computer system like Mac OS X, the single volume occupying the entire disk is accompanied by several much smaller special-purpose ones, and the tools used for examining them are designed to look at volumes individually. This means that figuring out how much disk space is available on the overall Unix system is difficult for everyone except experts. The df command is used for this task, but it doesn't summarize its results; the user must add the column of numbers.

1. This is the system's response to the df command on a thoroughly partitioned Unix server:

```
%  df
Filesystem          kbytes     used    avail capacity  Mounted
/dev/zd0a            17259    14514     1019     93%    /
/dev/zd8d           185379   143995    22846     86%    /userf
/dev/zd7d           185379    12984   153857      8%    /tmp
/dev/zd3f           385689   307148    39971     88%    /users
/dev/zd3g           367635   232468    98403     70%    /userc
/dev/zd2f           385689   306189    40931     88%    /usere
/dev/zd2g           367635   207234   123637     63%    /userb
/dev/zd1g           301823   223027    48613     82%    /usera
/dev/zd5c           371507   314532    19824     94%    /usr
/dev/zd0h           236820   159641    53497     75%    /usr/src
/dev/zd0g           254987    36844   192644     16%    /var
```

You end up with lots of information, but it's not easily added quickly to find the total space available. Nonetheless, the output offers quite a bit of information.

2. Because I know that my home directory is on the disk /users, I can simply look for that directory in the rightmost column to find out that I'm using the hard disk /dev/zd3f. I can see that 385,689 kilobytes are on the disk, and 88% of the disk is used, which means that 307,148 kilobytes are used and 39,971 kilobytes, or only about 38MB, are unused.

3. Some Unix systems have relatively few separate computer disks hooked up or volumes partitioned, making the df output more readable. The df output is shown below and explained in Figure 4.5.

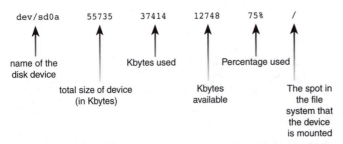

FIGURE 4.5
Understanding df output.

```
% df
Filesystem          kbytes    used    avail capacity Mounted
/dev/sd0a            55735    37414    12748    75%    /
/dev/sd2b           187195   153569   14907    91%    /usr
/dev/sd1a            55688    43089     7031    86%    /utils
```

You can add the columns to find that the system has a total of about 300MB of disk space (55,735 + 187,195 + 55,688), of which 230MB are used. The remaining space is therefore 33MB, or 16%, of the total disk size.

4. Many modern Unix systems enable you to use du with the -h flag. (Some man pages refer to this as the *human readable output* flag!) This offers a much more useful output format. Here's an example from yet another computer system:

```
% df -h
Filesystem    Size   Used  Avail Capacity  Mounted on
/dev/sd0a     15G    2.1G   13G     14%     /
/dev/sd1a     15G    157M   15G      1%     /web
```

5. Mac OS X is one of the more modern Unixes, and it has all sorts of nondisk devices included in `df` output, as you can see in this example:

```
$ df -h
Filesystem                  Size    Used   Avail  Capacity  Mounted on
/dev/disk0s8                 49G     43G    6.1G     88%     /
devfs                        94K     94K     0B     100%     /dev
fdesc                       1.0K    1.0K     0B     100%     /dev
<volfs>                     512K    512K     0B     100%     /.vol
automount -nsl [335]         0B      0B      0B     100%     /Network
automount -fstab [338]       0B      0B      0B     100%     /automount/Servers
automount -static [338]      0B      0B      0B     100%     /automount/static
```

With all this output, there's actually only one disk on the system, /dev/disk0s8, which is a 49GB hard drive that's 88% full.

6. Try using the `du` and `df` commands on your system to determine how much disk space is available on both the overall system and the disk you're using for your home directory. Then use `du` to identify how much space your files and directories are occupying.

Task 4.12: Shrinking Big Files with the `gzip` Program

Now that you can determine how much space you're using with the files in your directory, you're ready to learn how to save space without removing any files. Unix has a built-in program—the `gzip` program—that offers this capability.

The original compression program built into Unix is called `compress`, but there are now two other tools you can use to compress files that tend to do a better job: `gzip` and `bzip2`.

1. In this simple example, the `gzip` program is given a list of filenames and then compresses each of the files and renames them with a `.gz` suffix, which indicates that they are compressed:

```
% ls -l LISTDATA2
-rw-r--r--  1 taylor  taylor  24064 23 Apr 22:41 LISTDATA2
% gzip LISTDATA2
% ls -l LIST*
-rw-r--r--  1 taylor  taylor   3682 23 Apr 22:41 LISTDATA2.gz
```

Compressing the LISTDATA2 file has reduced its size from 24 kilobytes to a little more than 3 kilobytes (a savings of almost 85% in disk space). If you expect to have large files on your system that you won't access very often, using the `gzip` program can save lots of disk space.

2. Using `gzip` on bigger files can show even greater savings (note that I'm also adding the -v flag, which shows how much savings I've gained by using gzip on the file in question):

```
% ls -l big.file
-rwx------  1 taylor   taylor   3198588 23 Apr 22:48 big.file
% gzip -v big.file
big.file:                72.7% -- replaced with big.file.gz
% ls -l big.file*
-rwx------  1 taylor   taylor   871440 23 Apr 22:48 big.file.gz
```

This single command is able to free almost 3MB of disk space. If you're using a PC to run Unix, or if you are on a system with many users (which you can easily ascertain by using the w command), it might take a significant amount of time to compress files.

3. To reverse the operation, use the companion command `gunzip` and specify either the current name of the file (that is, with the `.gz` suffix) or the name of the file before it was compressed (that is, without the `.gz` suffix):

```
% gunzip LISTDATA2
% ls -l LISTDATA2
-rw-r--r--  1 taylor   taylor   24064 23 Apr 22:41 LISTDATA2
```

NOTE

Why would you compress files? You would do so to save file space. Before you use any of the compressed files, though, you must uncompress them, so the `gzip` utility is best used with large files you won't need for a while.

4. Before we leave this topic, let's take a quick peek at how the other two compression programs compare with both `LISTDATA2` and `big.file`:

```
% ls -l LISTDATA2 big.file
-rw-r--r--  1 taylor   taylor      24064 23 Apr 22:41 LISTDATA2
-rwx------  1 taylor   taylor   3198588 23 Apr 22:48 big.file
% compress -v LISTDATA2 big.file
LISTDATA2.Z: 25% compression
big.file.Z: 33% compression
% ls -l LISTDATA* big.file*
-rw-r--r--  1 taylor   taylor       5962 23 Apr 22:41 LISTDATA2.Z
-rwx------  1 taylor   taylor   1068457 23 Apr 22:48 big.file.Z*
% uncompress LISTDATA2* big.file*
% bzip2 -v LISTDATA2 big.file
  LISTDATA2:  5.979:1,  1.338 bits/byte, 83.27% saved, 24064 in, 4025 out.
  big.file:  5.305:1,  1.508 bits/byte, 81.15% saved, 3198588 in, 602958 out.
% bunzip2 LISTDATA* big.file*
% ls -l LISTDATA big.file
-rw-r--r--  1 taylor   taylor      24064 23 Apr 22:41 LISTDATA2
-rwx------  1 taylor   taylor   3198588 23 Apr 22:48 big.file
```

Different compression programs have different results because of the format of a given file. Sometimes the compression programs can't save any disk space at all. If you are having disk space issues, experiment with the different programs on your largest file or two to see which is doing the best job with the kind of files you have.

Try using the `gzip` program on some of the files in your directory, being careful not to compress any files (particularly preference or dot files) that might be required to run programs.

Summary

You've spent most of this hour learning about the powerful and complex `ls` command and its many ways of listing files and directories. You've also learned how to combine command flags to reduce typing. You've learned how to use the `touch` command to create new files and update the modification time on older files, if needed. The hour continued with a discussion of how to ascertain the amount of disk space you're using and how much space is left, using the `du` and `df` commands, respectively. You've also learned how the `gzip` command can keep you from running out of space by ensuring that infrequently used files are stored in the minimum space needed.

Workshop

The Workshop summarizes the key terms you've learned and poses some questions about the topics presented in this lesson. It also provides you with a preview of what you will learn in the next hour.

Key Terms

access permissions   This is the set of accesses (read, write, and execute) allowed for each of the three classes of users (owner, group, and everyone else) for each file or directory on the system.

block   At its most fundamental, a block is like a sheet of information in the virtual notebook that represents the disk: A disk is typically composed of many tens, or hundreds, of thousands of blocks of information, each 512 bytes in size. You also might read the explanation of **inode** in the glossary at the back of the book to learn more about how disks are structured in Unix.

column-first order   When you have a list of items that are listed in columns and span multiple lines, column-first order is a sorting strategy in which items are sorted so that the items are in alphabetical order down the first column. The sorting continues at the top of the second column, then the third column, and so on. The alternative strategy is **row-first order**.

permissions string   This string represents the access permissions, encoding the various privileges symbolically for easy reading.

row-first order   This is a sorting order in which items are sorted in rows so that the first item of each column in a row is in alphabetical order from left to right, then the second line contains the next set of items, and so on. The alternative strategy is **column-first order**.

Exercises

1. Try using the du command on different directories to see how much disk space each requires. If you encounter errors with file permissions, use `ls -ld` to list the permissions of the directory in question.

2. Why would you want all the different types of sorting alternatives available with `ls`? Can you think of situations in which each would be useful?

3. Use a combination of the `ls -t` and `touch` commands to create a few new files. Then update their modification times so that in a most recently modified listing of files, the first file you created shows up ahead of the second file you created.

4. Try using the `du -s ..` command from your home directory. Before you try it, however, what do you think will happen?

5. Use df and bc or dc to figure out the amounts of disk space used and available on your system.

6. Use the gzip command to shrink a file in /tmp or your home directory. Use the -v flag to learn how much the file was compressed and then restore the file to its original condition by using gunzip.

Preview of the Next Hour

The next hour is a bit easier. It offers further explanation of the various information given by the `ls` command and a discussion of file ownership, including how to change the owner and group of any file or directory. You will learn about the chmod command, which can change the specific set of permissions associated with any file or directory, and the umask command, which can control the modes that new files are given upon creation.

HOUR 5
Ownership and Permissions

Goals for This Hour

In this hour, you will learn

- About file permissions settings
- About directory permissions settings
- How to modify file and directory permissions with chmod
- About working with chmod numeric permissions strings
- How to establish default file and directory permissions with umask
- How to identify the owner and group for any file or directory

This hour focuses on teaching the basics of Unix file permissions. Topics include setting and modifying file permissions with chmod, analyzing file permissions as shown by the ls -l command, and setting up default file permissions with the umask command. Permission is only half the puzzle, however, and you'll also learn about file ownership and group ownership, and how to change either for any file or directory.

The preceding hour contained the first tutorial dealing with the permissions of a file or directory using the -l option with ls. If you haven't read that material recently, it would help to review it. In this hour, you'll learn about another option to ls that tells Unix to show the group and owner of files or directories. Two more commands are introduced and discussed in detail: chmod for changing the permissions of a file and umask for defining default permissions.

Working with File Permissions

As you have seen in examples throughout the book, Unix treats all directories as files; each has its own size (sometimes independent of its contents), its own permissions strings, and more. As a result, unless it's an important difference, from here on when I talk about *files*, I'm referring to both files and directories. Logic will confirm whether commands can apply to both, or to files only, or to directories only. (For example, you can't edit a directory, and you can't store files inside other files.)

Task 5.1: Understanding File Permissions Settings

In the past hour you learned a bit about how to interpret the information that ls offers on file permissions when it is used with the -l flag. Consider the following example:

```
% ls -l
total 403
drwx------  2 taylor         512 Sep 30 10:38 Archives/
drwx------  3 taylor         512 Oct  1 08:23 InfoWorld/
-rw-------  1 taylor      106020 Oct 10 13:47 LISTS
drwx------  2 taylor        1024 Sep 30 10:50 Mail/
drwx------  2 taylor         512 Oct  6 09:36 News/
drwx------  2 taylor         512 Sep 30 10:51 OWL/
-rw-------  1 taylor        4643 Oct 10 14:01 RUMORS.18Sept
drwx------  2 taylor         512 Oct 10 19:09 bin/
-rw-------  1 taylor        3843 Oct 10 16:22 iecc.list
-rw-rw-r--  1 taylor      280232 Oct 10 16:22 mailing.lists
-rw-rw----  1 taylor        1031 Oct  7 15:44 newlists
drwx------  2 taylor         512 Oct 10 19:09 src/
```

The first item of information on each line is what we're focused on here. You learned in the preceding hour that the first item is called the *permissions string* or, more succinctly, *permissions*. It also is sometimes referred to as the *mode* or *permissions mode* of the file, a mnemonic that can be valuable for remembering how to change permissions.

The permissions can be broken into four parts: type, owner, group, and world permissions. The first character indicates the file type: d is a directory and - is a regular file. Unix has various other types of files, each indicated by the first letter of its permissions string, as summarized in Table 5.1. You can safely ignore any file that isn't either a regular file or a directory.

TABLE 5.1   The ls File Type Indicators

Letter	Indicated File Type
d	Directory
b	Block-type special file
c	Character-type special file
l	Symbolic link
p	Pipe
s	Socket
-	Regular file

The next nine letters in the permissions string are broken into three groups of three each—representing the owner, group, and everyone else—as shown in Figure 5.1.

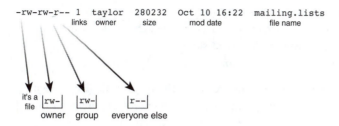

FIGURE 5.1
Interpreting file permissions.

To understand what the permissions actually mean to the computer system, remember that Unix treats everything as a file. If you install an application, it's just like everything else, with one exception: The system knows that an application is executable. A letter to your Mum is a regular file, but if you were to tell Unix that it was executable, the system would merrily try to run it as a program (and fail).

Three primary types of permission exist for files: read, write, and execute. Read permission enables users to examine the contents of the file with various programs, but they cannot alter, modify, or delete any information. They can copy the file to a directory where they have write permission and then edit the new version.

Write permission is the next step up. Users with write access to a file can add information to the file. If you have write permission and read permission for a file, you can edit the file: The read permission enables you to view the contents, and the write permission enables you to alter the contents. With write permission only, you'd be able to add information to the file, but you wouldn't be able to view the contents of the file at any time. Admittedly, write-only permission is unusual in Unix, but you might see it for log files, which are files that track activity on the system.

So far you've learned that you can have files with read-only permission, read-write permission, and write-only permission. The third type of access permission is execute, noted by `ls` with an x in the third slot of the permissions string. You can set any file to be executable; shell scripts, Perl, Ruby and other interpreted languages are text files that are executed. For example, here are some programs—and shell scripts—that are executable in my own "bin" directory:

```
% ls -l bin
total 57
-rwx------  1 taylor       1507 Aug 17 13:27 bounce.msg
-rwxrwx---  1 taylor      32916 Oct 10 19:09 calc
-rwx------  1 taylor      18567 Sep 14 22:14 fixit
-rw-------  1 taylor        334 Oct  1 09:53 punt
-rwx------  1 taylor       3424 Sep 10 22:27 rumor.mill.sh
```

1. Try listing the files in the directory /etc on your system and see whether you can identify which are executable files or programs, which are directories, which are symbolic links (denoted with an l as the first character of the permissions string; they're files that point to other files, or directories that point to other directories), and which are regular files.

2. Execute permission is slightly different from either read or write permission. Any file with execute permission can be treated like a program. You enter the name of the file on the command line, and if the directory is in your PATH, the file is executed:

```
% pwd
/home/taylor
% echo $PATH
/home/taylor/bin:/bin:/usr/bin:/usr/ucb:/usr/local:/usr/local/bin:
% ls -l bin/say.hi
-rwxrwx---  1 taylor          9 Oct 11 13:32 bin/say.hi
% say.hi
hi
```

You can now see the importance of your search path. Without a search path, the system wouldn't be able to find any commands, and you'd be left with a barely functional system. You can also see the purpose of checking the executable permission status. I'm going to jump ahead a bit to show you one use of the chmod (change mode/permission) program so that you can see what happens if I remove the execute permission from the say.hi program with the -x flag:

```
% chmod -x bin/say.hi
% ls -l bin/say.hi
-rw-rw----  1 taylor          9 Oct 11 13:32 bin/say.hi
% say.hi
/home/taylor/bin/say.hi: Permission denied.
```

This time Unix searched through my search path, found a file that matched the name of the program I requested, and then ascertained that it wasn't executable. The resultant error message was Permission denied.

3. Now try entering say.hi on your computer system. You'll get a different error message, Command not found, which tells you that Unix checked all the directories in your search path but couldn't find a match anywhere.

4. Check your PATH and find a directory that you can add files in. You'll probably have a bin directory in your HOME directory (for example, I have /home/taylor/bin in my search path). If you don't, use mkdir bin to create one. It's a good place to add a file using the touch command:

```
% echo $PATH
/home/taylor/bin:/bin:/usr/bin:/usr/ucb:/usr/local:/usr/local/bin:
% touch bin/my.new.cmd
% ls -l bin
-rw-rw----  1 taylor          0 Oct 11 15:07 my.new.cmd
```

5. Now try to actually execute the command by entering its name directly:

```
% my.new.cmd
/home/taylor/bin/my.new.cmd: Permission denied.
```

NOTE

If you're using the C shell (instead of `bash`) as your command interpreter, as might be the case on FreeBSD, it probably won't find the new command you just created. This is because, to speed things up, it keeps an internal table of where different commands are found in your search path. You need to force the program to rebuild its table, and you can do that with the simple command `rehash`. If, when you enter the filename, you don't get a permission denied error but instead see `Command not found`, enter `rehash` and try again.

6. Finally, use `chmod` to add execute permission to the file and try executing it one more time:

```
% chmod +x bin/my.new.cmd
% ls -l bin/my.new.cmd
-rwxrw----   1 taylor           0 Oct 11 15:07 bin/my.new.cmd
% my.new.cmd
%
```

Voilà! You've created your first Unix command, which is an achievement even though it doesn't do much. You can now see how the search path and the Unix philosophy of having applications be identical to regular files, except for the permission can be invaluable as you learn how to customize your environment.

Execute permission enables the user to run a file as if it were a program. Execute permission is independent of other permissions granted—or denied—so it's perfectly feasible to have a program with read and execute permission but no write permission. (After all, you wouldn't want others altering the program itself.) You also can have programs with execute permission only. This means that users can run the application, but they can't examine it to see how it works or copy it. (Copying requires the ability to read the file contents, of course.)

NOTE

Though actual programs with execute-only permission work fine, a special class of programs called *shell scripts* fail. Shell scripts act like a Unix command-line macro facility, which enables you to easily save a series of commands in a file and then run them as a single program. To work, however, the shell must be able to read the file and execute it, too, so shell scripts always require both read and execute permission.

There are clearly quite a few permutations on the three different permissions: read, write, and execute. In practice, a few occur most commonly, as listed in Table 5.2.

TABLE 5.2   The Most Common File Permissions

Permission	Meaning
---	No access is allowed
r--	Read-only access
r-x	Read and execute access, for programs and shell scripts
rw-	Read and write access, for files
rwx	All access allowed, for programs

These permissions have different meanings when applied to directories, but --- always indicates that no one can access the file in question.

Interpretation of the following few examples should help:

```
-rw-------  1 taylor       3843 Oct 10 16:22 iecc.list
-rw-rw-r--  1 taylor     280232 Oct 10 16:22 mailing.lists
-rw-rw----  1 taylor       1031 Oct  7 15:44 newlists
-rwxr-x---  1 taylor         64 Oct  9 09:31 the.script
```

The first file, iecc.list, has read and write permission for the owner (taylor) and is off-limits to all other users. The file mailing.lists offers similar access to the file owner (taylor) and to the group, but it offers read-only access to everyone else on the system. The third file, newlists, provides read and write access to both the file owner and group but no access to anyone not in the group.

The fourth file on the list, the.script, is a program that can be run by both the owner and group members, read (or copied) by both the owner and the group, and written (altered) by the owner. In practice, this probably would be a shell script, as described earlier, and these permissions would enable the owner (taylor) to use an editor to modify the commands therein. Other members of the group could read and use the shell script but would be denied access to change it.

Task 5.2: Directory Permissions Settings

Directories are similar to files in how you interpret the permissions strings. The differences occur because of the unique purpose of directories—namely, to store other files or directories. I always think of directories as bins or boxes. You can examine the box itself, or you can look at what's inside.

In many ways, Unix treats directories simply as files in the file system, where the content of the file is a list of the files and directories stored within rather than a letter, program, or shopping list.

The difference, of course, is that when you operate with directories, you're operating both with the directory itself and, implicitly, with its contents. By analogy, when you fiddle with a box full of toys, you're not altering just the state of the box itself but also potentially the toys within.

Three permissions are possible for a directory, just as for a file: read, write, and execute. The easiest is write permission. If a directory has write permission enabled, you can add new items to and remove items from the directory. It's like owning the box; you can do what you like with the toys inside.

The interaction between read and execute permission with a directory is confusing. There are two types of operations you perform on a directory: listing the contents of the directory (usually with ls) and examining specific known files within the directory.

1. Start by listing a directory, using the -d flag:

```
% ls -ld testme
dr-x------  2 taylor          512 Oct 11 17:03 testme/
% ls -l testme
total 0
-rw-rw----  1 taylor            0 Oct 11 17:03 file
% ls -l testme/file
-rw-rw----  1 taylor            0 Oct 11 17:03 testme/file
```

For a directory with both read and execute permission, you can see that it's easy to list the directory, find out the files therein, and list specific files within the directory.

2. Read permission on a directory enables you to read the "table of contents" of the directory but, by itself, does not allow you to examine any of the files therein. By itself, read permission is rather bizarre:

```
% ls -ld testme
dr--------  2 taylor          512 Oct 11 17:03 testme/
% ls -l testme
testme/file not found
total 0
% ls -l testme/file
testme/file not found
```

Notice that the system indicated the name of the file contained in the testme directory. When I tried to list the file explicitly, however, the system couldn't find the file. Weird.

3. Compare this with the situation when you have execute permission—which enables you to examine the files within the directory—but you don't have read permission, and you are prevented from viewing the table of contents of the directory itself:

```
% ls -ld testme
d--x------  2 taylor          512 Oct 11 17:03 testme/
% ls -l testme
testme unreadable
% ls -l testme/file
-rw-rw----  1 taylor            0 Oct 11 17:03 testme/file
```

With execute-only permission, you can set up directories so that people who know the names of files contained in the directories can access those files, but people without that knowledge cannot list the directory to learn the filenames.

4. I've actually never seen anyone have a directory in Unix with execute-only permission, and certainly you would never expect to see one set to read-only. It would be nice if Unix would warn you if you set a directory to have one permission and not the other. However, as a general rule in Unix, all combinations of parameters are possible, even the ones that don't make sense in practice; it's up to you to use the tools smartly. So, for directories remember always to be sure that you have both read and execute permissions set. Table 5.3 summarizes the most common directory permissions.

TABLE 5.3 The Most Common Directory Permissions

Permission	Meaning
`---`	No access allowed to directory
`r-x`	Read and execute access, essentially read-only, no modification allowed
`rwx`	All access allowed

5. One interesting permutation of directory permissions is for a directory that's write-only. Unfortunately, the write-only permission doesn't do what you'd hope—that is, enable people to add files to the directory without being able to see what the directory already contains. Instead, it is functionally identical to having it set for no access permission at all.

At the beginning of this hour, I used `ls` to list various files and directories in my home directory:

```
% ls -l
total 403
drwx------   2 taylor        512 Sep 30 10:38 Archives/
drwx------   3 taylor        512 Oct  1 08:23 InfoWorld/
-rw-------   1 taylor     106020 Oct 10 13:47 LISTS
drwx------   2 taylor       1024 Sep 30 10:50 Mail/
drwx------   2 taylor        512 Oct  6 09:36 News/
drwx------   2 taylor        512 Sep 30 10:51 OWL/
-rw-------   1 taylor       4643 Oct 10 14:01 RUMORS.18Sept
drwx------   2 taylor        512 Oct 10 19:09 bin/
-rw-------   1 taylor       3843 Oct 10 16:22 iecc.list
-rw-rw-r--   1 taylor     280232 Oct 10 16:22 mailing.lists
-rw-rw----   1 taylor       1031 Oct  7 15:44 newlists
drwx------   2 taylor        512 Oct 10 19:09 src/
```

Now you can see that all my directories are set so that I have list, examine, and modify (read, execute, and write, respectively) capability for myself and no access allowed for anyone else.

6. The very top-level directory is more interesting, with various directories and permissions:

```
% ls -l /
-rw-r--r--    1 root          61440 Nov 29  1991 boot
drwxr-xr-x    4 root          23552 Sep 27 11:31 dev
drwxr-xr-x    6 root           3072 Oct 11 16:30 etc
drwxr-xr-x    2 root           8192 Apr 12  1991 lost+found
lrwxr-xr-x    1 root              7 Jul 28  1988 sys -> usr/sys
drwxrwxrwx   65 root          12800 Oct 11 17:33 tmp
drwxr-xr-x  753 root          14848 Oct  5 10:07 usera
drwxr-xr-x  317 root          13312 Oct  5 10:17 userb
drwxr-xr-x  626 root          13312 Oct  8 13:02 userc
drwxr-xr-x  534 root          10752 Sep 30 13:06 users
drwxr-xr-x   34 root           1024 Oct  1 09:10 usr
drwxr-xr-x    5 root           1024 Oct  1 09:20 var
```

Clearly, this machine has a lot of users. Notice that the link counts for usera, userb, userc, and users are each in the hundreds. The dev directory has read and execute permissions for everyone and write permission for the owner (root). Indeed, all the directories at this level are identical except for tmp, which has read, write, and execute permission for all users on the system.

7. Did you notice the listing for the sys directory buried in that output?

```
lrwxr-xr-x  1 root              7 Jul 28  1988 sys -> usr/sys
```

From the information in Table 5.1, you know that because the first letter of the permissions string is l, the directory is a symbolic link. The filename shows just the specifics of the link, indicating that sys points to the directory usr/sys. In fact, if you count the number of letters in the name usr/sys, you'll find that it exactly matches the size of the sys link entry, too.

8. Try using ls -l / yourself. You should be able to understand the permissions of any file or directory that you encounter.

Permissions of files and directories will become easier to understand as you work with Unix more.

Task 5.3: Modifying File and Directory Permissions with chmod

Now that you can list directory permissions and understand what they mean, how about learning a Unix command that lets you change them to meet your needs? You've already had a sneak preview of the command for this: chmod. The mnemonic is "change mode," and it derives from early Unix folk talking about permission modes of files. You can remember it by thinking of it as a shortened form of "change permission modes."

NOTE

To sound like a Unix expert, pronounce chmod as "ch-mod," "ch" like the beginning of child, and "mod" to rhyme with *cod*.

The chmod command enables you to specify permissions in two different ways: symbolically or numerically. Symbolic notation is most commonly used to modify existing permissions, whereas numeric format always replaces any existing permission with the new value specified. In this task, you'll learn about symbolic notation, and the next task focuses on the powerful numeric format.

Symbolic notation for chmod is a bit like having a menu of different choices, enabling you to pick the combination that best fits your requirements. Figure 5.2 shows the menus.

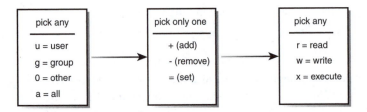

FIGURE 5.2
The menu of symbolic chmod values.

The command chmod is like a smorgasbord where you can choose any combination of items from either the first or last boxes, and you place the appropriate operator from the center box between them.

For example, if you wanted to add write permission to the file test for everyone in your group, you would, working backward from that description, choose g for group, + for add, and w for write. The finished Unix command would be chmod g+w test.

I think before we show an example of usage we should first list each u, g, o, and a.

NOTE

When you have an account assigned to you, you have a unique username, but you are also included in one or more groups. Group permissions let other people working on the same project share information without opening up the information to the rest of the world.

If you decided to take away read and execute permission for everyone not in your group, you could use `chmod o-rx test` to accomplish the task.

1. Turn to your computer and, using `touch` and `ls`, try changing permissions and see what happens. I'll do the same:

```
% touch test
% ls -l test
-rw-r--r--   1 taylor          0 Oct 11 18:29 test
```

2. The first modification I want to make is that people in my group should be able to read and write to the file. I'll add write permission for group members:

```
% chmod g+w test
% ls -l test
-rw-rw-r--   1 taylor          0 Oct 11 18:29 test
```

3. But then my boss reminds me that everyone in the group should have all access permissions. Okay, I'll make it so:

```
% chmod g+x test
% ls -l test
-rw-rwxr--   1 taylor          0 Oct 11 18:29 test
```

I also could do this with `chmod g=rwx`, of course.

4. Wait a second. This `test` file is just for my own use, and nobody in my group should be looking at it anyway. I'll change it back:

```
% chmod o-r test
% chmod g-rwx test
% ls -l test
-rw-------   1 taylor          0 Oct 11 18:29 test
```

Great. Now the file is set so that I can read and write it, but nobody else can touch it, read it, modify it, or anything else.

5. If I relented a bit, I could easily add, with one last `chmod` command, read-only permission for everyone:

```
% chmod a+r test
% ls -l test
-rw-r--r--   1 taylor          0 Oct 11 18:29 test
```

Permissions in Unix are based on a concentric access model from Multics. (In Hour 1, "What Is This Unix Stuff?" you learned that the name Unix is also a pun on Multics.) Figure 5.3 illustrates this concept.

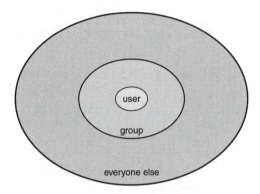

FIGURE 5.3
The concentric circles of access.

As a result, it's incredibly rare to see a file where the owner doesn't have the most access to a file. It'd be like buying a car and allowing everyone but you to drive it—rather silly. Similarly, members of the group are given better or equal permission to everyone else on the machine. You would never see `r----rwx` as a permissions string.

Experiment a bit more with the various combinations possible with the chmod symbolic notation. How would you change permission on a directory to enable all users to use `ls` to examine it but to deny them the ability to add or remove files? How about adding write access for the owner but removing it for everyone else?

Task 5.4: Setting New File Permissions with chmod

The second form of input that chmod accepts is absolute numeric values for permissions. Before you can learn how to use this notation, you have to learn a bit about different numbering systems.

The numbering system you're familiar with, the one you use to balance your checkbook and check the receipt from the market, is in decimal form, or base 10. This means that each digit—from right to left—has the value of the digit raised by a power of 10, based on the digit's location in the number. Figure 5.4 shows what the number 5,783 is in decimal form.

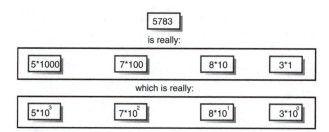

FIGURE 5.4
Interpreting decimal numbers.

You can see that in a base-10 numbering system, the value of a number is the sum of the value of each digit multiplied by the numeric base raised to the *n*th power. The *n* is the number of spaces the digit is away from the rightmost digit. That is, in the number 5,783, you know that the 7 is worth more than just 7 because it's two spaces away from the rightmost digit (the 3). Therefore, its value is the numeric base (10) raised to the *n*th power, where *n* is 2 (it's two spaces away). Ten to the second power equals 100 ($10^2 = 100$), and when you multiply that by 7, sure enough, you find that the 7 is worth 700 in this number.

What does all this have to do with the `chmod` command? Fundamentally, Unix permissions are a series of on/off switches. Does the group have write permission? One equals yes, zero equals no. A binary system is one in which each digit can have only two values: on or off, 1 or 0, yes or no. Therefore, you can easily and uniquely describe any permissions string as a series of zeros and ones, as a binary number. Figure 5.5 demonstrates this.

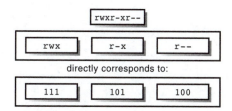

FIGURE 5.5
Permissions as binary numbers.

The convention is that if a letter is present, the binary digit is a 1—that permission is permitted—and if no letter is present, the digit is a zero. Thus, `r-xr-----` can be described as 101100000, and `r--r--r--` can be described in binary as 100100100.

You've already learned that the nine-character permissions string is really just a three-character permissions string duplicated thrice for the three different types of user (the owner, group, and everyone else). This means you can focus on learning how to translate a single tri-character permissions substring into binary and extrapolate for more than one permission. Table 5.4 lists all possible permissions and their binary equivalents.

TABLE 5.4 Permissions and Binary Equivalents

Permissions String	Binary Equivalent
- - -	000
- -x	001
-w-	010
-wx	011
r- -	100
r-x	101
rw-	110
rwx	111

Knowing how to interpret decimal numbers using the rather complex formula presented earlier, you should not be surprised that the decimal equivalent of any binary number can be obtained by using the same technique. Figure 5.6 shows how, with the binary equivalent of the r-x permission.

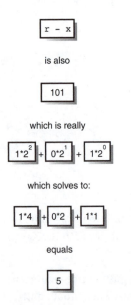

r - x

is also

101

which is really

$1*2^2$ + $0*2^1$ + $1*2^0$

which solves to:

1*4 + 0*2 + 1*1

equals

5

FIGURE 5.6
Expressing r-x as a single digit.

If r-x is equal to 5, it stands to reason that each of the possible three-character permissions has a single-digit equivalent, and Table 5.5 expands Table 5.4 to include the single-digit equivalents

TABLE 5.5 Permissions and Numeric Equivalents

Permissions String	Binary Equivalent	Decimal Equivalent
- - -	000	0
- -x	001	1
-w-	010	2
-wx	011	3
r- -	100	4
r-x	101	5
rw-	110	6
rwx	111	7

The value of having a single digit to describe any of the seven different permission states should be obvious. Using only three digits, you can fully express any possible combination of permissions for any file or directory in Unix—one digit for the owner permission, one for group, and one for everyone else. Figure 5.7 shows how to translate a full permissions string into its three-digit numeric equivalent.

NOTE

If this math is a bit intimidating, remember that r = 4, w = 2, and x = 1, so, for example, rwx = 4 + 2 + 1 = 7 and r-x = 4 + 1 = 5.

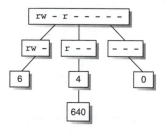

FIGURE 5.7
Translating a full permissions string into its numeric equivalent.

From this illustration, you can see how the permissions string `rw-r-----` (read and write permission for the owner, read permission for the group, and no access allowed for everyone else) is
exactly equivalent to the numeric string 640.

1. Try to create numeric strings on your own, using Table 5.4 to help. Turn to your computer and
   use `ls` to display some listings. Break each permissions string into three groups of three letters
   and figure out the numeric equivalents. Following are some examples from the `ls  -F` listing of
   my home directory:

   ```
   drwx------  2 taylor        512 Sep 30 10:38 Archives/
   -rw-------  1 taylor     106020 Oct 10 13:47 LISTS
   -rw-rw-r--  1 taylor     280232 Oct 10 16:22 mailing.lists
   -rw-rw----  1 taylor       1031 Oct  7 15:44 newlists
   ```

   Now, what are the numeric equivalents of each? The first is 700.

One last step is required before you can try using the numeric permissions strings with `chmod`.
You need to be able to work backward to determine a permission that you'd like to set and determine the numeric equivalent for that permission.

Task 5.5: Calculating Numeric Permissions Strings

Say that you want to have a directory set so that you have all access, people in your group can
look at the contents but not modify anything, and everyone else is shut out. How would you
do this?

All permissions for yourself means you want read+write+execute for owner (or numeric permission 7); read and listing permission for others in the group means read+execute for group
(numeric permission 5); and no permission for everyone else is numeric permission 0. Put the
three together, and you have the answer: 750.

That's the trick of working with `chmod` in numeric mode. You specify the absolute permissions
you want as a three-digit number, and the system sets the permissions on the file or directory
appropriately.

The absolute concept is important with this form of `chmod`. You cannot use the `chmod` numeric
form to add or remove permissions from a file or directory. It is usable only for reassigning the
permissions string of a file or directory.

The good news is that, as you learned earlier in this hour, there are a relatively small number of
commonly used file permissions, summarized in Table 5.6.

TABLE 5.6 Common Permissions and Their Numeric Equivalents

Permission	Numeric	Used With
---------	000	All types
r--------	400	Files
r--r--r--	444	Files
rw-------	600	Files
rw-r--r--	644	Files
rw-rw-r--	664	Files
rw-rw-rw-	666	Files
rwx------	700	Programs and directories
rwxr-x---	750	Programs and directories
rwxr-xr-x	755	Programs and directories
rwxrwxrwx	777	Programs and directories

1. Turn to your computer and try using the numeric mode of chmod, along with ls, to display the actual permissions to learn for yourself how this works:

```
% touch example
% ls -l example
-rw-rw----  1 taylor          0 Oct 12 10:16 example
```

By default, files are created in my directory with mode 660. This is determined by the umask setting, as we'll explore shortly.

2. To take away read and write permission for people in my group, I'd replace the 660 permission with what numeric permissions string? I'd use 600:

```
% chmod 600 example
% ls -l example
-rw-------  1 taylor          0 Oct 12 10:16 example
```

3. What if I change my mind and want to open up the file for everyone to read or write? I'd use 666:

```
% chmod 666 example
% ls -l example
-rw-rw-rw-  1 taylor          0 Oct 12 10:16 example
```

4. Finally, pretend that the example is actually a directory. What numeric mode would I specify to enable everyone to use `ls` in the directory and enable only the owner to add or delete files? I'd use 755:

```
% chmod 755 example
% ls -l example
-rwxr-xr-x  1 taylor        0 Oct 12 10:16 example
```

You've looked at both the numeric mode and the symbolic mode for defining permissions. Having learned both, which do you prefer?

NOTE

Somehow I've never gotten the hang of symbolic mode, so I almost always use the numeric mode for `chmod`. The only exception is when I want to add or delete simple permissions. Then, I use something like `chmod +r test` to add read permission. Part of the problem is that I don't think of the user of the file but rather the owner, which puts me in mind of "o"—and specifying `o+r` causes `chmod` to change permission for others, not the owner. It's important, therefore, that you remember that files have users so you remember `u` for user, and that everyone not in the group is other so you remember `o`. Otherwise, learn the numeric shortcut!

File permissions and modes are one of the most complex aspects of Unix. You can tell this because it's taken two hours to explain it fully. It's important that you spend the time to understand how the permissions strings relate to directory permissions, how to read the output of `ls`, and how to change modes using both styles of the `chmod` command. It will be time well spent.

Task 5.6: Establishing Default File and Directory Permissions with the `umask` Command

When I've created files, they've had read+write permission for the owner and group but no access allowed for anyone else. When you create files on your system, you might find that the default permissions are different.

NOTE

Different systems have different default permissions. The default mode on most Linux flavors is 664, whereas on other platforms 644 is more common.

The controlling variable behind the default permissions is called the *file creation mask*, or `umask` for short.

Inexplicably, `umask` doesn't always list its value as a three-digit number, but you can find its value in the same way you figured out the numeric permissions strings for `chmod`. For example, when I enter umask, the system indicates that my umask setting is 07. A leading zero has been dropped, so the actual value is 007, a value that British MI6 could no doubt appreciate!

NOTE

Some systems, such as Solaris and Linux, use a four-digit umask string rather than a two-digit one. The first digit in this case indicates any special modes (such as the "sticky bit" or the setGID option).

But 007 doesn't mean that the default file is created with read+write+execute for everyone else and no permissions for the owner or group. It means quite the opposite—literally.

The umask command is a filter through which permissions are pushed to ascertain what remains. Figure 5.8 demonstrates how this works.

Step One: translate the mask into binary

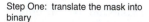

Step two: write down the binary equivalent of all permisssions allowed (777)

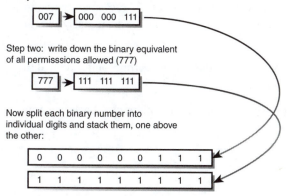

Now split each binary number into individual digits and stack them, one above the other:

Now add the two columns, remembering that any value greater than one is a zero (because binary numbers can only be 0 or 1).

And translate that back to a decimal value:

default creation permission

FIGURE 5.8
Interpreting the umask value.

Think of your mask as a series of filters: If the value is true, the information can't exude through the filter. If the value is false, it can. Your mask is therefore the direct opposite to how you want your permissions to be set. In Figure 5.8, I want to have 770 as the default permission for any new file or directory I create, so I want to specify the opposite of that, 007. Sure enough, with this umask value, when I create new files, the default permission allows read and write access to the owner and group but no access to anyone else.

Things are actually a bit trickier still. You've probably already asked yourself, Why, if I have 007 as my mask (which results in 770 as the default permissions), do my files have 660 as the actual default permission?

The reason is that Unix tries to be smart about the execute permission setting. If I create a directory, Unix knows that execute permission is important, and so it grants it. However, for data files (particularly text files), execute permission doesn't make sense, so the particular program creating the file (the shell, an editor, the email system, etc.) actually skips it, regardless of the umask setting.

Another way to look at this is that any time you create a file containing information, the original mask that the system uses to compare against your umask is not 777 (not rwxrwxrwx, to put it another way) but rather 666 (rw-rw-rw-). This is in recognition of the unlikely case that you'll want to mark the new file as executable.

The good news is that you now know an easy way to set the execute permission for a file if the system gets it wrong: chmod +x filename does the trick.

1. Turn to your computer and check your umask setting and then alternate between changing its values and creating new files with touch:

```
% umask
0007
% touch test.07
% ls -l test.07
-rw-rw----  1 taylor          0 Oct 12 14:38 test.07
```

2. To change the value of your umask, add the numeric value of the desired mask to the command line:

```
% umask 077
```

This changes my umask value from 007 (------rwx, which produces a 770 default permission: rwxrwx---) to 077 (---rwxrwx, which produces a 700 default permission: rwx------). Before you look at the following output, what would you expect this modification to mean? Remember that you should read it as exactly the opposite of how you want the default permissions:

```
% touch test.077
% ls -l test.077
-rw-------  1 taylor          0 Oct 12 14:38 test.077
```

Is that what you expected?

3. What would you have as your umask if you want to have the default permission keep files private to just the owner and make them read-only?

You can work through this problem in reverse. If you want `r-x------` as the default permission (because the system takes care of whether execute permission is needed, based on file type), write down the opposite permission, which is `-w-rwxrwx`. Translate that to a binary number, 010 111 111, and then to a three-digit value, 277 (010 = 2, 111 = 7, 111 = 7). That's the answer. The value 277 is the correct umask value to ensure that files you create are read-only for yourself and off-limits to everyone else:

```
% umask 277
% touch test.277
% ls -l test.277
-r--------  1 taylor          0 Oct 12 14:39 test.277
```

4. What if you want to have files created with the default permission being read-only for everyone, read-write for the group, but read-only for the owner? Again, work backward. The desired permission is `r-xrwxr-x`, so create the opposite value (`-w-----w-`), translate it into binary (010 000 010), and then translate that into a three-digit value: 202 (010 = 2, 000 = 0, 010 = 2).

NOTE

As a rule of thumb, it's best to leave the execute permission enabled when building umask values so the system doesn't err when creating directories.

---

umask is something set once and left alone or just left to its default value for your system, which is typically what you want anyway. If you've tried various experiments on your computer, remember to restore your umask back to a sensible value to avoid future problems (though each time you log in to the system, it's reset).

In the next hour, you'll learn how to use the `mkdir` command to create new directories, and you'll see how the umask value affects default directory access permissions.

Task 5.7: Identifying Owner and Group for Any File or Directory

One of the many items of information that the `ls` command displays when used with the `-l` flag is the owner of the file or directory. So far, all the files and directories in your home directory have been owned by you, with the probable exception of the `..` directory, which is owned by whoever owns the directory above your home.

In other words, when you enter ls -l, you should see your account name as the owner for every file in the listing.

If you're collaborating with another user, however, there might well be times when you'll want to change the owner of a file or directory after you've created and modified it. The first step in accomplishing this is to identify the owner and group.

Identifying the owner is easy: ls lists that by default. But how do you identify the group of which the file or directory is a part?

1. With the addition of a new command flag, -g, the ls command can show the group membership of any file or directory. By itself, -g doesn't alter the output of ls, but when used with the -l flag, it adds a column of information to the listing. Try it on your system. Here is an example:

```
% ls -lg /tmp
-rw-r--r--  1 root     root              0 Oct 12 14:52 sh145
drwxr-xr-x  2 shakes   root            512 Oct 12 07:23 shakes/
-rw-------  1 meademd  com435            0 Oct 12 14:46 snd.12
-rw-------  1 dessy    stuprsac       1191 Oct 12 14:57 snd.15
-rw-------  1 steen    utech             1 Oct 12 10:28 snd.17
-rw-r-----  1 jsmith   utech        258908 Oct 12 12:37 sol2
```

NOTE

On some System V–based systems, the output of ls -l always shows user and group. The –g flag actually turns off this display!

Both owners and groups vary for each of the files and directories in this small listing. Notice that files can have different owners while having the same group. (There are two examples here: sh145 and the shakes directory and snd.17 and sol2.)

2. Directories where there are often a wide variety of owners for directories are the directories above your own home directory and the tmp directory, as you can see in step 1. Examine both on your system and identify both the owner and group of every file. For files in the same group you're in (with the id command, you can find which group or groups you are in) but not owned by you, you'll need to check which of the three permission values to identify your own access privileges.

Files and directories have both owners and groups, although the group is ultimately less important than the owner, particularly where permissions and access are involved.

Summary

In this hour, you've learned the basics of Unix file permissions, including how to set and modify file permissions with `chmod` and how to analyze file permissions as shown by the `ls -l` command. You've also learned about translating between numeric bases (binary and decimal) and how to convert permissions strings into numeric values. Both are foundations for the `umask` command, which you've learned to interpret and alter as desired.

Workshop

The Workshop summarizes the key terms you've learned and poses some questions about the topics presented in this lesson. It also provides you with a preview of what you will learn in the next hour.

Key Terms

file creation mask   When files are created in Unix, they inherit a default set of access permissions. These defaults are under the control of the user and are known as the file creation mask.

mode   This is a shorthand way of saying permissions mode.

permissions mode   This is the set of accesses (read, write, and execute) allowed for each of the three classes of users (owner, group, and everyone else) for each file or directory on the system. This is a synonym for access permission.

shell script   This is a collection of shell commands in a file.

umask   This predetermined default file and directory permission set is used as a reference when new files or directories are created in the file system.

Exercises

1. In what situations might the following file permissions be useful?

   ```
   r--rw-r--          r--r--rw-
   rw--w--w-          -w--w--w-
   rwxr-xr-x          r-x--x--x
   ```

2. Translate the six file permissions strings in question 1 into their binary and numeric equivalents.

3. Explain what the following umask values would make the default permissions for newly
   created files:

007	077	777
111	222	733
272	544	754

4. Count the number of groups that are represented by group membership of files in the tmp
   directory on your system. Use id to see whether you're a member of any of them.

5. Which of the following directories could you modify if the id command listed the following information? Which could you view using the ls command?

```
% id
uid=19(smith) gid=50(users) groups=50(users)
% ls -lgF
drw-r--r--  2 root     users       512 Oct 12 14:52 sh/
drwxr-xr-x  2 shakes   root        512 Oct 12 07:23 shakes/
drw-------  2 meademd  com435     1024 Oct 12 14:46 tmp/
drwxr-x---  3 smith    users       512 Oct 12 12:37 viewer/
drwx------  3 jin      users       512 Oct 12 12:37 Zot!/
```

Preview of the Next Hour

In the next hour, you'll learn the various Unix file-manipulation commands, including how to
copy files, how to move them to new directories, and how to create new directories. You'll also
learn how to remove files and directories as well as about the dangers of file removal on Unix.

Creating, Moving, Renaming, and Deleting Files and Directories

---

Goals for This Hour

In this hour, you will learn

- ▶ How to create new directories using `mkdir`
- ▶ How to copy files to new locations using `cp`
- ▶ How to move files to new locations using `mv`
- ▶ About renaming files using `mv`
- ▶ How to remove directories using `rmdir`
- ▶ How to remove files using `rm`
- ▶ About minimizing the danger of using the `rm` command

In this hour, you'll learn the basic Unix file-manipulation commands. You'll learn how to create directories with `mkdir`, remove directories with `rmdir`, use `cp` and `mv` to move files about in the file system, and use `rm` to remove files. The `rm` command can be dangerous; this hour you'll learn that there isn't an "unremove" command in Unix, and you'll also learn how to circumvent the possible dangers that lurk in the program.

This hour introduces several tremendously powerful commands that enable you to create a custom file-system hierarchy (or wreak unintentional havoc on your files). As you learn these commands, you'll also read hints and ideas on how best to use the Unix file system to keep your files neat and organized.

Manipulating the Unix File System

You know how to find out what files are where in the file system, using `ls`, but there are also some incredibly useful commands that let you manipulate and modify files, directories, and the file system itself. That's what we'll focus on here.

Task 6.1: Creating New Directories Using `mkdir`

One important aspect of Unix that has been emphasized continually in this book is that, as in all other modern operating systems, in Unix the file system is hierarchical. The Unix file system includes directories containing files and directories, and each of those directories can contain yet more files and directories. Your own home directory, however, probably doesn't yet contain any directories (except `.` and `..` of course, because they're built-in shortcuts to the current and parent directory, respectively), which prevents you from exploiting what I call the *virtual file cabinet* of the file system.

Working with cloud storage? Me too. Turns out, though, that what you have stored in the cloud shows up on a Unix system as just more files and directories, with more files and directories within those. This is true with Dropbox, OneDrive, iCloud, and any other Unix-compatible cloud storage system you might have configured, even those internal to your corporation. I'll show you what I mean later in the lesson!

The command for creating directories is actually one of the least complex and most mnemonic (for Unix, anyway) in this book: `mkdir`, for "make directory."

NOTE

Pronounce the `mkdir` command as "make-drrr."

---

1. Move to your home directory and examine the files and directories there. Here's an example:

```
% cd
% ls -F
Archives/              OWL/                    rumors.26Oct.Z
InfoWorld/             PubAccessLists.Z        rumors.5Nov.Z
LISTS                  bin/                    src/
Mail/                  educ
News/                  mailing.lists.bitnet.Z
```

2. To create a directory, specify what you'd like to name the directory and where you'd like to locate it in the file system (the default location is your current working directory):

```
% mkdir NEWDIR
% ls -F
Archives/              News/                   mailing.lists.bitnet.Z
InfoWorld/             OWL/                    rumors.26Oct.Z
LISTS                  PubAccessLists.Z        rumors.5Nov.Z
Mail/                  bin/                    src/
NEWDIR/                educ
```

NOTE

Although Unix is very flexible about file and directory names, as a general rule, you'll want to avoid spaces, tabs, control characters, and the / character because they'll make things more difficult later on.

3. That's all there is to it. You've created your first Unix directory, and you can now list it with `ls` to see what it looks like:

```
% ls -ld NEWDIR
drwxrwx---   2 taylor          24 Nov  5 10:48 NEWDIR
% ls -la NEWDIR
total 2
drwxrwx---   2 taylor          24 Nov  5 10:48 .
drwx------  11 taylor        1024 Nov  5 10:48 ..
```

Remember that the -d flag to `ls` specifies that it should show the directory itself, not the contents of the directory. Try it both ways, and you'll immediately see the difference.

Not surprisingly, the directory is empty except for the two default entries . (the directory itself) and . . (the parent directory, your home directory).

4. Look closely at the permissions of the directory. Remember that the default directory permissions are a result of your umask setting. As you learned in the preceding hour, changing the umask setting changes the default directory permissions. Then, when you create a new directory, the new permissions will be in place:

```
% umask
07
% umask 0
% mkdir NEWDIR2
% ls -ld NEWDIR2
drwxrwxrwx  2 taylor          24 Nov  5 10:53 NEWDIR2
% umask 222
% mkdir NEWDIR3
% ls -ld NEWDIR3
dr-xr-xr-x  2 taylor          24 Nov  5 10:54 NEWDIR3
```

5. What happens if you try to create a directory with a name that has already been used?

```
% mkdir NEWDIR
mkdir: NEWDIR: File exists
```

6. To create a directory someplace other than your current location, prefix the new directory name with a location:

```
% mkdir /tmp/testme
% ls -l /tmp
-rwx------   1 zhongqi      22724 Nov  4 21:33 /tmp/a.out
```

```
-rw-------   1 xujia      95594 Nov  4 23:10 /tmp/active.10122
-rw-r--r--   1 beast        572 Nov  5 05:59 /tmp/anon1
-rw-rw----   1 root           0 Nov  5 10:30 /tmp/bar.report
-rw-------   1 qsc            0 Nov  5 00:18 /tmp/lh013813
-rwx------   1 steen      24953 Nov  5 10:40 /tmp/mbox.steen
-rwx------   1 techman     3711 Nov  5 10:45 /tmp/mbox.techman
-rw-r--r--   1 root      997536 Nov  5 10:58 /tmp/quotas
-rw-------   1 zhongqi   163579 Nov  4 20:16 /tmp/sp500.1
drwxrwx---   2 taylor        24 Nov  5 10:56 testme
-rw-r--r--   1 aru           90 Nov  5 02:55 /tmp/trouble21972
```

Most variations of Unix have no arguments for mkdir, so it is quite easy to use. Some variants, like Oracle Solaris, offer one or more flags, most commonly -m mode to explicitly specify permissions rather than leave it to whatever's set with the umask, and -p to have mkdir create any intermediate directories required as part of its action. Keep in mind two things: You must have write permission to the current directory if you're creating a new directory, and you should ensure that the name of the directory is not the same as (or, to avoid confusion, similar to) a directory name that already exists.

Task 6.2: Copying Files to New Locations Using cp

One of the most basic operations in any system is moving files, the modern-office computer equivalent of paper shuffling. On a computer, moving files is a simple matter of using one or two commands: You can move a file to a different location, or you can create a copy of the file and move the copy to a different location.

Both Windows and the Mac OS X GUI have an interesting strategy for differentiating between moving and copying. If you drag a file to another location on the same device (a hard disk, for example), by default the computer moves the file to that location. If you drag the file to a location on a different device (from a USB stick to a hard disk, for instance), the computer automatically copies the file, placing the new, identically named copy on the new device while leaving the old copy intact.

Unix lacks this subtlety (or, depending on your perspective, behavioral inconsistency). Instead, Unix lets you choose which of the two operations you'd like to perform. The two commands are typically succinct Unix mnemonics: mv to move files and cp to copy files. The mv command also serves the dual purpose of enabling you to rename files.

NOTE
Pronounce cp as "sea-pea." When you talk about copying a file, however, say "copy." Similarly, pronounce mv as "em-vee," but when you speak of moving a file, say "move."

I find myself using cp more than mv because it offers a slightly safer way to organize files: If I get confused and rename a file such that it steps on another file (you'll see what I mean in a moment), I still have original copies of all the files.

1. For a cp command, specify first the name of the file you want to copy and then the new filename. Both names can be either relative filenames (that is, without a leading slash or other indication of the directory) or absolute filenames. Start out by making a copy of your .login file and name the new copy login.copy, or, if you don't have a .login, do the same but with your .profile file instead:

```
% cp .login login.copy
% ls -ld .login login.copy
-rw-------  1 taylor        1858 Oct 12 21:20 .login
-rw-------  1 taylor        1858 Nov  5 12:08 login.copy
```

You can see that the new file is identical in size and permissions but that it has a more recent creation date, which certainly makes sense.

2. What happens if you try to copy a directory?

```
% cp olddir newdir
cp: olddir: Is a directory (not copied).
```

Generally, Unix won't permit you to use the cp command to copy directories.

NOTE

I found that this command worked—sort of—on one machine I have used. The system's response to the cp command indicated that something peculiar was happening with the following message:

```
cp: .: Is a directory (copying as plain file)
```

But the system also created newdir as a regular, executable file. You may find that your system reacts in this manner, but you probably do not have any use for it. On the other hand, you might find that your version of cp includes the useful -R command, which instructs it to recursively copy all files and directories below the specified location.

---

3. The cp command is quite powerful, and it can copy many files at once if you specify a directory as the destination rather than specifying a new filename. Further, if you specify a directory destination, the program automatically will create new files and assign them the same names as the original files.

You need to create a second file to work with:

```
% cp .profile profile.copy
```

Now try it yourself. Here is what I did:

```
% cp login.copy profile.copy NEWDIR
% ls -l NEWDIR
total 4
-rw-------  1 taylor       1178 Nov  5 12:18 profile.copy
-rw-------  1 taylor       1858 Nov  5 12:18 login.copy
```

You can use the cp command to copy an original file as a new file or to a specific directory (the format being cp *original-file new-file-or-directory*), and you can copy many files to a directory (cp *file1 file2 file3 new-directory*). With the -R flag that many versions of cp offer, you can recursively copy all files and directories below the specified directory. Experiment with creating new directories using mkdir and copying the files into the new locations. Use ls to confirm that the originals aren't removed as you go along.

On many Unix systems, a lowercase r gives you a recursive copy. You can check your Unix's capabilities with the man cp command.

Task 6.3: Moving Files to New Locations Using mv

Whereas cp leaves the original file intact, making a sort of electronic equivalent of a photocopy, mv functions like a more traditional desk: Papers are moved from one location to another. Rather than create multiple copies of the files you're copying, mv physically relocates them from the old directory to the new.

1. You use mv almost the same way that you use cp:

```
% ls -l login.copy
-rw-------  1 taylor       1858 Nov  5 12:08 login.copy
% mv login.copy new.login
% ls -l login.copy new.login
login.copy not found
-rw-------  1 taylor       1858 Nov  5 12:08 new.login
```

2. Also, you move a group of files together using mv almost the same way you do it using cp:

```
% cd NEWDIR
% ls
profile.copy  login.copy
% mv profile.copy login.copy ..
% ls -l
total 0
% ls -F ..
Archives/          OWL/                 mailing.lists.bitnet.Z
InfoWorld/         PubAccessLists.Z     new.login
LISTS              bin/                 rumors.26Oct.Z
Mail/              profile.copy         rumors.5Nov.Z
NEWDIR/            educ                 src/
News/              login.copy
```

3. Because you can use mv to rename files or directories, you can relocate the new directory NEWDIR. However, you cannot use mv to relocate the dot directory because you're inside it:

```
% mv . new.dot
mv: .: rename: Invalid argument
```

4. Both mv and cp can be dangerous. Carefully consider the following example before trying either mv or cp on your own computer:

```
% ls -l login.copy profile.copy
-rw-------   1 taylor        1178 Nov  5 12:38 profile.copy
-rw-------   1 taylor        1858 Nov  5 12:37 login.copy
% cp profile.copy login.copy
% ls -l login.copy profile.copy
-rw-------   1 taylor        1178 Nov  5 12:38 profile.copy
-rw-------   1 taylor        1178 Nov  5 12:38 login.copy
```

Without bothering to warn me, Unix copied the file profile.copy over the existing file login.copy. Notice that after the cp operation occurred, both files had the same size and modification dates.

The mv command will cause the same problem:

```
% ls -l profile.copy login.copy
-rw-------   1 taylor        1178 Nov  5 12:42 profile.copy
-rw-------   1 taylor        1858 Nov  5 12:42 login.copy
% mv profile.copy login.copy
% ls -l profile.copy login.copy
profile.copy not found
-rw-------   1 taylor        1178 Nov  5 12:42 login.copy
```

NOTE

The good news is that you can set up Unix so it won't overwrite files. The bad news is that for some reason, many systems don't default to this behavior. If your system is configured reasonably, when you try either of the two preceding dangerous examples, the system's response is remove login.copy?. You can either press the Y key to replace the old file or press Enter to change your mind. If your system cannot be set up to respond this way, you can use the -i flag to both cp and mv to avoid this problem. Later, you learn how to permanently fix this problem with a shell alias.

Together, mv and cp are the dynamic duo of Unix file organization. These commands enable you to put the information you want where you want it, leaving duplicates behind if desired.

Task 6.4: Renaming Files with mv

Both Windows and Macintosh systems have easy ways to rename files. On the Mac, you can select the name under the file icon and enter a new filename. On Windows, you right-click the icon and choose Rename from the pop-up menu.

Unix has neither of these options. To rename files, you use the mv command, which, in essence, moves the old name to the new name. It's a bit counterintuitive, but it works.

1. Rename the file profile.copy with your own first name. Here's an example:

```
% ls -l profile.copy
-rw-------  1 taylor        1178 Nov  5 13:00 profile.copy
% mv profile.copy dave
% ls -l dave
-rw-------  1 taylor        1178 Nov  5 13:00 dave
```

2. Rename a directory, too:

```
% ls -ld NEWDIR
drwxrwx---  2 taylor         512 Nov  5 12:32 NEWDIR
% mv NEWDIR New.Sample.Directory
% ls -ld New.Sample.Directory
drwxrwx---  2 taylor         512 Nov  5 12:32 New.Sample.Directory
```

3. Be careful! Just as moving files with cp and mv can carelessly overwrite existing files, renaming files using mv can overwrite existing files:

```
% mv dave login.copy
%
```

If you try to use mv to rename a directory with a name that already has been assigned to a file, the command fails:

```
% mv New.Sample.Directory dave
mv: New.Sample.Directory: rename: Not a directory
```

The reverse situation works fine because the file is moved into the directory as expected. This is the subtlety of using the mv command to rename files.

4. If you assign a new directory a name that belongs to an existing directory, some versions of mv will happily overwrite the existing directory and name the new one as requested:

```
% mkdir testdir
% mv New.Sample.Directory testdir
```

Being able to rename files is another important part of building a useful Unix virtual file cabinet for you. Some major dangers are involved, however, so tread carefully and always use ls in conjunction with cp and mv to ensure that in the process you don't overwrite or replace an existing file.

Task 6.5: Removing Directories with `rmdir`

Now that you can create directories with the mkdir command, it's time to learn how to remove directories using the rmdir command.

1. With `rmdir`, you can remove any directory for which you have appropriate permissions:

```
% mkdir test
% ls -l test
total 0
% rmdir test
```

Note that the output of `ls` shows that there are no files in the `test` directory.

2. By default, the `rmdir` command removes only directories that are empty:

```
% mkdir test
% touch test/sample.file
% ls -l test
total 0
-rw-rw----  1 taylor          0 Nov  5 14:00 sample.file
% rmdir test
rmdir: test: Directory not empty
```

To remove a directory, you must first remove all files therein using the `rm` command. In this example, `test` still has files in it. Note that some versions of `rmdir` offer the -p flag, which will recursively remove all directories and subdirectories from right to left until it encounters a non-empty directory. Other versions include the - f flag, which will let you forcibly remove any files or subdirectories contained within the specified directory. As you imagine, `rmdir  -f  /` could destroy your system, so be careful!

3. Permissions are important, too. Consider what happens when I try to remove a directory that I don't have permission to touch:

```
% rmdir /tmp
rmdir: /tmp: Permission denied
% ls -l /tmp
drwxrwxrwt 81 root          15872 Nov  5 14:07 /tmp
```

The permissions of the parent directory, rather than the directory you're trying to remove, are the important consideration.

There's no way to restore a directory you've removed, so be careful and think through what you're doing. The good news is that, because with `rmdir` you can't remove a directory that has anything in it (a second reason the attempt in the preceding example to remove /tmp would have failed), you're reasonably safe from major gaffes. You are not safe, however, with the next command, `rm`, because it will remove anything.

Task 6.6: Removing Files Using `rm`

The `rm` command is probably the most dangerous command in Unix. Lacking any sort of archival or restoration feature, the `rm` command removes files permanently. It's like throwing a document into a shredder instead of into a dustbin.

CAUTION
_____

On some Unixes, including Solaris, there's a command called `shred` that removes files but also overwrites the spot on the disk where the file information was previously stored. It's even more ruthless than `rm` and should be used with extreme caution, if at all.
_____

1. Removing a file using `rm` is easy. Here's an example:

```
% ls -l login.copy
-rw-------   1 taylor        1178 Nov  5 13:00 login.copy
% rm login.copy
% ls -l login.copy
login.copy not found
```

If you decide that you removed the wrong file and actually wanted to keep the `login. copy` file, it's too late. You're out of luck.

NOTE
_____

There's no "recycle bin" or "trashcan" from which you can recover accidentally deleted files in Unix if you're working on the command line. Be careful!
_____

2. You can remove more than one file at a time by specifying each of the files to the `rm` command:

```
% ls -F
Archives/              PubAccessLists.Z       new.login
InfoWorld/             bin/                   rumors.26Oct.Z
LISTS                  profile.copy            rumors.5Nov.Z
Mail/                  educ                   src/
News/                  login.copy             test/
OWL/                   mailing.lists.bitnet.Z testdir/
% rm profile.copy login.copy new.login
% ls -F
Archives/              OWL/                   rumors.26Oct.Z
InfoWorld/             PubAccessLists.Z       rumors.5Nov.Z
LISTS                  bin/                   src/
Mail/                  educ                   test/
News/                  mailing.lists.bitnet.Z testdir/
```

3. Fortunately, `rm` does have a command flag that to some degree helps avoid accidental file removal. When you use the `-i` flag to `rm` (the `i` stands for *interactive* in this case), the system will ask you whether you're sure you want to remove the file:

```
% touch testme
% rm -i testme
rm: remove testme? n
```

```
% ls testme
testme
% rm -i testme
rm: remove testme? y
% ls testme
testme not found
```

Note that n is *no* and y is *yes*.

4. Another flag that is often useful for rm but is very dangerous is the -r flag for recursive deletion of files. (A *recursive command* repeatedly invokes itself.) When the -r flag to rm is used, Unix will remove any specified directory along with all its contents:

```
% ls -ld test ; ls -lR test
drwxrwxrwx  3 taylor          512 Nov  5 15:32 test
total 1
-rw-rw----  1 taylor            0 Nov  5 15:32 alpha
drwxrwx---  2 taylor          512 Nov  5 15:32 test2

test/test2:
total 0
-rw-rw----  1 taylor            0 Nov  5 15:32 file1
% rm -r test
% ls -ld test
test not found
```

Without any warning or indication that it was going to do something so drastic, rm -r test caused not just the test directory but all files and directories inside it as well to be removed.

NOTE

This latest example demonstrates that you can give several commands on a single Unix command line. To do this, separate the commands with a semicolon. Instead of giving the commands ls -ld test and ls -lR test on separate lines, I opted for the more efficient ls -ld test; ls -lR test, which executes the commands one after the other.

The Unix equivalent of the paper shredder, the rm command allows for easy removal of files. With the -r flag, you can clean out an entire directory, even if it contains subdirectories and files within those subdirectories. With the -f flag, any warning messages or other permission issues will be ignored, making the command even more dangerous. The one command you never want to run on a Unix system is rm -rf /, for what I hope are obvious reasons!

Again, remember that nothing can be retrieved after the fact, however, so use great caution any time you invoke rm.

Task 6.7: Minimizing the Danger of the `rm` Command

At this point, you might be wondering why I am making such a big deal of the `rm` command and the fact that it does what it is advertised to do—that is, remove files. The answer is that learning a bit of paranoia now can save you immense grief in the future. It can prevent you from destroying a file full of information that you really needed to save.

For Windows, commercial programs (Norton Utilities, for instance) exist that can retrieve accidentally removed files. As with the Mac, the Windows *recycle bin* is a folder that you can open and extract files from until it's "emptied." Programs such as Norton Utilities for the Macintosh can be used to recover files that have been deleted by emptying the trash can. Unix just doesn't have that capability if you're working on the command line, though, and files that are removed are gone forever.

The only exception is if you work on a Unix system that has an automatic, reliable backup schedule onto the cloud or a local device. In such a case, you might be able to retrieve an older version of your file (maybe).

That said, you can do a few things to lessen the danger of using `rm` and yet give yourself the ability to remove unwanted files.

1. You can use a shorthand, a *shell alias*, to attach the `-i` flag automatically to each use of `rm`. To do this, ascertain what type of login shell you're running, which you can do most easily by using the following command:

   ```
   % grep taylor /etc/passwd
   taylor:x:19989:1412:Dave Taylor:/users/taylor:/bin/csh
   ```

   (Don't worry about what all of what this does right now. You'll learn about the `grep` command a few hours from now.) The last word on the line is what's important. The `/etc/passwd` file is one of the database files Unix uses to track accounts. Each line in the file is called a *password entry* or *password file entry*. On my password entry, you can see that the login shell specified is `/bin/csh`. If you try this and don't have an identical entry, you should have `/bin/sh` or `/bin/ksh`.

2. If your entry is `/bin/csh` or `/bin/tcsh`, enter exactly what is shown here:

   ```
   % echo "alias rm /bin/rm -i" >> ~/.cshrc
   % source ~/.cshrc
   ```

   Now `rm` includes the `-i` flag each time it's used:

   ```
   % touch testme
   % rm testme
   rm: remove testme? N
   ```

3. If your entry is `/bin/bash`, enter exactly what is shown here, paying particular attention to the two different quotation-mark characters used in the example:

```
$ echo 'alias rm="/bin/rm -i"' >> ~/.profile
$ . ~/.profile
```

Now `rm` includes the `-i` flag each time it's used.

NOTE
_____

One thing to pay special attention to is the difference between the single quote ('), the double quote ("), and the backquote (`). Unix interprets each differently, although single and double quotes are often interchangeable. The backquotes, also known as backticks, are less common and delineate commands within other commands.

_____

4. If your entry is `/bin/sh`, you cannot program your system to include the `-i` flag each time `rm` is used. The Bourne shell (`sh`) is the original command shell of Unix. The Bourne shell lacks an alias feature, a feature that both the Bash shell (`bash`) and the C shell (`csh`/`tcsh`) include. As a result, I recommend that you change your login shell to one of these alternatives, if available.

To see what's available, look in the `/bin` directory on your machine for the specific shells:

```
% ls -1F /bin/*sh
-rwxr-xr-x  1 root  wheel  603488  3 Nov 22:35 /bin/bash*
-r-xr-xr-x  1 root  wheel  348068  3 Nov 22:35 /bin/csh*
-r-xr-xr-x  1 root  wheel  603488  3 Nov 22:35 /bin/sh*
-r-xr-xr-x  1 root  wheel  348068  3 Nov 22:35 /bin/tcsh*
-rwxr-xr-x  1 root  wheel  479120  3 Nov 22:35 /bin/zsh*
```

Most of the examples in this book focus on the Bash shell because I think it's the easiest of the shells to use, and it's certainly in the most widespread use. To change your login shell, you need to e-mail your system administrator with the request, though some versions of Unix offer the `chsh` (change shell) or, in Solaris, `usermod` commands for just this purpose. If yours has one of these commands, check the man page to learn more about how to use it. Now you can go back to step 2 and set up a Bash shell alias. This will help you avoid mischief with the `rm` command.

The best way to avoid trouble with any of these commands is to learn to be just a bit paranoid about them. Before you remove a file, make sure it's the one you want to remove. Before you remove a directory, make doubly sure that it doesn't contain any files you might want. Before you rename a file or directory, double-check to see whether renaming it is going to cause any trouble. Before you press Enter, make sure the command is *exactly* what you want to invoke.

Take your time with the commands you learned in this hour, and you should be fine. Even in the worst case, you will hopefully have the safety net of a backup performed by a system administrator—though you shouldn't rely on it.

Summary

You now have completed six hours of Unix instruction, and you are armed with enough commands to make Unix do what you want it to do—as well as cause some trouble. In this hour, you learned the differences between cp and mv for moving files and how to use mv to rename both files and directories. You also learned how to create directories with the mkdir command and how to remove them with the rmdir command. And you learned about the rm command for removing files and directories, as well as how to avoid getting into too much trouble with it.

Finally, if you were really paying attention, you learned how to identify which login shell you're using (csh, ksh, bash, or sh).

Workshop

The Workshop summarizes the key terms you've learned and poses some questions about the topics presented in this lesson. It also provides you with a preview of what you will learn in the next hour.

Key Terms

recursive command This type of command repeatedly invokes itself while operating on a hierarchy of files.

shell alias Most Unix shells have a convenient way for you to create abbreviations for commonly used commands or series of commands, known as shell aliases. For example, if I always found myself typing ls -F, an alias can let me type just ls and have the shell automatically add the -F flag each time.

Exercises

1. What are the differences between cp and mv?

2. If you were installing a program from a USB stick onto a hard disk, would you use cp or mv?

3. If you know DOS, this question is for you. Although DOS has a RENAME command, it doesn't have both COPY and MOVE. Which of these two do you think DOS includes? Why?

4. Try using `mkdir` to create a directory. What happens, and why?

5. You've noticed that both `rmdir` and `rm -r` can be used to remove directories. Which is safer to use?

6. The `rm` command has another flag that wasn't discussed in this hour. The `-f` flag forces removal of files regardless of permission (assuming that you're the owner, that is). In combination with the `-r` flag, this can be amazingly destructive. Why?

Preview of the Next Hour

The seventh hour introduces the useful `file` command, which indicates the contents of any file in the Unix file system. With `file`, you will explore various directories in the Unix file system to see what the command reveals about different system and personal files. Then, when you've found some files worth reading, you will learn about `cat`, `more`, and `pg`, which give you different ways of looking at the contents of a file.

Looking into Files

Goals for This Hour

In this hour, you will learn

- ▶ How to use `file` to identify file types
- ▶ How to explore Unix directories with `file`
- ▶ About peeking at the first few lines with `head`
- ▶ How to view the last few lines with `tail`
- ▶ How to view the contents of files with `cat`
- ▶ How to view larger files with `more`

By this point, you've learned a considerable number of Unix commands and a lot about the operating and file systems. This hour focuses on Unix tools to help you ascertain what types of files you've been seeing in all the different directories. It then introduces five powerful tools for examining the content of files.

This hour begins with a tool to help ensure that the files you're about to view are intended for human perusal and then explores many of the commands available to view the contents of the file in various ways.

Looking Inside Files

You've learned how to manipulate files and directories, and now it's time to find out what kind of information is contained within these files and to look inside the files.

Task 7.1: Using `file` to Identify File Types

One of the most undervalued commands in Unix is `file`, which is often neglected and collecting dust in an unused virtual corner of the system. Unix does not rely on the filename extension for determining the type of file, like .txt or .jpg, the way Windows or Mac OS does, so you might not always be able to tell what kind of files you've got in a directory or what you can do with them. Using the `file` command, which examines a file and makes an educated guess about its contents, is a handy way to give you that missing information.

Unfortunately, a problem exists with the `file` command: It isn't 100% accurate. The program relies on a combination of the permissions of a file, the filename, and an analysis of the first few lines of the text. If you had a text file that started out looking like a C program or that had execute permission enabled, `file` might well identify it as an executable program rather than an English text file.

NOTE

You can determine how accurate your version of `file` is by checking the size of its database of file types. You can do this with the Unix command `wc -l /etc/magic` (Mac OS X calls this `/usr/share/file/magic`). The number of entries in the database should be at least 100 and ideally over 1,000. If you have fewer than this number, you're probably going to have trouble. If you have considerably more, you might have a very accurate version of `file` at your fingertips! Remember, however, that even if it's relatively small, `file` can still offer invaluable suggestions regarding file content.

---

1. Start by logging in to your account and using the `ls` command to find a file or two to check:

```
% ls -F
Archives/          OWL/                    rumors.26Oct.Z
InfoWorld/         PubAccessLists.Z        rumors.5Nov.Z
LISTS              bin/                    src/
Mail/              educ                    temp/
News/              mailing.lists.bitnet.Z
```

Next, enter the `file` command and list each of the files you'd like the program to analyze:

```
% file LISTS educ rumors.26Oct.Z src
LISTS:   ascii text
educ:    ascii text
rumors.26Oct.Z: block compressed 16 bit code data
src:     directory
```

From this example, you can see that `file` correctly identifies `src` as a directory, offers considerable information on the compressed file `rumors.26Oct.Z`, and tags both `LISTS` and `educ` as plain ASCII text files.

NOTE

ASCII is the *American Standard Code for Information Interchange*, and it means that the file contains the letters of the English alphabet, punctuation, and numbers but not much else. There are no multiple typefaces, italics, or underlined passages, and there are no graphics. It's the lowest common denominator of text in Unix.

---

2. Now try using the asterisk (*), a Unix wildcard (wildcards are explained in Hour 8, "Filters, Pipes, and Wildcards!"), to have the program analyze all files in your home directory:

```
% file *
Global.Software:        English text
Interactive.Unix:       mail folder
Mail:           directory
News:           directory
Src:            directory
bin:            directory
history.usenet.Z:       compressed data block compressed 16 bits
```

The asterisk (*) is a special character in Unix. Used by itself, it tells the shell to substitute the names of all the files in the current directory. Add letters before or after the asterisk (as in /bin/*sh earlier), and it matches all filenames that match the specified pattern. You'll learn a lot more about wildcards and patterns in subsequent lessons.

Now you can begin to see how file can help differentiate files. Using this command, I am now reminded that the file Global.Software is English text, but Interactive.Unix is actually an old electronic mail message. (file can't differentiate between a single mail message and a multiple-message folder, so it always errs on the side of saying that the file is a mail folder.)

3. Mail folders are actually problematic for the file command. On one of the systems I use, the file command doesn't know what mail messages are, so asking it to analyze mail folders results in a demonstration of how accuracy is related to the size of the file database.

On a Solaris system, I asked file to analyze two mail folders and got the following results:

```
% file Mail/mailbox Mail/sent
Mail/mailbox:   mail folder
Mail/sent: mail folder
```

Almost identical files on a Berkeley Unix system, however, have very different results when analyzed:

```
% file Mail/mailbox Mail/sent Mail/netnews
Mail/mailbox:           ascii text
Mail/sent:          shell commands
Mail/netnews:           English text
```

Not only does the Berkeley version of Unix not identify the files correctly, it doesn't even misidentify them consistently.

4. Another example of the `file` command's limitations is how it interacts with file permissions. Use `cp` to create a new file and work through this example to see how your `file` command interprets the various changes:

```
% cp .cshrc test
% file test
test: shell commands
% chmod +x test
% file test
test: shell script
```

Adding execute permission to this file caused this version of `file` to identify it as a shell script rather than shell commands.

Don't misinterpret the results of these examples as proof that the `file` command is useless and that you shouldn't use it. Quite the opposite is true. Unix has neither a specific file-naming convention (Windows has its three-letter filename suffixes) nor indication of file ownership by icon (Mac OS X does this with type and opener information added by each program). As a result, it's vital that you have a tool for helping ascertain file types without actually opening the file.

Why not just look at the contents? The best way to figure out the answer to this question is to accidentally display the contents of an executable file on the screen. You'll see that it's quite a mess, loaded with special control characters that can make your screen go berserk.

Task 7.2: Exploring Unix Directories with `file`

Now that you know how to work with the `file` command, it's time to wander through the Unix file system, learning more about types of files that tend to be found in specific directories. Your system might vary slightly; it'll certainly have more files in some directories than what I show here in the examples, but you'll quickly see that `file` can offer some valuable insight into the contents of files.

1. First things first. Take a look at the files at the very top level of the file system, in / (slash):

```
% cd /
% ls -F
bin@        etc/        media/      platform/   system/
boot/       export/     mnt/        proc/       tmp/
cdrom/      home/       net/        root/       usr/
dev/        kernel/     nfs4/       rpool/      var/
devices/    lib/        opt/        sbin@       zvboot
% ls -l bin
lrwxrwxrwx   1 root      root              9 Jun 25   2014 bin -> ./usr/bin
% file bin boot sbin zvboot
bin:        directory
boot:       directory
sbin:       directory
```

```
zvboot:      ELF 64-bit LSB executable AMD64 Version 1, statically linked, not
➥ stripped, no debugging information available
```

This example is from an Oracle Solaris system running Solaris 11.2.

Executable binaries are explained in detail by the `file` command on this computer: `zvboot` is listed as `ELF 64-bit LSB executable AMD64 Version 1, statically linked, not stripped, no debugging information available`. The specifics aren't vital to understand: The most important word to see in this output is `executable`, which indicates that the file is the result of compiling a program.

NOTE

Notice that `zvboot` is "not stripped." This doesn't mean that other files are naked but rather that various information included in most executables to help identify and isolate problems (in other words, debugging code) has not been removed to save space in this particular executable.

Notice the information shown for the `bin` directory. It's actually a symbolic link, as shown in the `ls -l` output, but `file` shows it as just another directory. Sometimes other tools reveal more information; it's up to you to be a detective.

2. There are differences in output formats on different machines. The following example shows what the same command as in step 1 would generate on an older Sun Microsystems workstation, examining analogous files:

```
% file boot core kadb tmp
boot:        sparc executable
core:        core file from 'popper'
kadb:        sparc executable not stripped
tmp:         symbolic link to /var/tmp
```

The older Sun computer offers the same information but fewer specifics about executable binaries. Sun workstations are built around SPARC chips (just as PCs are built around Intel chips), so these programs are identified as `sparc executable`.

3. Are you ready for another directory of weird files? It's time to move into the `/lib` directory to see what's there. Entering `ls` will demonstrate that there are many files in this directory! The `file` command can tell you about any of them. On my Solaris computer, I asked for information on a few select files, many of which you might also have on yours:

```
% file llib-lc llib-lssl mpxio nss_nis.so.1
llib-lc:     ascii text
llib-lssl:   ascii text
mpxio:       directory
nss_nis.so.1:  ELF 32-bit LSB dynamic lib 80386 Version 1, dynamically
➥ linked, not stripped, no debugging information available
```

The first file, llib-lc, demonstrates that the file command works regardless of the name of a file or whether it has an extension, and the second file, of course, has a similar name (though it's actually a symbolic link). As we saw earlier, the version of file in Oracle Solaris doesn't differentiate between a file/directory and a symbolic link to a file or directory.

The third file is an executable, demonstrating another way that file can indicate programs. The fourth entry, nss_nis.so.1, looks like it would be a man page source file (the .1 suffix is the clue) but is still identified as an executable file. There's clearly quite a bit of uncertainty here.

The good news is that you don't have to worry about what files are in /lib, /etc, or any other directory other than your own home directory. Thousands of happy Unix folk busily work each day without ever realizing that these other directories exist, let alone knowing what's in them.

What's important here is that you have learned that the file command identifies special Unix system files of various types. It can be a very helpful tool when you are looking around in the file system and even when you are trying to determine what's what in your own directory.

Task 7.3: Peeking at the First Few Lines with head

Now that you have the tools needed to move about in the file system, to double-check where you are, and to identify the different types of files, it's time to learn about some of the many tools Unix offers for viewing the contents of files. The first on the list is head, a simple program for viewing the first 10 lines of any file.

The head program is more versatile than it sounds: You can use it to view as much of a file as you'd like, actually. To specify the number of lines you want to see, you need to indicate how many as a starting argument and prefix the number of lines desired with a dash. By default, head shows the first 10 lines of the file.

NOTE

The head command is the first of a number of Unix commands that tend to work with their own variation on the regular rules of starting arguments. Instead of using a typical Unix command argument of -l33 to specify 33 lines, for example, head uses -33 to specify the same information. Even after all these years, Unix is less standardized in its interface than it should be.

1. Move back into your home directory and view the first few lines of your .cshrc file (or .profile if you don't have a .cshrc file):

```
% cd
% head .cshrc
#
# Default user .cshrc file (/bin/csh initialization).
```

```
set host=limbo

set path=(. ~/bin /bin /usr/bin /usr/ucb /usr/local /etc
/usr/etc/usr/local/bin /usr/unsup/bin)

# Set up C shell environment:

alias  diff     '/usr/bin/diff -c -w'
```

The contents of your own .cshrc file will doubtless be different, but notice that the program lists only the first few lines of the file.

2. To specify a different number of lines, use the -n format (where n is the number of lines). I'll look at just the first four lines of the .login file:

```
% head -4 .login
#
# @(#) $Revision: 62.2 $

setenv TERM vt100
```

3. You also can easily check multiple files by listing them one by one on the command line:

```
% head -3 .newsrc /etc/passwd
==> .newsrc <==
misc.forsale.computers.mac: 1-14536
utech.student-orgs! 1
general! 1-546

==> /etc/passwd <==
root:?:0:0: root,,,,:/:/bin/csh
news:?:6:11:USENET News,,,,:/usr/spool/news:/bin/ksh
ingres:*?:7:519:INGRES Manager,,,,:/usr/ingres:/bin/csh
```

4. More importantly, head and other Unix commands can work also as part of a *pipeline*, where the output of one program is the input of the next. The special symbol for creating Unix pipelines is the pipe character (|). Pipelines are read left to right, so you can easily have the output of who, for example, feed into head; this offers powerful new possibilities. If you want to see just the first five people logged in to the computer right now, try this:

```
% who | head -5
root      console Nov  9 07:31
mccool    ttya0   Nov 10 14:25
millekl2 ttyaP   Nov 10 14:58
paulwhit ttyaR   Nov 10 14:50
bobweir   ttyaS   Nov 10 14:49
Broken pipe
```

Pipelines are one of the most powerful features of Unix, and I have many examples of how to use them to great effect throughout the remainder of this book. Stay tuned!

5. Here is one last thing. Find an executable—/bin/ls will do fine—and enter **head -1 /bin/ ls**. Watch what happens. Or, if you'd like to preserve your sanity, take it from me that the random junk thrown on your screen is enough to cause your shell or terminal program to get quite confused and possibly even crash.

The point isn't to have that happen to your system but rather to remind you that using file to confirm the file type for unfamiliar files can save you lots of grief and frustration!

head is the simplest of programs for viewing the contents of a file; it's easy to use, it's efficient, and it works as part of a pipeline, too. The remainder of this hour focuses on other tools in Unix that offer other ways to view the contents of text and ASCII files.

Task 7.4: Viewing the Last Few Lines with `tail`

The head program shows you the first 10 lines of the file you specify. What would you expect tail to do, then? I hope you guessed the right answer: It shows the last 10 lines of a file. Like head, tail also understands the same format for specifying the number of lines to view.

1. Start out viewing the last 12 lines of your .cshrc (or .profile) file:

```
% tail -12 .cshrc

    set noclobber history=100 system=filec
    umask 007

    setprompt
endif

# special aliases:

alias info      ssinfo
alias ssinfo    'echo "connecting..." ; rlogin oasis'
```

2. Next, the last four lines of the file LISTS in my home directory can be shown with the following command line:

```
% tail -5 LISTS
            College of Education
            Arizona State University
            Tempe, AZ 85287-2411
            602-965-2692
```

TIP

Don't get too hung up trying to figure out what's inside my files; I'm not even sure myself sometimes.

3. Here's one to think about. You can use `head` to view the first *n* lines of a file and `tail` to view the last *n* lines of a file. Can you figure out a way to combine the two so that you can see just the 10th, 11th, and 12th lines of a file?

```
% head -12 .cshrc | tail -3
alias   diff        '/usr/bin/diff -c -w'
alias   from        'frm -n'
alias   ll          'ls -l'
```

It's easy with Unix command pipelines!

Combining the two commands `head` and `tail` can give you considerable power in viewing specific slices of a file on the Unix system. Try combining them in different ways for different results.

Task 7.5: Viewing the Contents of Files with `cat`

Both `head` and `tail` offer the capability to view a piece of a file, either the top or the bottom, but neither lets you conveniently see the entire file, regardless of length. For this job, the `cat` program is the right choice.

NOTE

The `cat` program got its name from its function in the early versions of Unix: concatenating (or join together) multiple files. It isn't, unfortunately, an homage to felines or anything so exotic!

The `cat` program also has a valuable secret capability: Through use of the `-v` flag, you can use `cat` to display any file on the system, executable or otherwise, with all characters that normally would not be printed (or would drive your screen bonkers) displayed in a special format I call *control key notation*. In control key notation, each nonprinting character is represented as `^n`, where *n* is a printable letter or symbol. A character with the value 0 (also referred to as a *null* or *null character*) is displayed as `^@`, a character with the value 1 is `^A`, a character with the value 2 is `^B`, and so on.

Another `cat` flag that can be useful for certain files is `-s`, which suppresses multiple blank lines from a file. Not all Unixes include a version of `cat` that has the `-s` flag, so check with `man cat` before you give it a try. Also, I admit, it isn't immediately obvious how this feature can help, but some files (particularly log files from system programs) can have a screenful (or more) of blank lines. To avoid having to watch them all fly past, you can use `cat -s` to chop 'em down to a single blank line. Don't have this flag, but need it? `cat | uniq` is a simple alternative.

Finally, a third flag that's tremendously useful is `-n`, which adds line numbers to the output, though not to the file itself, of course.

1. Move back to your home directory and use `cat` to display the complete contents of your
`.cshrc` file:

```
% cd
% cat .cshrc
#
# Default user .cshrc file (/bin/csh initialization).

set path=(. ~/bin /bin /usr/bin /usr/ucb /usr/local /etc
/usr/etc/usr/local/bin /usr/unsup/bin )

# Set up C shell environment:

alias   diff     '/usr/bin/diff -c -w'
alias   from     'frm -n'
alias   ll       'ls -l'
alias   ls       '/bin/ls -F'
alias   mail     Mail
alias   mailq    '/usr/lib/sendmail -bp'

alias   newaliases 'echo you mean newalias... '

alias   rd       'readmsg $ | page'
alias   rn       '/usr/local/bin/rn -d$HOME -L -M -m -e -S -/'

# and some special stuff if we're in an interactive shell

if ( $?prompt ) then            # shell is interactive.

   alias  cd              'chdir \!* ; setprompt'
   alias  env             'printenv'
   alias  setprompt       'set prompt="$system ($cwd:t) \! : "'

   set noclobber history=100 system=limbo filec
   umask 007

   setprompt
endif

# special aliases:

alias info      ssinfo
alias ssinfo    'echo "connecting..." ; rlogin oasis'
```

Don't be too concerned if the contents of your `.cshrc` file (or mine) don't make any sense
to you. You are slated to learn about the contents of this file within a few hours, and, yes,
it is complex.

You can see that `cat` is pretty simple to use. If you specify more than one filename to
the program, it lists the filenames in the order you specify. You can even list the contents

of a file multiple times by specifying the same filename on the command line multiple times.

2. The cat program also can be used as part of a pipeline. Compare the following command with my earlier usage of head and tail:

```
% cat LISTS | tail -5
        College of Education
        Arizona State University
        Tempe, AZ 85287-2411
        602-965-2692
```

3. Now find an executable file and try cat -v in combination with head to get a glimpse of the contents therein:

```
% cat -v /bin/ls | head -1
^?ELF^B^A^A^F^A^@^@^@^@^@^@^@^B^@>^@^A^@^@^@`4@^@^@^@^@^@@^@^@^@^@^@^@M-
^XM-\^@^@^@^@^@^@^@^@^@@^@8^@^H^@@^@^]^@^[^@^F^@^@^E^@^@@^@^@^@^@^@^@^@
@@^@@^@^@^@^@^@^@^@^@^@^@^@^@^@^M-@^A^@^@^@^@^@M-@^A^@^@^@^@^@^@^@^@^@^@
^@^@^C^@^@^@^D^@^@^@^@^B^@^@^@^@^@^@^B@^@^@^@^@^@^@^@^@^@^@^@W^@^@^@^@
^@^@^@^W^@^@^@^@^@^@^@^@^@^@^@^@^@^@^@^M-}M-^?M-^?o^D^@^@^@X^B^@^@^@^@^@X^B@
^@^@^@^@^@^@^@^@^@^@^@^@ ^@^@^@^@^@^@^@ ^@^@^@^@^@^@^@^@^@^@^@^@^@A^@^@
^@^E^@^@^@^@^@^@^@^@^@^@^@^@^@@^@^@^@^@^@^@^@^@^@^@^@^@^@^@RM-"^@^@^@^@^@^@RM-
"^@^@^@^@^@^@^@^A^@^@^@^@^@^A^@^@^@^F^@^@^@^@M-0^@^@^@^@^@^@M-0A^@^@^@^@^@^@
^@^@^@^@^@^@^@M-^P^G^@^@^@^@^@^@^\2^@^@^@^@^@^@^@^A^@^@^@^@^@^B^@^@^@^F^@^@
^@M-^HM-2^@^@^@^@^@^@M-^HM-2A^@^@^@^@^@^@^@^@^@^@^@^@@@^C^@^@^@^@^@^@^@^@^@
^@^@^@^@^@^@^@^@^@^@^@^@PM-edd^D^@^@^@8^B^@^@^@^@^@8^B@^@^@^@^@^@^@^@^@^@
^@^@^@@<^A^@^@^@^@^@^@<^A^@^@^@^@^@^@^H^@^@^@^@^@^@^@M-{M-^?M-^?o^F^@^@^@^@^@^@
^@^@^@^@^@^@^@^@^@^@^@^@^@^@^@^@^@^@^@^@^@^@^@^@^@^@^@^@^@^@^@^@^@^@^@^@
^@^@^@^@^@^@/usr/lib/amd64/ld.so.1^@^@^@A^@^@^@^@^@^@^@!^\^@^@^@^@^@^@^@^@^@
^@^@Broken pipe
```

This is complex and confusing, indeed! What's worse, this isn't the entire first line of the executable. You can see this because the data ends with Broken pipe. This indicates that a lot more was being fed to head than the system could process, due to the constraint of having only the first line listed—a line that head typically defines as no more than 512 characters long.

The cat command is useful for viewing files and is quite easy to work with for even a neophyte. The problem with it is that if the file you choose to view has more lines than can be displayed on your screen, it will fly past without any way to slow it down. That's where the next command, the more command, comes in handy for stepping through files.

Task 7.6: Viewing Larger Files with more

You can now wander about the file system, find files that might be of interest, check their type with file, and even view them with the cat command, but what if files are longer than your screen? That's the job of the more program, a program that knows how big your screen or terminal window is and displays the information properly paginated.

There are two primary flags in more:

-s   Suppresses multiple blank lines, just like the -s flag to cat

-c   Causes the program to clear the screen before displaying each screenful of text

The program also allows you to start at a specific line in the file by using the curious +n notation, where n is a specific number. Finally, you can start also at the first occurrence of a specific pattern by specifying that pattern to the program in a format similar to +/pattern. (Patterns are defined in Hour 8.)

1. View the .cshrc file using more:

```
% more ~/.cshrc
#
# Default user .cshrc file (/bin/csh initialization).

set host=limbo

set path=(. ~/bin /bin /usr/bin /usr/ucb /usr/local /etc
/usr/etc /usr/local/bin /usr/unsup/bin)

# Set up C shell environment:

alias  diff      '/usr/bin/diff -c -w'
alias  from      'frm -n'
alias  ll        'ls -l'
alias  ls        '/bin/ls -F'
alias  mail      Mail
alias  mailq     '/usr/lib/sendmail -bp'

alias  newaliases 'echo you mean newalias...'

alias  rd        'readmsg $ | page'
--More--(51%)
```

Unlike previous examples, where the program has run until completed and left you back on the command line, more is the first *interactive program* you've encountered. When you see the --More--(51%) prompt, the cursor sits at the end of that line, waiting for you to tell the program what to do. The more program lets you know how far into the file you've viewed; in this example, you've seen about half of the file (51%).

At this point, quite a variety of commands are available. Press the spacebar to see the next screen of information, and keep doing this until you have seen the entire file.

2. Try starting the program with the 12th line of the file:

```
% more +12 ~/.cshrc
alias   mailq     '/usr/lib/sendmail -bp'

alias   newaliases 'echo you mean newalias...'

alias   rd        'readmsg $ | page'
alias   rn        '/usr/local/bin/rn -d$HOME -L -M -m -e -S -/'

# and some special stuff if we're in an interactive shell

if ( $?prompt ) then            # shell is interactive.

  alias   cd            'chdir \!* ; setprompt'
  alias   env           'printenv'
  alias   setprompt     'set prompt="$system ($cwd:t) \! : "'

  set noclobber history=100 filec
  umask 007

  setprompt
endif
--More--(82%)
```

3. You can see that about halfway through the .cshrc file there is a line that contains the word newaliases. I can start more so that the line with this pattern is displayed on the top of the first screenful:

```
% more +/newaliases ~/.cshrc
...skipping
alias   mailq     '/usr/lib/sendmail -bp'

alias   newaliases 'echo you mean newalias...'

alias   rd        'readmsg $ | page'
alias   rn        '/usr/local/bin/rn -d$HOME -L -M -m -e -S -/'

# and some special stuff if we're in an interactive shell

if ( $?prompt ) then            # shell is interactive.

  alias   cd            'chdir \!* ; setprompt'
  alias   env           'printenv'
  alias   setprompt     'set prompt="$system ($cwd:t) \! : "'
```

```
set noclobber history=100 filec
umask 007

  setprompt
endif

# special aliases:

alias info      ssinfo
--More--(86%)
```

Notice that the line containing the pattern newaliases shows up as the third line of the first screen, not the first line. That's so you have a bit of context to the matched line, but it can take some getting used to. Also note that more says—with the message . . . skipping as the first line—that it's skipping some lines to find the pattern.

4. The list of commands available at the --More-- prompt is quite extensive, as shown in Table 7.1. The sidebar following the table explains what the conventions used in the table mean and how to enter the commands.

TABLE 7.1 Commands Available Within the more Program

Command	Function
[Space]	Press the spacebar to display the next screenful of text.
n[Return]	Display the next n lines (the default is the next line only of text).
h	Display a list of commands available in the more program.
d	Scroll down half a page.
q	Quit the more program.
ns	Skip forward n lines (default is 1).
nf	Skip forward n screenfuls (default is 1).
b or Ctrl-b	Skip backward a screenful of text.
=	Display the current line number.
/pattern	Search for an occurrence of pattern.
n	Search for the next occurrence of the current pattern.
v	Start the vi editor at the current line.
Ctrl-l	(That's a lowercase L.) Redraw the screen.
:f	Display the current filename and line number.

Entering Commands in the `more` Program

In this table and in the following text, [Space] (the word *space* enclosed in brackets) refers to pressing the spacebar as a command. Likewise, [Return] means you should press the Return key as part of the command.

A hyphen in a command—for example, Ctrl-b—means that you should hold down the first indicated key while you press the second key. The lowercase-letter commands in the table indicate that you should press the corresponding key, the B key for the `b` command, for example.

Two characters together, but without a hyphen (`:f`), mean that you should press the appropriate keys in sequence, as you would when typing text.

Finally, entries that have an *n* before the command mean that you can prefix the command with a number, which will let it use that value to modify its action. For example, 3[Return] displays the next three lines of the file, and `250s` skips the next 250 lines. Typically, pressing Return or Enter after typing a command within `more` is not necessary.

Try some commands on a file of your own. A good file that will have enough lines to make this interesting is `/etc/passwd`:

```
% more /etc/passwd
root:?:0:0: root:/:/bin/csh
news:?:6:11:USENET News:/usr/spool/news:/bin/ksh
ingres:*?:7:519:INGRES Manager:/usr/ingres:/bin/csh
usrlimit:?:8:800:(1000 user system):/mnt:/bin/false
vanilla:*?:20:805:Vanilla Account:/mnt:/bin/sh
charon:*?:21:807:The Ferryman:/users/tomb:
actmaint:?:23:809: Maintenance:/usr/adm/actmaint:/bin/ksh
pop:*?:26:819:,,,,:/usr/spool/pop:/bin/csh
lp:*?:70:10:System V Lp Admin:/usr/spool/lp:
trouble:*?:97:501:Trouble Report Facility:/usr/trouble:/usr/msh
postmaster:?:98:504:Mail:/usr/local/adm:/bin/csh
aab:?:513:1233:Robert Townsend:/users/aab:/bin/ksh
billing:?:516:1233:Accounting:/users/billing:/bin/csh
aai:?:520:1233:Pete Cheeseman:/users/aai:/bin/csh
--More--(1%) 60s

...skipping 60 lines

cq:?:843:1233:Rob Tillot:/users/cq:/usr/local/bin/tcsh
robb:?:969:1233:Robb:/users/robb:/usr/local/lib/msh
aok:?:970:1233:B Jacobs:/users/aok:/usr/local/lib/msh
went:?:1040:1233:David Math:/users/went:/bin/csh
```

```
aru:?:1076:1233:Raffie:/users/aru:/bin/ksh
varney:?:1094:1233:/users/varney:/bin/csh
brandt:?:1096:1233:Eric Brand:/users/brand:/usr/local/bin/tcsh
ask:?:1098:1233:/users/ask:/bin/csh
asn:?:1101:1233:Ketter Wesley:/users/asn:/usr/local/lib/msh
--More--(2%)
```

This example isn't exactly what you'll see on your screen because each time you type a command to more, it erases its own prompt and replaces the prompt with the appropriate line of the file. Try pressing [Return] to move down one line, and you'll see what I mean.

Quit more in the middle of viewing this file by typing q.

NOTE

Many Unixes have a program called less that offers the same functionality as more but also allows you to move backward in a file, so if you're on page three and decide you want to go back to page two, you can do so. Use man less to learn more about it.

The more program is one of the best general-purpose programs in Unix, offering an easy and powerful tool for perusing files.

Summary

You've learned about file to ascertain type, head and tail for seeing snippets of files, and cat and more to help easily view files of any size on your screen. Now that you have this new set of commands added to your Unix expertise, you are most certainly ready to wander about your own computer system and understand what files are what, where they are, and how to peer inside.

Workshop

The Workshop summarizes the key terms you've learned and poses some questions about the topics presented in this lesson. It also provides you with a preview of what you will learn in the next hour.

Key Terms

control key notation   This notational convention in Unix denotes the use of a Control key. There are three common conventions (Ctrl-C, ^c, and C-C) that all denote the Control-c character, produced by pressing the Control key (labeled Control or Ctrl on your keyboard) and, while holding it down, pressing the c key.

interactive program   An interactive Unix application is one that expects the user to enter information and then responds as appropriate. The `ls` command is not interactive, but the `more` program, which displays text a screenful at a time, is interactive.

null character   Each character in Unix has a specific value, and any character with a numeric value of zero is known as a null or null character.

pipeline   A pipeline is a series of Unix commands chained by |, the pipe character.

Exercises

1. Many people who use Unix systems tend to stick with file-naming conventions. Indeed, Unix has many of its own, including `.c` for C source files, `.gz` for gzip compressed files, and a single dot prefix for dot files. Yet `file` often ignores filenames when it ascertains what type of content is within. (Test it yourself.) Why?

2. Do you remember the television game show "Name That Tune?" If so, you'll recall that contestants had to identify a popular song by hearing just the first few notes. The `file` command is similar; the program must guess at the type of the file by checking only the first few characters. Do you think it would be more accurate or less accurate if it checked more of the file? Why should or shouldn't it do so? (Think about this one.)

3. Use `more` to check some possible file types that can be recognized with the `file` command by peeking in the configuration file `/etc/magic`.

4. How did the `cat` command get its name? Do you find that to be a helpful mnemonic?

5. Here's an oddity:

   `cat LISTS | more`

   What will this command do?

6. If you were looking at an absolutely huge file, and you were pretty sure that what you wanted was near the bottom, what command would you use, and why?

7. What if the information were near the top?

Preview of the Next Hour

Many non-alphanumeric characters have special functions in Unix, as you have doubtless learned by accidentally typing a slash, an asterisk, a question mark, a quotation mark, or just about any other punctuation character. What might surprise you is that they all have different specific meanings that are more or less consistent throughout the system. The next hour explains considerably more about how pipelines work and how programs are used as filters. Among the new commands you will learn are `sort`, `wc`, `nl`, `uniq`, and `spell`. You also will learn how to work with filename wildcards on the command line to refer to groups of files all at once.

HOUR 8
Filters, Pipes, and Wildcards!

Goals for This Hour

In this hour, you will learn

- ▶ The secrets of file redirection
- ▶ How to count words and lines using `wc`
- ▶ How to sort information in a file using `sort`
- ▶ Working with wildcards
- ▶ Searching files with `grep`
- ▶ Creating regular expressions
- ▶ The rest of the `grep` family

If you've ever learned a foreign language, you know that the most common approach is to start by building your vocabulary (which always includes the names of the months, for some inexplicable reason) and then learning about the rules of sentence construction. The Unix command line is much like a language in this regard. Now that you've learned many Unix "words," it's time to learn how to put them together as "sentences," using file redirection, filters, and pipes.

One of the trickiest aspects of Unix is the concept of wildcards and regular expressions. A *wildcard* allows you to "guess" at a filename or to specify a group of filenames. *Regular expressions* match patterns and are different from, and more powerful than, wildcards.

In this important lesson, you'll also meet the wonderful command `grep`, which is based on regular expressions, along with the commands `wc`, `sort`, and `uniq`.

This hour begins by focusing on one aspect of constructing powerful custom commands in Unix by using file redirection. The introduction of some filters—programs intended to be used as part of command pipes—follows. Next you'll learn another aspect of creating your own Unix commands: using pipelines.

Maximizing the Command Line

Now that you've learned some of the individual words of the Unix command vocabulary, it's time to get into some of the fun and power of the Unix system: combining individual commands into *pipes* or *filters* to perform complex and sophisticated tasks.

Task 8.1: The Secrets of File Redirection

So far, all the commands you've learned while teaching yourself Unix have required you to enter information at the command line, and all have produced output on the screen. But, as Gershwin said in *Porgy and Bess,* "it ain't necessarily so." In fact, one of the most powerful features of Unix is the capability for the input to come from a file as easily as it can come from the keyboard, and for the output to be saved to a file as easily as it can be displayed on your screen.

The secret is *file redirection,* the use of special operators in Unix command-line syntax that instruct the computer to read from a file, write to a file, or even append information to an existing file. Each of these acts can be accomplished with a file-redirection operation in a regular command line: < redirects input, > redirects output, and >> redirects output and appends the information to the end of an existing file.

A mnemonic for remembering which is which is to remember that, just as in English, Unix works from left to right, so a redirect that points to the left (<) changes the input, whereas a redirect that points right (>) changes the output.

1. Log in to your account and create an empty file by using the `touch` command:

   ```
   % touch testme
   ```

   You'll use this empty file to learn how to redirect output.

2. Use `ls` to list the files in your directory and save them all to the newly created file:

   ```
   % ls -l testme
   -rw-rw-r--  1 taylor         0 Nov 15 09:11 testme
   % ls -l > testme
   % ls -l testme
   -rw-rw-r--  1 taylor       120 Nov 15 09:12 testme
   ```

   Notice that when you redirect the output, nothing is displayed on the screen; no visual confirmation indicates that it has worked. But it has, as you can see by the increased size of the new file.

3. Instead of using `more` to view this file, try using file redirection:

   ```
   % cat < testme
   total 127
   drwx------  2 taylor       512 Nov  6 14:20 Archives/
   drwx------  3 taylor       512 Nov 16 21:55 InfoWorld/
   ```

```
drwx------  2 taylor      1024 Nov 19 14:14 Mail/
drwx------  2 taylor       512 Oct  6 09:36 News/
drwx------  3 taylor       512 Nov 11 10:48 OWL/
drwx------  2 taylor       512 Oct 13 10:45 bin/
-rw-rw----  1 taylor     57683 Nov 20 20:10 bitnet.lists.Z
-rw-rw----  1 taylor     46195 Nov 20 06:19 drop.text.hqx
-rw-rw----  1 taylor     12556 Nov 16 09:49 keylime.pie
drwx------  2 taylor       512 Oct 13 10:45 src/
drwxrwx---  2 taylor       512 Nov  8 22:20 temp/
-rw-rw----  1 taylor         0 Nov 20 20:21 testme
```

The results are the same as if you had used the `ls` command directly, but the output has been saved. You now can easily print the file or go back to it later to compare it to your file listings in the future.

4. Use the `ls` command to add some further information at the bottom of the `testme` file by using `>>`, the append double-arrow notation:

```
% ls -FC >> testme
```

The `-C` flag to `ls` forces the system to list output in multicolumn mode. Try redirecting the output of `ls -F` to a file to see what happens without the `-C` flag.

You can combine the various forms of file redirection to create custom commands and to process files in various ways. This hour just scratches the surface. Next, you'll learn about some popular Unix filters and how they can be combined with file redirection to create new versions of existing files. These examples also show the basic steps in all Unix file-redirection operations: Specify the input to the command, specify the command, and specify where the output should go.

Task 8.2: Counting Words and Lines Using `wc`

Writers generally talk about the length of their work in terms of number of words rather than number of pages. In fact, most magazines and newspapers are laid out according to formulas based on multiplying an average-length word by the number of words in an article.

These people are obsessed with counting the words in their articles, but how do they do it? You can bet that they don't count each word by hand. If they're using Unix, they simply use the Unix `wc` program, which computes a word count for the file. It also can indicate the number of characters and the number of lines in the file.

1. Count the lines, words, and characters in the `testme` file you created earlier in this hour:

```
% wc testme
      4      12     121
% wc < testme
      4      12     121
% cat testme | wc
   4       12      121
```

All three of these commands offer the same result (which probably seems a bit cryptic). Why do you need to have three ways of doing the same thing? Later, you'll learn why this flexibility is so helpful. For now, stick to using the first form of the command.

The output is three numbers, which reveal how many lines, words, and characters, respectively, are in the file. You can see that there are 4 lines, 12 words, and 121 characters in `testme`.

2. You can have `wc` list any one of these counts, or a combination of two, by using different command flags: `-w` counts words, `-c` counts characters, and `-l` counts lines:

```
% wc -w testme
   12 testme
% wc -l testme
    4 testme
% wc -wl testme
       12        4 testme
% wc -lw testme
        4       12 testme
```

3. Now the fun begins. Here's an easy way to find out how many files you have in your home directory:

```
% ls | wc -l
37
```

The `ls` command lists each file, one per line (because you didn't use the `-C` flag). The output of that command is fed to `wc`, which counts the number of lines it's fed. The result is that you can find out how many files you have (37) in your home directory.

4. How about a quick gauge of how many users are on the system?

```
% who | wc -l
   12
```

Notice here that I used the | to create a pipeline. Why not just use file redirection? Because by creating a pipeline, I can feed the output of the first command to a second command rather than just save it to disk. You'll see that this capability is the essence of pipelines, and that they are, in turn, the core of the powerful command-line capabilities of Unix itself.

The `wc` command is a great example of how the simplest of commands, when used in a sophisticated pipeline, can be very powerful.

Task 8.3: Sorting Information Using `sort`

Whereas `wc` is useful at the end of a pipeline of commands, the `uniq` and `sort` commands are *filters*, programs that are really designed to be tucked in the middle of a pipeline. Filters can be placed anywhere in a command line, anywhere that enables them to help direct Unix to do what you want it to do.

The common characteristic of all Unix filters is that they can read input from standard input, process it in some manner, and list the results in standard output. With file redirection, standard input and output can also be files. You can either specify the filenames to the command (usually input only) or use the file-redirection symbols you learned earlier in this hour (<, >, and >>).

NOTE

Standard input and *standard output* are two very common expressions in Unix. When a program is run, the default location for receiving input is called *standard input*. The default location for output is *standard output*. If you are running Unix from a terminal, standard input is your keyboard, and standard output is your computer screen.

A third I/O location, *standard error*, also exists in Unix. By default, this is the same as standard output, but you can redirect standard error to a different location than standard output. You'll learn more about I/O redirection later in the book.

One of the most useful filters is `sort`, a program that reads information and sorts it alphabetically. You can customize the behavior of this program, as with all other Unix programs, to ignore the case of words (for example, to sort `Big` between `apple` and `cat` rather than before `apple`, even though most sorts put uppercase letters before the lowercase letters) and to reverse the order of a sort (z to a). The program `sort` also enables you to sort lists of numbers properly.

Few flags are available for `sort`, but the ones that exist are powerful, as shown in Table 8.1.

TABLE 8.1 Flags for the `sort` Command

Flag	Function
-b	Ignore leading blanks.
-d	Sort in dictionary order (with only letters, digits, and blanks significant).
-f	Fold uppercase into lowercase; that is, ignore the case of words.
-n	Sort in numerical order.
-r	Reverse the order of the sort.

1. By default, the `ls` command sorts files in a case-sensitive manner, first listing files that begin with uppercase letters and then those that begin with lowercase letters:

```
% ls -1F
Archives/
InfoWorld/
Mail/
News/
```

```
OWL/
bin/
bitnet.mailing-lists.Z
drop.text.hqx
keylime.pie
src/
temp/
testme
```

Did you notice the `-1` (number 1) flag? It forces one-line-per-file output, which is useful for filters and pipes.

To sort filenames alphabetically, regardless of case, you can use `sort -f`:

```
% ls -1 | sort -f
Archives/
bin/
bitnet.mailing-lists.Z
drop.text.hqx
InfoWorld/
keylime.pie
Mail/
News/
OWL/
src/
temp/
testme
```

2. How about sorting the lines of a file? You can use the `testme` file you created earlier:

```
% sort < testme
Archives/           OWL/                    keylime.pie
InfoWorld/          bin/                    src/
Mail/               bitnet.mailing-lists.Z  temp/
News/               drop.text.hqx           testme
```

3. Here's a real-life Unix example. Of the files in your home directory, which are the largest? The `ls -s` command indicates the size of each file, in blocks, and `sort -n` sorts numerically:

```
% ls -s | sort -n
total 127
    1 Archives/
    1 InfoWorld/
    1 Mail/
    1 News/
    1 OWL/
    1 bin/
    1 src/
```

```
 1 temp/
 1 testme
13 keylime.pie
46 drop.text.hqx
64 bitnet.mailing-lists.Z
```

It would be more convenient if the largest files were listed first in the output. The `-r` flag reverses the sort order, which is quite useful:

```
% ls -s | sort -nr
64 bitnet.mailing-lists.Z
46 drop.text.hqx
13 keylime.pie
 1 testme
 1 temp/
 1 src/
 1 bin/
 1 OWL/
 1 News/
 1 Mail/
 1 InfoWorld/
 1 Archives/
total 127
```

4. One more refinement is available to you. Instead of listing all the files, use the `head` command and specify that you want to see only the top five entries:

```
% ls -s | sort -nr | head -5
64 bitnet.mailing-lists.Z
46 drop.text.hqx
13 keylime.pie
 1 testme
 1 temp/
```

This is a powerful and complex Unix command, yet it is composed of simple and easy-to-understand components.

5. One helpful filter that works with `sort` is the `uniq` command. In particular, `uniq -c` removes duplicate lines but *also shows you how many dupes were removed*. This is particularly helpful when you're analyzing large data files with recurring data.

For example, you can quickly duplicate the last line of a file by pulling it into a second file and then using `cat` to create a new test file:

```
% tail -1 testme > lastline
% cat lastline lastline lastline lastline > newtest2
% cat newtest2
News/                    drop.text.hqx            testme
News/                    drop.text.hqx            testme
```

```
News/                        drop.text.hqx              testme
News/                        drop.text.hqx              testme
```

Now you can see what `uniq` does:

```
% uniq newtest2
News/                        drop.text.hqx              testme
```

And you can see how the `-c` flag removes duplicate lines and shows the count:

```
% uniq -c newtest2
   4 News/                         drop.text.hqx              testme
```

You can see that this line occurs four times in the file. Lines that are unique have no numerical preface.

Like many of the other filters, `sort` and `uniq` aren't too exciting by themselves. As you explore Unix further and learn more about how to combine these simple commands to build sophisticated instructions, you will begin to see their true value.

Task 8.4: Filename Wildcards

By now you are doubtless tired of typing every letter of each filename into your system for each example. A better and easier way exists! Just as with the special cards in poker that can have any value, Unix has special characters that the various shells (the command-line interpreter programs) interpret as *wildcards*.

You need to learn two basic wildcards: * acts as a match for any number and sequence of characters, and ? acts as a match for any single character. In the broadest sense, a lone * acts as a match for all files in the current directory (in other words, `ls *` is identical to `ls`), whereas a single ? acts as a match for all one-character-long filenames in a directory (for instance, `ls ?`, which will list only those filenames that are one character long).

1. To experiment with wildcards, it's easiest to use the `echo` command. Recall that `echo` repeats anything given to it, but—and here's the secret to its value—the shell interprets anything that is entered before `echo` sees it. That is, the * is expanded before the shell hands the arguments over to the command:

```
% echo *
Archives InfoWorld Mail News OWL bin bitnet.mailing-lists.Z
drop.text.hqx keylime.pie src temp testme
```

Using the * wildcard enables you to easily reference all files in the directory.

2. A wildcard is even more helpful than the example suggests because it can be embedded in the middle of a word or otherwise used to limit the number of matches. To see all files that began with the letter *t*, use `t*`:

```
% echo t*
temp testme
```

3. Variations are possible, too. You could use wildcards to list all files or directories that end with the letter *s*:

```
% echo *s
Archives News
```

Watch what happens if I try the same command using the `ls` command rather than the `echo` command:

```
% ls -F *s
Archives:
Interleaf.story    Tartan.story.Z       nextstep.txt.Z
Opus.story         interactive.txt.Z    rae.assist.infoworld.Z

News:
mailing.lists.usenet  usenet.1              usenet.alt
```

Using the `ls` command here makes the shell think I want to list the contents of the two directories, not just the directory entries themselves. This is where I need to use the `-d` flag to `ls` to force a listing of the directories rather than of their contents.

4. Notice that, in the `News` directory, I have three files with the word `usenet` somewhere in their names. The wildcard pattern `usenet*` would match two of the files, and `*usenet` would match one. A valuable aspect of the `*` wildcard is that it can match *zero* or more characters, so the pattern `*usenet*` will match all three filenames:

```
% echo News/*usenet*
News/mailing.lists.usenet News/usenet.1 News/usenet.alt
```

Also notice that wildcards can be embedded in a filename or pathname. In this example, I specified that I was only interested in files in the `News` directory.

5. Can you match a single character? To see how this can be helpful, it's time to move into a different directory, such as `OWL` on my system:

```
% cd OWL
% ls -F
Student.config    owl.c          owl.o
WordMap/          owl.data       simple.editor.c
owl*              owl.h          simple.editor.o
```

If I request `owl*`, which files will be listed?

```
% echo owl*
owl owl.c owl.data owl.h owl.o
```

What do I do if I am interested only in the source, header, and object files, which are here indicated by a `.c`, `.h`, or `.o` suffix? Using a wildcard that matches zero or more letters won't work; I don't want to see `owl` or `owl.data`. One possibility would be to use the pattern `owl.*` (because by adding the period, I can eliminate the `owl` file itself).

What I really want, however, is to be able to specify all files that start with the four characters `owl.` and have exactly one more character. This is a situation in which the `?` wildcard works:

```
% echo owl.?
owl.c owl.h owl.o
```

Because no files have exactly one letter following the three letters `owl`, watch what happens when I specify `owl?` as the pattern:

```
% echo owl?
echo: No match.
```

6. You can use even more sophisticated wildcards. Next you'll learn about some of them so you can get a sense of what can be accomplished on the command line.

    A pair of square brackets denotes a range of characters, which can be either explicitly listed or indicated as a range with a dash between them I can explicitly list the letters of interest by listing them all tucked neatly into a pair of square brackets, as shown here:

```
% ls -ld [abkost]*
-rw-rw----  1 taylor         126 Dec  3 16:34 awkscript
-rw-rw----  1 taylor         165 Dec  3 16:42 bigfiles
drwx------  2 taylor         512 Oct 13 10:45 bin/
-rw-rw----  1 taylor       12556 Nov 16 09:49 keylime.pie
-rw-rw----  1 taylor        8729 Dec  2 21:19 owl.c
-rw-rw----  1 taylor         199 Dec  3 16:11 sample
-rw-rw----  1 taylor         207 Dec  3 16:11 sample2
drwx------  2 taylor         512 Oct 13 10:45 src/
drwxrwx---  2 taylor         512 Nov  8 22:20 temp/
-rw-rw----  1 taylor         582 Nov 27 18:29 testme
```

    In this case, the shell matches all files that start with *a*, *b*, *k*, *o*, *s*, or *t*. This notation is still a bit clunky and would be even more so if more files were involved.

7. You can specify a range of characters by putting a hyphen in the middle:

```
% ls -ld [a-z]*
-rw-rw----  1 taylor         126 Dec  3 16:34 awkscript
-rw-rw----  1 taylor         165 Dec  3 16:42 bigfiles
drwx------  2 taylor         512 Oct 13 10:45 bin/
-rw-rw----  1 taylor       12556 Nov 16 09:49 keylime.pie
-rw-rw----  1 taylor        8729 Dec  2 21:19 owl.c
-rw-rw----  1 taylor         199 Dec  3 16:11 sample
-rw-rw----  1 taylor         207 Dec  3 16:11 sample2
drwx------  2 taylor         512 Oct 13 10:45 src/
drwxrwx---  2 taylor         512 Nov  8 22:20 temp/
-rw-rw----  1 taylor         582 Nov 27 18:29 testme
```

In this example, the shell will match any file that begins with a lowercase letter from *a* to *z*, as specified.

8. The combination of character ranges, single-character wildcards, and multicharacter wildcards can be tremendously helpful. If I move to another directory, I can easily search for all files that contain a single digit, a dot, or an underscore in the name:

```
% ls *[0-9._]*
71075.446        ean_huts         matt_ruby     xd1f
72303.2166       gordon_hat       netnews.postings
bob_gull         john_welcher     siob_n
dan_some         john_prage       v892127
```

I think that the best way to learn about pervasive features of Unix such as shell filename wild-cards is to use them. As you've no doubt noticed so far in this book, examples build on earlier information. This will continue to be the case, and the wildcard notations shown here are used again and again to specify groups of files or directories.

If you want to experiment with filename wildcards, you can most easily use the echo command because it safely prints the expanded version of any pattern you specify without otherwise doing anything with those files. Lots of Unix experts use echo to develop and fine-tune a pattern and then use the pattern with a different command.

Task 8.5: Searching Files with `grep`

Two commonly used commands are important stepping stones in becoming a power user comfortable with the capabilities of the system: the ls command and the grep command. We've already looked at the ls command, so let's turn our attention to the oddly named grep command, which makes it easy to find files that contain specified text patterns.

The grep command not only has a ton of command options but has two variations in Unix systems, too. These variations are egrep, for specifying more complex patterns (regular expressions), and fgrep, for using file-based lists of words as search patterns.

NOTE

Before grep existed, Unix users would use a crude line-based editor called ed to find matching text. To search through a file with a *regular expression*, the user prefixed the command with global and had only the matches shown with print. Putting it all together, the operation was global/*regular expression*/print. This was shortened to g/re/p and eventually reinvented as grep.

You could spend the next 100 pages learning all the obscure and weird options to the grep family of commands. When you boil it down, however, you're probably going to use only the simplest patterns and maybe a flag or two. Think of it this way: The English language contains more than 500,000 words (according to the Oxford English Dictionary), but you don't have to learn them all to communicate effectively.

With this in mind, you'll learn the basics of grep this hour, but you'll pick up more insight into the program's capabilities and options during the next few hours.

A few of the most important grep command flags are listed in Table 8.2.

TABLE 8.2 **The Most Helpful grep Flags**

Flag	Function
-c	List a count of matching lines only.
-i	Ignore the case of the letters in the pattern.
-l	List only the names of files that contain the specified pattern.
-n	Include line numbers.
-v	Show lines that *don't* match the specified pattern.

1. The general form of grep is to specify the command, any flags you want to add, the pattern, and a filename:

   ```
   % grep bitnet testme
   Mail/                    bitnet.mailing-lists.Z  temp/
   ```

   As you can see, grep easily pulled out the line in the testme file that contained the pattern bitnet.

2. Be aware that grep finds patterns in a case-sensitive manner:

   ```
   % grep owl testme
   %
   % grep OWL testme
   Archives/                OWL/                     keylime.pie
   ```

   Note that OWL was not found in the first example because the pattern specified with the grep command was all lowercase, owl.

   That's where the -i (ignore case) flag can be helpful:

   ```
   % grep -i owl testme
   Archives/                OWL/                     keylime.pie
   ```

3. For the next few examples, I'll move into the /etc directory because the files there have lots of lines. On one of the systems I use, the file /etc/passwd has almost 4,000 lines:

   ```
   % cd /etc
   % wc -l /etc/passwd
       3877
   ```

My account is `taylor`. I'll use `grep` to see my account entry in the password file:

```
% grep taylor /etc/passwd
taylorj:?:1048:1375:James Taylor:/users/taylorj:/bin/csh
mtaylor:?:760:1375:Mary Taylor:/users/mtaylor:/usr/local/bin/tcsh
dataylor:?:375:518:David Taylor:/users/dataylor:/usr/local/lib/msh
taylorjr:?:203:1022:James Taylor:/users/taylorjr:/bin/csh
taylorrj:?:668:1042:Robert Taylor:/users/taylorrj:/bin/csh
taylorm:?:862:1508:Melanie Taylor:/users/taylormx:/bin/csh
taylor:?:1989:1412:Dave Taylor:/users/taylor:/bin/csh
```

4. As you can see, many accounts contain the pattern `taylor`.

You could figure out how many accounts there are with the pipeline `grep taylor /etc/passwd | wc -l`, right?

A smarter way to see how often the `taylor` pattern appears is to use the `-c` flag to `grep`, which will tell you how many matches are in the file:

```
% grep -c taylor /etc/passwd
7
```

The command located seven matches. Count the matches in the listing in the step 3 output to confirm this.

5. With 3,877 lines in the `password` file, an administrative file that records basic account information for everyone on the Unix system, it could be interesting to see whether all the Taylors started their accounts at about the same time. (This presumably would mean that they all appear in the file at about the same point.) To do this, I'll use the `-n` flag to number the output lines:

```
% grep -n taylor /etc/passwd
319:taylorj:?:1048:1375:James Taylor:/users/taylorj:/bin/csh
1314:mtaylor:?:760:1375:Mary Taylor:/users/mtaylor:/usr/local/_bin/tcsh
1419:dataylor:?:375:518:Dave Taylor:/users/dataylor:/usr/local/_lib/msh
1547:taylorjr:?:203:1022:James Taylor:/users/taylorjr:/bin/csh
1988:taylorrj:?:668:1042:Robert Taylor:/users/taylorrj:/bin/csh
2133:taylorm:?:8692:1508:Melanie Taylor:/users/taylorm:/bin/csh
3405:taylor:?:1989:1412:Dave Taylor:/users/taylor:/bin/csh
```

The `grep` command adds the line number, a colon, and the actual content of that line, which in this case proves to be quite confusing because the matching lines also use colons to separate information on the line. Normally, a line number followed by a colon would be no problem, but in the `passwd` file (which is already littered with colons), it's befuddling.

You can see that my theory about when the Taylors started their accounts was wrong. If proximity in the `passwd` file is an indicator that accounts are assigned at similar times, then no Taylors started their accounts even within the same week.

These examples of how to use `grep` barely scratch the surface of how this powerful and sophisticated command can be used. Explore your own file system by using `grep` to search files for specific patterns.

NOTE

Armed with wildcards, you now can try the `-l` flag to `grep`, which, as you recall, indicates the names of the files that contain a specified pattern rather than printing the lines that match the pattern. If I go into my email archive directory—Mail—I can easily, using the command `grep -l -i chicago Mail/*`, produces a list of folders that contain the case-insensitive pattern `chicago`. Try using `grep -l` to search across all files in your home directory for words or patterns.

Task 8.6: Creating Regular Expressions

A regular expression can be as simple as a word to be matched letter for letter, such as *acme*, or as complex as (`^[a-zA-Z]|:wi`), which matches all lines that begin with an upper- or lowercase letter or that contain `:wi`.

The language of *regular expressions* is full of punctuation characters and letters used in unusual ways. It is important to remember that regular expressions are different from shell wildcard patterns. It's unfortunate, but it's true. In the C shell, for example, `a*` lists any file that starts with the letter *a*. Regular expressions aren't *left-rooted*, which means that you need to specify `^a` if you want to match only lines that begin with the letter *a*. The shell pattern `a*` matches only filenames that start with the letter *a*, and the `*` has a different interpretation completely when used as part of a regular expression: `a*` is a pattern that matches zero or more occurrences of the letter *a*. The notation for regular expressions is shown in Table 8.3. The `egrep` command has additional notation, which you will learn shortly.

TABLE 8.3 Summary of Regular Expression Notation

Notation	Meaning
`c`	Match the character `c`
`\c`	Force `c` to be read as the letter `c`, not as another meaning that the character might have (for example, `\*` is how you would indicate a literal asterisk instead of a wildcard)
`^`	Beginning of the line
`$`	End of the line

Notation	Meaning
.	Any single character
[xy]	Any single character in the set specified
[^xy]	Any single character not in the set specified
c*	Zero or more occurrences of character c

The notation isn't as complex as it looks in this table. The most important things to remember about regular expressions are that the * denotes zero or more occurrences of the preceding character, and . is any single character. Remember that shell patterns use * to match any set of zero or more characters, independent of the preceding character, and ? to match a single character.

1. Earlier, when I searched for taylor in the /etc/passwd file, I found more matches than I wanted. If I'm looking for my own account, I don't want to see all these alternatives. Using the ^ character before the pattern left-roots the pattern:

```
% grep '^taylor' /etc/passwd
taylorj:?:1048:1375:James Taylor:/users/taylorj:/bin/csh
taylorjr:?:203:1022:James Taylor:/users/taylorjr:/bin/csh
taylorrj:?:662:1042:Robert Taylor:/users/taylorrj:/bin/csh
taylorm:?:869:1508:Melanie Taylor:/users/taylorm:/bin/csh
taylor:?:1989:1412:Dave Taylor:/users/taylor:/bin/cshx
```

2. Now I want to narrow the search further. I want to specify a pattern that says "show me all lines that start with taylor, followed by a character that is not a lowercase letter." To accomplish this, I use the [^xy] notation, which indicates an *exclusion set*, or a set of characters that cannot match the pattern:

```
% grep '^taylor[^a-z]' /etc/passwd
taylor:?:1989:1412:Dave Taylor:/users/taylor:/bin/csh
```

It worked! You can specify a set in two ways: You can either list each character or use a hyphen to specify a range starting with the character to the left of the hyphen and ending with the character to the right of the hyphen. That is, a-z is the range beginning with a and ending with z, and 0-9 includes all digits.

3. To see which accounts were excluded, remove the ^ to search for an *inclusion range*—a set of characters in which one must match the pattern:

```
% grep '^taylor[a-z]' /etc/passwd
taylorj:?:1048:1375:James Taylor:/users/taylorj:/bin/csh
taylorjr:?:203:1022:James Taylor:/users/taylorjr:/bin/csh
taylorrj:?:668:1042:Robert Taylor:/users/taylorrj:/bin/csh
taylormx:?:869:1508:Melanie Taylor:/users/taylorm:/bin/csh
```

4. Let's look at some other examples. Here I use `head` to view the first five lines of the password file:

```
% head -5 /etc/passwd
root:?:0:0:root:/:/bin/csh
news:?:6:11:USENET News:/usr/spool/news:/bin/ksh
ingres:*?:7:519:INGRES Manager:/usr/ingres:/bin/csh
usrlimit:?:8:800:(1000 user system):/mnt:/bin/false
vanilla:*?:20:805:Vanilla Account:/mnt:/bin/sh
```

Now I'll specify a pattern that tells `grep` to search for all lines that contain zero or more occurrences of the letter *z*:

```
% grep 'z*' /etc/passwd | head -5
root:?:0:0:root:/:/bin/csh
news:?:6:11:USENET News:/usr/spool/news:/bin/ksh
ingres:*?:7:519:INGRES Manager:/usr/ingres:/bin/csh
usrlimit:?:8:800:(1000 user system):/mnt:/bin/false
vanilla:*?:20:805:Vanilla Account:/mnt:/bin/sh
```

The result is identical to the result of the preceding command, but that shouldn't be a surprise. Specifying a pattern that matches *zero* or more occurrences will match every line! Specifying only the lines that have one or more *z*'s is accomplished with this odd-looking pattern:

```
% grep 'zz*' /etc/passwd | head -5
marg:?:724:1233:Guyzee:/users/marg:/bin/ksh
axy:?:1272:1233:martinez:/users/axy:/bin/csh
wizard:?:1560:1375:Oz:/users/wizard:/bin/ksh
zhq:?:2377:1318:Zihong:/users/zhq:/bin/csh
mm:?:7152:1233:Michael Kenzie:/users/mm:/bin/ksh
```

5. Earlier I found that a couple of lines in the `/etc/passwd` file were for accounts that didn't specify a login shell. Each line in the password file must have a certain number of colons, and the last character on the line for these accounts will be a colon, which is an easy `grep` pattern when you remember that as the last character in a pattern, a `$` represents the end of line. And don't forget that `^` as the very first character in a pattern represents the beginning of the line (versus within a set notation, where it indicates a "not," or reverse, of the pattern subsequently specified).

Here's how the `$` notation might look in this context:

```
% grep ':$' /etc/passwd
charon:*?:21:807:The Ferryman:/users/tomb:
lp:*?:70:10:System V Lp Adminuniverse(att):/usr/spool/lp:
```

6. Say that I get a call from my accountant, and I need to find a file that contains a message about a $100 outlay of cash to buy some software. Turns out that to find the message,

I can use `grep` to search for all files that contain a dollar sign, followed by a 1, followed by one or more 0s:

```
% grep '$100*' * */*
Mail/bob_gale:     Unfortunately, our fees are currently $100 per test drive,
➥ budgets
Mail/dan_sommer:We also pay $100 for Test Drives, our very short "First Looks"
➥ section. We often
Mail/james:has been dropped, so if I ask for $1000 is that way outta line
Mail/john_spragens:time testing things since it's a $100 test drive: I'm
➥ willing to
Mail/john_spragens:     Finally, I'd like to request $200 rather than $100 for
Mail/mac:again: expected pricing will be $10,000 - $16,000 and the BriteLite
➥ LX with
Mail/mark:I'm promised $1000 / month for a first
Mail/netnews.postings:  Win Lose or Die, John Gardner (hardback) $10
Mail/netnews.postings:I'd be willing to pay, I dunno, $100 / year for the
➥ space? I would
Mail/sent:to panic that they'd want their $10K advance back, but the good
➥ news is
Mail/sent:That would be fine.  How about $100 USD for both, to include any
Mail/sent:     Amount: $100.00
```

That's quite a few matches. Notice that among the matches are $1000, $10K, and $10. To match the specific value $100, of course, I can use $100 as the search pattern followed by an exclusion set: $100[^0].

NOTE

You can use the shell to expand files not just in the current directory but one level deeper into subdirectories, too: * expands your search beyond files in the current directory, and */* expands your search to all files contained one directory below the current point. If you have lots of files, you might occasionally see the error `arg list too long`; that's where wildcards reach the end of their usefulness and the `find` command (covered in Hour 22, "Searching for Information and Files") takes over.

This pattern demonstrates the sophistication and potential confusion surrounding Unix regular expressions. For example, the $ is a special character that can be used to denote the end of a line, but only if it is placed at the end of the pattern. Because I did not place it at the end of the pattern, the `grep` program correctly interpreted it as the $ character itself.

With the relatively small number of notations available in regular expressions, you can create quite a variety of sophisticated patterns to find information in a file. Use `man grep` to learn more.

Task 8.7: The Rest of the `grep` Family

Sometimes a single regular expression can't locate what you seek. For example, perhaps you're looking for lines that match either of two patterns. That's where the `egrep` command proves helpful. The command gets its name from "expression `grep`," and it has a notational scheme more powerful than that of `grep`, as shown in Table 8.4.

TABLE 8.4   Regular Expression Notation for `egrep`

Notation	Meaning
c	Match the character c
\c	Force c to be read as the letter c, not as another meaning the character might have
^	Beginning of the line
$	End of the line
.	Any single character
[xy]	Any single character in the set specified
[^xy]	Any single character not in the set specified
c*	Zero or more occurrences of character c
c+	One or more occurrences of character c

For example, you might want to have a file of patterns and invoke a Unix command that searches for lines that contain any of the patterns in that file. That's where the `fgrep`, or file-based `grep`, command comes into play. A file of patterns can contain any pattern that `grep` would understand (which means, unfortunately, that you can't use the additional notation available in `egrep`) and is specified with the `-f file` option.

1. I'll search the password file to demonstrate `egrep`. A pattern that seemed a bit weird was the one I used earlier with `grep` to search for lines containing one or more occurrences of the letter *z*: `'zz*'`. With `egrep`, this search is much easier:

    ```
    % egrep 'z+' /etc/passwd | head -5
    marg:?:724:1233:Guyzee:/users/marg:/bin/ksh
    axy:?:1272:1233:martinez:/users/axy:/bin/csh
    wizard:?:1560:1375:Oz:/users/wizard:/bin/ksh
    zhq:?:2377:1318:Zihong:/users/zhq:/bin/csh
    mm:?:7152:1233:Michael Kenzie:/users/mm:/bin/ksh
    Broken pipe
    ```

2. To search for lines that have either a *z* or a *q*, I can use the following:

    ```
    % egrep '(z|q)' /etc/passwd | head -5
    aaq:?:528:1233:Don Kid:/users/aaq:/bin/csh
    abq:?:560:1233:K Laws:/users/abq:/bin/csh
    marg:?:724:1233:Guyzee:/users/marg:/bin/ksh
    ahq:?:752:1233:Andy Smith:/users/ahq:/bin/csh
    ```

```
cq:?:843:1233:Rob Till:/users/cq:/usr/local/bin/tcsh
Broken pipe
```

3. Now this complicated egrep pattern should make sense to you:

```
% egrep '(^[a-zA-Z]|:wi)' /etc/printcap | head
aglw:\
        :wi=AG 23:wk=multiple Apple LaserWriter IINT:
aglw1:\
        :wi=AG 23:wk=Apple LaserWriter IINT:
aglw2:\
        :wi=AG 23:wk=Apple LaserWriter IINT:
aglw3:\
        :wi=AG 23:wk=Apple LaserWriter IINT:
aglw4:\
        :wi=AG 23:wk=Apple LaserWriter IINT:
Broken pipe
```

The pattern specified looks either for lines that begin (^)with an upper- or lowercase letter ([a-zA-Z]) or for lines that contain the pattern :wi. Remember that when used within a set, ^ reverses the meaning of the set, but when used at the very beginning of a pattern, ^ *left-roots* the search, having it match the very beginning of lines.

4. I use fgrep with wrongwords, an alias, and .wrongwords, a file that contains a list of words I commonly misuse:

```
% alias wrongwords ='fgrep -i -f .wrongwords'
% cat .wrongwords
effect
affect
insure
ensure
idea
thought
```

Any time I want to check a file, such as dickens.note, to see whether it has any of these commonly misused words, I simply enter the following:

```
% wrongwords dickens.note
drama of The Frozen Deep, I first conceived the main idea of this
As the idea became familiar to me, it gradually shaped itself into its
```

I need to determine whether these are ideas or thoughts. It's a subtle distinction I often forget in my writing. To be fair, Charles Dickens probably got the usage correct in his great work *A Tale of Two Cities*, so we should probably cut the guy some slack, right?

5. Here's another sample file that contains a couple of words from wrongwords:

```
% cat sample3
At the time I was hoping to insure that the cold weather
would avoid our home, so I, perhaps foolishly, stapled the
```

```
weatherstripping along the inside of the sliding glass
door in the back room. I was surprised how much affect it
had on our enjoyment of the room, actually.
```

Can you see the two incorrectly used words in that sentence? The `spell` program can't:

`% spell sample3`

(Use `man spell` to learn more about the Unix `spell` command. But be aware that many modern Unixes no longer include `spell` for reasons I find inexplicable.)

The `wrongwords` alias, on the other hand, can detect these words:

```
% wrongwords sample3
At the time I was hoping to insure that the cold weather
door in the back room. I was surprised how much affect it
```

You have now met the entire family of `grep` commands. For most of your searches for information, you can use the `grep` command itself. Sometimes, though, it's nice to have options!

Summary

In this hour, you have had a chance to build on the knowledge you're picking up about Unix with your introduction to an exciting and powerful Unix utility: `grep`. Finally, what's a poker hand without some new wildcards? Because suicide kings and one-eyed jacks don't make much sense in Unix, you instead learned how to specify ranges of characters in filename patterns, further ensuring that you can type the minimum number of keys for maximum effect.

You have learned quite a bit in this hour as you've continued down the road to Unix expertise. You've learned about file redirection. You can't go wrong by spending time studying this information closely. The concept of using filters and building complex commands by combining simple commands with pipes has been more fully demonstrated here, too. This higher level of Unix command language is makes Unix powerful and easy to mold.

This hour hasn't skimped on commands, either. You've learned about `wc` for counting lines, words, and characters in a file, and you've met `uniq`, `sort`, and the super-useful `grep` command family.

Workshop

The Workshop summarizes the key terms you've learned and poses some questions about the topics presented in this lesson. It also provides you with a preview of what you will learn in the next hour.

Key Terms

exclusion set   This is a set of characters that a pattern must not contain.

file redirection   Most Unix programs expect to read their input from the user (standard input) and write their output to the screen (standard output). By use of file redirection, however, input can come from a previously created file, and output can be saved to a file instead of being displayed on the screen.

filter   Filters are a particular type of Unix program that expects to work either with file redirection or as part of a pipeline. These programs read input from standard input, write output to standard output, and often don't have any starting arguments.

inclusion range   This is a range of characters that a pattern must include.

left-rooted   Patterns that must occur at the beginning of a line are said to be left-rooted.

regular expression   This is a convenient notation for specifying complex patterns. Notable special characters are ^ to match the beginning of the line and $ to match the end of the line.

standard error   This is the same as standard output, but you can redirect standard error to a different location than standard output.

standard input   Unix programs always default to reading information from the user by reading the keyboard and watching what's typed. With file redirection, input can come from a file, and with pipelines, input can be the result of a previous Unix command.

standard output   When processing information, Unix programs default to displaying the output on the screen, also known as standard output. With file redirection, output can easily be saved to a file; with pipelines, output can be sent to other programs.

wildcards   Wildcards are special characters that are interpreted by the Unix shell or other programs to have meanings other than the characters themselves. For example, * is a shell wildcard and creates a pattern that matches zero or more characters. When prefaced, for example, with the letter X (X*), this shell pattern will match all files beginning with *X*.

Exercises

1. The placement of file-redirection characters is important to ensure that a command works correctly. Which of the following do you think will work, and why?

```
< file wc            wc file <           wc < file
cat file | wc        cat < file | wc     wc | cat
```

Now try them and see whether you're correct.

2. Does the file size listed by `wc -c` always agree with the file size listed by the `ls` command? With the size indicated by `ls -s`? If there is any difference, why?

3. What do you think would happen if you tried to sort a list of words by pretending they're all numbers? Try it with the command `ls -1 | sort -n` to see what happens. Experiment with the variations.

4. What wildcard expression would you use to find the following?

   ▶ All files in the `/tmp` directory

   ▶ All files that contain a `w` in that directory

   ▶ All files that start with a `b`, contain an `e`, and end with `.c`

   ▶ All files that either start with `test` or contain the pattern `hi` (notice that it can be more than one pattern)

5. Create regular expressions to match the following:

   ▶ Lines that contain the words `hot` and `cold` (tricky!)

   ▶ Lines that contain the word `cat` but not `cats`

   ▶ Lines that begin with a numeral

6. Use the `-v` flag with various `grep` commands and show the command and pattern needed to match lines that:

   ▶ Don't contain `cabana`

   ▶ Don't contain either `jazz` or `funk`

   ▶ Don't contain `jazz`, `funk`, `disco`, `blues`, or `ska`

Preview of the Next Hour

The next hour introduces you to many more commands that are ideal for working with pipelines and filters—commands that will help you move from being a Unix amateur to being a true expert, a wizard at the command line!

Slicing and Dicing Command-Pipe Data

Goals for This Hour

In this hour, you will learn

▶ About the `awk` programming system

▶ How to use `cut` in pipes

▶ About using `sed` and `tr` for in-line transformations

By this point, you've learned enough about Unix to be able to build quite sophisticated command-line pipes, sequences of standard commands that offer flexibility and power. You need to add a couple of key tools to your toolkit to keep moving forward, however, and they're the focus of this lesson.

The first and most powerful of the tools is `awk`, a programming system built specifically to work with data streams. You can build very complex processing systems in `awk`, but in fact the most common `awk` programs are typically just a line or two long.

Many modern Unix folk prefer Perl, but I find that Perl isn't as pervasive across Unix, Linux, and other *nix platforms, so I'll stick with `awk` for this lesson. I do cover Perl later in the book, though, in case you're curious. If you'd prefer to just learn Perl, you can find a lot of really good tutorials on this sophisticated—and confusing—programming language.

In addition to explaining `awk`, this hour also talks about three additional pipeline commands that you will doubtless find essential for your toolbox: `sed`, a stream editor; `tr`, a character mapping facility; and `cut`, a utility that makes it remarkably easy to slice individual columns of data out of a pipeline of information.

There's one interesting characteristic of `awk` that's worth mentioning before we go further: It's a powerful programming language, and you can use it to duplicate many of the actual utilities that are an essential part of the Unix operating system. In a moment, I'll show you how to duplicate the `wc` command with a few lines of `awk`.

Later in the book, in Hour 23, "Perl Programming in Unix," we'll explore the Perl programming language and how it's integrated into modern Unix systems. Like `awk`, Perl has the ability to duplicate many of the most common Unix commands. Perl is also considerably more powerful and sophisticated than awk.

Okay, true confession: I don't recommend actually rewriting existing commands, but it is good to know which of the tools in the Unix toolbox are actually all-purpose utilities rather than just focused on a single, specific task.

The awk Programming System

Whether it's C, Pascal, BASIC, Java, or even Swift, every programming language has its forte, the area where it really shines. If it's BASIC, it's simple introductory programming. If it's Java, it's platform-independent software. Ruby, Python, C++, LISP, and all other programming languages have a specific type of programming for which they're designed. awk is different, though, living somewhere in between simple shell scripts and these sophisticated languages. It doesn't have many of the features and characteristics of a formal programming environment, but in its own way, awk is powerful, and it's definitely ideal for lightweight, in-line data processing.

Task 9.1: Learning to Use awk

The basic structure of every awk script is a pattern followed by a command. If you skip the pattern, the command applies to all lines in the data stream. If you skip the command section, all matching lines are printed (sent to the output data stream).

As a very simple example, the program NF == 3 (yep, that's all you'd need for this program!) will print all lines of input that have exactly three fields (NF is a shortcut meaning *number of fields in the input line*). The program $1 > 3 { print $1 } will print the first field of all lines where that field has a numeric value greater than three.

Let's take a closer look at awk.

1. I want to figure out the average size of all the email files on a new system I've been building. To accomplish this, I'll start with ls to get the file sizes:

```
$ ls -l
total 8474
-rw-r--r--  1 taylor   taylor      3111 Dec 14 16:09 baby-responses
-rw-r--r--  1 taylor   taylor     19930 Dec 14 16:09 barbara
-rw-r--r--  1 taylor   taylor    298719 Dec 14 16:09 dunlap
-rw-r--r--  1 taylor   taylor      5758 Dec 14 16:09 evan
-rw-r--r--  1 taylor   taylor     14577 Dec 14 16:09 glee
-rw-r--r--  1 taylor   taylor      1610 Dec 14 16:09 hbrayman
-rw-r--r--  1 taylor   taylor     10788 Dec 14 16:09 jwickert
-rw-r--r--  1 taylor   taylor   2746614 Dec 14 16:09 mail.sent
-rw-r--r--  1 taylor   taylor     18106 Dec 14 16:09 mbeaudoin
-rw-r--r--  1 taylor   taylor      6753 Dec 14 16:09 pennyln
-rw-r--r--  1 taylor   taylor    128815 Dec 14 16:09 permission
```

```
-rw-r--r--  1 taylor   taylor  1011092 Dec 14 16:09 taylor
-rw-r--r--  1 taylor   taylor    17549 Dec 14 16:09 wellnitz
$
```

As you can see, the lines of output from ls are very consistent, and if you assume that "one or more spaces without any other characters between them" is the separator between fields and that the fifth field in the output is always the size of the file, you have a recipe for finding and processing the necessary data for a file size total within a directory.

2. Let's use awk to extract the fifth field:

```
$ ls -l | awk '{print $5}'

3111
19930
298719
5758
14577
1610
10788
2746614
18106
6753
128815
1011092
17549
$
```

$1 matches the first field, $2 the second, and so on. $0 matches the entire input line. Pretty simple, isn't it?

It's not quite what I want, however, because the very first line of output from ls is a summary of the blocks taken up by the entire directory (the total 8474 line), and the awk script sees that and counts it as a line, even though it doesn't have a fifth field. If we leave this as-is, the eventual average mailbox size will be wrong because it'll be taking "n+1" files into account due to this erroneous match.

3. The standard Unix way to solve this would be to drop something else into the pipeline that'll extract that line, or filter just the lines of valid data. It might look like this:

```
$ ls -l | grep taylor | awk '{print $5}'
3111
19930
298719
5758
14577
1610
10788
```

```
2746614
18106
6753
128815
1011092
17549
$
```

This works, but it's not very elegant, particularly because awk can do the job itself.

4. The awk solution is to apply a pattern that uses the special NF (number of fields) variable:

```
$ ls -l | awk 'NF > 2 { print $5 }'
3111
19930
298719
5758
14577
1610
10788
2746614
18106
6753
128815
1011092
17549
$
```

Great. Here you can see a pattern (NF > 2) and a statement (print $5) combined to make a very powerful and simple addition to the pipeline. This succinct awk program prints the fifth field of input lines, but only when there are more than two fields on the line. Notice that when this notation is used, there's no explicit if in the if statement, unlike in most other programming languages.

5. Now let's make our script a bit more sophisticated. It needs to total all the sizes and count how many files it counted, too. Those statements are added within the curly brackets, but before I get to that point, I'm going to simplify things by putting the growing awk script in its own file.

Here's how it looks once I've added the two counting variables:

```
$ cat average.awk
NF > 2 { count += 1
         totalsize += $5
       }
$
```

There's no point in running this yet because there isn't any output. Try it yourself by typing awk -f average.awk, and you'll see what I mean.

NOTE
_____

The += notation is a shorthand way of saying "add the following value to the current value of the variable," and it saves having to type `count = count + 1` and `totalsize = totalsize + 1`.
_____

6. To add output, I need to add an END block. END is a special pattern that is matched once after every line of input is processed:

```
$ cat average.awk
NF > 2 { count += 1
         totalsize += $5
       }

END { print "Counted " count " mailboxes"
      print "average size = " totalsize/count
    }
$
```

This is all that's needed to compute the average file size. It's invoked with the -f flag to awk:

```
$ ls -l | awk -f average.awk
Counted 14 mailboxes
average size = 305969
$
```

Where there's an END, there's also a BEGIN, if you need to initialize variables prior to the script being run. Though it's not a great programming practice, you can be lazy as I have been and assume that a new variable that hasn't been used before starts with a value of zero. In fact, better programming style would be to have a block like the following at the very beginning of the script:

```
BEGIN {
       count = 0
     totalsize = 0
}
```

This script demonstrates a very typical use of the awk command and also shows how most sophisticated pipelines are built one step at a time.

Next let's look at some of the common one-liner programs for which you'll find awk particularly useful.

NOTE
_____

You've already seen two special variables in this simple awk script: NF is the number of fields in a line of input, and $5 is the fifth field in each line. It turns out that there's also NR, which contains the current record number, and, in the END block, the total number of records (lines) encountered.

The $5 variable is also an instance of a general naming scheme: $n will give you the nth field, and $0 is the entire line.

---

7. How many lines are in the input stream?

```
'END {print NR}'
```

8. Print the eighth line of input only?

```
'NR == 8'
```

9. Print just the last field of each line?

```
'{ print $NF }'
```

This one requires a wee bit of explanation: Because NF is the number of fields, the reference $NF is evaluated as the last field. If the input line has five fields, NF=5 and $NF is the contents of the fifth field.

10. Print the maximum number of fields in any line?

```
'NF > maxnf { maxnf = NF }   END { print maxnf }'
```

Notice that you can compress scripts onto a single line if that's easier to type.

11. One more example: You learned about the wc (word count) command in the last hour, and you know that it returns the number of characters, words, and lines in its input stream. It turns out that duplicating this with an awk script is remarkably easy:

```
$ cat wc.awk
{ chars += length($0) + 1    # 1 for the carriage return
  words += NF;
}

END {
  print chars " characters, " words " words, and " NR " lines."
}
$
```

It can be used very much like the earlier script:

```
$ ls -l | awk -f wc.awk
908 characters, 137 words, and 16 lines.
```

To make sure that the results are accurate, here's the same ls output run through the official wc command:

```
$ ls -l | wc
      16     137     908
```

They are indeed the same!

With a programming tool as sophisticated as awk, we can only scratch the surface in this book. It's frustrating that there are remarkably few resources for learning more about the helpful awk programming language. About the only one I can recommend is the dry *The AWK Programming Language*, written by the authors of the program, Alfred Aho, Peter Weinberger, and Brian Kernighan.

Whether you choose to get a copy of that book or simply explore and poke around by yourself, my experience suggests that a good grasp of awk is a valuable addition to your Unix knowledgebase.

Alternatively, many Perl fanatics will tell you that it can do absolutely everything that awk can do and much, much more. They're right, but the price is complexity: I find awk to be much more simple and straightforward for tasks like those shown above. You'll need to decide for yourself whether you want to stick with Perl for all programmatic tasks or explore the other tools in your Unix toolbox.

Perl is covered in some detail later in the book, too, so you are welcome to flip forward and get a taste of the Perl programming language and decide for yourself.

How to Use cut in Pipes

While awk is a general-purpose tool that you can bend to your needs (sort of like a geek Swiss army knife), there are specific tasks for which other Unix tools are better suited.

Earlier you saw how to use the simple '{print $5}' to extract the fifth column of the data stream, but in fact there's a faster way to do that—with the simple cut command.

Action 9.2: Slicing and Dicing with cut

In the earlier example, the fields are all neatly separated by *white space*. What happens if you need to get a specific set of characters, regardless of spaces, however? This is one great example of where cut can be your friend. More typically, however, you work with a database-like file, and there's a specific *delimiter* that separates each of the fields. This is also a good place to use cut.

1. An interesting data file to explore is the /etc/passwd file, which contains account record information for each login account on the system.

    Here's the tail of one on a busy system I use:

    ```
    $ tail /etc/passwd
    djk:*:23678:100:Doug King:/home/djk:/ bin/csh
    voxroom:*:24108:100:Gregory Smith:/home/voxroom:/bin/csh
    allied:*:24138:100:Gordon Wilkinson:/home/allied:/ bin/csh
    rottn1:*:24173:100:The Rott'n One:/home/rottn1:/bin/tcsh
    effugas:*:24263:100:Dan Kaminsky:/home/effugas:/bin/tcsh
    stinkbug:*:24331:100:Edward Fuller:/home/stinkbug:/ bin/bash
    hrweb:*:24434:100:Human Rights Web:/home/hrweb:/ bin/tcsh
    lcamag:*:24522:100:David Heller:/home/lcamag:/bin/csh
    ```

```
kodachen:*:24547:100:Jaimie Mc Curry:home/kodachen:/bin/tcsh
nobody:*:65534:65534:Unprivileged user:/nonexistent:/nonexistent
```

If we isolate one line, it's a bit less overwhelming:

```
$ grep 'taylor:' /etc/passwd
taylor:*:101:99:Dave Taylor:/home/taylor:/bin/bash
```

Fields in this file are separated by the colon character (:). Without going into exhaustive detail, the first field is the account name, the fifth field is the username, the sixth field is the home directory, and the seventh field is the login shell.

Now, let's see how cut can make the analysis of this file a bit more interesting. -d is an important flag to know because it lets you specify the field delimiter (the default is a tab).

2. First, let's get a list of usernames:

```
$ cut -d: -f5 /etc/passwd
Charlie &
Bourne-again Superuser
Owner of many system processes
Administrative Sandbox
Binaries Commands and Source
Administrative Sandbox

lots and lots of output removed

Edward Fuller
Human Rights Web
David Heller
Jaimie Mc Curry
Unprivileged user
$
```

3. Let's do a quick analysis of what shells people are using by pulling out the seventh field with cut and then piping it to sort and uniq with the important -c flag to have uniq show a count of matching results:

```
$ cut -d: -f7 /etc/passwd | sort | uniq -c
  51 /bin/bash
 857 /bin/csh
  40 /bin/ksh
   1 /bin/sh
 382 /bin/tcsh
   9 /bin/zsh
   8 /noshell
   5 /usr/local/bin/bash
   7 /usr/local/bin/tcsh
$
```

NOTE

If you want to have the output sorted from most popular to least popular, you can use another `sort` on the end of the pipe: `sort-rn` will sort in reverse numerical order. This means that the line prefaced with the largest number (/bin/csh) will appear first, and the line prefaced with the smallest number (/bin/sh) will appear last.

---

4. One more interesting example of `cut` before we go: You might have noticed that the first character of the `ls -l` output is a d when it's a directory and a - when it's just a regular file.

    Another useful flag for `cut` is `-c`, which lets you indicate specific *character locations* to use as the start location (or the start and end locations). For Western languages (which internationalization folk call this "Latin-1" languages, including Spanish, German, and Italian), one character = one letter, but in other, so called double-byte languages (Chinese, Arabic), a character doesn't have quite the same meaning. For now you can ignore this nuance.

    If we put those two flags together, we can use `cut` to answer the question "How many files and how many directories are in the current location?" This is a relatively complex pipe that summarizes how many of each suffix are found in a given `ls -l` output:

    ```
    $ ls -l | awk 'NF > 2' | cut -c1 | sort | uniq -c
      15 -
      12 d
    $
    ```

    The `awk` weeds out all lines that don't have at least three fields. (Remember the "Total" line we had to deal with earlier? Yeah, it's again something we need to omit from our analysis.) Then `cut` slices just the first character of output, and then we simply `sort` and `uniq` it, and voilà! We see that we have 15 plain files and 12 directories in the test directory.

The `cut` command has a very narrow set of capabilities, but when you're extracting specific columns of information, either by field value or by counting characters, it's a winner and worth knowing.

Don't stop here, though. Read `man cut` for more details on how to work with this useful program.

Inline Editing with `sed` and `tr`

Before we leave the topic of UNIX pipeline power tools, you need to learn about two more programs that are designed to change information as it goes through the data stream. The `sed` command, the more common of the two, is used primarily to substitute one pattern for another as information goes past. The `tr` command is even more limited: It translates one set of characters to another (but there are some surprising capabilities hidden in this otherwise dull utility).

Action 9.3: Inline Editing with `sed` and `tr`

To more fully understand how each of these commands work, it's useful to see them in action.

1. A common task for a pipeline is to change all uppercase letters into lowercase or vice versa. There are a number of ways to accomplish this within the Unix world, but the `tr` command makes it very easy:

    ```
    $ cut -d: -f5 /etc/passwd | tr '[a-z]' '[A-Z]' | tail
    GREGORY SMITH
    GORDON WILKINSON
    THE ROTT'N ONE
    DAN KAMINSKY
    EDWARD FULLER
    HUMAN RIGHTS WEB
    DAVID HELLER
    JAIMIE MC CURRY
    UNPRIVILEGED USER
    $
    ```

    The `tr` command does a 1:1 matching of what's specified in the first argument with what's specified in the second argument. In this case, you can see two ranges specified (`tr '[a-z]' '[A-Z]'`): all lowercase letters and then all uppercase letters.

    If you're working in multiple languages, a more sophisticated approach is to reference one of `tr`'s built-in character sets. Instead of using `'[a-z]'`, for example, use `'[[:lower:]]'`, which will work with Spanish, German, or whatever other language you or another user might be working with on the system.

    Table 9.1 lists of the character sets that `tr` knows. It's worth dog-earing this particular page so you can find it again later.

TABLE 9.1 Character Set Class Name Reference

Class Name	Description
alnum	Alphanumeric characters
alpha	Alphabetic characters
cntrl	Control characters
digit	Numeric characters
graph	Graphic characters
lower	Lowercase alphabetic characters

Class Name	Description
print	Printable characters
punct	Punctuation characters
space	Space characters
upper	Upper-case characters
xdigit	Hexadecimal characters

Using this information, the proper and better way to translate all lowercase characters into uppercase characters is therefore:

```
tr '[[:lower:]]' '[[:upper:]]'
```

2. To translate all vowels into a dash, you can again use `tr` to accomplish the task:

```
$ cut -d: -f5 /etc/passwd | tr 'aeiou' '-----' | tail
Gr-g-ry Sm-th
G-rd-n W-lk-ns-n
Th- R-tt'n On-
D-n K-m-nsky
Edw-rd F-ll-r
H-m-n R-ghts W-b
D-v-d H-ll-r
J--m-- Mc C-rry
Unpr-v-l-g-d -s-r
$
```

Looks like some sort of code, doesn't it? Or maybe you're just partway through a game of hangman?

3. A more common use of `tr` is for simple rotation ciphers. Back in the day, Usenet discussion groups used to use a simple one called ROT13 to apply rudimentary encryption to text messages. It's a simple 13-character rotation of the text. This means that *a* becomes *n*, *b* becomes *o*, and so on. Get it? *n* is 13 characters further along in the alphabet than *a*, *o* is 13 characters from *b*, etc. Sound complex? It's very easy with `tr` on the job:

```
$ cat badjoke | tr '[a-zA-Z]' '[n-za-mN-ZA-M]'
Jul qvq gur puvpxra pebff gur ebnq?
Gb purpx uvf rznvy!
$
```

The reverse translation can be most easily done by switching the first and second arguments to the `tr` command:

```
$ cat badjoke.rot13 | tr '[n-za-mN-ZA-M]' '[a-zA-Z]'
Why did the chicken cross the road?
To check his email!
$
```

4. This would actually be a perfect place for a shell alias, something like:

```
alias rot13="tr '[a-zA-Z]' '[n-za-mN-ZA-M]'"
alias unrot13="tr '[n-za-mN-ZA-M]' '[a-zA-Z]'"
```

You can then encode things with rot13 *filename* and decode things with *unrot13*
filename.

5. The sed command is considerably more powerful than tr, and it doesn't need any sort of
1:1 matching on the patterns specified. For example, here's a smarter way to translate all
vowels into dashes:

```
$ cat badjoke | sed 's/[aeiouAEIOU]/-/g'
Why d-d th- ch-ck-n cr-ss th- r--d?
T- ch-ck h-s -m--l!
$
```

Unlike the earlier version with tr, this works with upper- and lowercase vowels.

6. A more common usage would be to change words, rather than letters, however. Perhaps
I'd like to change the punch line a wee bit:

```
$ cat badjoke | sed 's/email/portfolio/'
Why did the chicken cross the road?
To check his portfolio!
$
```

7. sed is actually a powerful programming environment in its own right, even though we've
only looked at the *substitute* capability. The general form of sed commands is

{*address*{,*address*}}*command*{*arguments*}

where the {} denote optional information. The previous use of sed had s as the command
and the old and new patterns as the argument.

Table 9.2 shows a summary of a few of the capabilities of sed.

TABLE 9.2 The Most Useful sed Commands

Command	Example	Explanation
d	4,8d	Delete the fourth through eighth lines
p	11p	Print the 11th line
s	s/old/new/	Replace all occurrences of *old* with *new*

8. Addresses can be individual numbers, as shown in Table 9.2, or $ to match the last line
in the stream, but they can also be regular expressions. Want to delete all the lines that
contain the word *road*? You can use /road/d for the task.

9. Regular expressions can have special characters too: ^ is the beginning of the line, and $ is the end of the line, for example. Want to quickly preface all lines with a > sequence to indicate quoting? Use s/^/> / to do the job.

10. Finally, using sed and its -n (don't echo lines by default) flag, we now have yet another way to list a subset of lines to the output. To see only lines 8–13 of the sed man page, for example:

```
$ man sed | sed -n '8,13p'
        [-an] [-e command] [-f command_file] [file ...]

DESCRIPTION
        The sed utility reads the specified files, or the standard input if no
        files are specified, modifying the input as specified by a list of com-
        mands.  The input is then written to the standard output.
```

As with awk, we've only scratched the surface of the sed command in this hour. If your interest is piqued, I strongly encourage you to learn more about it, either by reading the man page or seeking out some useful online resources that can expand your knowledge.

Summary

The more you learn about the tools in Unix, the more you realize that there's really almost nothing you can't do with a combination of two or three commands. That's what I really like about Unix, frankly, and why I still use its command line even on my beloved Mac OS X system through the Terminal app.

In the pantheon of Unix commands, two powerful utilities—awk and sed—have earned special spots.

Workshop

The Workshop poses some questions about the topics presented in this lesson.

Exercises

1. How did awk get its name? (Perhaps the man page answers this question?)

2. The -f flag in awk lets you change field delimiters. How would you use awk to extract all the home directories out of the /etc/passwd file?

3. ROT13 is useful, but ROT7 could be even better. How would you write aliases for both encoding and decoding a ROT7 system?

4. The output of `ls -l` has the file permission shown as a character sequence: `rwx`, `r-x`, and so on. Can you come up with a combination of `cut` and `grep` to identify whether you have any files that have only `write` or `execute` permission?

5. Using `tr`'s class identifiers and its `-d` flag (read the man page to find out what it does), how would you remove all punctuation characters from your input stream?

Preview of the Next Hour

In the next hour you'll learn about the powerful and phenomenally useful `vi` editor, which will doubtless seem weird and puzzling when you get started. But `vi` is a mainstay in any good Unix user's repertoire and can make editing quite a bit faster than even the best graphically based application.

An Introduction to the `vi` Editor

Goals for This Hour

In this hour, you will learn

- ▶ How to start and quit `vi`
- ▶ Simple cursor motion in `vi`
- ▶ How to move by words and pages
- ▶ How to insert text into a file
- ▶ How to delete text

The next few hours focus on full-screen editing tools for Unix. First you'll learn how to use `vi` to create and modify files. This hour covers the basics, including how to move around in a file and how to insert and delete characters, words, and lines. The next hour shows how to search for specific patterns in the text and how to replace them with other information, as desired. In Hour 12, "An Overview of the `emacs` Editor," you'll learn to use an alternative Unix editor called `emacs`. As you work with `emacs` and `vi`, you're likely to develop a preference for one or the other.

In some ways, an editor is like another operating system living within Unix; we'll need two hours just to cover the basics of `vi`. If you're used to Windows or Macintosh editors, you'll be unhappy to find that `vi` doesn't know anything about your mouse. After you spend some time working with `vi`, however, I promise it will grow on you because it's so super-efficient to work without ever lifting your hands off the keyboard to use the mouse! By the end of this hour, you will be able to create and modify files on your Unix system to your heart's content.

TIP

I pronounce the editors as "vee-eye" and "e-max."

Editing the Unix Way

You've learned about how to manipulate your files and even peek inside them from the command line, and now it's time to learn the key Unix tool for creating and editing files: `vi`.

Task 10.1: Starting and Quitting `vi`

You might have noticed that many Unix commands covered so far have one characteristic in common: They all do their work, display their results, and quit. Among the few exceptions is `more`, in which you work within the specific program environment until you have viewed the entire contents of the file being shown or until you quit. The `vi` editor is another program in this small category that you move in and use until you explicitly tell the program to quit.

NOTE

Where did `vi` get its name? It's not quite as interesting as some of the earlier, more colorful commands. The `vi` command is so named because it's the visual interface to the `ex` editor. It was written by Bill Joy while he was at the University of California at Berkeley.

Before you start `vi` for the first time, you must learn about two aspects of its behavior. The first is that `vi` is a *modal* editor. A *mode* is like an environment. Different modes in `vi` interpret the same key differently. For example, if you're in *insert mode*, typing a adds an a to the text, whereas in *command mode*, typing a puts you in insert mode because a is the key abbreviation for the `append` command. If you ever get confused about what mode you're in, press the Escape (or Esc) key on your keyboard. Pressing Escape always returns you to the command mode (and if you're already in command mode, it simply beeps to remind you of that fact).

When you are in command mode, you can manage your document; this includes the capability to change text, rearrange it, and delete it. In insert mode, you add text directly to your document from the keyboard.

NOTE

In `vi`, the Return key is a specific command (meaning to move to the beginning of the next line). As a result, you never need to press Return to have `vi` process a command.

By contrast, the other popular UNIX editor, `emacs`, is a *modeless* editor. In `emacs`, the A key always adds the letter a to the file. You indicate all commands in `emacs` by holding down the Control (Ctrl) key while pressing the command key; for example, Ctrl-C deletes a character. We'll have a close look at `emacs` in Hour 12.

The second important characteristic of `vi` is that it's a screen-oriented program. It must know what kind of terminal, computer, or system you are using to work with Unix. This probably won't be a problem for you because most systems are set up so that the default terminal type matches the terminal app you're using. In this hour, you'll learn how to recognize when `vi` cannot figure out what terminal you're using and how to fix it.

You can start `vi` in various ways, and you'll learn about lots of helpful alternatives later this hour. Right now, let's look at the basics. The `vi` command, by itself, starts the editor, ready for you to create a new file. The `vi` command with a filename starts `vi` with the specified file loaded and ready to edit.

Let's get started!

1. To begin, enter `vi` at the prompt. If all is working well, the screen will clear, the first character on each line will become a tilde (~), and the cursor will be sitting at the upper-left corner of the screen:

```
% vi
```

NOTE

In the interest of efficiency, I will only show the portion of the screen that is relevant to the command being discussed for `vi` rather than show the entire screen each time. When the full screen is required to explain something, however, I'll use that instead. A smooth edge will indicate the edge of the screen, and a jagged edge will indicate that the rest of the display has been omitted.

Type a colon. Doing so moves the cursor to the bottom of the screen and replaces the last tilde with the colon:

Type q and press the Return key, and you should be back at the shell prompt:

```
~
~
~
~
~
~
~
~
:q
%
```

2. If that operation worked without a problem, skip to step 3. If the operation did not work, you received the unknown-terminal-type error message. You might see this on your screen:

```
% vi
"unknown": Unknown terminal type
I don't know what type of terminal you are on. All I have is "unknown"
[using open mode]

—
```

Alternatively, you might see this:

```
% vi
Visual needs addressible cursor or upline capability
:
```

Don't panic. You can fix this problem!

To fix this, you need to get back to the shell prompt, so do exactly what you did in step 1: Type :q followed by the Return key. You should then see this:

```
% vi
"unknown": Unknown terminal type
I don't know what type of terminal you are on. All I have is "unknown"
[using open mode]
:q
%
```

The problem here is that vi needs to know the type of terminal you're using, but it can't figure that out on its own. Therefore, you need to tell the operating system by setting the TERM environment variable. If you know what kind of terminal you have (something determined by the terminal or telnet application), use the value associated with the terminal; otherwise, try the default of vt100:

```
% setenv TERM vt100
```

If you have the $ prompt, which means you're using the Bourne shell (sh/bash) or Korn shell (ksh), rather than the C shell (csh), try this:

```
$ export TERM=vt100
```

Either way, you can now try entering vi again, and it should work.

If it does work, append the command (whichever of these two was successful) to your .profile file if you use ksh or sh or your .login file if you use csh. You can do this by entering whichever of the following commands is appropriate for your system:

```
% echo "setenv TERM vt100" >> ~/.login
```

or

```
$ echo "export TERM=vt100" >> ~/.profile
```

This way, the next time you log in, the system will remember what kind of terminal you're using, and you won't have to fuss with setting the TERM variable ever again.

CAUTION

Be careful to use >> to add to your file, not >, which will replace the contents of your .login or .profile file!

NOTE

vi and other screen commands use a Unix package called curses to control the screen. Like most other Unix applications, curses is not designed for a specific configuration; instead, it is designed to be device independent. Therefore, to work on a specific device, you need to give it some additional information—in this case, the terminal type.

If vt100 didn't work, it's time to talk with your system administrator about the problem or call your Unix vendor to find out what the specific value should be. If you are connected through the Internet and you actually are using a terminal emulator or communications app, try using ansi as a TERM setting. If that fails, call the company that makes your software to find out what terminal type the program is emulating.

---

3. Great! You have successfully launched vi, seen what it looks like, and even entered the most important command: the quit command. Now create a simple file and start vi so that it shows you the contents of the file:

```
% ls -lF > demo
% vi demo
```

```
total 29
drwx------   2 taylor        512 Nov 21 10:39 Archives/
drwx------   3 taylor        512 Dec  3 02:03 InfoWorld/
drwx------   2 taylor       1024 Dec  3 01:43 Mail/
```

```
drwx------   2 taylor        512 Oct  6 09:36 News/
drwx------   4 taylor        512 Dec  2 22:08 OWL/
-rw-rw----   1 taylor        126 Dec  3 16:34 awkscript
-rw-rw----   1 taylor        165 Dec  3 16:42 bigfiles
drwx------   2 taylor        512 Oct 13 10:45 bin/
-rw-rw----   1 taylor          0 Dec  3 22:26 demo
-rw-rw----   1 taylor      12556 Nov 16 09:49 keylime.pie
-rw-rw----   1 taylor       8729 Dec  2 21:19 owl.c
-rw-rw----   1 taylor        199 Dec  3 16:11 sample
-rw-rw----   1 taylor        207 Dec  3 16:11 sample2
drwx------   2 taylor        512 Oct 13 10:45 src/
drwxrwx---   2 taylor        512 Nov  8 22:20 temp/
-rw-rw----   1 taylor        582 Nov 27 18:29 testme
~
~
~
~
~
~
~
"demo" 17 lines, 846 characters
```

You can see that vi reads the file specified on the command line. In this example, my file is 17 lines long, but my screen can hold 25 lines. To show that some lines lack any text, vi uses the tilde on a line by itself. Finally, note that, at the bottom, the program shows the name of the file, the number of lines it found in the file, and the total number of characters.

Type :q again to quit vi and return to the command line for now. When you type the colon, the cursor will jump down to the bottom line and wait for the q, as it did before.

You have learned the most basic command in vi—the :q command—and survived the experience. It's all easy going from here.

TIP

If you really get used to the vi way of thinking, you should explore using set -o vi when you start up your interactive shell. It'll set things up to let you work with those familiar vi keystrokes when editing commands at the command line and make your life just a bit simpler!

Task 10.2: Simple Cursor Motion in vi

Getting to a file isn't much good if you can't actually move around in it. So let's learn how to use the cursor-control keys in vi. To move left one character, type h. To move up, type k. To move down, type j, and to move right a single character, type l (lowercase L). You can also move left one character by pressing the Backspace key, and you can move to the beginning of the next line with the Return key.

In most modern Unix systems, you can also use the arrow keys, but as you'll learn, there's much benefit to knowing the basic vi commands so that you never have to move your hands off the standard "ready" position on the keyboard. As a result, try your best to stick with h, j, k, and l for moving around in files.

1. Launch vi again and specify the demo file:

```
% vi demo
```

```
total 29
drwx------  2 taylor         512 Nov 21 10:39 Archives/
drwx------  3 taylor         512 Dec  3 02:03 InfoWorld/
drwx------  2 taylor        1024 Dec  3 01:43 Mail/
drwx------  2 taylor         512 Oct  6 09:36 News/
drwx------  4 taylor         512 Dec  2 22:08 OWL/
-rw-rw----  1 taylor         126 Dec  3 16:34 awkscript
-rw-rw----  1 taylor         165 Dec  3 16:42 bigfiles
drwx------  2 taylor         512 Oct 13 10:45 bin/
-rw-rw----  1 taylor           0 Dec  3 22:26 demo
-rw-rw----  1 taylor       12556 Nov 16 09:49 keylime.pie
-rw-rw----  1 taylor        8729 Dec  2 21:19 owl.c
-rw-rw----  1 taylor         199 Dec  3 16:11 sample
-rw-rw----  1 taylor         207 Dec  3 16:11 sample2
drwx------  2 taylor         512 Oct 13 10:45 src/
drwxrwx---  2 taylor         512 Nov  8 22:20 temp/
-rw-rw----  1 taylor         582 Nov 27 18:29 testme
~
~
~
~
~
~
"demo" 17 lines, 846 characters
```

You should see the cursor sitting on top of the t in total on the first line or perhaps flashing underneath the t character. Perhaps you have a flashing-box cursor or one that shows up in a different color. In any case, that's your starting spot in the file.

2. Type h once to try to move left. The cursor stays in the same spot, and vi beeps to remind you that you can't move left any farther on the line. Try the k key to try to move up; the same thing will happen.

Now try typing j to move down a character:

```
total 29
drwx------  2 taylor         512 Nov 21 10:39 Archives/
drwx------  3 taylor         512 Dec  3 02:03 InfoWorld/
drwx------  2 taylor        1024 Dec  3 01:43 Mail/
```

Now the cursor is on the `d` directory indicator of the second line of the file.

Type `k` to move back up to the original starting spot.

3. Using the four cursor-control keys—h, j, k, and l—move around in the file for a little bit until you are comfortable with what's happening on the screen. Now try using the Backspace and Return keys to see how they help you move around. Remember that since you're in command mode, they won't delete a character or add a new line to the file.

4. Move to the middle of a line:

```
total 29
drwx------   2 taylor        512 Nov 21 10:39 Archives/
drwx------   3 taylor        512 Dec  3 02:03 InfoWorld/
drwx------   2 taylor       1024 Dec  3 01:43 Mail/
```

I'm at the middle digit in the file size of the second file in the listing. Here are a couple of new cursor motion keys: the 0 (zero) key moves the cursor to the beginning of the line, and $ moves it to the end of the line. First, I type 0:

```
total 29
drwx------   2 taylor        512 Nov 21 10:39 Archives/
drwx------   3 taylor        512 Dec  3 02:03 InfoWorld/
drwx------   2 taylor       1024 Dec  3 01:43 Mail/
```

Now I type $ to move to the end of the line:

```
total 29
drwx------   2 taylor        512 Nov 21 10:39 Archives/
drwx------   3 taylor        512 Dec  3 02:03 InfoWorld/
drwx------   2 taylor       1024 Dec  3 01:43 Mail/
```

5. If you have arrow keys on your keyboard, try using them to see whether they work the same way that the h, j, k, and l keys work. If the arrow keys don't move you about, they might have shifted you into insert mode. If you type characters and they're added to the file, press the Escape key (or Esc, depending on your keyboard) to return to command mode.

6. Let's wrap this up by leaving this edit session. Because `vi` now knows that you have modified the file, it will try to ensure that you don't quit without saving the changes:

```
~
~
~
:q
No write since last change (:quit! overrides)
```

Use :q! (shorthand for :quit, throwing away any changes you've made, which is what the ! means) to quit without saving the changes.

NOTE

In general, if you try to use a colon command in vi and the program complains that it might do something bad, stop and make sure it's really what you want to do. If it is, then type in the command again, followed by an exclamation point. I like to think of this as saying, "Do it anyway!"

Stay in this file for the next task if you'd like or use :q to quit.

Moving about a file using these six simple key commands is, on a small scale, much like the entire process of using the vi editor when working with files. Stick with these simple commands until you're comfortable moving around, and you'll be well on your way to becoming proficient using vi.

Task 10.3: Moving by Words and Pages

Earlier, in the description of the emacs editor, I commented that because emacs is always in insert mode, all commands must include the Control key. Well, it turns out that vi has its share of Control-key commands, too—commands that require you to hold down the Control key and press another key. In this section, you'll learn about Ctrl-f, Ctrl-b, Ctrl-u, and Ctrl-d. These move you forward or backward a screen and up or down half a screen of text, respectively.

I'll toss a few more commands into the pot, too: w moves you forward word by word, b moves you backward word by word, and the uppercase versions of these two commands have very similar, but not identical, functions. (That's right—vi distinguishes between whether or not you're holding Shift when you enter a keyboard command. So the A command is different from a.)

1. To see how this works, you need to create a file that is longer than the size of your screen. An easy way to do this is to save the output of a common command to a file over and over until the file is long enough. The system I use has many users, so I can create the file just by using the who command once. You might have to append the output of who to the big.output file a couple of times before the file is longer than 24 lines. (You can check using wc, of course.)

    ```
    % who > big.output; wc -l big.output
        40
    % vi big.output
    ```

    ```
    leungtc   ttyrV    Dec  1 18:27    (magenta)
    tuyinhwa  ttyrX    Dec  3 22:38    (expert)
    hollenst  ttyrZ    Dec  3 22:14    (dov)
    brandt    ttyrb    Nov 28 23:03    (age)
    holmes    ttyrj    Dec  3 21:59    (age)
    yuxi      ttyrn    Dec  1 14:19    (pc115)
    ```

```
frodo      ttyro    Dec  3 22:01   (mentor)
labeck     ttyrt    Dec  3 22:02   (dov)
chenlx2    ttyru    Dec  3 21:53   (mentor)
leungtc    ttys0    Nov 28 15:11   (gold)
chinese    ttys2    Dec  3 22:53   (excalibur)
cdemmert   ttys5    Dec  3 23:00   (mentor)
yuenca     ttys6    Dec  3 23:00   (mentor)
janitor    ttys7    Dec  3 18:18   (age)
mathisbp   ttys8    Dec  3 23:17   (dov)
janitor    ttys9    Dec  3 18:18   (age)
cs541      ttysC    Dec  2 15:16   (solaria)
yansong    ttysL    Dec  1 14:44   (math)
mdps       ttysO    Nov 30 19:39   (localhost)
md         ttysU    Dec  2 08:45   (muller)
jac        ttysa    Dec  3 18:18   (localhost)
eichsted   ttysb    Dec  3 23:21   (pc1)
sweett     ttysc    Dec  3 22:40   (dov)
"big.output" 40 lines, 1659 characters
```

Because I have only a 25-line display and the output is 40 lines long (you can see that on the status line at the bottom), there is more information in this file than the screen can display at once.

2. To see the next screenful, press Ctrl-`f`. When I do this, I get the following output:

```
eichsted ttysb    Dec  3 23:21   (pc1)
sweett   ttysc    Dec  3 22:40   (dov)
wellman  ttysd    Dec  3 23:01   (dov)
tuttleno ttyse    Dec  3 23:03   (indyvax)
wu       ttysf    Dec  3 23:10   (term01)
daurismj ttysg    Dec  3 23:10   (dov)
cs414    ttysh    Dec  3 23:12   (xds)
cq       ttysi    Dec  3 23:13   (expert)
cdemmert ttysk    Dec  3 22:37   (xsun22)
jrlee    ttysn    Dec  3 22:53   (mac1)
fitzgejs ttyso    Dec  3 23:18   (dov)
doerrhb  ttysp    Dec  3 23:20   (dov)
cdemmert ttysq    Dec  3 23:00   (xsun22)
frazierw ttysr    Dec  3 23:01   (dov)
buckeye  ttyss    Dec  3 23:20   (mac2)
mtaylor  ttyst    Dec  3 23:22   (dov)
look     ttysu    Dec  3 23:12   (age)
janitor  ttysw    Dec  3 18:29   (age)
ajones   ttysx    Dec  3 23:23   (rass)
~
~
~
~
```

Notice that the entire screen was rewritten and that the familiar tilde characters have appeared again to let me know that I have reached the end of the file.

By default, vi has a two-line overlap when you move from screen to screen. If you look carefully, you can see that both eichsted and sweett show up on both screens of data. This doesn't mean that they appear twice in the file; rather, vi is trying to help me not get lost while I wander through the file.

3. Now, what do you think will happen if I press Ctrl-u?

```
leungtc   ttys0    Nov 28 15:11    (gold)
chinese   ttys2    Dec  3 22:53    (excalibur)
cdemmert  ttys5    Dec  3 23:00    (mentor)
yuenca    ttys6    Dec  3 23:00    (mentor)
janitor   ttys7    Dec  3 18:18    (age)
mathisbp  ttys8    Dec  3 23:17    (dov)
janitor   ttys9    Dec  3 18:18    (age)
cs541     ttysC    Dec  2 15:16    (solaria)
yansong   ttysL    Dec  1 14:44    (math)
mdps      ttysO    Nov 30 19:39    (localhost)
md        ttysU    Dec  2 08:45    (muller)
jac       ttysa    Dec  3 18:18    (localhost)
eichsted  ttysb    Dec  3 23:21    (pc1)
sweett    ttysc    Dec  3 22:40    (dov)
wellman   ttysd    Dec  3 23:01    (dov)
tuttleno  ttyse    Dec  3 23:03    (indyvax)
wu        ttysf    Dec  3 23:10    (term01)
daurismj  ttysg    Dec  3 23:10    (dov)
cs414     ttysh    Dec  3 23:12    (xds)
cq        ttysi    Dec  3 23:13    (expert)
cdemmert  ttysk    Dec  3 22:37    (xsun22)
jrlee     ttysn    Dec  3 22:53    (mac1)
fitzgejs  ttyso    Dec  3 23:18    (dov)
```

The command has moved me up half a screen. Notice the location of eichsted and sweett now. Instead of the text being replaced at once, as when I used Ctrl-f, the text was scrolled downward a line at a time, each new line being added as the program went along. The Ctrl-u command might work either way—one line at a time or an entire screen at a time—for you.

4. Now it's time to try moving around in this file word by word. Type the w key once to see what happens:

```
leungtc   ttys0    Nov 28 15:11    (gold)
chinese   ttys2    Dec  3 22:53    (excalibur)
cdemmert  ttys5    Dec  3 23:00    (mentor)
```

Now type w six times more, noting that the cursor stops three times in the field to indicate what time the user logged in to the system (15:11 in this listing). Now your cursor should be sitting on the parenthesized field:

```
leungtc  ttys0   Nov 28 15:11   (gold)
chinese  ttys2   Dec  3 22:53   (excalibur)
cdemmert ttys5   Dec  3 23:00   (mentor)
```

5. It's time to move backward. Type b a few times; your cursor moves backward, to the beginning of each word.

   What happens if you try to move backward, and you're already on the first word, or if you try to move forward with the w command, and you're already on the last word of the line? Let's find out.

6. Using the various motion keys you've learned, move back to the beginning of the line that starts with leungtc, which you used in instruction 4:

```
leungtc  ttys0   Nov 28 15:11   (gold)
chinese  ttys2   Dec  3 22:53   (excalibur)
cdemmert ttys5   Dec  3 23:00   (mentor)
```

   This time, type W (uppercase W, not lowercase w) to move through this line. Can you see the difference? Notice what happens when you hit the time field and the parenthesized words. Instead of typing w seven times to move to the left parenthesis before gold, you can type W only five times.

7. Try moving backward using the B command. Notice that the B command differs from the b command the same way in which the W command differs from the w command.

Moving about by words, both forward and backward, being able to zip through half screens or full screens at a time, and being able to zero in on specific spots with the h, j, k, and l cursor-motion keys give you quite a range of motion. Practice using these commands in various combinations to get your cursor to specific characters in your sample file.

Task 10.4: Inserting Text Using i, a, o, and O

Being able to move around in a file is useful. The real function of an editor, however, is to enable you to easily add and remove—in editor parlance, insert and delete—information. The vi editor has a special insert mode, which you must use to add to the contents of a file. Four possible ways exist to switch into insert mode from command mode, and you'll learn about all of them in this task.

The first way to switch to insert mode is to type the letter i, which, mnemonically enough, *inserts* text into the file. The other commands that accomplish more or less the same thing are a, to append text to the file; o, to open a line below the current line; and O, to open a line above the current line.

1. For this task, you need to start with a clean file, so quit from the big.output editing session and start vi again, this time specifying a nonexistent file called buckaroo:

    ```
    % vi buckaroo
    ```

    ```
    __
    ~
    ~
    ~
    ~
    ~
    ~
    ~
    ~
    ~
    ~
    ~
    ~
    ~
    ~
    ~
    ~
    ~
    ~
    ~
    ~
    "buckaroo" [New file]
    ```

    Notice that vi reminds you that this file doesn't exist; the bottom of the screen says New file instead of indicating the number of lines and characters.

2. Now it's time to try using insert mode. Try to insert a k into the file by typing k once:

    ```
    __
    ~
    ~
    ~
    ```

    The system beeps at you because you haven't moved into insert mode yet, and the k still has its command meaning of moving down a line (and, of course, there isn't another line yet).

Type i to move into insert mode and then type k again:

```
k_
~
~
~
```

There you go! You've added a character to the file.

3. Press the Backspace key to move the cursor over the letter k:

```
k
~
~
~
```

Now see what happens when you press Escape to leave insert mode and return to the vi command mode:

```
_
~
~
~
```

Notice that the k vanished when you pressed Escape. That's because vi only saves text you've entered to the left of or above the cursor, not the letter the cursor is resting on.

4. Now move back into insert mode by typing i and enter a few sentences from a favorite book of mine:

NOTE

Movie buffs perhaps will recognize that the text used in this hour comes from the Earl Mac Rauch book *Buckaroo Banzai*. The cult film *The Adventures of Buckaroo Banzai Across the Eighth Dimension* is based on this very fun book.

```
"He's not even here," went the conservation.
"Banzai."
"Where is he?"
"At a hotpsial in El paso."
"What? Why werent' we informed? What's wrong with him?"_
~
~
```

I've deliberately introduced some typing errors in the text here. Fixing them will demonstrate some important features of the vi editor. If you fixed them as you went along, that's okay, and if you added errors of your own, that's even better!

Press Escape to leave insert mode. Press Escape a second time to ensure that it worked; remember that vi beeps to remind you that you're already in command mode.

5. Use the cursor motion keys (h, j, k, and l) to move the cursor to any point on the first line:

```
"He's not even here," went the conservation.
"Banzai."
"Where is he?"
"At the hotpsial in El paso."
"What? Why werent' we informed? What's wrong with him?"
~
~
```

It turns out that I forgot a line of dialog between the line I'm on and the word Banzai. One way to enter the line would be to move to the beginning of the line "Banzai.", insert the new text, and press Return before pressing Escape to quit insert mode. But vi has a special command, o, to *open* a line immediately below the current line for inserting text.

Type o and follow along:

```
"He's not even here," went the conservation.
_
"Banzai."
"Where is he?"
"At the hotpsial in El paso."
"What? Why werent' we informed? What's wrong with him?"
~
~
```

Now type the missing text:

```
"He's not even here," went the conservation.
"Who?"_
"Banzai."
"Where is he?"
"At the hotpsial in El paso."
"What? Why werent' we informed? What's wrong with him?"
~
~
```

That's it. Press Escape to return to command mode.

6. The problem with the snippet of dialog we're using is that there's no way to figure out who
is talking. Adding a line above this dialog helps identify the speakers. Again, use cursor
motion keys to place the cursor on the top line:

```
"He's not_even here," went the conservation.
"Who?"
"Banzai."
"Where is he?"
"At the hotpsial in El paso."
"What? Why werent' we informed? What's wrong with him?"
~
~
```

Now you face a dilemma. You want to open a line for new text, but you want the line
to be above the current line, not below it. It happens that vi can do that, too. Instead
of using the o command, use its big brother O (that's an uppercase letter O, not a zero).
When I type O, here's what I see:

```
_
"He's not even here," went the conservation.
"Who?"
"Banzai."
"Where is he?"
"At the hotpsial in El paso."
"What? Why werent' we informed? What's wrong with him?"
~
~
```

Type the new sentence and then press Escape.

```
I found myself stealing a peek at my own watch and overheard
General Catbird's
aide give him the latest._
"He's not even here," went the conservation.
"Who?"
"Banzai."
"Where is he?"
"At the hotpsial in El paso."
"What? Why werent' we informed? What's wrong with him?"
~
~
```

Now the dialog makes a bit more sense. The conversation overheard by the narrator takes
place between the general and his aide.

7. I missed a couple of words in one of the lines, so the next task is to insert them. Use the cursor keys to move the cursor to the seventh line, just after the word `Where`:

```
I found myself stealing a peek at my own watch and overheard
General Catbird's
aide give him the latest.
"He's not even here," went the conservation.
"Who?"
"Banzai."
"Where_is he?"
"At the hotpsial in El paso."
"What? Why werent' we informed? What's wrong with him?"
~
~
```

At this juncture, I need to add the words `the  hell` to make the sentence a bit stronger (and correct). I can use `i` to insert the text, but then I end up with a trailing space. Instead, I can add text immediately after the current cursor location by using the a command to *append*, or insert, the information. When I type a, the cursor moves one character to the right:

```
I found myself stealing a peek at my own watch and overheard
General Catbird's
aide give him the latest.
"He's not even here," went the conservation.
"Who?"
"Banzai."
"Where is he?"
"At the hotpsial in El paso."
"What? Why werent' we informed? What's wrong with him?"
~
~
```

Here's where `vi` can be difficult to use. I'm in insert mode, but there's no way for me to know that. When I type the letters I want to add, the screen shows that they are appended, but what if I thought I was in insert mode when I actually was in command mode? One trick I could use to ensure that I'm in insert mode is to type the command a second time. If the letter a shows up in the text, I simply would backspace over it; now I would know that I'm in append mode.

When I'm done entering the new characters, and I'm still in insert mode, here's what my screen looks like:

```
I found myself stealing a peek at my own watch and overheard
General Catbird's
aide give him the latest.
"He's not even here," went the conservation.
"Who?"
"Banzai."
"Where the hell is he?"
"At the hotpsial in El paso."
"What? Why werent' we informed? What's wrong with him?"
~
~
```

Notice that the cursor always stayed on the i in `is` throughout this operation. Press Escape to return to command mode. Notice that the cursor finally hops off the i and moves left one character.

NOTE

To differentiate between the i and a commands, remember that the insert command always adds the new information immediately before the character that the cursor is sitting on, whereas the append command adds the information immediately to the right of the current cursor position.

8. With this in mind, try to fix the apostrophe problem in the word `werent'` on the last line. Move the cursor to the n in that word:

```
"Where the hell is he?"
"At the hotpsial in El paso."
"What? Why werent' we informed? What's wrong with him?"
~
```

To add the apostrophe immediately after the current character, do you want to use the insert command (i) or the append (a) command? If you said *append*, give yourself a pat on the back! Type a to append the apostrophe:

```
"Where the hell is he?"
"At the hotpsial in El paso."
"What? Why werent' we informed? What's wrong with him?"
~
```

Type ' once and then press Escape.

9. Quit `vi` using `:q`, and the program reminds you that you haven't saved your changes to this new file at the very bottom of the screen:

```
~

~

No write since last change (:quit! overrides)
```

To write the changes, you need a new command, so I'll give you a preview of a set of colon commands you'll learn later in this hour. Type `:` (the colon character), which moves the cursor to the bottom of the screen:

```
~

~

:_
```

Now type `w` to write out (save) the file and then press the Return key:

```
~

~

"buckaroo" 9 lines, 277 characters
```

It's okay to leave `vi` now. I'll use `:q` to quit, and I'm safely back at the command prompt. A quick `cat` confirms that the tildes were not included in the file itself:

```
% cat buckaroo
I found myself stealing a peek at my own watch and overheard
General Catbird's
aide give him the latest.
"He's not even here," went the conservation.
"Who?"
"Banzai."
"Where the hell is he?"
"At the hotpsial in El paso."
"What? Why weren't' we informed? What's wrong with him?"
%
```

As you can tell, the `vi` editor is quite powerful and has a plethora of commands. Just moving about and inserting text, you have learned 24 commands, as summarized in Table 10.1.

TABLE 10.1 Summary of `vi` Motion and Insertion Commands

Command	Meaning
0	Move to the beginning of the line.
$	Move to the end of the line.
a	Append text; enter insert mode after the current character.

Command	Meaning
^b	Back up one screen of text. Note that ^b is the same as Ctrl-b; both indicate that you should hold down the Control key, then press the second key, then release both.
B	Back up one space-delimited word.
b	Back up one word.
Backspace	Move left one character.
^d	Move down half a page.
Escape	Leave insert mode and return to command mode.
^f	Move forward one screen of text.
h	Move left one character.
i	Insert text; enter insert mode before the current character.
j	Move down one line.
k	Move up one line.
l	Move right one character.
O	Open a new line for inserting text above the current line.
o	Open a new line for inserting text below the current line.
Return	Move to the beginning of the next line.
^u	Move up half a page.
W	Move forward one space-delimited word.
w	Move forward one word.
:w	Write the file to disk.
:q	Quit `vi` and return to the Unix system prompt.
:q!	Quit `vi` and return to the Unix system prompt, throwing away any changes made to the file.

NOTE

In this table, I use the simple shorthand notation introduced in Hour 7, "Looking into Files." Unix users often use a caret (^) followed by a character instead of the awkward Ctrl- notation. Therefore, ^f has the same meaning as Ctrl-f. Expressing this operation as ^f does not change the way it's performed: You still press and hold down the Control key and then type f. It's just a more succinct notation.

You've already learned quite a few commands, but we have barely scratched the surface of the powerful `vi` command!

Task 10.5: Deleting Text

You now have many of the pieces you need to work efficiently with the vi editor, to zip to any point in the file, and to add text wherever you'd like. Now you need to learn how to delete characters, words, and lines.

The simplest form of deletion is to use the x command, which functions as though you were writing an *X* over a letter you don't want on a printed page: It deletes the character under the cursor. Type x five times, and you delete five characters. Deleting a line of text this way can be quite tedious, so vi has some alternative commands. (Are you surprised?)

One command that many vi users don't know about is D (for "delete through the end of the line"). Wherever you are on a line, if you type D, you immediately delete everything after the cursor to the end of that line of text.

If there's an uppercase D command, you can bet there's a lowercase d command, too. The d delete command is the first of a set of more sophisticated vi commands that require a second command that indicates the range to which it's applied. You already know that w and W move you forward a word in the file; they're known as *addressing commands* in vi. You can follow d with one of these addressing commands to specify what you want to delete. For example, to delete a word, simply use the delete command and the move word command together: dw.

NOTE

Sometimes you might get a bit overzealous and delete more than you anticipated. That's not a problem—well, not too much of a problem—because vi remembers the state of the file prior to the most recent action taken. To undo a deletion (or an insertion, for that matter), use the u command. To undo a line of changes, use the U command. Be aware that once you've moved off the line in question, the U command is unable to restore it!

1. Start vi again with the big.output file you used earlier:

```
leungtc   ttyrV    Dec  1 18:27    (magenta)
tuyinhwa ttyrX    Dec  3 22:38    (expert)
hollenst ttyrZ    Dec  3 22:14    (dov)
brandt    ttyrb    Nov 28 23:03    (age)
holmes    ttyrj    Dec  3 21:59    (age)
yuxi      ttyrn    Dec  1 14:19    (pc)
frodo     ttyro    Dec  3 22:01    (mentor)
labeck    ttyrt    Dec  3 22:02    (dov)
chenlx2   ttyru    Dec  3 21:53    (mentor)
leungtc   ttys0    Nov 28 15:11    (gold)
chinese   ttys2    Dec  3 22:53    (excalibur)
cdemmert ttys5    Dec  3 23:00    (mentor)
yuenca    ttys6    Dec  3 23:00    (mentor)
janitor   ttys7    Dec  3 18:18    (age)
```

```
mathisbp ttys8   Dec  3 23:17   (dov)
janitor  ttys9   Dec  3 18:18   (age)
cs541    ttysC   Dec  2 15:16   (solaria)
yansong  ttysL   Dec  1 14:44   (math)
mdps     ttysO   Nov 30 19:39   (localhost)
md       ttysU   Dec  2 08:45   (muller)
jac      ttysa   Dec  3 18:18   (localhost)
eichsted ttysb   Dec  3 23:21   (pc1)
sweett   ttysc   Dec  3 22:40   (dov)
"big.output" 40 lines, 1659 characters
```

Type x a few times to delete a few characters from the beginning of the file:

```
gtc        ttyrV   Dec  1 18:27   (magenta)
tuyinhwa ttyrX   Dec  3 22:38   (expert)
hollenst ttyrZ   Dec  3 22:14   (dov)
brandt   ttyrb   Nov 28 23:03   (age)
holmes   ttyrj   Dec  3 21:59   (age)
```

Now type u to undo the last deletion:

```
ngtc       ttyrV   Dec  1 18:27   (magenta)
tuyinhwa ttyrX   Dec  3 22:38   (expert)
hollenst ttyrZ   Dec  3 22:14   (dov)
brandt   ttyrb   Nov 28 23:03   (age)
holmes   ttyrj   Dec  3 21:59   (age)
```

If you type u again, what do you think will happen?

```
gtc        ttyrV   Dec  1 18:27   (magenta)
tuyinhwa ttyrX   Dec  3 22:38   (expert)
hollenst ttyrZ   Dec  3 22:14   (dov)
brandt   ttyrb   Nov 28 23:03   (age)
holmes   ttyrj   Dec  3 21:59   (age)
```

The undo command alternates between the last command having happened and not having happened. To explain it a bit better, the undo command is an action unto itself, so the second time you type u, you're undoing the undo command. Type u a few more times to convince yourself that this is the case.

NOTE

Caveat: Some versions of `vi` have a considerably more sophisticated undo capability, and the u key goes back, and back, and back until you're looking at an empty file or the file in its original pre-edit form. If you have that version of `vi`, you'll want to use the `:redo` command (type in the colon first) to go "forward in time" if you undo too far.

2. It's time to make some bigger changes to the file. Type dw twice to delete the current word and the next word in the file. It should look something like this after the first dw:

```
ttyrV   Dec  1 18:27   (magenta)
tuyinhwa ttyrX   Dec  3 22:38   (expert)
hollenst ttyrZ   Dec  3 22:14   (dov)
brandt   ttyrb   Nov 28 23:03   (age)
holmes   ttyrj   Dec  3 21:59   (age)
```

Then it should look like this after the second dw:

```
Dec  1 18:27   (magenta)
tuyinhwa ttyrX   Dec  3 22:38   (expert)
hollenst ttyrZ   Dec  3 22:14   (dov)
brandt   ttyrb   Nov 28 23:03   (age)
holmes   ttyrj   Dec  3 21:59   (age)
```

Type u. You see that you can undo only the most recent command. At this point, though, because I haven't moved from the line I'm editing, the U, or restore-this-line command, will restore the line to its original state:

```
leungtc  ttyrV   Dec  1 18:27   (magenta)
tuyinhwa ttyrX   Dec  3 22:38   (expert)
hollenst ttyrZ   Dec  3 22:14   (dov)
brandt   ttyrb   Nov 28 23:03   (age)
holmes   ttyrj   Dec  3 21:59   (age)
```

3. I really don't want to see some of these folks in the output file, however. Fortunately, I can change the contents of this file by using the dd command to delete lines. When you're using one of these two-letter commands, repeating the letter means to apply the command to the entire line. What if I want to delete the entries for chinese and janitor, both of which are visible on this screen?

The first step is to use the cursor keys to move down to any place on the line for the chinese account, about halfway down the screen:

```
chenlx2  ttyru   Dec  3 21:53   (mentor)
leungtc  ttys0   Nov 28 15:11   (gold)
chinese  ttys2   Dec  3 22:53   (excalibur)
cdemmert ttys5   Dec  3 23:00   (mentor)
yuenca   ttys6   Dec  3 23:00   (mentor)
janitor  ttys7   Dec  3 18:18   (age)
mathisbp ttys8   Dec  3 23:17   (dov)
```

If your cursor isn't somewhere in the middle of this line, move it so that you aren't at an edge.

I had planned to remove this line completely, but perhaps I'd rather just remove the date, time, and name of the system (in parentheses) instead. To accomplish this, I don't need to type dw many times, or even x many times but rather D to delete through the end of the line:

```
chenlx2   ttyru    Dec   3 21:53    (mentor)   ·
leungtc   ttys0    Nov 28 15:11    (gold)
chinese   ttys2    _
cdemmert  ttys5    Dec   3 23:00    (mentor)
yuenca    ttys6    Dec   3 23:00    (mentor)
janitor   ttys7    Dec   3 18:18    (age)
mathisbp  ttys8    Dec   3 23:17    (dov)
```

Oh, that's not quite what I wanted to do. No problem. The undo command can fix it. Simply typing u restores the text I deleted:

```
chenlx2   ttyru    Dec   3 21:53    (mentor)
leungtc   ttys0    Nov 28 15:11    (gold)
chinese   ttys2    Dec   3 22:53    (excalibur)
cdemmert  ttys5    Dec   3 23:00    (mentor)
yuenca    ttys6    Dec   3 23:00    (mentor)
janitor   ttys7    Dec   3 18:18    (age)
mathisbp  ttys8    Dec   3 23:17    (dov)
```

4. The problem is that I wanted to delete the two entries chinese and janitor from the file, but I used the wrong command. Instead of using the D command, I should use dd. Typing dd has these results:

```
Dec   1 18:27       (magenta)
tuyinhwa ttyrX    Dec   3 22:38    (expert)
hollenst ttyrZ    Dec   3 22:14    (dov)
brandt    ttyrb    Nov 28 23:03    (age)
holmes    ttyrj    Dec   3 21:59    (age)
yuxi      ttyrn    Dec   1 14:19    (pc)
frodo     ttyro    Dec   3 22:01    (mentor)
labeck    ttyrt    Dec   3 22:02    (dov)
chenlx2   ttyru    Dec   3 21:53    (mentor)
leungtc   ttys0    Nov 28 15:11    (gold)
cdemmert  ttys5    Dec   3 23:00    (mentor)
yuenca    ttys6    Dec   3 23:00    (mentor)
janitor   ttys7    Dec   3 18:18    (age)
mathisbp  ttys8    Dec   3 23:17    (dov)
janitor   ttys9    Dec   3 18:18    (age)
```

```
cs541     ttysC    Dec  2 15:16    (solaria)
yansong   ttysL    Dec  1 14:44    (math)
mdps      ttysO    Nov 30 19:39    (localhost)
md        ttysU    Dec  2 08:45    (muller)
jac       ttysa    Dec  3 18:18    (localhost)
eichsted  ttysb    Dec  3 23:21    (pc1)
sweett    ttysc    Dec  3 22:40    (dov)
wellman   ttysd    Dec  3 23:01    (dov)
```

Notice that a new line of information has been pulled onto the screen at the bottom to replace the blank line removed.

If you try using the u command now, what happens?

I'm almost finished. A few presses of the Return key, and I'm down to the entry for the janitor account. Using dd removes that line, too:

```
Dec  1 18:27       (magenta)
tuyinhwa ttyrX    Dec  3 22:38    (expert)
hollenst ttyrZ    Dec  3 22:14    (dov)
brandt    ttyrb   Nov 28 23:03    (age)
holmes    ttyrj   Dec  3 21:59    (age)
yuxi      ttyrn   Dec  1 14:19    (pc)
frodo     ttyro   Dec  3 22:01    (mentor)
labeck    ttyrt   Dec  3 22:02    (dov)
chenlx2   ttyru   Dec  3 21:53    (mentor)
leungtc   ttys0   Nov 28 15:11    (gold)
cdemmert  ttys5   Dec  3 23:00    (mentor)
yuenca    ttys6   Dec  3 23:00    (mentor)
mathisbp  ttys8   Dec  3 23:17    (dov)
janitor   ttys9   Dec  3 18:18    (age)
cs541     ttysC   Dec  2 15:16    (solaria)
yansong   ttysL   Dec  1 14:44    (math)
mdps      ttysO   Nov 30 19:39    (localhost)
md        ttysU   Dec  2 08:45    (muller)
jac       ttysa   Dec  3 18:18    (localhost)
eichsted  ttysb   Dec  3 23:21    (pc1)
sweett    ttysc   Dec  3 22:40    (dov)
wellman   ttysd   Dec  3 23:01    (dov)
tuttleno  ttyse   Dec  3 23:03    (indyvax)
```

Each line below the one deleted moves up a line to fill in the blank space, and a new line, for tuttleno, moves into view.

5. Now I want to return to the buckaroo file to remedy some of the horrendous typographical errors! I don't really care whether I save the changes I've just made to this file, so I'm going to use :q! to quit and discard the modifications to the big.output file.

Entering `vi buckaroo` starts `vi` again:

```
I found myself stealing a peek at my own watch and overheard
General Catbird's
aide give him the latest.
"He's not even here," went the conservation.
"Who?"
"Banzai."
"Where the hell is he?"
"At the hotpsial in El paso."
"What? Why weren't' we informed? What's wrong with him?"
~
~
~
~
~
~
~
~
~
~
~
~
~
~
~
~
"buckaroo" 9 lines, 277 characters
```

You can make a couple of fixes in short order. The first is to change `conservation` to `conversation` on the third line. To move there, press the Return key twice and then use `W` to zip forward until the cursor is at the first letter of the word you're editing:

```
I found myself stealing a peek at my own watch and overheard
General Catbird's
aide give him the latest.
"He's not even here," went the conservation.
"Who?"
"Banzai."
"Where the hell is he?"
```

Then use the `dw` command:

```
I found myself stealing a peek at my own watch and overheard
General Catbird's
aide give him the latest.
"He's not even here," went the .
"Who?"
"Banzai."
"Where the hell is he?"
```

Now enter insert mode by typing i, type the correct spelling of the word conversation, and then press Escape:

```
I found myself stealing a peek at my own watch and overheard
General Catbird's
aide give him the latest.
"He's not even here," went the conversation .
"Who?"
"Banzai."
"Where the hell is he?"
```

6. That's one fix. Now move down a couple of lines to fix the atrocious misspelling of hospital:

```
"Banzai."
"Where the hell is he?"
"At the hotpsial in El paso."
"What? Why weren't' we informed? What's wrong with him?"
~
```

Again, use dw to delete the word, type i to enter insert mode, type hospital, and then press Escape. Now all is well on the line:

```
"Banzai."
"Where the hell is he?"
"At the hospital in El paso."
"What? Why weren't' we informed? What's wrong with him?"
~
```

Well, almost all is well. The first letter of Paso needs to be capitalized. Move to it by typing w to move forward a few words:

```
"Banzai."
"Where the hell is he?"
"At the hospital in El paso."
"What? Why weren't' we informed? What's wrong with him?"
~
```

7. It's time for a secret vi expert command! Instead of typing x to delete the letter, i to enter insert mode, P as the correct letter, and then Escape to return to command mode, you can use a much faster method to *transpose case*: the ~ (tilde) command. Type ~ once, and here's what happens:

```
"Banzai."
"Where the hell is he?"
"At the hospital in El Paso."
"What? Why weren't' we informed? What's wrong with him?"
~
```

Cool, isn't it? Back up to the beginning of the word again and type ~ a few times to see what happens. Notice that each time you type ~, the character's case switches—transposes—and the cursor moves to the next character. Type ~ four times, and you should end up with this:

```
"Banzai."
"Where the hell is he?"
"At the hospital in El pASO."
"What? Why weren't' we informed? What's wrong with him?"
~
```

Return to the beginning of the word and press ~ until the word is correct.

8. One more slight change, and the file will be fixed. Move to the last line of the file, to the extra apostrophe in the word `weren't'`, and type x to delete the offending character. The screen should now look like this:

```
I found myself stealing a peek at my own watch and overheard
General Catbird's
aide give him the latest.
"He's not even here," went the conversation.
"Who?"
"Banzai."
"Where the hell is he?"
"At the hospital in El Paso."
"What? Why weren't we informed? What's wrong with him?"
~
~
~
~
~
~
~
~
~
~
~
```

```
~
~
~
~
```

This looks great! It's time to save it for posterity. Use `:wq`, a shortcut that has `vi` write out the changes and immediately quit the program:

```
~
~
~
"buckaroo" 9 lines, 276 characters
%
```

Not only have you learned about the variety of deletion options in `vi`, but you also have learned a few simple shortcut commands: `~` to transpose case and `:wq` to write out the changes and quit the program all in one step.

You should feel pleased; you're now a productive and knowledgeable `vi` user, and you can modify files, making easy or tough changes. Go back to your system and experiment further by modifying some of the other files. Be careful, though, not to make changes in any of your dot files (for example, `.profile`) lest you cause trouble that would be difficult to fix.

Summary

Table 10.2 summarizes the basic `vi` commands you learned in this hour.

TABLE 10.2   Basic `vi` Commands

Command	Meaning
0	Move to the beginning of the line.
$	Move to the end of the line.
a	Append text; enter insert mode after the current character.
^b	Back up one screen of text.
B	Back up one space-delimited word.
b	Back up one word.
Backspace	Move left one character.
^d	Move down half a page.
D	Delete through the end of the line.
d	Delete: `dw` = delete word, `dd` = delete line.

Command	Meaning
Escape	Leave insert mode and return to command mode.
^f	Move forward one screen of text.
G	Go to the last line of the file.
*n*G	Go to the *n*th line of the file.
h	Move left one character.
i	Insert text; enter insert mode before the current character.
j	Move down one line.
k	Move up one line.
l	Move right one character.
n	Repeat the last search.
O	Open a new line for inserting text above the current line.
o	Open a new line for inserting text below the current line.
Return	Move to the beginning of the next line.
^u	Move up half a page.
U	Undo; restore the current line, if it changed.
u	Undo the last change made to the file.
W	Move forward one space-delimited word.
w	Move forward one word.
x	Delete a single character.

Workshop

The Workshop summarizes the key terms you've learned and poses some questions about the topics presented in this lesson. It also provides you with a preview of what you will learn in the next hour.

Key Terms

addressing commands   These `vi` commands enable you to specify what type of object you want to work with. The `d` commands serve as an example: `dw` means *delete word*, and `db` means *delete preceding word*.

command mode   This is the mode in which you can manage your document; it allows you to change text, rearrange it, and delete it.

insert mode   This is the `vi` mode that allows you to enter text directly into a file. The `i` command starts insert mode, and Escape exits it.

modal   A modal program has multiple environments, or modes, that offer different capabilities. In a modal program, the Return key, for example, might do different things in different modes.

modeless   A modeless program always interprets a key the same way, regardless of what the user is doing.

transpose case   Transposing case means switching uppercase letters to lowercase or lowercase to uppercase.

Exercises

1. What happens if you try to quit `vi` by using `:qw`? Before you try it, do you expect it to work?

2. If you're familiar with word processing programs in the Mac or Windows environments, would you describe them as modal or modeless?

3. The `d` command is an example of a command that understands addressing commands. You know of quite a few. Test them to see whether they will all work following `d`. Make sure you see whether you can figure out the command that has the opposite action to the `D` command.

4. Do all the following three commands give the same result?
   ```
   D
   d$
   dG
   ```

5. Imagine that you're in command mode in the middle of a line that's in the middle of the screen. Describe what would happen if you were to type each of the following:
   ```
   Badluck
   Window
   blad$
   ```

Preview of the Next Hour

The next hour expands your knowledge of the `vi` editor. It introduces you to the sophisticated search and replace capability, explores the useful colon commands, and details the command-line options you'll want to know.

Advanced vi Tricks, Tools, and Techniques

Goals for This Hour

In this hour, you will learn

▶ How to search within a file

▶ How to search and replace

▶ How to have vi start correctly

▶ The key colon commands in vi

▶ The change and replace commands

▶ How to use the :! command to access Unix commands

In the preceding hour, you learned what probably seems like a ton of vi commands to enable you to easily move about in files, insert text, delete other text, and move from file to file without leaving the program. This hour expands your expertise by showing you some more powerful vi commands. Before you begin this hour, I strongly recommend that you use vi to work with a few files to ensure that you're comfortable with the different modes of the program.

This might seem like a small list, but there's a lot packed into this hour. I'll be totally honest: You can do fine in vi without ever reading this particular lesson. You already know how to move around, how to insert and delete text, and how to save your changes or quit the program without saving! But vi is like any other complex topic: The more you're willing to study and learn, the more the program will bow to your needs. This means you can accomplish a wider variety of daily tasks more efficiently.

Advanced Editing with vi

The preceding hour focused on the basics of inserting and deleting text and moving around within a file. This hour adds a critical capability: searching and replacing text within a file.

Task 11.1: Searching Within a File

With the addition of two more capabilities, you'll be ready to face down any vi expert, demonstrating your skill and knowledge of the editor, and, much more importantly, you will be able to really fly through files, moving immediately to the information you desire for further edits.

The two new capabilities we're going to explore are for finding specific words or phrases in a file and for moving to specific lines in a file. Similar to searching for patterns in less, the /pattern command searches forward in the file for a specified pattern, and ?pattern searches backward for the specified pattern. To repeat the preceding search, use the n command to tell vi to search again, in the same direction, for the next instance of the same pattern.

You can move easily to any specific line in a file by using the G, or go-to-line, command. If you type a number before you type G, the cursor will move to that line in the file. If you type G without a line number, the cursor will zip you to the last line of the file (by default).

1. Start vi again with the big.output file with the command vi big.output:

```
leungtc   ttyrV    Dec   1 18:27    (magenta)
tuyinhwa  ttyrX    Dec   3 22:38    (expert)
hollenst  ttyrZ    Dec   3 22:14    (dov)
brandt    ttyrb    Nov  28 23:03    (age)
holmes    ttyrj    Dec   3 21:59    (age)
yuxi      ttyrn    Dec   1 14:19    (pc)
frodo     ttyro    Dec   3 22:01    (mentor)
labeck    ttyrt    Dec   3 22:02    (dov)
chenlx2   ttyru    Dec   3 21:53    (mentor)
leungtc   ttys0    Nov  28 15:11    (gold)
chinese   ttys2    Dec   3 22:53    (excalibur)
cdemmert  ttys5    Dec   3 23:00    (mentor)
yuenca    ttys6    Dec   3 23:00    (mentor)
janitor   ttys7    Dec   3 18:18    (age)
mathisbp  ttys8    Dec   3 23:17    (dov)
janitor   ttys9    Dec   3 18:18    (age)
cs541     ttysC    Dec   2 15:16    (solaria)
yansong   ttysL    Dec   1 14:44    (math)
mdps      ttysO    Nov  30 19:39    (localhost)
md        ttysU    Dec   2 08:45    (muller)
jac       ttysa    Dec   3 18:18    (localhost)
eichsted  ttysb    Dec   3 23:21    (pc1)
sweett    ttysc    Dec   3 22:40    (dov)
"big.output" 40 lines, 1659 characters
```

Remember that I used :q! to quit earlier, so my changes were not retained. (I know you're paying super-close attention to these examples!)

To move to the last line of the file, I type G once, and I see this:

```
cdemmert ttysk   Dec  3 22:37   (xsun)
jrlee    ttysn   Dec  3 22:53   (mac1)
fitzgejs ttyso   Dec  3 23:18   (dov)
doerrhb  ttysp   Dec  3 23:20   (dov)
cdemmert ttysq   Dec  3 23:00   (xsun)
frazierw ttysr   Dec  3 23:01   (dov)
buckeye  ttyss   Dec  3 23:20   (mac2)
mtaylor  ttyst   Dec  3 23:22   (dov)
look     ttysu   Dec  3 23:12   (age)
janitor  ttysw   Dec  3 18:29   (age)
ajones   ttysx   Dec  3 23:23   (rassilon)
~
~
~
~
~
~
~
~
~
~
~
~
```

To move to the third line of the file, I type 3 followed by G:

```
leungtc  ttyrV   Dec  1 18:27   (magenta)
tuyinhwa ttyrX   Dec  3 22:38   (expert)
hollenst ttyrZ   Dec  3 22:14   (dov)
brandt   ttyrb   Nov 28 23:03   (age)
holmes   ttyrj   Dec  3 21:59   (age)
yuxi     ttyrn   Dec  1 14:19   (pc)
frodo    ttyro   Dec  3 22:01   (mentor)
labeck   ttyrt   Dec  3 22:02   (dov)
chenlx2  ttyru   Dec  3 21:53   (mentor)
leungtc  ttys0   Nov 28 15:11   (gold)
chinese  ttys2   Dec  3 22:53   (excalibur)
cdemmert ttys5   Dec  3 23:00   (mentor)
yuenca   ttys6   Dec  3 23:00   (mentor)
janitor  ttys7   Dec  3 18:18   (age)
mathisbp ttys8   Dec  3 23:17   (dov)
janitor  ttys9   Dec  3 18:18   (age)
cs541    ttysC   Dec  2 15:16   (solaria)
yansong  ttysL   Dec  1 14:44   (math)
mdps     ttysO   Nov 30 19:39   (localhost)
md       ttysU   Dec  2 08:45   (muller)
```

```
jac       ttysa    Dec  3 18:18   (localhost)
eichsted ttysb    Dec  3 23:21   (pc1)
sweett    ttysc    Dec  3 22:40   (dov)
```

Notice that the cursor is on the third line of the file.

2. Now it's time to search. From my previous travels in this file, I know that the very last line is for the account ajones, but instead of using G to move there directly, I can search for the specified pattern by using the / search command.

    Typing / immediately moves the cursor to the bottom of the screen:

```
md        ttysU    Dec  2 08:45   (mueller)
jac       ttysa    Dec  3 18:18   (localhost)
eichsted ttysb    Dec  3 23:21   (pc1)
sweett    ttysc    Dec  3 22:40   (dov)
/_
```

Now I can type in the pattern ajones:

```
md        ttysU    Dec  2 08:45   (mueller)
jac       ttysa    Dec  3 18:18   (localhost)
eichsted ttysb    Dec  3 23:21   (pc1)
sweett    ttysc    Dec  3 22:40   (dov)
/ajones_
```

When I press Return, vi spins through the file and moves me to the first line following the line that the cursor was sitting on that contains the specified pattern:

```
cdemmert ttysk    Dec  3 22:37   (xsun)
jrlee    ttysn    Dec  3 22:53   (mac1)
fitzgejs ttyso    Dec  3 23:18   (dov)
doerrhb  ttysp    Dec  3 23:20   (dov)
cdemmert ttysq    Dec  3 23:00   (xsun)
frazierw ttysr    Dec  3 23:01   (dov)
buckeye  ttyss    Dec  3 23:20   (mac2)
mtaylor  ttyst    Dec  3 23:22   (dov)
look     ttysu    Dec  3 23:12   (age)
janitor  ttysw    Dec  3 18:29   (age)
ajones   ttysx    Dec  3 23:23   (rassilon)
~
~
~
~
```

```
~
~
~
~
~
~
~
~
```

3. If I type n to search for this pattern again, a slash appears at the bottom to show that vi understood my request. But the cursor stays exactly where it is, which means that this is the only occurrence of the pattern in this file.

4. Looking at this file, I noticed that the account janitor has all sorts of sessions running. To search backward for occurrences of the account, I can use the ? command:

```
~

~

?janitor_
```

The first search moves the cursor up one line, which leaves the screen looking almost the same:

```
cdemmert ttysk   Dec  3 22:37   (xsun)
jrlee    ttysn   Dec  3 22:53   (mac1)
fitzgejs ttyso   Dec  3 23:18   (dov)
doerrhb  ttysp   Dec  3 23:20   (dov)
cdemmert ttysq   Dec  3 23:00   (xsun)
frazierw ttysr   Dec  3 23:01   (dov)
buckeye  ttyss   Dec  3 23:20   (mac2)
mtaylor  ttyst   Dec  3 23:22   (dov)
look     ttysu   Dec  3 23:12   (age)
janitor  ttysw   Dec  3 18:29   (age)
ajones   ttysx   Dec  3 23:23   (rassilon)
~
~
~
~
~
~
~
~
~
~
~
~
?janitor
```

Here's where the n, or next match, can come in handy. If I type n this time and another occurrence of the pattern is in the file, vi moves me directly to the match:

```
yuxi         ttyrn    Dec  1 14:19   (pc)
frodo        ttyro    Dec  3 22:01   (mentor)
labeck       ttyrt    Dec  3 22:02   (dov)
chenlx2      ttyru    Dec  3 21:53   (mentor)
leungtc      ttys0    Nov 28 15:11   (gold)
chinese      ttys2    Dec  3 22:53   (excalibur)
cdemmert     ttys5    Dec  3 23:00   (mentor)
yuenca       ttys6    Dec  3 23:00   (mentor)
janitor      ttys7    Dec  3 18:18   (age)
mathisbp     ttys8    Dec  3 23:17   (dov)
janitor   ttys9    Dec  3 18:18     (age)
cs541        ttysC    Dec  2 15:16   (solaria)
yansong      ttysL    Dec  1 14:44   (math)
mdps         ttysO    Nov 30 19:39   (localhost)
md           ttysU    Dec  2 08:45   (muller)
jac          ttysa    Dec  3 18:18   (localhost)
eichsted     ttysb    Dec  3 23:21   (pc1)
sweett       ttysc    Dec  3 22:40   (dov)
wellman      ttysd    Dec  3 23:01   (dov)
tuttleno     ttyse    Dec  3 23:03   (indyvax)
wu           ttysf    Dec  3 23:10   (term01)
daurismj     ttysg    Dec  3 23:10   (dov)
cs414        ttysh    Dec  3 23:12   (xds)
```

Try it with a pattern that occurs multiple times in your own file. When you're done, quit vi by using :q.

vi has not dozens but hundreds of commands. Rather than overwhelm you with all of them, I have opted to show you the most important ones. In fact, that's how this entire book is organized; after all, if you wanted a huge command reference, you'd be reading the man pages, right? By the time you're done with this hour, your knowledge of vi commands will be substantial, and you will be able to use the editor with little difficulty.

This task focused on searching for patterns, which is a common requirement and helpful feature of any editor. In addition, you learned how to move to the top of the file (1G) and to the bottom of the file (G), as well as anywhere in between.

Task 11.2: The Colon Commands in vi

Without too much explanation, you have learned a couple of colon commands—that is, commands that have a colon as the first character. The colon immediately zooms the cursor to the bottom of the screen for further input. These commands are actually a subset of quite a large range of commands, all part of the ex editor on which vi is based. Remember what I told you at the beginning of the last hour about how vi is the visual shell to the ex editor? Turns out that ex is still a part of the system after all.

NOTE

One difference to note with colon commands is that unlike with vi commands that you type in command mode, the commands you type at the colon prompt must be followed by a Return for the editor to process them. This is a typical confusion in vi, but you'll get used to it once you try it.

Table 11.1 lists the most helpful colon commands.

TABLE 11.1 **Most Helpful Colon Commands**

Command	Function
:e *filename*	Stop editing the current file and edit the specified file.
:n	Stop editing the current file and edit the next file specified on the command line. Remember, you can always start up vi as vi *txt or similar.
:N	Go to the previous specified file.
:q	Quit the editor.
:q!	Quit regardless of whether any changes have occurred, overriding all warnings.
:r *filename*	Include the contents of the specified file at this position in the file that is currently being edited.
:w	Write the file to disk.
:w *filename*	Write the file to disk with the specified filename.

1. Start vi again, this time specifying a list of files to edit; vi indicates that you have specified more than one file:

```
% vi buckaroo big.output
2 files to edit.
```

Then it clears the screen and shows you the first file:

```
I found myself stealing a peek at my own watch and overheard
General Catbird's
aide give him the latest.
"He's not even here," went the conversation.
"Who?"
"Banzai."
"Where the hell is he?"
"At the hospital in El Paso."
"What? Why weren't we informed? What's wrong with him?"
~
~
```

```
 ~
 ~
 ~
 ~
 ~
 ~
 ~
 ~
 ~
 ~
 ~
 ~
 ~
 ~
"buckaroo" 9 lines, 276 characters
```

Typing the command sequence :w and pressing Return results in the file being written to disk with the current name. There's not much to see in that case.

```
 ~
 ~
 ~
"buckaroo" 9 lines, 276 characters
```

2. Instead, try writing to a different file, using :w newfile:

```
 ~
 ~
:w newfile_
```

When you press Return, you see this:

```
 ~
 ~
"newfile" [New file] 9 lines, 276 characters
```

3. Now pay attention to where the cursor is in the file. The :r, or read-file, command always includes the contents of the file below the current line. Just before I press Return, then, here's what my screen looks like:

```
I found myself stealing a peek at my own watch and overheard
General Catbird's
aide give him the latest.
"He's not even here," went the conversation.
"Who?"
"Banzai."
```

```
"Where the hell is he?"
"At the hospital in El Paso."
"What? Why weren't we informed? What's wrong with him?"
~
~
~
~
~
~
~
~
~
~
~
~
~
~
~
~
:r newfile_
```

Pressing Return yields this:

```
I found myself stealing a peek at my own watch and overheard
General Catbird's
I found myself stealing a peek at my own watch and overheard
General Catbird's
aide give him the latest.
"He's not even here," went the conversation.
"Who?"
"Banzai."
"Where the hell is he?"
"At the hospital in El Paso."
"What? Why weren't we informed? What's wrong with him?"

aide give him the latest.
"He's not even here," went the conversation.
"Who?"
"Banzai."
"Where the hell is he?"
"At the hospital in El Paso."
"What? Why weren't we informed? What's wrong with him?"
~
~
~
~
~
~
~
~
```

This can be a helpful way to include files within one another or to build a file that contains lots of other files.

4. Now that I've garbled the file, I want to save it to a new file, buckaroo.confused:

```
~
~
:w buckaroo.confused_
```

When I press Return, I see this:

```
~
~
"buckaroo.confused" [New file] 17 lines, 546 characters
```

5. Now it's time to move to the second file in the list of files given to vi at startup. To do this, I use the :n, or next-file, command:

```
~
~
:n_
```

Pressing Return results in the next file being brought into the editor to replace the first:

```
leungtc   ttyrV   Dec  1 18:27   (magenta)
tuyinhwa  ttyrX   Dec  3 22:38   (expert)
hollenst  ttyrZ   Dec  3 22:14   (dov)
brandt    ttyrb   Nov 28 23:03   (age)
holmes    ttyrj   Dec  3 21:59   (age)
yuxi      ttyrn   Dec  1 14:19   (pc)
frodo     ttyro   Dec  3 22:01   (mentor)
labeck    ttyrt   Dec  3 22:02   (dov)
chenlx2   ttyru   Dec  3 21:53   (mentor)
leungtc   ttys0   Nov 28 15:11   (gold)
chinese   ttys2   Dec  3 22:53   (excalibur)
cdemmert  ttys5   Dec  3 23:00   (mentor)
yuenca    ttys6   Dec  3 23:00   (mentor)
janitor   ttys7   Dec  3 18:18   (age)
mathisbp  ttys8   Dec  3 23:17   (dov)
janitor   ttys9   Dec  3 18:18   (age)
cs541     ttysC   Dec  2 15:16   (solaria)
yansong   ttysL   Dec  1 14:44   (math)
mdps      ttysO   Nov 30 19:39   (localhost)
md        ttysU   Dec  2 08:45   (muller)
jac       ttysa   Dec  3 18:18   (localhost)
eichsted  ttysb   Dec  3 23:21   (pc1)
sweett    ttysc   Dec  3 22:40   (dov)
"big.output" 40 lines, 1659 characters
```

6. In the middle of working on this, I suddenly realize that I need to make a slight change to the recently saved `buckaroo.confused` file. That's where the `:e` command comes in handy. Using it, I can edit any other file:

```
~

~

:e buckaroo.confused_
```

I press Return and see this:

```
I found myself stealing a peek at my own watch and overheard
General Catbird's
I found myself stealing a peek at my own watch and overheard
General Catbird's
aide give him the latest.
"He's not even here," went the conversation.
"Who?"
"Banzai."
"Where the hell is he?"
"At the hospital in El Paso."
"What? Why weren't we informed? What's wrong with him?"

aide give him the latest.
"He's not even here," went the conversation.
"Who?"
"Banzai."
"Where the hell is he?"
"At the hospital in El Paso."
"What? Why weren't we informed? What's wrong with him?"
~

~

~

~

~

~

~

"buckaroo.confused" 17 lines, 546 characters
```

That's it! You now know a considerable amount about one of the most important, and certainly most used, commands in Unix. There's more to learn (isn't there always?), but you now can edit your files with aplomb!

Task 11.3: Starting `vi` Correctly

The `vi` command wouldn't be part of Unix if it didn't have some startup options available, but there really are only two worth mentioning. The `-R` flag sets up `vi` to show you the specified files in read-only mode, to ensure that you don't accidentally modify them. The second option doesn't start with a dash but with a plus sign: Any command following the plus sign is used as an initial command to the program. This is more useful than it might sound. The command `vi +$ sample`, for example, starts the editor at the bottom of the file `sample`, and `vi +17 sample` starts the editor on the 17th line of `sample`.

1. Try the read-only format:

```
% vi -R buckaroo
```

```
I found myself stealing a peek at my own watch and overheard
General Catbird's
aide give him the latest.
"He's not even here," went the conversation.
"Who?"
"Banzai."
"Where the hell is he?"
"At the hospital in El Paso."
"What? Why weren't we informed? What's wrong with him?"
~
~
~
~
~
~
~
~
~
~
~
~
~
~
"buckaroo" [Read only] 9 lines, 276 characters
```

Notice the addition of the [Read only] message on the status line at the bottom of the screen. You can edit the file, but if you try to save the edits with :w, you see this:

```
~
~
"buckaroo" File is read only
```

Quit `vi` with `:q!`.

2. Recall that `janitor` occurs in many places in the `big.output` file. Start `vi` on the file line that contains the pattern `janitor` in the file:

```
% vi +/janitor big.output
```

```
brandt    ttyrb    Nov 28 23:03    (age)
holmes    ttyrj    Dec  3 21:59    (age)
yuxi      ttyrn    Dec  1 14:19    (pc)
frodo     ttyro    Dec  3 22:01    (mentor)
labeck    ttyrt    Dec  3 22:02    (dov)
chenlx2   ttyru    Dec  3 21:53    (mentor)
leungtc   ttys0    Nov 28 15:11    (gold)
chinese   ttys2    Dec  3 22:53    (excalibur)
cdemmert  ttys5    Dec  3 23:00    (mentor)
yuenca    ttys6    Dec  3 23:00    (mentor)
janitor   ttys7    Dec  3 18:18    (age)
mathisbp  ttys8    Dec  3 23:17    (dov)
janitor   ttys9    Dec  3 18:18    (age)
cs541     ttysC    Dec  2 15:16    (solaria)
yansong   ttysL    Dec  1 14:44    (math)
mdps      ttysO    Nov 30 19:39    (localhost)
md        ttysU    Dec  2 08:45    (muller)
jac       ttysa    Dec  3 18:18    (localhost)
eichsted  ttysb    Dec  3 23:21    (pc1)
sweett    ttysc    Dec  3 22:40    (dov)
wellman   ttysd    Dec  3 23:01    (dov)
tuttleno  ttyse    Dec  3 23:03    (indyvax)
wu        ttysf    Dec  3 23:10    (term01)
"big.output" 40 lines, 1659 characters
```

This time, notice where the cursor is sitting. Quit again, with `:q`.

3. Finally, launch `vi` with the cursor on the third line of the file `buckaroo`:

```
% vi +3 buckaroo
```

```
I found myself stealing a peek at my own watch and overheard
General Catbird's
aide give him the latest.
"He's not even here," went the conversation.
"Who?"
"Banzai."
"Where the hell is he?"
"At the hospital in El Paso."
"What? Why weren't we informed? What's wrong with him?"
~
~
~
```

```
~
~
~
~
~
~
~
~
~
~
~
~
"buckaroo" 9 lines, 276 characters
```

Again, notice where the cursor rests.

It can be helpful to know these two starting options. In particular, I often use +/*pattern* to start the editor at the first occurrence of a specific pattern, but you can use vi for years without ever knowing more than just the name of the command itself.

Task 11.4: Searching and Replacing

Though most of vi is easy to learn and use, one command that always causes great trouble for users is search-and-replace. The key to understanding this command is to remember that vi is built atop the line editor (ex). Instead of trying to figure out some arcane vi sequence, in this case it's far easier to just drop into the line editor and use a simple colon command to replace the old pattern with a new one. To replace an existing word on the current line with a new word (the simplest case), use :s/*old*/*new*/. If you want to have all occurrences on the current line matched, add the g (global) suffix: :s/*old*/*new*/g. You'll know if you've forgotten the g suffix because you'll only change the *first* occurrence of the pattern on each line of the file rather than all occurrences.

To change all occurrences of one word or phrase to another across the entire file, the command is identical to the preceding, except that you must add a range specifier. Recall that $ is the vi notation for the last line in the file (invoking vi as vi +$ *filename* starts out on the last line, for example). Also recall that ranges are specified by two numbers separated by a comma. It should be no surprise that the full, all-file global search and replace command is :1,$ s/*old*/*new*/g.

1. Start vi again with the buckaroo file, add the additional text on the first and last lines using the existing vi commands you know, and then use 1G to jump to the top of the file:

```
Excerpt from "Buckaroo Banzai" by Earl MacRauch
I found myself stealing a peek at my own watch and overheard
General Catbird's
aide give him the latest.
"He's not even here," went the conversation.
```

```
"Who?"
"Banzai."
"Where the hell is he?"
"At the hospital in El Paso."
"What? Why weren't we informed? What's wrong with him?"

Go Team Banzai! Go Team Banzai! Go Team Banzai!


~
~
~
~
~
~
~
~
~
~
~
~
~
```

The cursor is on the first line. I'm going to rename `Earl`. I type `:`, the cursor immediately moves to the bottom, and then I type `s/Earl/Duke/`. Pressing Return produces this:

```
Excerpt from "Buckaroo Banzai" by Duke MacRauch
I found myself stealing a peek at my own watch and overheard
General Catbird's aide give him the latest.
"He's not even here," went the conversation.
```

As you can see, this search and replace was simple and effective.

2. Say that you decide that developmental psychology is your bag. Now, instead of having this Banzai character, you want my fictional character to be called Bandura. You could use the preceding command to change the occurrence on the current line, but you really want to change all occurrences within the file.

This is no problem. Type `:1,$ s/Banzai/Bandura/` and press Return. Here's the result:

```
Excerpt from "Buckaroo Bandura" by Duke MacRauch
I found myself stealing a peek at my own watch and overheard
General Catbird's
aide give him the latest.
"He's not even here," went the conversation.
"Who?"
```

```
"Bandura."
"Where the hell is he?"
"At the hospital in El Paso."
"What? Why weren't we informed? What's wrong with him?"

Go Team Bandura! Go Team Banzai! Go Team Banzai!

~
~
~
~
~
~
~
~
~
~
~
~
~
~
```

The result is not quite right. Because you forgot the trailing g in the substitute command, vi changed only the very first occurrence on each line, leaving the "go team" exhortation on the last line rather confusing.

To try again, type :1,$ s/Banzai/Bandura/g and press Return. This time the file changes as you wanted it to:

```
Excerpt from "Buckaroo Bandura" by Duke MacRauch
I found myself stealing a peek at my own watch and overheard
General Catbird's
aide give him the latest.
"He's not even here," went the conversation.
"Who?"
"Bandura."
"Where the hell is he?"
"At the hospital in El Paso."
"What? Why weren't we informed? What's wrong with him?"

Go Team Bandura! Go Team Bandura! Go Team Bandura!

~
~
~
~
```

```
        ~
        ~
        ~
        ~
        ~
        ~
        ~
7 substitutions
```

Notice that vi also indicates the total number of substitutions on the very bottom line of the screen (7, in this case).

3. Press u to undo the last change.

I have to admit, search and replace is one area where a graphical user interface comes in handy. A windowing system offers different text input fields for the old and new patterns; it shows each change and a dialog box that asks "Should I change this one?" We're focused on the Unix command line, so that's just not an option within vi. Later in the book, we'll have a look at the X window system and the GNOME interface, however, so don't despair!

Task 11.5: Using the Change and Replace Commands

In the preceding sections, you learned how to fix various problems by deleting words and then replacing them with new words. There is, in fact, a much smarter way to do this, and that is by using either the change or replace command.

Both of these commands have a lowercase version and an uppercase version, and each is quite different from the other. The r command *replaces* the character that the cursor is sitting on with the next character you type, whereas the R command puts you into *replace mode* so that anything you type overwrites whatever is already on the line until you press Esc. By contrast, C replaces everything on the line with whatever you type, regardless of whether you match the number of characters. (It's a subtle difference—but I demonstrate it, so don't fear.) The c command is the most powerful of the four. The *change* command, c, works just like the d command, described in the preceding hour. You can use the c command with any address reference, and it will enable you to change text through to that address, whether it's a word, a line, or even the rest of the document.

This will all make more sense with a few examples.

1. Start vi with the buckaroo.confused file:

```
I found myself stealing a peek at my own watch and overheard
General Catbird's
I found myself stealing a peek at my own watch and overheard
General Catbird's
```

```
aide give him the latest.
"He's not even here," went the conversation.
"Who?"
"Banzai."
"Where the hell is he?"
"At the hospital in El Paso."
"What? Why weren't we informed? What's wrong with him?"

aide give him the latest.
"He's not even here," went the conversation.
"Who?"
"Banzai."
"Where the hell is he?"
"At the hospital in El Paso."
"What? Why weren't we informed? What's wrong with him?"


~
~
~
~
~
~
~
"buckaroo.confused" 17 lines, 546 characters
```

Without moving the cursor at all, type R. Nothing happens, or so it seems. Now type the words Excerpt from "Buckaroo Banzai", and watch what occurs:

```
Excerpt from "Buckaroo Banzai" at my own watch and overheard
General Catbird's
I found myself stealing a peek at my own watch and overheard
General Catbird's
aide give him the latest.
"He's not even here," went the conversation.
```

Now press Escape and notice that what you see on the screen is exactly what's in the file.

2. This isn't, however, quite what you want. You could use either D or d$ to delete through the end of the line, but that's a bit awkward. Instead, use 0 to move back to the beginning of the line:

```
Excerpt from "Buckaroo Banzai" at my own watch and overheard
General Catbird's
I found myself stealing a peek at my own watch and overheard
General Catbird's
aide give him the latest.
"He's not even here," went the conversation.
```

This time, type C to change the contents of the line. Before you even type a single character of the new text, notice what the line now looks like:

```
Excerpt from "Buckaroo Banzai" at my own watch and overheard
General Catbird'$
I found myself stealing a peek at my own watch and overheard
General Catbird's
aide give him the latest.
"He's not even here," went the conversation.
```

Here's where a subtle difference comes into play. Look at the last character on the current line. When you pressed C, the program replaced the last character of the line with a $ to show the range of the text that'll be changed. Press the Tab key once and then type Excerpt from "Buckaroo Bansai" by Earl MacRauch.

```
Excerpt from "Buckaroo Bansai" by Earl MacRauchheard General Catbird'$
I found myself stealing a peek at my own watch and overheard
General Catbird's
aide give him the latest.
"He's not even here," went the conversation.
```

This time, watch what happens when you press Escape:

```
Excerpt from "Buckaroo Bansai" by Earl MacRauch
I found myself stealing a peek at my own watch and overheard
General Catbird's
aide give him the latest.
"He's not even here," went the conversation.
```

3. Here's another mistake. The actual title of the book is *Buckaroo Banzai* with a *z*, but it's been spelled it with an *s* instead. This is a chance to try the new r command.

Use cursor-control keys to move the cursor to the offending letter. Use b to back up words and then h a few times to move into the middle of the word. The screen now looks like this:

```
Excerpt from "Buckaroo Bansai" by Earl MacRauch
I found myself stealing a peek at my own watch and overheard
General Catbird's
aide give him the latest.
"He's not even here," went the conversation.
```

Now type r. Again, nothing happens; the cursor doesn't move. Type r again to make sure it worked:

```
Excerpt from "Buckaroo Banrai" by Earl MacRauch
I found myself stealing a peek at my own watch and overheard
General Catbird's
aide give him the latest.
"He's not even here," went the conversation.
```

That's no good. It replaced the s with an r, which definitely isn't correct. Fix it with rz, and you should have the following:

```
Excerpt from "Buckaroo Banzai" by Earl MacRauch
I found myself stealing a peek at my own watch and overheard
General Catbird's
aide give him the latest.
"He's not even here," went the conversation.
```

4. Okay, those are the easy ones. Now it's time to see what the c command can do. In fact, it's incredibly powerful. You can change just about any range of information from the current point in the file in either direction!

To start, move to the middle of the file, where the second copy of the passage is located:

```
Excerpt from "Buckaroo Banzai" by Earl MacRauch
I found myself stealing a peek at my own watch and overheard
General Catbird's
aide give him the latest.
"He's not even here," went the conversation.
"Who?"
"Banzai."
"Where the hell is he?"
"At the hospital in El Paso."
"What? Why weren't we informed? What's wrong with him?"

aide give him the latest.
"He's not even here," went the conversation.
"Who?"
"Banzai."
"Where the hell is he?"
"At the hospital in El Paso."
"What? Why weren't we informed? What's wrong with him?"
```

```
~
~
~
~
~
~
~
"buckaroo.confused" 17 lines, 546 characters
```

Say that you want to change the word `aide` that the cursor is sitting on to `The tall beige wall clock opted to` instead. Type `c` and note that, as with many other commands in `vi`, nothing happens. Now type `w` to change just the current word. The screen should look like this:

```
"At the hospital in El Paso."
"What? Why weren't we informed? What's wrong with him?"

aid$ give him the latest.
"He's not even here," went the conversation.
"Who?"
"Banzai."
```

The editor has replaced the last character in the affected range to a `$` so that you can see what's going to be changed when you're done. Now type `The tall beige wall clock opted to`. Once you reach the `$`, the editor stops overwriting characters and starts inserting them instead; the screen now looks like this:

```
"At the hospital in El Paso."
"What? Why weren't we informed? What's wrong with him?"

The tall beige wall clock opted to_give him the latest.
"He's not even here," went the conversation.
"Who?"
"Banzai."
```

Press Escape, and you're done (though you can undo the change with the u or U commands, of course).

5. Tall and beige or not, this section makes no sense now, so change this entire line by using the $ motion command you learned in the preceding hour. First, use 0 to move to the beginning of the line and then type c$:

```
"At the hospital in El Paso."
"What? Why weren't we informed? What's wrong with him?"

The tall beige wall clock opted to give him the latest$
"He's not even here," went the conversation.
"Who?"
"Banzai."
```

Note that the last character changed to $. Press Escape without typing in any replacement text, and the entire line is deleted:

```
"At the hospital in El Paso."
"What? Why weren't we informed? What's wrong with him?"


"He's not even here," went the conversation.
"Who?"
"Banzai."
```

6. Six lines are still below the current line. I could delete them and then type the information I want, but that's rather crude. Instead, the c command comes to the rescue. Move down one line, type c6, and press Return. Watch what happens:

```
"At the hospital in El Paso."
"What? Why weren't we informed? What's wrong with him?"
~
~
~
~
~
~
~
~
~
~
~
7 lines changed
```

In general, you can change the current and next line by using c followed by a Return (because the Return key is a motion key, too, remember). By prefacing the command with a number above, you changed the range of the command from two lines to six.

NOTE

You might be asking, "Why two lines?" The answer is subtle. In essence, whenever you use the c command, you change the current line plus any additional lines that might be touched by the command. Pressing Return moves the cursor to the following line; therefore, the current line (starting at the cursor location) through the following lines are changed. The command probably should change just to the beginning of the following line, but that's beyond even my control!

Now press Tab four times, type `(page 8)` and then press the Escape key. The screen should look like this:

```
"Where the hell is he?"
"At the hospital in El Paso."
"What? Why weren't we informed? What's wrong with him?"



                        (page 8)
~
   ~
   ~
```

7. What if you change your mind? That's where the u command comes in handy. Typing u once undoes the last command:

```
Excerpt from "Buckaroo Banzai" by Earl MacRauch
I found myself stealing a peek at my own watch and overheard
General Catbird's
aide give him the latest.
"He's not even here," went the conversation.
"Who?"
"Banzai."
"Where the hell is he?"
"At the hospital in El Paso."
"What? Why weren't we informed? What's wrong with him?"


"He's not even here," went the conversation.
"Who?"
"Banzai."
"Where the hell is he?"
```

```
"At the hospital in El Paso."
"What? Why weren't we informed? What's wrong with him?"

~
~
~
~
~
~
~
6 more lines
```

The combination of replace and change commands adds a level of sophistication to an editor that you might have suspected could only insert or delete. But wait, there's more to cover in this hour!

Task 11.6: Accessing Unix with !

This final task on vi introduces you to one of the most powerful, and least-known, commands in the editor: the ! escape-to-Unix command. When prefaced with a colon (:!, for example), it enables you to run Unix commands without leaving the editor. More powerfully, the ! command in vi itself accepts address specifications, feeds that block of text to the command as input, and replaces it with the results of having run that command on the text.

All this might be a bit confusing, so let's have a look.

1. Let's leave Buckaroo Banzai alone for a bit to switch to another classic, Charles Dickens's *A Tale of Two Cities*. I've created a file called dickens.note for this exercise, and you can either type it yourself or grab a copy of the file from our website, http://www.intuitive.com/tyu24/. The file is shown here:

```
% cat dickens.note

                    A Tale of Two Cities
                         Preface

     When I was acting, with my children and friends, in Mr Wilkie
     Collins's drama of The Frozen Deep, I first conceived the main
     idea of this story. A strong desire was upon me then, to
     embody it in my own person;
     and I traced out in my fancy, the state of mind of which it would
     necessitate the presentation
     to an observant spectator, with particular
     care and interest.

     As the idea became familiar to me, it gradually shaped itself into
     its present form. Throughout its execution, it has had complete
```

```
possession of me; I have so far verified what
is done and suffered on these pages,
as that I have certainly done and suffered it all myself.

Whenever any reference (however slight) is made here to the
condition of the French people before or during
the Revolution, it is truly
made on the faith of the most trustworthy
witnesses. It has been one of my hopes to add
something to the popular and picturesque means of
understanding that terrible time, though no one can hope to
add anything to the philosophy of Mr Carlyle's wonderful book._


Tavistock House
November 1859
```

With this file on my system, I'll start by invoking vi with the filename and then use a command escape to double-check what files I have in my home directory. To do this, I type : !, which moves the cursor to the bottom line:

```
of the French people before or during the Revolution, it is truly
made on the faith of the most trustworthy
witnesses.  It has been one of my hopes to add
something to the popular and picturesque means of
:!_
```

Then I type ls -F and press Return, as if I were at the prompt of the command line itself:

```
of the French people before or during the Revolution, it is truly
made on the faith of the most trustworthy
witnesses.  It has been one of my hopes to add
something to the popular and picturesque means of
:!ls -F
Archives/          big.output        dickens.note      src/
InfoWorld/         bigfiles          keylime.pie       temp/
Mail/              bin/              newfile           tetme
News/              buckaroo          owl.c
OWL/               buckaroo.confused sample
awkscript          demo              sample2
[Hit any key to continue] _
```

If I press Return, I'm back in the editor, and nothing's been changed.

2. Now for some real fun, I move to the beginning of the first paragraph and add the text
`Chuck, here are my current files:`. Then I press Return twice before using the
Escape key to return to command mode. The screen now looks like this:

```
                        A Tale of Two Cities
                              Preface

Chuck, here are my current files:

_

When I was acting, with my children and friends, in Mr Wilkie
Collins's drama of The Frozen Deep, I first conceived the main
idea of this story.  A strong desire was upon me then, to
```

Notice that the cursor was moved up a line. (Caveat: Some Unix implementations have a
version of `vi` that leaves you at the original insertion point.) I'm now on a blank line, and
the line following is also blank.

To feed the current line to the Unix system and replace it with the output of the command,
`vi` offers an easy shortcut: `!!`. When I type the second `!` (or, more precisely, after `vi` fig-
ures out the desired range specified for this command), the cursor moves to the bottom of
the screen and prompts with a single `!` character:

```
of the French people before or during the Revolution, it is truly
made on the faith of the most trustworthy
witnesses. It has been one of my hopes to add
something to the popular and picturesque means of
:!_
```

To list all the files in my directory, I can type `ls -F` and press Return. After a moment or
two, `vi` adds the output of that command to the file itself:

```
                        A Tale of Two Cities
                              Preface


Chuck, here are my current files:
Archives/              bigfiles              newfile
InfoWorld/             bin/                  owl.c
Mail/                  buckaroo              sample
News/                  buckaroo.confused     sample2
OWL/                   demo                  src/
awkscript              dickens.note          temp/
big.output             keylime.pie           tetme
```

```
When I was acting, with my children and friends, in Mr Wilkie
Collins's drama of The Frozen Deep, I first conceived the main
idea of this story.  A strong desire was upon me then, to
embody it in my own person;
and I traced out in my fancy, the state of mind of which it would
necessitate the presentation
to an observant spectator, with particular
care and interest.

As the idea became familiar to me, it gradually shaped itself into
its present form.  Throughout its execution, it has had complete
6 more lines
```

Notice that this time the status on the bottom indicates how many lines were added to the file: 6 more lines.

Type u to undo this change. Notice that the `vi` status indicator on the bottom line says there are now six fewer lines.

3. Move back to the W in When. You are now ready to learn one of my favorite vi commands, one that lets you filter text through an arbitrary Unix command or sequence of commands.

This time I'm going to use the Unix stream editor, sed, to perform a neat trick: prefacing each selected line with >. The actual command I'll use is sed `'s/^/> /'`. Ready?

This is where the } motion command comes in handy, too: It selects *from the current point to the end of the paragraph*. To accomplish this, I type ! }, moving the cursor to the bottom of the screen, then type in the sed command shown earlier: sed `'s/^/> /'`. Pressing Return feeds the affected lines—the current paragraph—to sed. The sed command then applies the substitution indicated and replaces those lines in the file with the output of the sed command. Voilà! Here's what I get:

NOTE

The sed editor is one of your best friends in Unix because you can use it in any command pipe to modify the data as it passes through. A quick read of the sed man page will be time well spent.

```
                    A Tale of Two Cities
                         Preface

Chuck, here are my current files:


> When I was acting, with my children and friends, in Mr Wilkie
> Collins's drama of The Frozen Deep, I first conceived the main
```

```
> idea of this story.  A strong desire was upon me then, to
> embody it in my own person;
> and I traced out in my fancy, the state of mind of which it would
> necessitate the presentation
> to an observant spectator, with particular
> care and interest.

As the idea became familiar to me, it gradually shaped itself into
its present form.  Throughout its execution, it has had complete
possession of me; I have so far verified what
is done and suffered in these pages,
as that I have certainly done and suffered it all myself.

Whenever any reference (however slight) is made here to the condition
of the French people before or during the Revolution, it is truly
!sed 's/^/> /'
```

I hope you're excited to see this command in action! It's a powerful way to interact with Unix while within vi.

4. I'll provide a few more examples of ways to interact with Unix while within vi. First, I don't really want the prefix to each line, so I'm going to type u to undo the change.

   Instead, I would rather have the system actually tighten up the lines and ensure that a reasonable number of words occur on each line and that no lines are so long that they wrap around onto the next line on my screen. On most systems, there is a command called either fmt or adjust to accomplish this. To figure out which works on your system, simply use the :! command and feed a word or two to the fmt command to see what happens:

```
Whenever any reference (however slight) is made here to the condition
of the French people before or during the Revolution, it is truly
:!echo hi | fmt
[No write since last change]
hi
[Hit any key to continue] _
```

In this case, fmt did what I hoped, so I can be sure that the command exists on my system. If your response was command unknown, adjust is a likely alternative. If neither exists, complain to your vendor!

Armed with this new command, you can try another variant of !}, this time by feeding the current paragraph to the fmt command. I'm still at the beginning of the word When in the text, so when I type the sequence ! } fmt, the paragraph is cleaned up, and the screen changes to this:

```
                        A Tale of Two Cities
                             Preface

Chuck, here are my current files:


When I was acting, with my children and friends, in Mr Wilkie
Collins's drama of The Frozen Deep, I first conceived the main
idea of this story.  A strong desire was upon me then, to embody it in my own
person; and I traced out in my fancy, the state of mind of which it
would necessitate the presentation to an observant spectator, with
particular care and interest.

As the idea became familiar to me, it gradually shaped itself into
its present form.  Throughout its execution, it has had complete
possession of me; I have so far verified what
is done and suffered in these pages,
as that I have certainly done and suffered it all myself.

Whenever any reference (however slight) is made here to the condition
of the French people before or during the Revolution, it is truly
made on the faith of the most trustworthy
witnesses.  It has been one of my hopes to add
2 fewer lines
```

Again, `vi` tells us that the number of lines in the file has changed as a result of the command. In this situation, tightening up the paragraph actually reduced it by two lines.

This command is so helpful that I often have it bound to a specific key with the `map` command. A typical way to do this in an `.exrc`, the `preferences/config` file for `vi`, might be this:

```
:map ^P !}fmt^M
```

The `^M` is what `vi` uses to record a Return. (You need to use `^v` beforehand to have vi save a control sequence.) With this defined in the `.exrc` file in my home directory, I can then press `^P` to format the current paragraph. Fast and darn handy.

Clearly, the ! command opens up `vi` to work with the rest of the Unix system. There's almost nothing you can't now do within the editor, whether it's add or remove prefixes, clean up text, or even show what happens when you try to run a command or reformat a passage within the current file.

Summary of `vi` Commands

A summary of the commands you learned in this hour is shown in Table 11.2.

TABLE 11.2   Advanced `vi` Commands

Command	Meaning
`!!`*command*	Replace the current line with the output of the specified Unix command.
`!}`*command*	Replace the current paragraph with the results of piping it through the specified Unix command or commands.
`(`	Move backward one sentence.
`)`	Move forward one sentence.
`C`	Change text from the point of the cursor through the end of the line.
`c`	Change text in the specified range; `cw` changes the following word, whereas `c}` changes the next paragraph.
`e`	Move to the end of the current word.
`^g`	Show the current line number and other information about the file.
`R`	Replace text from the point of the cursor until Escape is pressed.
`r`	Replace the current character with the next one pressed.
`^v`	Prevent `vi` from interpreting the next character.
`{`	Move backward one paragraph.
`}`	Move forward one paragraph.
`:!`*command*	Invoke the specified Unix command.
`:ab` *a bcd*	Define the abbreviation *a* for the phrase *bcd*.
`:ab`	Show the current abbreviations, if any.
`:map` *a bcd*	Map key *a* to the `vi` commands *bcd*.
`:map`	Show current key mappings, if any.
`:s/`*old*`/`*new*`/`	Substitute *new* for the first instance of *old* on the current line.
`:s/`*old*`/`*new*`/g`	Substitute *new* for all occurrences of *old* on the current line.
`:set nonumber`	Turn off line numbering (display only, file not affected).
`:set number`	Turn on line numbering.

Summary

Clearly, vi is a very complex and sophisticated tool that enables you not only to modify your text files but also to customize the editor for your keyboard. Just as importantly, you can access all the power of Unix while within vi.

Workshop

The Workshop summarizes the key terms you've learned and poses some questions about the topics presented in this lesson. It also provides you with a preview of what you will learn in the next hour.

Key Terms

colon commands The vi commands that begin with a colon are usually used for file manipulation.

replace mode In this mode of vi, any characters you type replace those that are already in the file.

Exercises

1. What does the following command do?

   ```
   :1,5 s/kitten/puppy
   ```

2. What do these commands do?

   ```
   15i?ESCh
   i15?ESCh
   i?ESC15h
   ```

3. What would happen if you were to use the following startup flags?

   ```
   vi +O test
   vi +/joe/ names
   vi +hhjjhh
   vi +:q testme
   ```

4. Try ^G on the first and last lines of a file. Explain why the percentage indicator might not be what you expected.

5. What's the difference between the following four strings?

   ```
   rr
   RrESC
   cwrESC
   CrESC
   ```

6. What key mappings do you have in your version of `vi`? Do you have labeled keys on your keyboard that could be helpful in `vi` but aren't defined? If so, define them in your `.exrc` file using the `:map` command.

7. What do you think the following command will do? Try it and see whether you're right.

   `!}ls`

Preview of the Next Hour

Now that you've read this hour and the preceding one, you know more about `vi` than the vast majority of people using Unix and Linux. There's a second popular editor, however—one that is modeless and offers its own interesting possibilities for working with files and the Unix system. It's called `emacs`, and if you have it on your system, it's definitely worth a look. We'll spend the next hour getting acquainted with it.

An Overview of the emacs Editor

Goals for This Hour

In this hour, you will learn

- ▶ How to launch emacs and insert text
- ▶ About moving around in a file
- ▶ How to delete characters and words
- ▶ How to search and replace in emacs
- ▶ About using the emacs tutorial and help system
- ▶ About working with other files

The only screen-oriented editor that's guaranteed to be included with the Unix system is vi, but that doesn't mean it's the only good editor available in Unix! An alternative editor that has become quite popular in the computer science world is called emacs. This hour teaches you the fundamentals of this very different and quite powerful editing tool and environment.

Remember what I said in the preceding hour, when I mentioned the emacs editor: emacs is modeless. So this hour, be prepared for an editor that is quite unlike vi. And because it's modeless, there's no insert or command mode. As a result, you will have ample opportunity to use the Control key. And then some.

NOTE

Over the years, I have tried to become an emacs enthusiast, once even forcing myself to use it for an entire month. I had crib sheets of commands taped up all over my office. At the end of the month, I had attained an editing speed that was about half of my speed in vi, an editor I've used thousands of times in the past 30+ years that I've worked in Unix. I think emacs has a lot going for it, and generally I think that modeless software is better than modal software. The main obstacle I see for emacs, however, is that it's begging for pull-down menus like you'd get in a Mac or Windows program. Using Control, Meta, Shift-Meta, and other weird key combinations just isn't as easy. On the other hand, your approach to editing might be different, and you might not have years of vi experience affecting your preference of editing environments. I encourage you to give emacs a fair shake by working through all the examples I have included. You might find that it matches your working style better than vi.

The Other Popular Editor: emacs

Computer folk are passionate about their tools, so it's no surprise that when it comes to terminal-based editors, that's a "religious" war, too. When it comes to Unix, the main combatants are vi and emacs, and the fact is that both are very competent editors, and you can be highly productive with either. It's kind of your call on which is going to work better for you.

One wrinkle, though: I've never seen a Unix or Linux system without some version of the vi editor installed, but plenty ship without emacs. If yours is missing emacs and you really want to try it, check out your system package manager or window GUI-based package management tool. It should just be a few mouse clicks away.

Task 12.1: Launching emacs and Inserting Text

Starting emacs is as simple as starting any other Unix program: Type the name of the program, followed by any file or files you'd like to work with. The puzzle with emacs is figuring out what it's actually called on your system, if you have it. There are a couple of ways to try to identify emacs; I'll demonstrate these methods in action 2 of this task.

Take a look at your computer keyboard. emacs requires you to use not just the Control key but another key, known as the *Meta key*, a sort of alternative Control key. If you have a key labeled Meta or Alt (for Alternative) on your keyboard, that's the one. If, like me, you don't, simply press Escape every time a Meta key is indicated.

Because both Control and Meta keys are used in emacs, the notation for indicating commands is unique. Throughout this book, a Control-key sequence has been shown either as Ctrl-F or as ^F. emacs people write this differently, to allow for the difference between Control and Meta keys. In emacs notation, ^F is shown as C-f, where C- always means Control. Similarly, M-x is the Meta key plus the character specified by x. If you don't have a Meta key, the sequence is Escape followed by x. Finally, some arcane commands involve both the Control and the Meta keys being pressed (simultaneously with the other key involved). This notation is C-M-x and indicates that you need either to press and hold down both the Control and the Meta keys while typing x, or, if you don't have a Meta (or Alt) key, press Escape followed by C-x. (I did warn you that it's a bit more complicated, right?)

With this notation in mind, you leave emacs by pressing C-x C-c (Ctrl-X, followed by Ctrl-C).

1. Check whether your system has emacs available. The easiest way to find out is to type emacs at the command line and see what happens:

```
% emacs
emacs: Command not found.
%
```

This is a good indication that emacs isn't available. If your command worked and you now are in the emacs editor, move down to step 2 in this task.

A popular version of emacs is from the Free Software Foundation, and it's called GNU emacs. To see whether you have this version, type gnuemacs or gnumacs at the command line.

Still can't find emacs on your system? Check with your system administrator or do a Google search for the name of your particular OS and the word emacs and see what you can find out. At worst, you can go to the GNU Project site and download a copy: http://www.gnu.org/software/emacs/.

2. Rather than start with a blank screen, quit the program (C-x C-c) and restart emacs with one of the earlier test files, dickens.note:

```
% gnuemacs dickens.note
```

```
                    A Tale of Two Cities
                         Preface

When I was acting, with my children and friends, in Mr Wilkie
Collins's drama of The Frozen Deep, I first conceived the main idea of
this story. A strong desire was upon me then, to
embody it in my own person;
and I traced out in my fancy, the state of mind of which it would
necessitate the presentation
to an observant spectator, with particular
care and interest.

As the idea became familiar to me, it gradually shaped itself into
its present form. Throughout its execution, it has had complete
possession of me; I have so far verified what
is done and suffered in these pages,
as that I have certainly done and suffered it all myself.

Whenever any reference (however slight) is made here to the condition
of the French people before or during the Revolution, it is truly
made, on the faith of the most trustworthy
witnesses. It has been one of my hopes to add
-----Emacs: dickens.note          (Fundamental)----Top-------------
```

As you can see, it's quite different from the display shown when vi starts up. The status line at the bottom of the display offers useful information as you edit the file at different points, and it also reminds you at all times of the name of the file, which can be surprisingly helpful. emacs can work with different kinds of files, and here you see by the word Fundamental in the status line that emacs is prepared for a regular text file. If you're programming, emacs can offer special features customized for your particular language.

3. Quit emacs by using the C-x C-c sequence but let a few seconds pass after you press C-x to watch what happens. When I press C-x, the bottom of the screen suddenly changes to this:

```
on the faith of the most trustworthy
witnesses. It has been one of my hopes to add
-----Emacs: dickens.note           (Fundamental)----Top--------------
C-x-
```

> **NOTE**
>
> Confusingly, the cursor remains at the top of the file, but emacs reminds me that I've pressed C-x and that I need to enter a second command after I've decided what to do. I now press C-c and immediately exit emacs.

Already you can see some dramatic differences between emacs and vi. If you're comfortable with multiple key sequences such as C-x C-c to quit, I think you're going to enjoy learning emacs. If not, stick with it anyway. Even if you never use emacs after trying the examples in this lesson, it's still good to know a little bit about it.

> **NOTE**
>
> Why learn about a tool you're not going to use? Because as you go from system to system, you never really know what graphical interface, what window manager, and even what editor packages might be available. Being competent at emacs or vi means that even in a worst-case scenario with a very rustic install, you can edit files and proceed with your project. So the answer really is that it's smart to learn because it's smart to have options.

Task 12.2: Moving Around in a File

Files are composed of characters, words, lines, sentences, and paragraphs, and emacs has commands to help you move about among them. Most systems have the arrow keys enabled, which helps you avoid worrying about some of the key sequences, but it's best to know them all anyway.

The most basic motions are C-f and C-b, which are used to move the cursor forward and backward one character, respectively. Switch those to the Meta command equivalents, and the cursor will move by words: M-f moves the cursor forward a word, and M-b moves it back a word. Pressing C-n moves the cursor to the next line, C-p to the previous line, C-a to the beginning of the line, and C-e to the end of the line. (The vi equivalents for all of these are l, h, w, and b for moving forward and backward a character or word; j and k for moving up or down a line; and 0 or $ to move to the beginning or end of the current line. Which makes more sense to you?)

To move forward a sentence, you can use M-e, which actually moves the cursor to the end of the sentence. Pressing M-a moves it to the beginning of a sentence. Notice the parallels between

Control and Meta commands: C-a moves the cursor to the beginning of the line, and M-a moves it to the beginning of the sentence.

To scroll within the document, you use C-v to move forward a screen and M-v to move back a screen. To move forward a page (usually 60 lines of text; this is based on a printed page of information), you can use either C-x] or C-x [for forward motion or backward motion, respectively.

Finally, to move to the top of the file, use M-<, and to move to the bottom, use the M-> command.

1. Go back into emacs and locate the cursor. It should be at the top of the screen:

```
                         A Tale of Two Cities
                              Preface

When I was acting, with my children and friends, in Mr Wilkie Collins's
drama of The Frozen Deep, I first conceived the main idea of this
story. A strong desire was upon me then, to
embody it in my own person;
and I traced out in my fancy, the state of mind of which it would
necessitate the presentation
to an observant spectator, with particular
care and interest.

As the idea became familiar to me, it gradually shaped itself into
its present form. Throughout its execution, it has had complete
possession of me; I have so far verified what
is done and suffered in these pages,
as that I have certainly done and suffered it all myself.

Whenever any reference (however slight) is made here to the condition
of the French people before or during the Revolution, it is truly
made, on the faith of the most trustworthy
witnesses. It has been one of my hopes to add
-----Emacs: dickens.note          (Fundamental)----Top--------------
```

Move down four lines by using C-n four times. Your cursor should now be sitting on the d of drama:

```
Preface

When I was acting, with my children and friends, in Mr Wilkie Collins's
drama of The Frozen Deep, I first conceived the main idea of this
story. A strong desire was upon me then, to
embody it in my own person;
and I traced out in my fancy, the state of mind of which it would
```

2. Next, move to the end of this sentence by using the M-e command (`emacs` expects two spaces to separate sentences):

```
When I was acting, with my children and friends, in Mr Wilkie Collins's
drama of The Frozen Deep, I first conceived the main idea of this
story._ A strong desire was upon me then, to
embody it in my own person;
and I traced out in my fancy, the state of mind of which it would
```

Now type the following text: I fought the impulse to write this novel vociferously, but, dear reader, I felt the injustice of the situation too strongly in my breast to deny. Don't press Return or Escape when you're done. The screen should now look similar to this:

```
drama of The Frozen Deep, I first conceived the main idea of this
story. I fought the impulse to write this novel vociferously, but, dear
reader,\
 I felt
the injustice of the situation too strongly in my breast to deny_  A strong
des\
ire was upon me then, to
embody it in my own person;
and I traced out in my fancy, the state of mind of which it would
necessitate the presentation
```

You can see that `emacs` wrapped the line when it became too long (between the words `felt` and `the`), and because the lines are still too long to display, a few of them end with a backslash. The backslash isn't actually a part of the file; with it, `emacs` is saying that those lines are longer than can be displayed.

3. Now try to move back a few characters by pressing Backspace.

Uh oh! If your system is like mine, the Backspace key doesn't move the cursor back up a character at all. Instead, it starts the `emacs` help system, where you're suddenly confronted with a screen that looks like this:

```
You have typed C-h, the help character. Type a Help option:

A   command-apropos.  Give a substring, and see a list of commands
              (functions interactively callable) that contain
                that substring. See also the  apropos  command.
B   describe-bindings. Display table of all key bindings.
C   describe-key-briefly. Type a command key sequence;
```

```
              it prints the function name that sequence runs.
F   describe-function. Type a function name and get documentation of it.
I   info. The  info  documentation reader.
K   describe-key. Type a command key sequence;
              it displays the full documentation.
L   view-lossage. Shows last 100 characters you typed.
M   describe-mode. Print documentation of current major mode,
              which describes the commands peculiar to it.
N   view-emacs-news. Shows emacs news file.
S   describe-syntax. Display contents of syntax table, plus explanations
T   help-with-tutorial. Select the Emacs learn-by-doing tutorial.
V   describe-variable. Type name of a variable;
              it displays the variable's documentation and value.
W   where-is. Type command name; it prints which keystrokes
              invoke that command.
--**-Emacs: *Help*                  (Fundamental)----Top-------------
A B C F I K L M N S T V W C-h C-h C-h C-d C-n C-w or Space to scroll: _
```

To escape the help screen (you'll learn more about it later in this hour), press Escape, and your screen should be restored. The status line shows what file you're viewing. But beware: You aren't always viewing the file you want to work with.

The correct key to move the cursor back a few characters is C-b. Use that to back up and then use C-f to move forward again to the original cursor location.

4. Check that the last few lines of the file haven't changed by using the emacs move-to-end-of-file command, M->. (Think of file redirection to remember the file motion commands.) Now the screen looks like this:

```
Whenever any reference (however slight) is made here to the condition
of the French people before or during the Revolution, it is truly
made, on the faith of the most trustworthy
witnesses. It has been one of my hopes to add
something to the popular and picturesque means of
understanding that terrible time, though no one can hope
to add anything to the philosophy of Mr Carlyle's wonderful book.

Tavistock House
November 1859

    _


--**-Emacs: dickens.note            (Fundamental)----Bot-------------
```

5. Changing the words of Charles Dickens was fun, so save these changes and quit. If you try to quit the program with C-x C-c, emacs reminds you that there are unsaved changes:

```
--**-Emacs: dickens.note          (Fundamental)----Bot--------------
Save file /users/taylor/dickens.note? (y or n)  _
```

Typing y saves the changes; n quits without saving the changes; and if you instead decide to return to the edit session, Escape will cancel the action entirely. Typing n gets you a second reminder that the changes will be lost if you don't save them:

```
--**-Emacs: dickens.note          (Fundamental)----Bot--------------
Modified buffers exist; exit anyway? (yes or no)  _
```

This time type yes (emacs will complain if you just type y!) and, finally, you're back on the command line.

Entering text in emacs is incredibly easy. It's as though the editor is always in insert mode. The price you pay for this, however, is that just about anything else you do requires Control or Meta sequences. Even the Backspace key did something other than what you wanted.

The motion commands are summarized in Table 12.1.

TABLE 12.1   emacs Motion Commands

Command	Meaning
M->	Move to the end of the file.
M-<	Move to the beginning of the file.
C-v	Move forward a screen.
M-v	Move backward a screen.
C-x]	Move forward a page.
C-x [	Move backward a page.
C-n	Move to the next line.
C-p	Move to the previous line.
C-a	Move to the beginning of the line.
C-e	Move to the end of the line.
M-e	Move to the end of the sentence.
M-a	Move to the beginning of the sentence.
C-f	Move forward a character.
C-b	Move backward a character.
M-f	Move forward a word.
M-b	Move backward a word.

Task 12.3: Deleting Characters and Words

Inserting text into an emacs buffer is simple, and after you get the hang of it, moving about in the file isn't too bad, either. How about deleting text? The series of Control and Meta commands that enable you to insert text are a precursor to all commands in emacs, and it should come as no surprise that C-d deletes the current character, M-d deletes the next word, M-k deletes the rest of the current sentence, and C-k deletes the rest of the current line. If you have a key on your keyboard labeled DEL, RUBOUT, or Delete, you're in luck because Delete deletes the previous character, M-Delete deletes the previous word, and C-x Delete deletes the previous sentence.

Unfortunately, although I have a Delete key, it's tied to the Backspace function on my system, so every time I press it, it actually sends a C-h sequence, not the DEL sequence, to the system. The result is that I cannot use any of these backward deletion commands.

1. Restart emacs with the dickens.note file and move the cursor to the middle of the fifth line. (Remember that C-n moves to the next line, and C-f moves forward a character.) It should look like this:

```
Preface

When I was acting, with my children and friends, in Mr Wilkie Collins's
drama of The Frozen Deep, I first conceived the main idea of this
story. A strong desire was upon me then, to
embody it in my own person;
and I traced out in my fancy, the state of mind of which it would
necessitate the presentation
to an observant spectator, with particular
```

Notice that my cursor is on the w in was on the fifth line here.

2. Press C-d C-d C-d to remove the word was. Now type came to revise the sentence slightly. The screen should now look like this:

```
Preface

When I was acting, with my children and friends, in Mr Wilkie Collins's
drama of The Frozen Deep, I first conceived the main idea of this
story. A strong desire came upon me then, to
embody it in my own person;
and I traced out in my fancy, the state of mind of which it would
necessitate the presentation
to an observant spectator, with particular
```

Now press Delete once to remove the last letter of the new word, and then type e to reinsert it. Instead of backing up a character at a time, I am going to use M-Delete (Meta plus the Delete key) to delete the word just added. The word is deleted, but the spaces on either side of the word are retained:

```
Preface

When I was acting, with my children and friends, in Mr Wilkie Collins's
drama of The Frozen Deep, I first conceived the main idea of this
story. A strong desire _upon me then, to
embody it in my own person;
and I traced out in my fancy, the state of mind of which it would
necessitate the presentation
to an observant spectator, with particular
```

Try another word to see whether you can get this sentence to sound interesting. Type crept to see how it reads.

3. Of course, it's probably not good writing karma to revise classic stories such as *A Tale of Two Cities*, so delete this entire sentence. If you press C-x Delete, which is an example of a *multi-keystroke command* in emacs, will it do the right thing? Recall that C-x Delete deletes the previous sentence. When you press C-x Delete, the results are helpful, if not completely what you want to accomplish:

NOTE

emacs also requires some multi-keystroke commands, where you might press a Control sequence and follow it with a second keystroke. Although this allows you to have many commands to control your text, it also means you need to know many commands.

```
Preface

When I was acting, with my children and friends, in Mr Wilkie Collins's
drama of The Frozen Deep, I first conceived the main idea of this
story. _upon me then, to
embody it in my own person;
and I traced out in my fancy, the state of mind of which it would
necessitate the presentation
to an observant spectator, with particular
```

That's okay. Now you can delete the second part of the sentence by using the M-k command. Now the screen looks like what you want:

```
When I was acting, with my children and friends, in Mr Wilkie Collins's
drama of The Frozen Deep, I first conceived the main idea of this
story. _

As the idea became familiar to me, it gradually shaped itself into its
present form. Throughout its execution, it has had complete possession
of me; I have so far verified what
```

4. Let's look at a great feature of emacs. Deleting sentences is just as wildly inappropriate as changing words, so you might want to undo the last two changes. If you were using vi, you'd be stuck because vi remembers only the last change, while some versions of vi have more sophisticated undo features that let you move back and forth in the entire edit stream; but emacs has that beat. With emacs, you can back up as many changes as you'd like, usually until you restore the original file. To step backward, use C-x u.

The first time you press C-x u, the screen changes to this:

```
When I was acting, with my children and friends, in Mr Wilkie Collins's
drama of The Frozen Deep, I first conceived the main idea of this
story. _upon me then, to
embody it in my own person;
and I traced out in my fancy, the state of mind of which it would
necessitate the presentation
to an observant spectator, with particular
care and interest.

As the idea became familiar to me, it gradually shaped itself into its
present form. Throughout its execution, it has had complete possession
```

The second time you press it, the screen goes even further back in the revision history:

```
When I was acting, with my children and friends, in Mr Wilkie Collins's
drama of The Frozen Deep, I first conceived the main idea of this
story. A strong desire crept_upon me then, to
embody it in my own person;
and I traced out in my fancy, the state of mind of which it would
necessitate the presentation
to an observant spectator, with particular
care and interest.
```

```
As the idea became familiar to me, it gradually shaped itself into its
present form. Throughout its execution, it has had complete possession
```

Finally, using C-x u three more times causes the original text to be restored:

```
                     A Tale of Two Cities
                          Preface

When I was acting, with my children and friends, in Mr Wilkie Collins's
drama of The Frozen Deep, I first conceived the main idea of this
story. A strong desire came upon me then, to
embody it in my own person;
and I traced out in my fancy, the state of mind of which it would
necessitate the presentation
to an observant spectator, with particular
care and interest.

As the idea became familiar to me, it gradually shaped itself into its
present form. Throughout its execution, it has had complete possession
of me; I have so far verified what
is done and suffered in these pages,
as that I have certainly done and suffered it all myself.

Whenever any reference (however slight) is made here to the condition
of the French people before or during the Revolution, it is truly made,
on the faith of the most trustworthy
witnesses. It has been one of my hopes to add
--**-Emacs: dickens.note          (Fundamental)----Top--------------
Undo!
```

If you don't have a Delete key, some of the deletion commands will, regrettably, be unavailable to you. Generally, though, emacs has as many ways to delete text as vi has—if not more. The best feature, however, is that, unlike vi, emacs remembers edit changes from the beginning of your editing session. You can always back up as far as you want by using the C-x u undo request, all the way back to the original version of the file you launched the editor with.

The deletion commands are summarized in Table 12.2.

TABLE 12.2 Deletion Commands in emacs

Command	Meaning
Delete	Delete the previous character.
C-d	Delete the current character.
M-Delete	Delete the previous word.
M-d	Delete the next word.
C-x Delete	Delete the previous sentence.
M-k	Delete the rest of the current sentence.
C-k	Delete the rest of the current line.
C-x u	Undo the last edit change.

Task 12.4: Searching and Replacing in emacs

Because emacs reserves the last line of the screen for its own system prompts, searching and replacing are easier than in vi. Moreover, the system prompts for the fields and asks, for each occurrence, whether to change it. On the other hand, this command isn't a simple keystroke or two; rather, it is an example of a *named* emacs command. A named emacs command is a command that requires you to type its name, such as query-replace, rather than a command key or two.

Searching forward for a pattern is done by pressing C-s, and searching backward is done with C-r (the mnemonics are *search* forward and *reverse* search). To leave the search when you've found what you want, press Escape, and to cancel the search and return to your starting point, use C-g.

NOTE

Unfortunately, you might find that pressing C-s does very strange things to your system. In fact, ^s and ^q are often used as *flow control* on a terminal, and by pressing C-s, you're actually telling the terminal emulator to stop sending information until it sees a C-q. Flow control is the protocol used by your computer and terminal to make sure that neither outpaces the other during data transmission. If this happens to you, you need to turn off XON/XOFF flow control. Ask your system administrator for help or check the settings on your Terminal or telnet app.

Query and replace is really a whole new feature within emacs. To start a query and replace, use M-x query-replace. emacs will prompt for what to do next. When a match is shown, you can type various commands to affect what happens: y makes the change; n leaves the matching sequence as is but moves to the next match; Escape or q quits replace mode; and ! automatically replaces all occurrences of the pattern without further prompting.

1. I'm still looking at the `dickens.note` file, and I have moved the cursor to the upper-left corner by using M-<. Somewhere in the file is the word `Revolution`, but I'm not sure where. Worse, every time I press C-s, the terminal freezes up until I press C-q because of flow control problems.

   Instead of searching forward, I'll search backward by first moving the cursor to the bottom of the file with M-> and then pressing C-r:

   ```
   -----Emacs: dickens.note          (Fundamental)----Bot--------------
   I-search backward:
   ```

   As I type each character of the pattern `Revolution`, the cursor dances backward, matching the pattern as it grows longer and longer, until emacs finds the word I seek:

   ```
   Whenever any reference (however slight) is made here to the condition
   of the French people before or during the Revolution, it is truly
   made, on the faith of the most trustworthy
   witnesses. It has been one of my hopes to add
   something to the popular and picturesque means of
   understanding that terrible time, though no one can hope
   to add anything to the philosophy of Mr Carlyle's wonderful book.

   Tavistock House
   November 1859



   -----Emacs: dickens.note          (Fundamental)----Bot--------------
   I-search backward: Revol
   ```

2. Now to try the `query-replace` feature. To begin, I move to the top of the file with M-< and then press M-x, which causes the notation to show up on the bottom status line:

   ```
   of the French people before or during the Revolution, it is truly made,
   on the faith of the most trustworthy
   witnesses. It has been one of my hopes to add
   --**-Emacs: dickens.note          (Fundamental)----Top--------------
   M-x _
   ```

I then type the words `query-replace` and press Return. emacs understands that I want to find all occurrences of a pattern and replace them with another. emacs changes the prompt to this:

```
of the French people before or during the Revolution, it is
truly made, on the faith of the most trustworthy
witnesses. It has been one of my hopes to add
--**-Emacs: dickens.note          (Fundamental)----Top-------------
Query replace: _
```

Now I type the word I want to replace. To cause confusion in the file, I think I'll change French to Danish because maybe *A Tale of Two Cities* really takes place in London and Copenhagen. To do this, I type French and press Return. The prompt changes to this:

```
of the French people before or during the Revolution, it is truly made,
on the faith of the most trustworthy
witnesses. It has been one of my hopes to add
--**-Emacs: dickens.note          (Fundamental)----Top-------------
Query replace French with: _
```

I type Danish and again press Return.

```
as that I have certainly done and suffered it all myself.

Whenever any reference (however slight) is made here to the condition
of the French_people before or during the Revolution, it is truly
made, on the faith of the most trustworthy
witnesses. It has been one of my hopes to add
--**-Emacs: dickens.note          (Fundamental)----Top-------------
Query replacing French with Danish:
```

It might not be completely obvious, but emacs has found a match (immediately before the cursor) and is prompting me for what to do next. The choices here are summarized in Table 12.3.

TABLE 12.3 Options During Query and Replace

Command	Meaning
y	Change this occurrence of the pattern.
n	Don't change this occurrence but look for another.
q	Don't change this occurrence. Leave `query-replace` completely (you can also use Escape to do this).
!	Change this occurrence and all others in the file.

I opt to make this, and all other possible changes in the file, by pressing !, and the screen changes to tell me that there were no more occurrences:

```
Whenever any reference (however slight) is made here to the condition
of the Danish_people before or during the Revolution, it is truly
made, on the faith of the most trustworthy
witnesses. It has been one of my hopes to add
--**-Emacs: dickens.note              (Fundamental)----Top--------------
Done
```

Searching in emacs is awkward, particularly because of the flow control problems you may incur because of your terminal. However, searching and replacing with the query-replace command is fantastic; it's much better and more powerful than the vi alternative. As I said earlier, your assessment of emacs all depends on what features you prefer.

Task 12.5: Using the emacs Tutorial and Help System

Unlike vi and, indeed, unlike most of Unix, emacs includes its own extensive built-in documentation and a tutorial to help you learn how to use the program. As I noted earlier, you access the help system by pressing C-h. Pressing C-h two times brings up the general help menu screen. There is also an information browser called info (accessed with C-h i), and there's a tutorial system you can start by pressing C-h t.

emacs enthusiasts insist that the editor is modeless, but in fact it does have modes. You used one just now—the query-replace mode. To obtain help on the current mode you're working in, you can use C-h m.

1. Boldly, I press C-h, and the entire screen is replaced with this:

```
You have typed C-h, the help character. Type a Help option:

A   command-apropos.  Give a substring, and see a list of commands
              (functions interactively callable) that contain
              that substring. See also the  apropos  command.
B   describe-bindings. Display table of all key bindings.
C   describe-key-briefly. Type a command key sequence;
              it prints the function name that sequence runs.
F   describe-function. Type a function name and get documentation of it.
I   info. The  info  documentation reader.
K   describe-key. Type a command key sequence;
              it displays the full documentation.
L   view-lossage. Shows last 100 characters you typed.
M   describe-mode. Print documentation of current major mode,
              which describes the commands peculiar to it.
```

```
N  view-emacs-news. Shows emacs news file.
S  describe-syntax. Display contents of syntax table, plus explanations
T  help-with-tutorial. Select the Emacs learn-by-doing tutorial.
V  describe-variable. Type name of a variable;
            it displays the variable's documentation and value.
W  where-is. Type command name; it prints which keystrokes
            invoke that command.
--**-Emacs: *Help*                  (Fundamental)----Top--------------
A B C F I K L M N S T V W C-x  b C-d C-n C-w or Space to scroll: _
```

What to do now? Seventeen options are possible from this point, as shown in Table 12.4.

TABLE 12.4   `emacs` **Help System Command Options**

Command	Meaning
A	List all commands matching the specified word.
B	List all key mappings.
C	Describe any key sequence pressed instead of doing it.
F	Describe the specified function.
I	Start the `info` browser.
K	Fully describe the result of a particular key sequence.
L	Show the last 100 characters you typed.
M	Describe the current mode you're in.
N	Show the `emacs` news file.
S	List a command syntax table.
T	Start the `emacs` tutorial.
V	Define and describe the specified variable.
W	Indicate what keystroke invokes a particular function.
C-x b	Display `emacs` copyright and distribution information.
C-d	Display `emacs` ordering information.
C-n	Display recent `emacs` changes.
C-w	Display the `emacs` warranty.

2. I choose K and then press M-< to see what that command really does. The first thing that happens after I type K is that the table of help information vanishes, to be replaced by my original text, and then the prompt appears along the bottom:

```
of the Danish_people before or during the Revolution, it is truly
made, on the faith of the most trustworthy
witnesses. It has been one of my hopes to add
--**-Emacs: dickens.note          (Fundamental)----Top--------------
Describe key:-
```

Pressing M-< brings up the desired information:

```
                       A Tale of Two Cities
                            Preface

When I was acting, with my children and friends, in Mr Wilkie
Collins's drama of The Frozen Deep, I first conceived the main idea
of this story. A strong desire came upon me then, to
embody it in my own person;
and I traced out in my fancy, the state of mind of which it would
necessitate the presentation
to an observant spectator, with particular
-----Emacs: dickens.note~          (Fundamental)----Top--------------
beginning-of-buffer:
Move point to the beginning of the buffer; leave mark at previous
position.
With arg N, put point N/10 of the way from the true beginning.
Don't use this in Lisp programs!
(goto-char (point-min)) is faster and does not set the mark.




-----Emacs: *Help*                 (Fundamental)----All--------------
Type C-x 1 to remove help window.
```

A quick C-x 1 removes the help information when I'm done with it.

A considerable amount of help is available in the emacs editor. If you're interested in learning more about this editor, the online tutorial is a great place to start. Use C-h t to start it and go from there.

Task 12.6: Working with Other Files

By this point, it should be no surprise to you that about a million commands are available within the emacs editor, though some of them can be a bit tricky. There are many file-related commands, too, but I'm going to focus on just a few essentials so that you can get around in the program. The emacs help system can offer lots more. (Try using C-h a file to find out what functions are offered in your version of the program.)

To add the contents of a file to the current edit buffer, use the command C-x i. It will prompt for a filename. Pressing C-x C-w prompts for a file to write the buffer into rather than the default file. To save to the default file, use C-x C-s (that is, if you can; the C-s might again hang you up, just as it did when you tried to use it for searching). If that doesn't work, you always can use the alternative, C-x s, which also works. To move to another file, use C-x C-f. (emacs users never specify more than one filename on the command line; they use C-x C-f to move between files instead.) What's nice is that when you use the C-x C-f command, you load the contents of that file into another buffer, so you can zip quickly between files by using the C-x b command to switch buffers. emacs allows you to edit several files at once, using different areas of the screen; these areas are called *buffers*.

1. Without leaving emacs, I press C-x C-f to read another file into the buffer. The system then prompts me as follows:

```
of the Danish people before or during the Revolution, it is truly
made, on the faith of the most trustworthy
witnesses. It has been one of my hopes to add
-----Emacs: dickens.note          (Fundamental)----Top-------------
Find file: ~/ _
```

I type buckaroo, and the editor opens a new buffer and moves me to that file:

```
I found myself stealing a peek at my own watch and overheard
General Catbird's
aide give him the latest.
"He's not even here," went the conversation.
"Who?"
"Banzai."
"Where the hell is he?"
"At the hospital in El Paso."
"What? Why weren't we informed? What's wrong with him?"



-----Emacs: buckaroo            (Fundamental)----All-------------
```

2. Now I'll flip back to the other buffer with C-x b. When I enter that command, however, it doesn't automatically move me there. Instead, it offers this prompt:

```
--**-Emacs: buckaroo            (Fundamental)----All-------------
Switch to buffer: (default dickens.note) _
```

When I type ?, I receive a split screen indicating what the possible answers are here:

```
I found myself stealing a peek at my own watch and overheard
General Catbird's
aide give him the latest.
"He's not even here," went the conversation.
"Who?"
"Banzai."
"Where the hell is he?"
"At the hospital in El Paso."
"What? Why weren't we informed? What's wrong with him?"




--**-Emacs: buckaroo            (Fundamental)----All--------------
Possible completions are:
*Buffer List*                   *Help*
*scratch*                       buckaroo
dickens.note




-----Emacs:  *Completions*      (Fundamental)----All--------------
Switch to buffer: (default dickens.note) _
```

The default is okay, so I press Return. Voilà! I'm back in the Dickens file. One more C-x b; this time the default is buckaroo, so I again press Return to move back.

3. I'm in the buckaroo file, and I want to see what happens if I read dickens.note into this file. This is done easily. I move the cursor to the end of the file with M->, press C-x i, and answer dickens.note to the prompt Insert file: ~/. Pressing Return yields the following screen display:

```
I found myself stealing a peek at my own watch and overheard
General Catbird's
aide give him the latest.
"He's not even here," went the conversation.
"Who?"
"Banzai."
"Where the hell is he?"
"At the hospital in El Paso."
"What? Why weren't we informed? What's wrong with him?"
```

```
                      A Tale of Two Cities
                           Preface

When I was acting, with my children and friends, in Mr Wilkie
Collins's drama of The Frozen Deep, I first conceived the main idea
of this story. A strong desire came upon me then, to
embody it in my own person;
and I traced out in my fancy, the state of mind of which it would
necessitate the presentation
to an observant spectator, with particular
care and interest.


As the idea became familiar to me, it gradually shaped itself into
its present form. Throughout its execution, it has had complete possession
--**-Emacs: buckaroo              (Fundamental)----Top--------------
```

4. It's time to quit and split. To do this, I press C-x s and wait for an emacs prompt or two. The first one displayed is this:

```
As the idea became familiar to me, it gradually shaped itself into
its present form. Throughout its execution, it has had complete possession
--**-Emacs: buckaroo              (Fundamental)----Top--------------
Save file /users/taylor/buckaroo? (y or n) _
```

I answer y to save this muddled file. I'm returned to the top of the file, and a quick C-x C-c drops me back to the system prompt.

One of the more useful facets of emacs you have learned about is the capability to work with multiple files.

Summary

You have now learned quite a bit about the emacs editor. Some capabilities exceed those of the vi editor, and some are considerably more confusing. Which of these editors you choose is up to you, and your choice should be based on your own preferences for working on files. You should spend some time working with the editor you prefer, making sure that you can create simple files and modify them without any problems.

Workshop

The Workshop summarizes the key terms you've learned and poses some questions about the topics presented in this lesson. It also provides you with a preview of what you will learn in the next hour.

Key Terms

buffer   An area of the screen used to edit a file in `emacs`, the buffer actually represents a portion of memory used to store that information.

flow control   The protocol used by a computer and terminal to make sure that neither outpaces the other during data transmission.

key bindings   This is the `emacs` term for key mapping.

Meta key   A key that is labeled either Meta or Alt on a keyboard. It is used much like the Control key in keyboard shortcuts.

named `emacs` command   Some commands in `emacs` require you to type the command name, such as `query-replace`, rather than use a command key or two.

XON/XOFF   This is a particular type of flow control in which the receiving end can send an XON (delay transmission) character until it's ready for more information, when it sends an XOFF (resume transmission).

Exercises

1. How do you get to the `emacs` help system?

2. Check your keyboard. If you don't have a Meta or Alt key, what alternative strategy can you use to enter commands such as M-x?

3. What's the command sequence for leaving `emacs` when you're done?

4. What was the problem you might have with the Delete key? How can you solve that problem? What's the alternative delete command if Delete isn't available?

5. How do you do global search-and-replace in `emacs`, and what key do you press to stop a global search-and-replace when you are prompted for confirmation at the first match?

6. Use the `emacs` help system to list the `emacs` copyright information. What's your reaction?

Preview of the Next Hour

The next hour takes an in-depth look at the different shells available in Unix, how to configure them, and how to choose which you'd like to use. You will also learn about the contents of the default configuration files for both `csh` and `sh`, the two most common shells in Unix.

Introduction to Command Shells

Goals for This Hour

In this hour, you will learn

▶ What shells are available and how they differ from one another

▶ How to identify which shell you're running

▶ How to choose a new shell

▶ More about the environment of your shell

▶ How to explore `bash` configuration files

Welcome to your 13th hour of learning Unix. Don't worry, this is a lucky hour: No horror film tropes to worry about. Actually, you should take a moment to pat yourself on the back. You've come a long way, and you're already quite a sophisticated user. In the past few hours, I've occasionally touched on the differences between the various command shells, but I haven't really stopped to explain what shells are available, how they differ from one another, and which is the best for your style of interaction. That's what this hour is all about.

Shells, you'll recall, are the command-line interface programs through which you tell the computer what to do. All Unix systems include the C shell (`csh`) and its predecessor, the Bourne shell (`sh`). All modern Unix systems also include some nifty newer shells, notably Korn shell (`ksh`) and a new rewrite of `sh` humorously called the Bourne Again shell (`bash`). It's the `bash` shell that I'm going to focus on for all our shell-specific discussion because it's one of the most popular shells, and it's so powerful and flexible—it includes all the cool features of both `csh` and `sh` and adds tons of additional stuff—that it's a great place to start.

Various shells are available in Unix, but two are guaranteed to be included in just about all Unix versions: the Bourne shell (`sh`) and the C shell (`csh`). Primarily, however, you'll learn about `bash` and `ksh` in this lesson.

The (Command) Shell Game

You can't get very far with Unix on most systems without having a command-line interpreter. This lesson gets quickly you up and running with the `bash` command shell.

Task 13.1: What Shells Are Available?

If I asked an expert how many command interpreters are available for the PC, the immediate answer would be "one, of course." After a few minutes of reflection, however, the answer might be expanded to include the classic DOS command line (which is still in Windows!) and various third-party interfaces as well as the standard Windows user interface. This expanded answer reflects the reality that whenever different people use a computer, different styles of interacting with the machine and different products to meet these needs evolve. Similarly, the Macintosh has several command interpreters. If you decide that you don't like the standard GUI, perhaps you will find that the command-line Terminal app or even the X11 environment works better.

From the very beginning, Unix has been a programmer's operating system, designed to allow programmers to extend the system easily and gracefully. It should come as no surprise that quite a few command shells are available. Not only that, but technically any program can serve as a command shell, so you could even start right in emacs if you wanted and then use escapes to Unix for actual commands. (Don't laugh! I know people who've done this.)

The original shell was written by Ken Thompson, back in the early Unix laboratory days, as part of his design of the Unix file system. Somewhere along the way, Steven Bourne, also at AT&T, got ahold of the shell and started expanding it. By the time Unix began to be widely distributed, sh was known as the Bourne shell. Characterized by speed and simplicity, it was the default shell for writing shell scripts, but now it is rarely used as a command shell for users.

The next shell was designed by the productive Bill Joy, author of vi. Entranced by the design and features of the C programming language, Joy decided to create a command shell that shared much of the C language structure and that would make it easier to write sophisticated shell scripts: the C shell, or csh. He also expanded the shell concept to add command aliases, command history, and job control. *Command aliases* enable users to rename and reconfigure commands easily. *Command history* ensures that users never have to enter commands a second time. *Job control* enables users to run multiple programs at once. Before bash appeared on the scene, the C shell was the shell I used from the day I first logged in to a BSD Unix system in 1980.

NOTE

A *command alias* is a shortcut for a command that allows you to enter a shorter string for the entire command. The *command history* is a mechanism by which the shell remembers commands you have typed and allows you to repeat the command without retyping the whole command. *Job control* is a mechanism that allows you to start, stop, and suspend commands.

In the 1990s, another AT&T Labs (now Lucent) software wizard, David Korn, built an eponymous shell. The Korn shell, also known as ksh, is designed to be a superset of the Bourne shell, sharing its configuration files (.profile) and command syntax but including many of the more powerful features of the C shell, too, including command aliases (albeit in a slightly different format), command history, and job control. You might not have it on your version of Unix.

The shell we focus on in this book, however, was written as part of the extensive GNU Project by a large group of programmers known as the Free Software Foundation. The original goal of the GNU Project was to create a version of Unix that was free of any licensing or intellectual property restrictions because both System V and BSD shared core code from an earlier AT&T release and weren't available for free distribution. Although much of what the foundation released was a re-implementation of exactly the same commands that were already part of Unix, it did innovate in a few areas, sometimes spectacularly.

In my eyes, the three best pieces of the GNU Project were the terrific compiler system it developed (gcc, a compiler so good that it then was incorporated into many commercial versions of Unix because it produced better code than the commercial alternative!), the extensively hacked GNU emacs, and the humorously named "Bourne Again shell" (remember that Steve Bourne wrote the original Unix shell), known as bash.

What makes bash such a standout is that the designers included a remarkable set of features and capabilities that enable sh, csh, and ksh users to switch with minimal, if any, changes to their existing keystroke sequences. It's nice to innovate, but forcing users to learn something completely new is a tough road to travel, and the designers avoided that mistake. In addition, bash sports some remarkable features and capabilities all its own.

Check on your Solaris Unix system, and you'll find a ton of shells, actually, including bssh (a specialized version of Bash for browsing possible secure [SSH] connections), jsh (job control shell), pfbash and similar (limited access profile shells), rbash (the "ultra-restricted shell"), remsh (remote shell), rksh (yet another restricted shell), slsh (slang shell), wish (a TCL programming language–related shell), and zsh (yes, yet another command shell option). Linux has its share of different modern shells, too, but I suggest that you stick with bash unless there's a compelling reason to use something else.

Other shells exist in special niches. A modified version of the C shell, tcsh, a version that incorporates the slick history-editing features of the Korn shell, has appeared and is prevalent in the BSD world; for instance, it's the default shell on FreeBSD. Maintained by programmers at Cornell University, it is 95% csh and 5% new features. The most important tcsh additions to the C shell are these:

- ▸ emacs-style command-line editing

- ▸ Visual perusal of the command history list

- ▸ Identifying files with the first few unique characters

- ▸ Spelling correction of commands, filenames, and usernames

- ▸ Automatic logout after an extended idle period

- ▸ The capability to monitor logins, users, or terminals

- ▸ New pre-initialized environment variables $HOST and $HOSTTYPE

- ▸ Support for a meaningful and helpful system status line

Another shell you might bump into is called the MH shell, or `msh`, and it's designed around the MH electronic mail program, originally designed at the Rand Corporation. In essence, the MH shell provides you with instant access to any electronic mail message you receive without requiring you to enter an explicit email program.

For sites that have security considerations, a restricted version of the Bourne shell is also available, called `rsh` (ingeniously, it's the restricted `sh` shell). Persistent rumors of security problems with `rsh` suggest that you should double-check before you trust dubious users on your system with `rsh` as their login shell. (The login shell is the shell you use, by default, when you log in to the system.)

Another variant of the Bourne shell is worth mentioning: `jsh` is a version of the Bourne shell that includes C shell–style job control features.

1. The easiest way to ascertain what shells are available on your system is to look for `*sh` in the `/bin` directory. I'll do this most easily with an `ls` wildcard:

```
$ ls -F /bin/*sh
/bin/csh*   /bin/ksh*   /bin/rksh*   /bin/sh*
```

2. Where's `bash`? Well, different systems have "non-Posix"—which is to say, nonstandard— shells in other places. A smart place to figure out where other shells might be located is to look at your `PATH` environment variable:

```
$ echo $PATH
/usr/bin:/bin:/usr/sbin:/sbin:/usr/X11R6/bin:/usr/local/bin:/home/taylor/bin:
➥ /home/taylor/bin:/home/taylor/bin:/home/taylor/bin:/home/
➥ taylor/bin
```

A lot is in this `PATH`, but I'm looking for other `bin` directories. I can list them all one by one (for example, `ls /sbin/*sh`), but I'm going to use a different strategy: I'm going to explicitly look for the Bourne Again shell:

```
$ which bash
/usr/local/bin/bash
```

Now I know where the system has `bash`; let's see if there are any other shells in this directory:

```
% ls -F /usr/local/bin/*sh
/usr/local/bin/bash*
```

Ah well, that's the only shell in that particular directory.

As you can see, this particular version of Unix offers five different login shells: `csh`, `ksh`, `rksh`, `sh`, and `bash`. I've opted to use `bash` for my interaction with the Unix system. Most likely you'll find more matches when you search for `*sh`. Don't be overwhelmed, though: Most of them are likely not actually command shells. Not sure? Check the man page for the particular command.

Task 13.2: Identifying Your Shell

You can use many different approaches to identify which shell you're using. The easiest, however, is to type echo $SHELL or, if that fails, swoop into the /etc/passwd file to see what your account lists. It's helpful to know some alternatives because searching the /etc/passwd file isn't always an option. (Some systems hide the /etc/passwd file in the interest of security, and others use a shared account database that's on the network but not on that specific system.)

1. One simple technique to identify your shell is to check your prompt. If your prompt contains a %, you probably are using the C shell or modified C shell (tcsh). If your prompt contains $, you could be using the Bourne shell, the Korn shell, bash, or a variant thereof. Another easy way to find out is to check the value of your SHELL environment variable with the echo command:

   ```
   $ echo SHELL
   SHELL
   ```

   Oops! Let's try again, remembering the $ to indicate that we're asking for the value of the variable named SHELL, not the word itself!

   ```
   $ echo $SHELL
   /usr/local/bin/bash
   ```

   (On your system, it might be /bin/bash instead).

2. A cool way to ascertain which shell you're using is to ask the operating system what program you're currently running. The shell variable $$ identifies the process ID of the shell. You can use the helpful ps (*processor status*) command with its -p process flag to see what shell you have. Here's what happens when I try it:

   ```
   $ ps -p $$
     PID TT   STAT      TIME COMMAND
    9503 p0   Ss     0:00.12 -bash (bash)
   ```

   You can see that I'm running bash. There is a leading dash with the indication of what shell I'm running because that's how the system denotes that this particular shell process is my login shell.

3. Another way to find out what shell is running is to peek into the /etc/passwd file, which you can do with grep:

   ```
   % grep taylor /etc/passwd
   taylor:*:1001:999:Dave Taylor,,,:/home/taylor:/usr/local/bin/bash
   taylorsu:*:0:0:Dave as Root:/home/taylorsu:/bin/csh
   ```

   Helpful results, but I ended up with two matches: both the taylor account (which is my current login account) and the taylorsu account, which I don't want to see.

4. Here's the fancy regular expression way to ensure that I match only my current account (refer to Hour 8, "Filters, Pipes, and Wildcards!"):

```
$ grep '^taylor:' /etc/passwd
taylor:*:1001:999:Dave Taylor,,,:/home/taylor:/usr/local/bin/bash
```

That's what I want! In the `/etc/passwd` file, fields of information are separated by colons, and the last field is the login shell. As expected, you can see that it's `/usr/local/bin/bash`.

One more refinement: Use the `cut` command to slice out just the login shell rather than seeing all the stuff in the `/etc/passwd` file:

```
$ grep '^taylor:' /etc/passwd | cut -d: -f7
/usr/local/bin/bash
```

In a nutshell, you tell `cut` to use the `:` as a field delimiter and then show just the seventh field (which is the login shell—count it for yourself).

5. For fun, I used the preceding `cut` command as the basis of a command sequence on a busy system to see what shells people were using. The program extracts the last field of each line in the `password` file and then sorts and counts matches, showing the number of occurrences of the shell, one per line. Ready?

```
$ cut -d: -f7 /etc/passwd | sort | uniq -c
   1 /abuse
 230 /bin/bash
  75 /bin/csh
  23 /bin/ksh
 159 /bin/tcsh
   2 /bin/zsh
 382 /noshell
   3 /usr/local/bin/bash
   6 /usr/local/bin/tcsh
```

As you can see, many people have been disabled with the `noshell` option, and, on this system, `bash` is the most popular. Also note that apparently two versions of `bash` and `tcsh` are present on this system, in two different directories.

NOTE

The `cut` command is a great one to remember when you want to slice a column out of a data file like `/etc/passwd`. Take a minute and learn more about it with `man cut` on your system.

When you've identified your shell, you can contemplate choosing a different one. I suggest that you try `bash` if you aren't using it already because it enables you to try all the examples in the next few lessons for yourself.

Task 13.3: Choosing a New Shell

In the old days of Unix, the only way to switch login shells on many systems was to ask the system administrator to edit the /etc/passwd file directly. This usually meant waiting until the sysadmin had time, which could be hours or even days. The good news is that a simple program now exists to change login shells: chsh, or change shell. It has no starting flags or options, does not require that any files be specified, and can be used regardless of your location in the file system. Just type chsh and press Return.

1. To change my login shell to any of the alternative shells, or even to verify what shell I'm running, I can use the chsh command. The original implementation of chsh had the system prompt for a new shell on the command line:

```
% chsh
Changing login shell for taylor.
Old shell: /bin/csh
New shell: _
```

At this point, the program shows me that I currently have /bin/csh as my login shell and asks me to specify an alternative shell. I'll try to confuse it by requesting that emacs become my login shell:

```
% chsh
Changing login shell for taylor.
Old shell: /bin/csh
New shell: /usr/local/bin/gnuemacs
/usr/local/bin/gnuemacs is unacceptable as a new shell.
```

2. The program has some knowledge of valid shell names as specified by the administrator, and it requires you to specify one. Unfortunately, it doesn't divulge that information, so typing ? to find what's available results in the program complaining that ? is unacceptable as a new shell.

You can, however, peek into the file that this version of chsh uses to confirm which programs are valid shells, if this is what you're seeing as you try this command. The data file is called /etc/shells, and it looks like this:

```
% cat /etc/shells
# List of acceptable shells for chpass(1).
# Ftpd will not allow users to connect who are not using
# one of these shells.

/bin/sh
/bin/csh
/bin/tcsh
/bin/bash
/bin/zsh
/bin/ksh
```

```
/usr/local/bin/ksh
/usr/local/bin/tcsh
/usr/local/bin/bash
```

I'll leave my shell alone and quit `chsh` without making any changes by pressing Enter.
If you'd like to change yours, type in the new name:

```
% chsh
Changing login shell for taylor
Old shell: /bin/csh
New shell: /usr/local/bin/bash
```

Notice that, in typical Unix style, you do not see any actual confirmation that anything
was done. I conclude that, because I did not get any error messages, the program worked.
Fortunately, I can check easily by either using `chsh` again or redoing the `awk` program
with a C shell history command:

```
$ !grep
grep '^taylor:' /etc/passwd | cut -d: -f7
/usr/local/bin/bash
```

In the next hour, you'll learn more about the powerful bash command-history mechanism, but here just notice that I only had to type the first few letters of the previous command to have it automatically run. Quite a time-saver!

NOTE
_____

Because of the popularity of the Bourne Again shell (bash), the next few hours are focused on it. To
get the most out of these hours, I strongly recommend that you use the bash shell.

NOTE
_____

If you can't change your login shell, perhaps because of not having chsh (as is the case on Solaris),
you always can enter bash after you log in by typing bash or replace your login shell with bash by
typing in exec bash instead. That'll work until you log out, at which point you'll be back in your
default login shell on your next login.

It's easy to change your login shell. You can try different shells until you find the one that best
suits your style of interaction. For the most part, though, shells all have the same basic syntax
and use the same commands: `ls -1` does the same thing in any shell. The differences, then,
really come into play when you use the more sophisticated capabilities, including programming the shell (with shell scripts), customizing its features through command aliases, and saving

on keystrokes by using a history mechanism. That's where bash has an edge and why it's so popular. It is easy and straightforward, and it has powerful aliasing, history, and job-control capabilities.

Task 13.4: Learning the Shell Environment

Earlier in this book, you used the env or printenv command to learn the various characteristics of your working environment. Now it's time to use this command again to look more closely at the shell environment and define each of the variables therein.

1. To start out, I enter env to list the various aspects of my working environment. Do the same on your system, and although your environment will not be identical to mine, you should see considerable similarity between the two:

```
% env | cat -n
     1  PWD=/home/taylor
     2  HOSTNAME=staging
     3  USER=taylor
     4  MAIL=/var/mail/taylor
     5  EDITOR=/bin/vi
     6  LOGNAME=taylor
     7  SHLVL=1
     8  SHELL=/usr/local/bin/bash
     9  HOME=/home/taylor
    10  TERM=vt100
    11  PATH=/home/taylor/bin:/usr/bin:/bin:/usr/sbin:/sbin:/usr/X11R6/bin:/
        ➥ usr/local/bin
    12  SSH_TTY=/dev/ttyp0
    13  EXINIT=:set ignorecase
    14   =/usr/bin/env
```

This probably seems pretty overwhelming. What are all these things, and why on earth should they matter? They matter because it's important for you to learn exactly how your own environment is set up so that you can change things if you desire. As you soon will be able to recognize, I have modified much of my system's environment so that the shell does what I want it to do rather than what its default would tell it to do.

2. When I log in to the system, the system defines some environment variables, indicating where my home directory is located, what shell I'm running, and so on. These variables are listed in Table 13.1.

TABLE 13.1 Default Variables Set by Unix on Login

Variable	Description
HOME	This is my home directory, obtained from the fourth field of the password file. Try the command `grep $LOGNAME /etc/passwd	cut -d: -f6` to see what your home directory is set to or just use echo $HOME. This is not only the directory that I start in but also the directory that cd moves me back to when I don't specify a different directory. My HOME variable is /home/taylor.
SHELL	When Unix programs such as vi process the ! command to execute Unix commands, they check this variable to see which shell I'm using. If I were to type :! followed by Return in vi, the program would create a new bash shell for me. If I had SHELL=/bin/sh, vi would start a Bourne shell. My SHELL variable is set to /bin/bash.
TERM	By default, your terminal is defined by the value of this environment variable, which starts out as unknown. (Recall that when you first were learning about vi, the program would complain unknown: terminal not known.) Many sites know what kind of terminals are using which lines, however, so this variable is often set to the correct value before you even see it. If it isn't set, you can define it to the appropriate value within your .profile or .bash_profile file. (You will learn to do this later in the hour.) My TERM is set to vt100, for a Digital Equipment Corporation Visual Terminal model 100, which is probably the most commonly emulated terminal in communications packages.
USER	Programs can quickly look up your user ID and match it with an account name. However, predefining your account name as an environment setting saves time. That's exactly what USER, and its companion LOGNAME, are—time-savers. My USER is set to taylor.
PATH	Earlier, you learned that the Unix shell finds a command by searching from directory to directory until it finds a match. The environment variable that defines which directories to search and the order in which to search them is the PATH variable. Rather than keep the default settings, I've added some directories to my search path, which is now as follows: `/home/taylor/bin:/usr/bin:/bin:/usr/sbin:/sbin:/usr/X11R6/bin:` ➥ `/usr/local/bin` I have told the shell always to look first for commands in my bin directory (/home/taylor/bin) and after that in the standard system directories (/usr/bin, /bin, /usr/sbin, /sbin). If the commands are not found in any of those areas, the shell should try looking in some unusual directories (/usr/X11R6/bin, /usr/local/bin).

Variable	Description
MAIL	One of the most exciting and enjoyable aspects of Unix is its powerful electronic mail capability. Various programs can be used to check for new mail, read mail, and send mail messages. All of these programs need to know where my default incoming mailbox is located, which is what the MAIL environment variable defines. My MAIL is set to /var/mail/taylor.
LOGNAME	LOGNAME is a synonym for USER. My LOGNAME is set to taylor.

CAUTION

Be careful not to use . as the first entry in your PATH because it is a security hazard. Why? Imagine this: A devious chap has written a program that will do bad things to my directory when invoked. But how will he make me invoke it? The easiest way is to give the bad program the same name as a standard Unix utility, such as ls, and leave it in a commonly accessed directory, such as /tmp. Imagine that the . (current directory) is the first entry in my PATH, and I change directories to /tmp to check something. While I'm in /tmp, I enter ls, and I've just run the bad program without knowing it. Having the . at the end of the search path would avoid all this because then the default ls command will always be matched first.

NOTE

Having both LOGNAME and USER defined in my environment demonstrates how far Unix has progressed since the competition and jostling between the Berkeley and AT&T versions (BSD and SVR3, respectively) of Unix. When I started working with Unix, if I was on a BSD system, the account name would be defined as LOGNAME, and if I used an SVR3 system, the account name would be defined as USER. Programs had to check for both, which was frustrating. Over time, each system has begun to use both terms (instead of using the solution that you and I might think is most obvious, which is to agree on a single word).

3. A glance back at the output of the env command reveals that more variables are in my environment than are listed in Table 13.1. That's because you can define anything you want in the environment. Certain programs can read many environment variables that customize their behavior.

Many Unix programs allow you to enter text directly, and then they spin off into an editor, if needed. Others start your favorite editor for entering information. Both types of programs use the EDITOR environment variable to identify which editor to use. I have mine set to /bin/vi.

You learned earlier that vi can have default information stored in the .exrc file, but the program also can read configuration information from the environment variable EXINIT. To make all my pattern searches *not case sensitive* (meaning that a search for precision will match Precision), I set the appropriate vi variable in the EXINIT. Mine is set to

`:set ignorecase`. If you want line numbers to always show up, you could easily have your `EXINIT` set to `:set number`.

The `bash` shell sets some internal variables, too, most notably `SHLVL` (shell level), which tracks how many levels of subshell you're within.

You can define many possible environment variables for yourself. Most large Unix programs have environment variables of their own, enabling you to tailor the program's behavior to your needs and preferences. Unix itself has quite a few environment variables, too. Until you're an expert, however, I recommend that you stick with viewing these variables and ensuring that they have reasonable values rather than changing them. Particularly focus on the set of variables defined in Table 13.1. If they're wrong, you could have trouble, whereas if other environment variables are wrong, you'll be okay; you'll just find that a particular program behaves differently than expected.

Task 13.5: Exploring `bash` Configuration Files

The `bash` shell uses two files to configure itself, and although neither of them needs to be present, both probably can be found in your home directory: `.profile` (or `.bash_profile`) and `.bashrc`. The difference between them is subtle but important. The `.profile` file is read only once, when you log in, and the `.bashrc` file is read every time a shell is started. For example, if you're working in `vi` and you enter `:!ls`, `vi` carries out the command by launching a new subshell and then feeding the command to that shell. Therefore, the new `bash` shell will read what's in `.bashrc` but won't ever read what's in `.profile`.

This split between two configuration files isn't too bad, actually, because most modifications to the environment are automatically included in all subshells (a shell other than the login shell) invoked. To be specific, all environment variables are inherited by subshells, but shell command aliases are lost and, therefore, must be defined in the `.bashrc` file to be available within all occurrences of `bash`. You'll learn more about command aliases in Hour 14, "Advanced Shell Interaction."

1. I use `cat` to list the contents of my `.profile` file. Remember that any line beginning with a # is a comment and is ignored.

```
$ cat .profile
# .profile

# Read in my aliases before going any further
. ~/.bashrc

# Tweak my environment variables to reflect my favorites

PATH=$HOME/bin:$PATH

SHELL=/usr/local/bin/bash
EDITOR="/bin/vi"
EXINIT=":set ignorecase"
```

```
export PATH SHELL EDITOR EXINIT

# now set the prompt to the current directory (base name) and
# the current command number (for "!n" escapes)

PS1='\W \!: '

# I'd like 'vi' style command-line editing, don't want to log
# out when I accidentally type "^D" at the command line, and
# don't want to accidentally delete files if I attempt to
# blindly overwrite them:

set -o vi ignoreeof noclobber

# Finally, I'd like to have the default file permission be
# 755 (rwxr-xr-x) on files/directories, hence this umask

umask 022

newmail
mesg y
```

This is pretty straightforward, after you remove all the comments. Environmental variables are set with the NAME=value lines, and then I ensure that they're available to the current shell (in addition to any subshells) with the export command. To allow me to use any .bashrc aliases or functions within .profile, I start by having the shell read in the file (that's what . means at the beginning of the first non-comment line). You can see that some of the variables shown in the previous unit are defined in my .profile file.

By setting the PS1 variable, I create a custom prompt rather than the default bash prompt of the shell name and a dollar sign (bash2.3$, which isn't very friendly). Instead, I have the prompt set to the base name of the current directory, the command number (in the history list), and a colon (bin 343:, which shows that I'm in the bin directory and that this is the 343rd command in my history list). In the next lesson you'll learn some of the many nifty things you can place in your command prompt.

Finally, the set commands are configuration options for the shell. I have told the shell to ignore ^D sequences at the command line so I don't accidentally log myself out (instead, I'll need to type in exit or logout), and warn me before it overwrites existing files with file redirection (noclobber).

The three commands at the end of the .profile file are invoked as though I'd entered them on the command line. umask sets my default file creation mask, the newmail command informs me when new electronic mail arrives (in the mailbox defined by the environment variable MAIL, in fact). The mesg y variable makes sure that I have my terminal configured so that other folks can beep me or say hello using `talk`, a communication tool discussed in Hour 20, "Communicating with Email."

2. How about the other file—the one that's read by the shell each time a shell or subshell is started?

```
$ cat .bashrc
# .bashrc
# This contains all user specific aliases and functions

# If there are shared global definitions, read them in

if [ -f /etc/bashrc ]; then
  . /etc/bashrc
fi

# now some useful aliases

alias ls="ls -F"
alias who="who | sort"

alias cp="/bin/cp -i"
alias rm="/bin/rm -i"

# Note that these aliases for 'cp' and 'rm' are redundant
# because of the 'set -o noclobber' in my .bash_profile
# file. They're here to show you that there's more than one
# way to minimize the risk of accidentally stepping on and
# deleting files with these commands.
```

Any line that begins with a # is considered a comment and is there just for us humans to read. There are, therefore, very few commands in this file: one that reads a system-wide `.bashrc` if it exists in the `/etc` directory and another that sets a couple of useful command aliases that I prefer.

You'll learn all about aliases in the next hour, but for now you should know that the format is `alias` word=*command* (or commands). When I enter `ls`, for example, you can see that the shell has that aliased to `ls -F`, which saves me from having to type the `-F` flag each time.

The shell also has conditional statements and various other commands that indicate what commands to run. Here I'm using `if [expression]; then` to execute a command only if the file it wants to access exists on the system. The condition `-f /etc/bashrc` is true if the file exists. If not, the condition is false, and the shell zips to the `fi` before resuming execution of the commands.

If you're thinking that there are a tremendous number of ways to configure your shell, you are correct. You can have an incredibly diverse set of commands in both your `.profile` and `.bashrc` files, enabling you to customize many aspects of the shell and the Unix environment. If you use the C shell or the `tcsh` shell, the configuration information is kept in a similar file, called `.login`.

Summary

Armed with the information learned in this hour about shells and shell environments, explore your own environment; examine your `.profile` and `.bashrc` files also.

Workshop

The Workshop summarizes the key terms you've learned and poses some questions about the topics presented in this lesson. It also provides you with a preview of what you will learn in the next hour.

Key Terms

command alias   An alias is a shorthand command mapping, with which you can define new command names that are aliases of other commands or sequences of commands. This is helpful for renaming commands so that you can remember them or for having certain flags added by default.

command history   The shell uses this mechanism to remember what commands you have entered already and to allow you to repeat them without having to type the entire command again.

job control   Job control enables you to manage the various programs that are running. It lets you push programs into the background and pull them back into the foreground as desired.

login shell   This is the shell you use, by default, when you log in to the system.

subshell   This is a shell other than the login shell, which is invoked from within the login shell or another program (for example, by typing `bash` at the command line or by calling the shell from within `emacs`).

Exercises

1. Draw lines to connect the original shells with their newer variants:

   ```
   sh
   ksh
   tcsh
   csh
   bash
   ```

2. What does chsh do?

3. What shell are you running? What shells are your friends on the system running?

4. What's the difference between the .profile file and the .bashrc file?

5. What's the csh equivalent of the bash .profile file?

6. What aliases do you think could prove helpful for your daily Unix interaction?

Preview of the Next Hour

I hope this hour has whetted your appetite for learning more about the shell! In the next hour, you'll learn how to really customize the shell and make your interaction with Unix quite a bit easier. Topics include how to create command aliases, how to use the history mechanism, and how to edit your previously edited commands interactively.

Advanced Shell Interaction

Goals for This Hour

In this hour, you will learn

- ▶ How to turn on the `bash` and `ksh` history mechanism
- ▶ How to use `bash` history and `ksh` history to cut down on typing
- ▶ About command aliases in `bash` and `ksh`
- ▶ Some power aliases for `bash`
- ▶ How to set custom prompts

The preceding hour gave you an overview of the different shells available in Unix. In this hour, you'll learn much more about the `bash` shell and how to use it to your best advantage. You'll also learn valuable tips about working with the immediate predecessor to `bash`, the Korn shell (`ksh`), a popular alternative shell. The goal of this hour is for you to be able to easily customize your Unix environment to fit your working style.

This hour focuses on two key facets of `bash` and `ksh`: the history mechanism and the command alias capability. I guarantee that within a few minutes of learning about these two functions, you will realize that you couldn't have survived in Unix without them. There are actually three ways to ensure that you never need to enter commands more than once: Shell history enables you to repeat previous commands without reentering them, an alias enables you to name one command as another, and shell scripts enable you to place many commands into a file that you can then reference as a new command. The last of these three, shell scripts, is covered in depth in Hour 16, "Shell Programming Overview."

One of the fun parts of Unix is that you can customize the prompt that greets you each time you use the system. There's no need to be trapped with a boring $ prompt anymore! So we'll wrap up by exploring different ways you can customize your shell prompt. Because, well, it's just something you gotta do.

Which Shell Is Which?

Let's dig in and find out about some of the key capabilities of the most popular Unix command shells.

Task 14.1: The Shell History Mechanisms

You have doubtless heard the aphorism "Those who do not study history are doomed to repeat it." Unix stands this concept on its head. For Unix, it's better stated "Those who are aware of their history can easily repeat it."

Both `bash` and `ksh` build a list of commands as you enter them and assign each of them a command number. Each time you log in, the first command you enter is command #1, and the command number is incremented for each subsequent command you enter. You can review or repeat any previous command easily with just a few keystrokes.

Unlike earlier command shells, such as C shell, both `bash` and `ksh` have a default history list of 128 or more commands, which is plenty for anyone. To review your history, you can use the `history` command. Secretly, though, it's an alias: The real command for both shells is the more cryptic `fc -l`.

1. Log in to your system so that you have a shell prompt. If you're currently in the C shell or a shell other than `bash`, this would be a great time to use `chsh` to change shells (see Hour 13, "Introduction to Command Shells," for more details on how to change your login shell):

```
% history 10
  270   more /etc/shells
  271   exit
  272   ls
  273
  274   grep '^taylor:' /etc/passwd
  275   grep '^taylor:' /etc/passwd | cut -d: -f7
  276   env
  277   printenv
  278   alias
  279   exit
  280   history 10
$
```

I just logged in. Where'd all this come from?

Notice command #279: `exit`. That's giving you the clue. The shell remembers commands across different invocations, so the commands I see on this list are from the last time I logged in! (In fact, #271 is `exit`, too, so command #270 is actually from two logins ago.)

2. You can change whether your history is remembered across login sessions, and you can also change the size of the history list. Both of these are done with environment variables. Let's see if any of them are set. First:

```
% echo $HISTSIZE $HISTFILESIZE
500  500
```

This indicates that bash is keeping track of the 500 most recent commands I've typed in and will also store 500 commands in my history file so that they'll be automatically available next time I log in.

3. If 500 seems too large, this is easily set to a different value, ideally in .bash_profile or .profile:

```
export HISTSIZE=200
```

If for some strange reason you don't seem to have any history (the default value is 500, so having it explicitly set to 0 would be a bit weird), you can turn on the feature by specifying a HISTSIZE, as shown above.

You shouldn't end up having to do anything to get your history mechanism enabled for your shell, but now you know how, if it's necessary.

One final note: C shell requires most people to fiddle with the environment variables, too. Look for set history=200 or set savehist=200 in the .cshrc (though a better alternative is to simply switch to bash instead).

Task 14.2: Using History to Cut Down on Typing

There are three main mechanisms for working with the history list. You can specify a previous command by its command number, by the first few characters of the command, or, if you've set your command editing parameters, interactively on the command line.

Non-interactive history commands begin with an exclamation point. If the 33rd command you entered was the who command, for example, you can execute it by referring to its command number: Enter !33 at the command prompt. You can also execute it by entering one or more characters of the command: !w, !wh, or !who. Be careful, though: The most recent match is invoked without confirmation, so if you typed who but afterward typed an alias to the rm command called wipeout, it would be the latter that would match the !w sequence, but the former would match !wh or !who.

A very useful shorthand is !!, which repeats the most recently executed command. Two other history references are valuable to know: !$ expands to the last word of the preceding command (which makes sense because $ always refers to the end of something, whether it be a line, the file, or, in this case, a command), and !* expands to all the words in the preceding command except the first word. So, for example, if I entered the command ls /usr /etc /dev and then immediately entered echo !*, it would be expanded automatically to echo /usr /etc /dev.

1. First, I need to spend a few minutes building up a history list by running various commands:

```
$ cat buckaroo
I found myself stealing a peek at my own watch and overhead
General Catbird's
aide give him the latest.
"He's not even here," went the conversation.
"Who?"
"Banzai."
"Where the hell is he?"
"At the hospital in El Paso."
"What? Why weren't we informed? What's wrong with him?"
$ who
taylor   ttyp0    May  1 11:50  (198.76.82.151)
$ date
Sat Mar  7 13:26:26 MST 2015
$ echo $HISTSIZE $HOME
500 /home/taylor
$
```

2. Now I will check my history list to see what commands are squirreled away for later:

```
% history 10
  310  echo $HISTFILESIZE
  311  who
  312  ls
  313  vi buckaroo
  314  cat buckaroo
  315  who
  316  date
  317  echo $HISTSIZE $HOME
  318  history 10
```

3. To repeat the date command, I can specify its command number:

```
% !316
date
Sat Mar  7 13:26:38 MST 2015
```

Notice that the shell shows the command I've entered as command number 316 (date) and then executes it. The ksh equivalent here would be r 316.

4. A second way to accomplish this repeat—a way that is much easier—is to specify the first letter of the command:

```
% !w
who
taylor   ttyp0    Feb  1 11:50  (198.76.82.151)
```

5. Now glance at the history list:

```
% history 10
  314  cat buckaroo
  315  who
  316  date
  317  echo $HISTSIZE $HOME
  318  history 10
  319  cat buckaroo
  320  date
  321  who
  322  history 10
```

Commands expanded by the history mechanism are stored as the expanded command, not as the history repeat sequence that was actually entered. Thus, this is an exception to the earlier rule that the history mechanism always shows what was previously entered. It's an eminently helpful exception, however!

History commands are quite helpful for people working on a software program. The most common cycle for programmers to repeat is edit-compile-run, over and over again. The commands Unix programmers use most often probably will look something like vi test.c, cc -o test test.c, and ./test, to edit, compile, and run the program, respectively. Using the shell history mechanism, a programmer easily can enter !v to edit the file, !c to compile it, and then !. to test it. As your commands become longer and more complex, this function proves more and more helpful.

6. It's time to experiment a bit with file wildcards:

```
% ls
Archives          awkscript          dickens.note     src
InfoWorld         bin                keylime.pie      temp
Mail              buckaroo           owl.c
News              buckaroo.confused  sample
OWL               cshrc              sample2x
```

Oops! I meant to specify the -F flag to ls. I can use !! to repeat the command; then I can add the flag:

```
% !! -F
ls -F
Archives/         awkscript          dickens.note     src/
InfoWorld/        bin/               keylime.pie      temp/
Mail/             buckaroo           owl.c
News/             buckaroo.confused  sample
OWL/              cshrc              sample2
```

NOTE

The general idea of all these history mechanisms is that you specify a pattern that is replaced by the appropriate command in the history list. So you could enter echo !! to have the system echo the last command, and it would end up echoing twice. Try it.

I want to figure out a pattern or two that will let me specify both buckaroo files, the dickens file, and sample2, but not sample. This is a fine example of where the echo command can be helpful:

```
% echo b* d* s*
bin buckaroo buckaroo.confused dickens.note sample sample2 src
```

That's not quite it. I'll try again:

```
% echo bu* d* sa*
buckaroo buckaroo.confused dickens.note sample sample2
```

That's closer. Now I just need to remove the sample file:

```
% echo bu* d* sa*2
buckaroo buckaroo.confused dickens.note sample2
```

That's it. Check out that complex pattern, too: sa*2.

Now I want to compute the number of lines in each of these files. If I use the csh history mechanism, I can avoid having to enter the filenames again:

```
% wc -l !*
wc -l bu* d* sa*2
      36 buckaroo
      11 buckaroo.confused
      28 dickens.note
       4 sample2
      79 total
```

Notice that the !* expanded to the entire preceding command *except the very first word*.

7. What happens if I use !$ instead?

```
% wc -l !$
wc -l sa*2
       4 sample2
```

8. If you are using bash, here's where it truly shines! Set the editor preference within the shell to either vi or emacs. I prefer the former, so I use:

```
$ set -o vi
$
```

Now, any time I'm entering a command, I can press the Escape key and be in bash history-edit command mode. The usual vi commands work, including h and l to move left and right; i and Escape to enter and leave insert mode; w, W, b, and B to zip about by words; and 0 and $ to move to the beginning or end of the line.

Much more useful are k and j, which replace the current command with the preceding or next, enabling you to zip through the history list.

If I'd just entered who and then ls, to append | wc -l to the who command, I could press the Escape key:

```
$ [_]
```

Now each time I type k, I will see the preceding command. Typing k one time reveals this:

```
$ ls
```

Typing k a second time reveals this:

```
$ who
```

That's the right command, so $ moves the cursor to the end of the line:

```
$ who
```

Typing a appends, at which point I can add | wc -l like this:

```
$ who | wc -l
```

Pressing Return results in ksh actually executing the command:

```
$ who | wc -l
     1
$
```

NOTE

A lot of modern Unix shells let you move up and down through your command history with the arrow keys. For example, on Mac OS X, the up arrow moves earlier and earlier into the history list, while the down arrow shows increasingly recent commands. That's probably a lot easier for you to remember than the emacs or vi motion key sequences!

TIP

Even with arrow-key navigation, you might find yourself having to repeatedly scroll into your history to find a frequently invoked but complicated command. The bash shell has another trick up its sleeve: the ^r command, which searches your history for the most recent match of whatever you type. Press ^r and then type a few letters, and your command line will automatically be filled out with the latest matching command you entered.

The history mechanisms of the shells are wonderful time-savers when you're working with files. I find myself using the bash !! and !*word* mechanisms daily either to repeat intricate commands (such as the preceding example, in which I built up a very complex command, step by step) or to repeat the most recently used edit commands. Table 14.1 summarizes the available bash history mechanisms. I encourage you to learn and use them. They will soon become second nature and save you lots of typing as you proceed.

TABLE 14.1 Bash History Commands

Command	Function
!!	Repeat the last command.
!$	Repeat the last word of the preceding command.
!*	Repeat all but the first word of the preceding command.
^*a*^*b*	Replace *a* with *b* in the preceding command and then re-invoke it.
!*ptrn*	Repeat the most recent command that starts with *ptrn*.
!*n*	Repeat command number *n* from the history list.

Task 14.3: Command Aliases

If you think the history mechanism has the potential to save you typing, you'll be glad to learn about the command-alias mechanism in bash and ksh. Using aliases, you can easily define new commands that do whatever you'd like, or you can even redefine existing commands to work differently, have different default flags, or more!

The general format for using the alias mechanism in both shells is alias *word=commands*. If you enter alias without any specified words, the output shows a list of aliases you have defined. If you enter alias *word*, the output lists the current alias, if there is one, for the specified word.

1. One of the most helpful aliases you can create specifies certain flags to ls so that each time you enter ls, the output will look as though you used the flags with the command. I like to have the -F flag set:

```
% ls
Archives           awkscript          dickens.note       src
InfoWorld          bin                keylime.pie        temp
Mail               buckaroo           owl.c
News               buckaroo.confused  sample
OWL                cshrc              sample2
```

Now I'll create a bash alias and try it again:

```
% alias ls='ls -CF'
% ls
Archives/              awkscript            dickens.note        src/
InfoWorld/             bin/                 keylime.pie         temp/
Mail/                  buckaroo             owl.c
News/                  buckaroo.confused    sample
OWL/                   cshrc                sample2
```

This is very helpful!

2. If you're really an old timer, just came out of your digital cave, and are migrating to Unix from the MS-DOS world, you might find some of the Unix file commands confusing. In MS-DOS, for example, you use DIR to list directories, REN to rename files, COPY to copy them, and so on. With aliases, you can re-create all those commands and map them to specific Unix equivalents:

```
% alias DIR 'ls -lF'
% alias REN 'mv'
% alias COPY 'cp -I'
% alias DEL 'rm -I'
% DIR
total 33
drwx------    2 taylor          512 Nov 21 10:39 Archives/
drwx------    3 taylor          512 Dec  3 02:03 InfoWorld/
drwx------    2 taylor         1024 Dec  3 01:43 Mail/
drwx------    2 taylor          512 Oct  6 09:36 News/
drwx------    4 taylor          532 Dec  6 18:31 OWL/
-rw-rw----    1 taylor          126 Dec  3 16:34 awkscript
drwx------    2 taylor          512 Oct 13 10:45 bin/
-rw-rw----    1 taylor         1393 Dec  5 18:48 buckaroo
-rw-rw----    1 taylor          458 Dec  4 23:22 buckaroo.confused
-rw-------    1 taylor         1339 Dec  2 10:30 cshrc
-rw-rw----    1 taylor         1123 Dec  5 18:16 dickens.note
-rw-rw----    1 taylor        12556 Nov 16 09:49 keylime.pie
-rw-rw----    1 taylor         8729 Dec  2 21:19 owl.c
-rw-rw----    1 taylor          199 Dec  3 16:11 sample
-rw-rw----    1 taylor          207 Dec  3 16:11 sample2
drwx------    2 taylor          512 Oct 13 10:45 src/
drwxrwx---    2 taylor          512 Nov  8 22:20 temp/
% COPY sample newsample
%
```

3. To see what aliases have been defined, use the alias command:

```
% alias
alias COPY='cp -i'
alias DEL='rm -i'
alias DIR='ls -lF'
```

4. You could improve the alias for DIR by having the output of ls fed directly into the less program so that a directory listing with a lot of output will automatically pause at the end of each page. To redefine an alias, just define it again:

```
% alias DIR= 'ls -1F | less'
```

To confirm that the alias is set as you desire, try this:

```
% alias DIR
alias DIR='ls -1F | less'
```

NOTE

If you're defining just one command with an alias, you don't really need to use the quotation marks around the command argument. But what would happen if you entered alias DIR ls -1F | more? The alias would be set to ls -1F, and the output of the alias command would be fed to the more program, which is quite different from what you desired. Therefore, it's just good form to use the quotation marks, and it's a good habit to get into.

Aliases are a great addition to any command shell, and with the arcane Unix commands, they also can be used to define full-word commands as synonyms. For example, if you decide you'd like the simplicity of remembering only the command move to move a file somewhere else, you could add the new alias alias move='mv' to your .bashrc, and the shell would include a new command.

The only warning I'll share is that if you become highly reliant on specific aliases, you might find it frustrating if you ever have to use a different Unix or Linux system that doesn't include your .bashrc (or equivalent). Just something to keep in mind before you do something, um, bizarre like duplicate the MS-DOS command line interface.

Task 14.4: Some Power Aliases

Because I have used the C shell for many years, I have created various aliases to help me work efficiently. A few of the best are shown in this section.

1. To see what aliases I have defined, I can use the same command I used earlier after having read in a different .bashrc file that defines all these additional aliases:

```
% alias
alias diff='/usr/bin/diff -c -w'
alias from='frm -n'
alias ls='/bin/ls -F'
alias mail='Mail'
alias mailq='/usr/lib/sendmail -bp'
alias newaliases='echo you mean newalias...'
alias rn='/usr/local/bin/rn -d$HOME -L -M -m -e -S -/'
alias intuitive='echo Intuitive.com;echo '\''MyPassWord.'\''|pbcopy;ssh
dtaylor@intuitive.com'
```

Recall that each of these aliases started out in my `.bashrc` file:

```
% grep alias .bashrc
alias   diff='/usr/bin/diff -c -w'
alias   from='frm -n'
alias   ll='ls -l'
alias   ls='/bin/ls -F'
alias   mail=Mail
alias   mailq='/usr/lib/sendmail -bp'
alias   newaliases='echo you mean newalias...'
alias   rn='/usr/local/bin/rn -d$HOME -L -M -m -e -S -/'
alias intuitive='echo Intuitive.com; \
   echo '\''MyPassWord.'\''| pbcopy;ssh dtaylor@intuitive.com'
```

Also notice that the shell always shows an alphabetically sorted list of aliases, regardless of the order in which they were defined.

Most of these aliases are easy to understand. For example, the first alias, `diff`, ensures that the command `diff` always has the default flags `-c` and `-w`. If I enter `from`, I want the system to invoke `frm -n`; if I enter `ll`, I want the system to invoke `ls -l`; and so on.

2. Some commands can cause trouble if entered, so creating an alias for each of those commands is a good way to stay out of trouble. For example, I have an alias for `newaliases`; if I accidentally enter that command, the system gently reminds me that I probably meant to use the `newalias` command:

```
$ newaliases
you mean newalias...
```

3. I have created aliases for connecting to accounts on other systems. I like to name each alias after the system to which I'm connecting (for example, `intuitive`):

```
$ alias intuitive
alias intuitive='echo Intuitive.com;echo '\''MyPassWord.'\''| pbcopy;ssh
➥ dtaylor@intuitive.com'
```

Separating commands with a semicolon is the Unix way of having multiple commands on a single line, so when I enter the alias `sunworld`, for example, it's as if I'd entered all these commands one after another:

```
echo Intuitive.com
echo 'MyPassWord.' | pbcopy
ssh dtaylor@intuitive.com
```

Before you get too excited, no, "MyPassWord." is not my real account password!

Using aliases is a great way to really customize your command interface. I always tweak the set of commands and the default flags. (For example, look at all the options I set as default values for the `rn` command.) I even effectively disable commands that I don't want to enter accidentally.

Let your imagination run wild with aliases! If you decide you really like one and you're using bash, add the alias to your .bashrc file so that it's permanent. (You can also put these into your .profile file if you prefer.) If you want to temporarily have the system "forget" an alias, you can use the unalias command, and it's gone until you log in again. For example, unalias intuitive would temporarily remove from the shell the intuitive alias shown earlier.

Task 14.5: Setting Custom Prompts

Up to this point, the command prompt you've seen is a boring $. It turns out that bash lets you set your prompt to just about any possible value, with PS1="value". Note that PS1 must be all uppercase for this to work.

1. I'm getting tired of Unix being so blunt and impolite. Fortunately, I easily can change how it responds to me:

   ```
   % PS1="Yes, master? "
   Yes, master?
   ```

   That's more like it!

2. There are a lot of things you can tuck away in your prompt that can be of great help, and they all take the form of \x. The first useful variable is \w, which holds the current working directory:

   ```
   Yes, master? PS1="In \w, oh master: "
   In /users/taylor, oh master:
   ```

   What happens if I change directories?

   ```
   In /users/taylor, oh master: cd /
   In /, oh master:
   ```

   Cool, eh?

3. There are a lot of different variables you can add, the most useful of which are shown in Table 14.2.

TABLE 14.2 Special Values for the System Prompt

Value	Expands to
\d	The date, in *Weekday Month Day* format (example: Thu Feb 1)
\H	The full system hostname (example: limbo.intuitive.com)
\h	The system name (example: limbo)
\n	Carriage return sequence (yes, you can have a two-line prompt, if you want!)
\s	The name of the shell (example: bash2.4)

Value	Expands to
\T	Current time, in HH:MM:SS format (example: 04:23:28)
\t	Same as \T, but in 24 hour format (example: 16:23:28)
\@	Current time in am/pm format (example: 04:23pm)
\u	Username of the current user (example: taylor)
\w	Current working directory (example: /home/taylor/bin)
\W	Base name of current directory (example: bin)

Remember how you learned earlier this hour about using the command numbers to repeat commands (like !37 to repeat command #37)? It turns out that there's an environment variable HISTCMD that contains the current command number. Fortunately, you can use a shortcut:

```
In /, oh master: PS1="(The current command is #\!) $ "
(The current command is #132) $
```

The number shown is the command number, as used by the shell history mechanism, with a slightly more succinct variation:

```
(132) $ echo hi
hi
(133) $ ls News
mailing.lists.usenet   usenet.1              usenet.alt
(134) $ !132
echo hi
hi
(135) $
```

Here's another example that you might find valuable:

```
(135) % PS1="\h (\!) % "
limbo (136) $
```

This is close to what I use myself, but I like to include the *basename* of the current directory. Basename means the name of the closest directory, so the basename of /home/taylor is taylor, for example. Also, I replace the dollar sign with a colon, which is a bit easier on the eyes:

```
limbo (136) $ PS1="\h (\W) \! : "
limbo (taylor) 137 :
```

Experiment until you find a set of variables that can help you customize your Unix prompt. I strongly recommend that you use command numbers to familiarize yourself with the history mechanism.

Taking advantage of the command-alias capability is a helpful way to cut down on entering short commands time and again, but what if you have a series of 5 or 10 commands you often enter in sequence? That's where shell scripts can help (see Hour 16).

Summary

This hour introduced you to many of the most powerful aspects of Unix command shells. Practice creating aliases and working with the history list to minimize your typing. Also, find a prompt you like and set it in your `.bashrc` or `.profile` so that it will be your default.

Workshop

The Workshop summarizes the key terms you've learned and poses some questions about the topics presented in this lesson. It also provides you with a preview of what you will learn in the next hour.

Key Terms

basename   The basename is the name of the closest directory. For example, the basename of `/usr/home/taylor` is `taylor`.

command number   The unique number by which the shell indexes all commands. You can place this number in your prompt by using `\$HISTCMD` and use it with the history mechanism as `!command-number`.

Exercises

1. How do you tell `bash` that you want it to remember the last 30 commands during a session and to remember the last 10 commands across login sessions?

2. Assume that you get the following output from entering `history`:

   ```
   1    ls -CF
   2    who | grep andrews
   3    wc -l < test
   4    cat test
   5    history
   ```

   What would be the result of entering each of the following history commands?

   ```
   !2     !w     !wh     echo !1
   ```

3. Some Unix systems won't enable you to use the following. What danger do you see lurking in this alias?

   ```
   alias who    who -a
   ```

4. Which of the following aliases do you think would be useful?

```
alias alias='who'
alias ls='cp'
alias copy='cp -'
alias logout='vi'
alias vi='logout'
alias bye='logout'
```

5. Set your prompt to the following value. Remember that 33 should be replaced with the appropriate command number each time:

```
#33 - I know lots about Unix. For example:
```

Preview of the Next Hour

In the next hour, you'll learn how to get even more out of your shell. You'll learn about shell programming and how to create shell programs on-the-fly.

HOUR 15
Job Control

Goals for This Hour

In this hour, you will learn

- ▶ About job control in the shell: stopping jobs
- ▶ How to put jobs in the background and bring them back to the foreground
- ▶ How to find out what tasks are running by using `jobs` and `ps`
- ▶ How to terminate errant processes by using `kill`

In this hour you will learn about how Unix handles jobs and how you can manipulate them. Commands you will learn include `jobs` and `ps`, to see what processes are running; `fg` and `bg`, to move jobs back and forth between the foreground and background; and `kill`, to terminate jobs you no longer want around.

This hour presents an explanation of a Unix philosophical puzzle: What is a running program? To learn the answer, you are introduced to `ps` and `jobs`, for controlling processes; `fg` and `bg`, to move your own processes back and forth between the foreground and background; and the quasi-omnipotent `kill` command, for stopping programs in their proverbial tracks.

Wrestling with Your Jobs

Every program you run is a job, according to the Unix system, and although it might not be obvious, you have the ability to start and stop jobs at any time.

Task 15.1: Job Control in the Shell: Stopping Jobs

Whether you're requesting a man page, listing files with `ls`, starting `vi`, or running just about any Unix command, you're starting one or more processes. In Unix, any program that's running is a *process*. You can have multiple processes running at once. The pipeline `ls -l | sort | more` invokes three processes: `ls`, `sort`, and `more`. Processes in both the C and Korn shells are also known as *jobs*, and the program you're running is known as the *current* or *active job*.

Any job or process can have various states, with "running" being the most typical state. In both shells, you can stop a job by pressing ^z. To restart it, enter fg (foreground) when you are ready.

1. Earlier I was perusing the man page entry for sort. I had reached the bottom of the first screen:

```
$ man sort

SORT(1)                 DYNIX Programmer's Manual               SORT(1)

NAME
     sort - sort or merge files

SYNOPSIS
     sort [ -mubdfinrtx ] [ +pos1 [ -pos2 ] ] ... [ -o name ] [
     -T directory ] [ name ] ...

DESCRIPTION
     Sort sorts lines of all the named files together and writes
     the result on the standard output.  The name `-' means the
     standard input.  If no input files are named, the standard
     input is sorted.

     The default sort key is an entire line.  Default ordering is
     lexicographic by bytes in machine collating sequence.  The
     ordering is affected globally by the following options, one
     or more of which may appear.

     b    Ignore leading blanks (spaces and tabs) in field com-
--More--
```

I'd like to try using the -b flag mentioned at the bottom of this screen, but I want to read the rest of the man page, too. Instead of typing q to quit and then restarting the man program later, I can stop the program. I press ^z and see this:

```
     ordering is affected globally by the following options, one
     or more of which may appear.

     b    Ignore leading blanks (spaces and tabs) in field com-
--More--
Stopped
$
```

At this point, I can do whatever I'd like:

```
$ ls -sF | sort -b | head -4
   1 Archives/
   1 InfoWorld/
   1 Mail/
   1 News/
   1 OWL/
```

2. I can resume the stopped job at any time, too. I enter fg, the program reminds me where I was, and man (which is actually the more program invoked by man) returns to its prompt:

```
$ fg
man sort
--More--
$
```

3. Screen-oriented programs are even smarter about stopping and starting. For example, vi refreshes the entire screen when you return from it having been stopped. If I were in vi working on the dickens.note file, the screen would look like this:

```
                    A Tale of Two Cities
                         Preface

When I was acting, with my children and friends, in Mr Wilkie
Collins's drama of The Frozen Deep, I first conceived the main idea
 of this story.  A strong desire came upon me then, to
embody it in my own person;
and I traced out in my fancy, the state of mind of which it would
necessitate the presentation
to an observant spectator, with particular
care and interest.

As the idea became familiar to me, it gradually shaped itself into its
present form.  Throughout its execution, it has had complete possession of me;
 I have so far verified what
is done and suffered in these pages,
as that I have certainly done and suffered it all myself.

Whenever any reference (however slight) is made here to the condition
of the Danish people before or during the Revolution, it is truly made,
 on the faith of the most trustworthy
witnesses.  It has been one of my hopes to add
something to the popular and picturesque means of
"dickens.note" 28 lines, 1123 characters
```

Pressing `^z` would result in this:

```
witnesses.  It has been one of my hopes to add
something to the popular and picturesque means of
"dickens.note" 28 lines, 1123 characters


Stopped
$
```

I can check to see whether someone is logged in and then return to `vi` with the `fg` command:

```
$ who | grep marv
$ fg
```

```
                    A Tale of Two Cities
                          Preface

When I was acting, with my children and friends, in Mr Wilkie
Collins's drama of The Frozen Deep, I first conceived the main idea of this
story.  A strong desire came upon me then, to
embody it in my own person;
and I traced out in my fancy, the state of mind of which it would
necessitate the presentation
to an observant spectator, with particular
care and interest.

As the idea became familiar to me, it gradually shaped itself
into its present form.  Throughout its execution, it has had complete
 possession of me; I have so far verified what
is done and suffered in these pages,
as that I have certainly done and suffered it all myself.

Whenever any reference (however slight) is made here to the condition
of the Danish people before or during the Revolution, it is truly made,
on the faith of the most trustworthy
witnesses.  It has been one of my hopes to add
something to the popular and picturesque means of
"dickens.note" 28 lines, 1123 characters
```

Processes and jobs in Unix have many aspects, particularly regarding the level of control offered by the shell. The rest of this hour explains how to exploit these capabilities to make your work easier and faster.

Task 15.2: Foreground/Background and Unix Programs

Now that you know how to suspend programs (freezing them in their tracks), it's time to learn how to allow them to keep running in the background (by using the `bg` command) while you're doing something else and how to have programs start in the background by using the `&` suffix.

In the first hour, you learned that one of the distinguishing characteristics of Unix is that it's a true multitasking operating system. It is capable of running hundreds of programs at the same time. This applies to any program from a simple command-line utility to a full-screen persistent application. If you want to save a couple of man pages to a file, for example, you can run those processes in the background while you are working on something else.

Once a job is stopped, you can enter `fg` to restart it as the program you're working with. (The `fg` command takes its name from *foreground*, which refers to the program that your display and keyboard are working with.) If the process will continue without any output to the screen and without any requirement for input, you can use `bg` to move it into the *background*, where it runs until it is done. If the program needs to write to the screen or read from the keyboard, the system will stop its execution automatically and inform you. You then can use `fg` to bring the program into the foreground to continue running.

TIP

If you find that running background jobs are still writing information to your screen, try using the shell command `stty tostop` prior to starting the command as a solution.

You can also use job control to start multiple programs and then use the `fg` command, with the job ID as an argument, to start the job you want to work with. Not entering the job ID will bring the most recently stopped job back to the foreground. If your system takes a long time to start big applications (such as `emacs` or `vi`), this could save you lots of time.

NOTE

Although a job can be stopped, it still typically consumes resources, so you should be careful not to have too many stopped programs around, in deference to the other users of the system. To free resources, kill or terminate the jobs instead.

A different strategy is to start a program in the background and let Unix manage it. If the program needs user input or has output to display, it stops, just like processes you've put into the background with `bg` after they've already started running. To have a program (or pipeline!) automatically start in the background, simply type an `&` at the end of the command line.

1. Here's an example of a complex sequence of `awk` commands that processes files without needing any input or offering any output:

```
$ awk -F: '{print $1" = "$5}' < /etc/passwd | \
awk -F, '{print $1}'| \
awk '{ if (NF > 2) print $0 }' | \
sort > who.is.who
```

   After about 10 seconds, the `$` prompt returns; it takes that long to feed the password file through the three-part `awk` filter, sort the entire output, and save it to the file `who.is.who`.

CAUTION

When you're working with long commands, it's useful to know that you can always move to the next line—even in the middle of entering something—by ending the current line with a single backslash. Note that the backslash must be the *very last character* on the line.

   With this new file, I easily can look up an account to see the full name of that user:

```
$ alias lookup='grep -i \!* who.is.who'
$ who | head
root       console Dec  6 18:02
maritanj ttyAa    Dec  8 21:20
efb        ttyAb    Dec  8 12:12
wifey      ttyAc    Dec  8 19:41
phamtu     ttyAe    Dec  8 21:14
curts      ttyAf    Dec  8 21:14
seifert    ttyAg    Dec  8 21:11
taylor     ttyAh    Dec  8 21:09
halcyon    ttyAi    Dec  8 18:34
jamilrr  ttyAj    Dec  8 20:25
Broken pipe
$ lookup maritanj
maritanj = Jorge Maritan
$ lookup efb
efb = Edward F. Billiard
$
```

2. To have the build process run in the background, I can stop the process immediately after I start it, by using `^z`:

```
$ !awk
awk -F: '{print $1" = "$5}' < /etc/passwd | awk -F, '{print $1}'
| awk '{ if (NF > 2) print $0 }' | sort > who.is.who
Stopped
$
```

NOTE

Notice that the command I repeated using the history mechanism was listed as being all on a single line even though I originally entered it across multiple lines.

At this point, `bg` will continue the program, running it in the background:

```
$ bg
[1]     awk -F: {print $1" = "$5} < /etc/passwd | awk -F, {print $1}
➡  | awk { if (NF > 2) print $0 } | sort > who.is.who &
$
```

The number in square brackets is this job's *control number* in the shell. In a moment, you'll learn why this is a handy number to note.

On some systems a completed background job will notify you immediately that it's done, but on most systems, after a completed background job has finished running, it waits until you press Return to get a new system prompt before it lets you know. After about 30 or 40 seconds, I press Return and see this:

```
$
[1]     Done                    awk -F:
{print $1" = "$5} < /etc/passwd | awk -F,
{print $1} | awk { if (NF > 2) print $0 } | sort > who.is.who
$
```

3. A better strategy for moving a program into the background is to move the process to the background automatically by adding a & to the end:

```
$ !awk &
awk -F: '{print $1" = "$5}' < /etc/passwd | awk -F, '{print $1}'
➡  | awk '{ if (NF > 2) print $0 }' | sort > ! who.is.who &
[1] 27556 27557 27558 27559
$
```

This is more interesting. This command is shown with a control number of 1, but the four numbers listed after it are the actual process ID numbers of each piece of the pipeline: `27556` is the first `awk` process, `27557` is the second `awk` process, `27558` is the third `awk` process, and `27559` is the `sort` program.

Again, when it's complete, pressing Return lets me know:

```
$
[1]     Done                    awk -F: {print $1" = "$5} < /etc/passwd | awk -F,
➡  {print $1} | awk { if (NF > 2) print $0 } | sort > who.is.who
$
```

4. What happens if I try to automatically move to the background a program that has input or output?

```
$ vi &
[1] 28258
$
```

This looks fine. Pressing Return indicates otherwise, though:

```
$
[1]   + Stopped (tty output) vi
$
```

You can see that this program has stopped because of some information (output) it wants to display. If the program expected input, the message would be Stopped (tty input) *program name*.

I can use fg to bring this program back into the foreground.

Because so much of the Unix design focuses on running streams of data through filters and saving the output to a file, you could be running various commands in the background, freeing you up to do other work while it's chugging away. Remember that you can put in the background jobs that take a fair amount of processing time and then display information on the screen. When it's time for a background job to write something to the screen, the program will stop automatically until you enter fg to pull it into the foreground.

Remember also that when you want a program to be running in the background, you can redirect its output, too. A common command would be something like longcmd > longcmd.output &.

Task 15.3: Finding Out What Tasks Are Running

There are two ways to keep tabs on what programs are running on a Unix system. The easier way is to use jobs, which shows what processes you've stopped and moved into the background in the current shell. Enter jobs, and the system tells you what programs, if any, are stopped or running.

The alternative is a complex command called ps, which shows the processor status for the entire computer. The processor is another name for the computer itself. Fortunately, without any arguments, it only shows the active or stopped programs associated with your current login session. Don't be fooled, however: The ps program has more flags than even ls does. The vast majority of them are never going to be of value to you or any normal Unix user. Confusingly, the flags are very different between BSD systems and System V, too. Table 15.1 summarizes the ps flags that are most helpful.

TABLE 15.1   Useful Flags to the `ps` Command, BSD-Style

Flag	Meaning
-a	Shows all processes associated with terminals attached to the system.
-e	Shows all processes on the system.
-l	Gives the long listing format for each line.
-t *xx*	Lists only processes associated with the specified `tty`*xx*.
-u	Produces user-oriented output.
-w	Uses wide output format. If repeated (`-ww`), it will show as much of each command as possible.
-x	Shows all processes in the system.

The `-a`, and `-x` flags affect how much information is displayed by `ps`. To use the `-x` command, you also must use the `-a` command. On most machines, `-ax` yields considerably more output than `-a`. The most commonly used flags (and flag combinations) are `-a`, to have all interesting processes listed; `-ax`, to see everything on the machine (you almost always want to pipe this to `grep` or `more`, lest you be overrun with hundreds of lines of information); and `-wt`*xx*, to show all the processes associated with `tty`*xx*, in wide format.

NOTE

The `ps` program varies from System V to Berkeley Unix more than any other command. Fortunately, the two or three most common flags are similar across the two systems. To explore more about the `ps` command on your system, you should start by reading the man page.

1. I start `vi` in the background:

```
$ vi dickens.note &
[1] 4352
$
```

I start that `awk` job again, too:

```
$ !awk
awk -F: '{print $1" = "$5}' < /etc/passwd | awk -F, '{print $1}'
➥ | awk '{ if (NF > 2) print $0 }' | sort > ! who.is.who &
[2] 4532 4534 4536 4537
$
```

The `jobs` command shows what processes I have running:

```
$ jobs
[1]  + Stopped (tty output) vi dickens.note
[2]  - Running               awk -F: {print $1" = "$5} < /etc/passwd
➥ | awk -F,
```

```
{print $1} | awk { if (NF > 2) print $0 } | sort > who.is.who
$
```

2. Now that I know the job numbers (the numbers in square brackets here), I can easily move specific jobs into the foreground or the background by specifying the job number prefixed by %. To show what I mean, I'll put a couple more vi jobs in the background:

```
$ vi buckaroo.confused &
[2] 13056
$ vi awkscript csh.man cheryl mbox &
[3] 13144
$
```

Now I use the jobs command to see what's running:

```
$ jobs
[1]    Stopped (tty output) vi dickens.note
[2]  - Stopped (tty output) vi buckaroo.confused
[3]  + Stopped (tty output) vi awkscript csh.man cheryl mbox
$
```

NOTE

Notice that the awk job finished and no longer shows up as an active job.

To edit the buckaroo.confused note, I need only to enter fg %2 to pull the file into the foreground. To terminate these processes (which you'll learn more about later in this hour), I can use the kill command:

```
$ kill %2 %3
$
```

Nothing happened. Or did it? Pressing Return again reveals what occurred in the operating system:

```
$
[3]  - Done            vi awkscript csh.man cheryl mbox
[2]  - Done            vi buckaroo.confused
$
```

3. I restart the awk command with !awk. Contrast the output of jobs with the output of the BSD ps command:

```
$ ps
  PID TT STAT  TIME COMMAND
 4352 Ah T     0:00 vi dickens.note
 4532 Ah R     0:03 awk - : {print $1"
```

```
 4534 Ah R      0:02 awk - , {print $1}
 4536 Ah S      0:01 - k { if (NF > 2) print $0 } (awk)
 4537 Ah S      0:00 sort
 4579 Ah R      0:00 ps
$
```

You can see here that four unique processes are really running for that pipeline: three awk processes and one sort process. In addition, vi and ps are listed as running. Note that my login shell (bash) isn't in this listing.

Figure 15.1 explains each field, and Table 15.2 lists possible values for the STAT program status column.

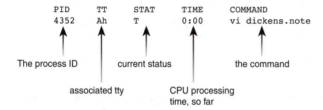

FIGURE 15.1
The ps default process output.

TABLE 15.2   Possible Process Status Values

Value	Meaning
R	Running
S	Sleeping (20 seconds or less)
I	Idle (sleeping more than 20 seconds)
T	Stopped
Z	Zombie process

Other process states exist, but they rarely show up for most users. A *zombie process* is one that has ended but hasn't freed up its resources. Usually, it takes a second or two for the system to completely recover all memory used by a program. Sometimes, zombies are stuck in the process table for one reason or other. Unix folk refer to this as a *wedged process*, and such a process has an annoying habit of staying around until the system is rebooted. Sometimes these zombie processes can be listed as <defunct> in process listings. Any process that is preceded by a sleep command is noted as sleeping.

4. Adding some flags can change the output of `ps` quite dramatically:

```
$ ps -x
  PID TT STAT   TIME COMMAND
 4352 Ah T      0:00 vi dickens.note
 6171 Ah R      0:02 awk - : {print $1"
 6172 Ah R      0:01 awk - , {print $1}
 6173 Ah S      0:01 - k { if (NF > 2) print $0 } (awk)
 6174 Ah S      0:00 sort
 6177 Ah R      0:00 ps -x
19189 Ah S      0:06 -bash (bash)
19649 Ah I      0:02 newmail
$
```

Two new processes show up here: `-bash` (the shell), which is, finally, my login shell; and `newmail`, a program that automatically starts in the background when I log in to the system (it's located at the end of my `.login`).

<hr>

NOTE

<hr>

The shell process is shown with a leading dash to indicate that it's a login shell. Any other copies of `bash` that I run won't have that leading dash. This is one way the shell knows not to read through the `.login` file every time it's run.

<hr>

5. To see more about what's happening, I add yet another flag, `-f`, to expand the output on the display:

```
$ ps -xf
USER        PID  %CPU %MEM   SZ  RSS TT STAT ENG   TIME COMMAND
taylor     7011  10.4  0.2  184  100 Ah R      6   0:02 awk - :
➧ {print $1"
taylor     7012   6.3  0.1  160   92 Ah S          0:01 awk - ,
➧ {print $1}
taylor     7013   5.9  0.1  160   92 Ah R      3   0:01 - k
➧ { if (NF > 2) print
taylor    19189   1.1  0.2  256  148 Ah S          0:07 -bash (bash)
taylor     7014   1.0  0.1  316   64 Ah S          0:00 sort
taylor     7022   0.1  0.2  180  116 Ah R      0   0:00 ps -xu
taylor     4352   0.0  0.3  452  168 Ah T          0:00 vi
➧ dickens.note
taylor    19649   0.0  0.1  124   60 Ah I          0:02 newmail
$
```

Figure 15.2 explains these fields.

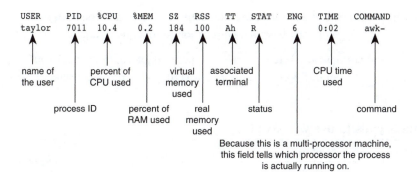

FIGURE 15.2
The -f user-oriented output of ps.

6. On a Solaris workstation, the output of the ps command is a bit different:

```
$ ps
  PID TTY    TIME COMMAND
 8172 pts/2 0:00 -bash (bash)
 8182 pts/2      0:00 vi
 8186 pts/2      0:00 ps
$
```

In many ways, though, these different Unixes still have very similar output from the ps commands. For example, consider this Mac OS X output from ps -ef to the ps -xu output on the Solaris system that I showed earlier:

```
$ ps -ef | head -4
  UID   PID  PPID   C STIME    TTY          TIME CMD
    0     1     0   0 Thu11AM ??        2:49.85 /sbin/launchd
    0    19     1   0 Thu11AM ??        0:21.14 /usr/libexec/UserEventAgent
                                     ➥ (System)
    0    20     1   0 Thu11AM ??        0:49.64 /usr/sbin/syslogd
$
```

Unix works with processes. Your login shell, the edit session you run, and even the ls program listing your files are all processes in the operating system. This means that you can work with processes. You can stop programs temporarily to do something else, restart them as you choose, and even look at all the programs you're running at any time, including otherwise hidden processes such as your login shell itself.

Task 15.4: Terminating Processes with `kill`

Now that you know how to create multiple processes, tuck some into the background, and find stray processes, you need some way to permanently stop them from running, as needed. The command to accomplish this in Unix is kill. For the most part, to use kill, you specify the process ID numbers of the programs you want to terminate. Both the C shell and the Korn shell have a convenient shorthand you've already seen: the percent–job-number notation.

The `kill` command can send various signals to a process. To specify a job control action, you need to specify to `kill` one of the various signals. Table 15.3 lists the most common signals you'd use with `kill`.

TABLE 15.3   Some Signals to Use with `kill`

Number	Name	Meaning
1	SIGHUP	Hang up
2	SIGINT	Interrupt
9	SIGKILL	`kill` (cannot be caught or ignored)
15	SIGTERM	Software termination signal from `kill`

Unix knows about more than 30 signals, but Table 15.3 lists the ones that are most helpful. The SIGHUP signal is sent to every process you are running just before you hang up (log out of the system). SIGINT is the signal sent when you press ^c; many programs respond in specific ways when this signal is received, typically to cancel the current operation. SIGKILL is the "Terminator" of the Unix signals: Programs cannot ignore it and cannot do anything special when receiving it. The process is terminated immediately, without even a chance to clean up after itself. SIGTERM is the more graceful alternative: It requests an immediate termination of the program, but it allows the program to remove temporary files it might have created.

By default, `kill` sends a SIGTERM to the processes specified. You can specify other signals, however, by using either the number or the name of the signal (minus the SIG prefix, that is). On many systems, you also can specify the -1 flag to `kill` to see what signals are available.

CAUTION

Use the `kill` command with caution. It can get you into a lot of trouble. For example, do you want to log out rather suddenly? To do that, find the process ID of your login shell and terminate it. Learn to use `kill`, but learn to use it cautiously.

1. The simplest way to use the `kill` command is from the shell. First, I start a job in the background:

```
$ vi &
[1] 6016
$
```

I can terminate this process now by using either `kill %1` or `kill 6016` (without a specified signal, by the way, `kill` sends a SIGTERM signal), but if I try both of them, the second command will fail because the first already will have terminated the process:

```
$ kill %1
$ kill 6016
6016: No such process
[1]    Done                vi
$
```

Just as if I had dropped a process into the background and it instantly stopped because it needed to produce output, the `kill` process also had no feedback and took a second or two to occur. In the interim, I entered the second `kill` command, which then output the error message `No such process`. Following that, I got an indication from the shell that the job ended.

2. Using the `ps` command, I can find that pesky `newmail` program that's always running in the background:

```
$ ps -ef | grep newmail
taylor    6899   0.1   0.1   52   28 Av S          0:00 grep newmail
taylor   25817   0.0   0.1  124   60 Av I          0:01 newmail
$
```

I want to send that process a hang-up signal (SIGHUP), which I can do with either `kill -1` (the signal number) or `kill -HUP` (the base signal name):

```
$ kill -HUP 25817
$ !ps
ps -ef | grep newmail
taylor    7220   0.0   0.1   52   28 Av S          0:00 grep newmail
$
```

Because the `newmail` program isn't in this output, I can conclude that the SIGHUP signal stopped `newmail`.

NOTE

Because `kill` tells you whether a process cannot be found, the typical Unix solution to finding out whether the command worked is to enter `!!` immediately to repeat the `kill` command a second time. If `kill` worked, you see `No such process`.

---

3. Some processes are persistent and can resist the less powerful signals SIGTERM and SIGHUP. (In Unix, this is called "catching" a signal. In some processes, you need to send and catch signals to perform certain actions.) That's when you need to use what I call the "big guns," or SIGKILL. You see this referred to sometimes as the terminate-with-extreme-prejudice command; the format is `kill -9 processID`, and it's dangerous!

I strongly recommend that you just let `kill` send the SIGTERM signal and see whether that does the job. If it doesn't, try SIGHUP, and if that also fails, use SIGKILL as a last resort.

4. What happens if you try to use `kill` on jobs that aren't yours? Fortunately, it doesn't work:

```
$ ps -ef | head -5
USER       PID  %CPU %MEM   SZ  RSS TT STAT ENG   TIME COMMAND
news      7460  97.7  0.4  336  252 ?  R N    4   4:33 sort -u
➥ /tmp/nnsubj6735a
phaedrus  8693  18.1  1.1 1260  720 rm S           0:03 nn
root      8741  14.4  0.4  416  252 ?  R      9   0:03 nntpd
root      8696  13.9  0.4  416  252 ?  S          0:03 nntpd
Broken pipe
$ kill 7460
7460: Not owner
$
```

5. Finally, if you forget and leave stopped jobs in the background and try to log out, here's what happens:

```
$ logout
There are stopped jobs.
$
```

You must either use `fg` to bring each job into the foreground and terminate each normally or use `kill` to terminate each of the jobs and then log out.

In this task, you have been introduced to the `kill` command and some of the signals associated with it.

Summary

Although the file is the underlying unit in the Unix file system, including all directories, the most fundamental piece of Unix is the process. In this hour, you've learned how to have background processes, how to stop and restart processes, and how to use `kill` to quit any errant program— running or not.

Workshop

The Workshop summarizes the key terms you've learned and poses some questions about the topics presented in this lesson. It also provides you with a preview of what you will learn in the next hour.

Key Terms

control number   This is a unique number that the C shell assigns to each background job for easy reference and for use with other commands, such as `fg` and `kill`.

current job   The current job is the job that is currently running on the terminal and keyboard—that is, the program you're actually running and working within.

errant process   An errant process is not performing the job you expected it to perform.

foreground job   Foreground job is a synonym for current job.

job   Job is a synonym for process.

kill   Killing a process means terminating the process.

login shell   The login shell is the process that started when you logged in to the system. This is usually where you're working when you're logged in to Unix.

process   A process is a program that is stopped or running within the Unix operating system. Also known as a job.

signals   Signals are special messages that can be sent to stopped or running processes.

stop a job   Stopping a job means stopping the running program without terminating it.

wedged process   A wedged process is stuck in memory and can't free up its resources even though it has ceased running. This is rare but annoying.

zombie   A zombie is a terminated process that has not been cleaned up by the parent process.

Exercises

1. Start a program, such as `vi`, and use `^z` to stop it. Now terminate the process by using `kill`.

2. Start `vi` again, stop it, and put it in the background. Work on something else and then return `vi` to the foreground.

3. Use `ps` to check the status of processes to see what processes you have running that aren't shown on `jobs`. Why might `ps` and `jobs` list different processes?

Preview of the Next Hour

The next hour focuses on the basics of shell script programming, a topic that's not only near to my heart but will become something you'll be glad to learn, too. Stay tuned!

HOUR 16
Shell Programming Overview

Goals for This Hour

In this hour, you will learn

- ▶ About shell variables
- ▶ About shell arithmetic
- ▶ About comparison functions
- ▶ How to use conditional expressions
- ▶ About looping expressions
- ▶ How to use `bash` functions

In the preceding few hours, you have learned about some of the many options available to you when you use a command shell. Using these shells enables you to enter commands for Unix. What most people don't realize when they first start using Unix is that these shells are also programming environments and that you can write your own shell programs with remarkably little effort. And, oh yeah, it's really fun, too!

Because shells are really just line-by-line interpreted languages, any sequence of commands you can use at the command line can also be placed in a file and run repetitively. This is a shell program. Originally, Unix experts wrote their shell scripts for the Bourne shell (`/bin/sh`) because that shell was standard on every Unix platform; but the extra flexibility and capabilities of the `bash` shell have made it the most popular alternative, and that's what I use this hour.

NOTE

I strongly urge you to explore the shells you have available, as discussed in Hour 13, "Introduction to Command Shells." The best shell to use is the one that makes you the most productive. And remember, the shell that you use for scripting doesn't have to be the same as the one you use for your interactive commands.

Building Your Own Commands

Unix is remarkably capable and includes over 1,000 different commands, but amazingly, sometimes that's not sufficient. When it becomes time to create your own unique commands, a simple shell script almost always suffices.

Task 16.1: Shell Variables

Programming languages usually include variables, and the shell naturally does, too. Variables are just tags to identify values that can change as a program is used. In the shell, these variables can take a single value and are always interpreted as strings (that is, sequences of alphanumeric or punctuation characters). Even numeric values are strings to the shell.

You can use any string-manipulation command, such as sed or cut, to change a shell variable.

1. Here is an example of setting the value of a shell variable:

   ```
   $ color=blue
   ```

   This sets the variable color to the string blue. You can output the value of any variable with the echo command:

   ```
   $ echo $color
   blue
   ```

   This also indicates how to reference a shell variable: It must be preceded by the dollar sign ($) and be referenced by its mnemonic name. This can cause some problems, however, because what if you want to use it in a way that embeds it in other text?

2. If you are using a shell variable as a prefix, and you want to append text immediately, you might think that this would work:

   ```
   $ leaning='anti-'
   $ echo Joe is basically $leaningtaxes
   ```

   The output here is just Joe is basically. The shell does not know what appears to be a new variable, $leaningtaxes. Because no value is assigned to $leaningtaxes, the output is NULL, or an empty string. To solve this problem, enclose the variable name in curly braces:

   ```
   $ echo Joe is basically ${leaning}taxes
   Joe is basically anti-taxes
   ```

   If leaning is undefined, the output might not make sense. It would be Joe is basically taxes. Fortunately, the shell provides a means to have a default value if a variable is undefined:

   ```
   $ echo Joe is basically ${leaning:-pro }taxes
   Joe is basically pro taxes
   ```

3. If `leaning` is undefined, the `:-` notation tells the shell to use the subsequent string, including the space character, instead of leaving the output blank. This does not assign a new value to the variable, however. If you need to use the variable repeatedly, you might want to assign a new value to it if it's undefined. The `:=` notation does this:

```
$ echo Joe is basically ${leaning:=pro }taxes and ${leaning}spending.
Joe is basically pro taxes and pro spending.
```

The first occurrence of the variable has it undefined, so the shell assigns "`pro `" (pro with a trailing space) to $leaning and outputs that. The second time the variable is interpreted, it has the value "`pro `".

4. Variables are typically assigned within scripts but can also be assigned interactively by use of the `read` command. This assigns an individual word to a specified variable, with the last variable in the list being assigned the remaining words if there are more words entered than variables listed:

```
$ read city state message
CapeMay, New Jersey Hi Mom!
$ echo $city is city
CapeMay, is city
$ echo $state is state
New is state
$ echo $message is message
Jersey Hi Mom! is message
```

As you can see, only `New` is assigned to `state`. Frustrating!

The best way around this is to escape the space (make sure that the space isn't interpreted as separating variable values) with a backslash:

```
$ read city state message
CapeMay, New\ Jersey Hi Mom!
$ echo $city is city
CapeMay, is city
$ echo $state is state
New Jersey is state
$ echo $message is message
Hi Mom! is message
```

This can be a bit tricky at first.

5. The third common way to assign variables is by using command-line arguments. The shell has built-in variables to access the command line. If you've written a script to copy files and named it `copy-files`, you might want to list all the files on the command line:

```
$ copy-files.sh file1 file2 file3
```

The program would access these arguments as $1, $2, and $3:

```
cp $1 destination
cp $2 destination
cp $3 destination
```

The $0 variable is a special case for looking at the command name, and $* lists all the command-line variables.

The standard data in any shell program is the variable. Such variables can be assigned in several ways: directly assigned, read in from a user's typing, or assigned from the command line. The shell also provides means to provide some helpful manipulation of variables.

Task 16.2: Shell Arithmetic

Although the shell treats variable values as strings, methods are available for performing basic mathematics on shell variables.

1. If a variable is assigned a numeric value, you can perform arithmetic on the value by using the command expr. This command takes several arguments to perform arithmetic functions. You can test it out directly on the command line:

    ```
    $ expr 1 + 1
    2
    ```

    Arguments must be separated by spaces—and must be present—for the expr command to work. If a variable is undefined or does not have a value assigned to it (sometimes called *zero length*), the result is a syntax error. Here is where the : - notation can be particularly helpful:

    ```
    $ echo $noval

    $ expr $noval + 1
    expr: syntax error
    $ expr ${noval:-0} + 1
    1
    ```

    expr also supports subtraction, multiplication, integer division, and remainders. These are illustrated here:

    ```
    $ expr 11 - 5
    6
    $ expr 11 \* 5
    55
    $ expr 11 / 5
    2
    $ expr 11 % 5
    1
    ```

Note that I had to escape the asterisk with a backslash and use spaces between numbers and operators, too. If I didn't do that, the shell would expand it to be the list of files in the current directory, and the `expr` program wouldn't understand that.

2. Despite what I've just shown you, I'll tell you that I never use `expr` directly because all modern shells have a shorthand notation you can use that's faster and more elegant than calling `expr`: `$((` and `))`. For example:

```
$(( 11 * 3 ))
```

is functionally identical to `expr 11 * 3`. Since it's faster, I'll use this notation from this point on for simple one-operation math (it can't support anything more complex), but if your system doesn't support it, use calls to `expr` instead. If you'd like, you can use `$( expr 1 + 1 )` or similar, so it's almost the same thing!

3. The `expr` command can also work with complex arithmetic so if you need a more complex calculation than the basic four, you'll want to use `expr` after all. You can write an expression to add two numbers and then multiply by a third number. Normally, you wouldn't need to worry about operator precedence, but `expr` isn't that sophisticated:

```
$ expr 11 + 5 \* 6
41
```

Instead, you need to group the operations in parentheses:

```
$ expr \( 11 + 5 \) \* 6
96
```

This command first adds 11 and 5, and then it multiplies the result by 6. Because the parentheses are important shell characters, you need to escape them with backslashes, just as I had to do with the asterisk earlier. Of course, you could quote the entire sequence, too: `expr "( 11 + 5 ) * 6"`.

The `expr` command is a very useful command for performing arithmetic in any shell. Strings must be numbers, or errors will occur; the results of the `expr` command can be assigned to other variables.

NOTE

The `expr` command is much more powerful than described here; it includes the capability to perform logical operations and perform operations on strings. Not powerful enough for your needs? Check out the `bc` command. It's considerably more powerful, but it's also trickier to use in a script. For more information, check the man pages for both commands.

Task 16.3: Comparison Functions

Often, when writing a program, you may want the actions taken to be dependent on certain values. A simple example is the rm -i command, where the -i flag tells rm to prompt you before deleting a file. Type y, and a file is deleted. Type n, and it remains. The shell also has similar options. This task and the next one cover how to use those options.

Just as expr is a powerful program for solving arithmetic expressions, the test command can be used to compare variables and conditions. test can perform comparisons on both strings and numeric values. test will always return zero if the condition is true and non-zero if it is false. It is standard for Unix shells to use these values as true and false.

test is used for three types of operations: numeric comparisons, string comparisons, and status tests for the file system. First up, let's look at the numeric comparisons.

1. Because the shell treats the less-than and greater-than symbols as redirection characters, they can't be used within the test command to compare two numbers. Instead, test uses a series of two-letter flags, as described in Table 16.1. These flags are always placed between the two arguments:

   ```
   test 3 -eq 4
   ```

   This example would return non-zero because 3 and 4 are not equal.

TABLE 16.1   Test Operators

Comparison Flag	Meaning
-eq	True if the numbers are equal
-ne	True if the numbers are not equal
-lt	True if the first number is less than the second number
-le	True if the first number is less than or equal to the second number
-gt	True if the first number is greater than the second number
-ge	True if the first number is greater than or equal to the second number

2. You can use the result of expr, or any other command that returns a numeric value, in test. There is also a special expression in test, -l *string*, which returns the length of a string. So you can write the following tests, after setting a couple of useful variables:

   ```
   value=3 ; string="my horse Horace"
   test $value < $(echo $string | wc -c)
   test `wc -l filename` -ge 10000
   ```

   The first test determines whether $value is the same as the length of $string. The second compares the number of characters in variable string to the number value.

The third example takes a count of the number of lines in a file, and it evaluates to `true` if 10,000 or more lines are present.

3. The second type of comparison is on strings. The first two are unary, which means that each applies to only one variable or parameter:

```
test -z "$string"
test -n "$string"
```

The first test is true if the string is of zero length or undefined. The second is true if the string has some content.

4. The next two tests compare strings with each other. The simple exclamation point and equals sign (commonly used to mean "not!" in Unix) are used for these comparisons:

```
test alphabet = Alphabet
test alphabet != Alphabet
```

The first is false; the second is true.

NOTE

When comparing string variables that don't have spaces within them, you might see shell script programmers write something like this:

```
test X$string1 = X$string2
```

The presence of the X prevents a null string from confusing `test`. If `string1` is `null`, and `string2` is `string`, you'd expand to this:

```
test X = Xstring
```

Without the X, the test would be expanded to this:

```
test = string
```

This is a syntax error. The other option is to enclose the string in quotation marks:

```
test "$string1" = "$string2"
```

which expands to this:

```
test "" = "string"
```

---

5. The final test operators work on the file system. They are single flags, as listed in Table 16.2, followed by a path.

TABLE 16.2 The Most Useful File System Test Flags

Option	Meaning
-L	True if the file exists and points to another file (symbolic link)
-d	True if the file is a directory

Option	Meaning
-e	True if the file exists
-ef	True if the two files specified are the same
-f	True if the file exists and is a regular file
-nt	True if the first file is newer than the second
-ot	True if the first file is older than the second
-g	True if the file exists and runs in a specific group
-r	True if the file exists and is readable
-s	True if the file exists and has data
-w	True if the file exists and is writable
-x	True if the file exists and is executable

Here's a sample test:

```
test -d $HOME/bin
```

This checks to see whether you have a subdirectory named `bin` in your home directory. The most common flags you see in shell programs are the -f flag and the -d flag. The others are used only in unusual situations.

6. The file system also has three binary comparisons. The -ef test determines whether the two files are the same. (When you create a link between files, this is *de facto* true.) The -nt flag is true if the first file is newer than the second, and the -ot flag is true if the first file is older than the second. You might see a test in a looping statement like this:

```
test file1 -ot file2
```

This test compares the two files, and it is true if `file1` is older than `file2`.

7. Test commands can be negated with the exclamation point or combined with -a for *and* and -o for *or*. You can make arbitrarily long conditions, at the potential cost of script readability:

```
test $var -eq 0 -a ! -e file
```

This checks to see whether the value of $var is zero and whether `file` doesn't exist (note the use of the ! in the expression).

8. `test` also has a second form. Instead of explicitly calling `test`, you can surround the conditional expression with square brackets:

```
[ -f file ]
```

Doing this makes shell programs more readable. Indeed, you'll rarely see `test` appear explicitly, as shown earlier.

Pay attention to spacing, too: If you don't use the spacing shown here, particularly the spacing between the brackets and the expression elements, the shell will complain.

The `test` command is one of the most used commands in shell programming. It is essential to understanding the next two shell script programming tasks, conditional expressions and loops.

Task 16.4: Conditional Expressions

Sometimes, when writing a program, you want to perform an action only when a specific conditional expression is met. Shell programming provides you with this capability by way of the `if` command, the `case` command, and two special command separators.

1. The `if` command is the most commonly seen conditional command. It takes the following form:

```
if
    conditional-expression
then
    command-block
fi
```

A *command* block is a sequence of one or more shell commands. The first command block, the conditional expression, is always executed. The return value of the last statement executed is used to determine whether the second block is executed. The most commonly used sequence for the conditional expression is the `test` command in its `[]` notation:

```
if
    [ -f $file ]
then
    echo $file is a regular file
fi
```

This `if` statement notifies the user that a file is a regular file. If the file is not a regular file (such as a directory), the condition fails and the shell doesn't execute the `echo`, with the result that you don't see an output message.

2. Sometimes, you might want output regardless of the situation. In the preceding case, you might be interested in the status of the file even if it is not a regular file. You can expand the `if` command with the `else` keyword to provide that second option:

```
if
    [ -f $file ]
then
    echo $file is a regular file
```

```
else
    echo $file is not a regular file
fi
```

This statement provides output regardless of the status of the file.

3. For these simple tests and output, the shell provides a second, quicker means of executing the if statement. If the two commands are joined by &&, the second command is executed if the first command is evaluated as true. If the commands are joined by ||, the second command is executed if the first is false. The preceding command would, therefore, look like this:

```
[ -f $file ] && echo $file is a regular file
[ -f $file ] || echo $file is not a regular file
```

This shorthand is very useful but can be confusing for a novice. If you accidentally place a space between the characters, you have a wildly different command; the & will run the first command at the same time as the echo, and the | will pipe the output of the test (none) to the echo.

I rarely use the && or || notation because I prefer to have my scripts be slightly longer but easier to understand with if-then conditional statements.

4. If you have even more possibilities, your if statement can have more than two options. For multiple tests, use the elif keyword:

```
if
    [ -f $file ]
then
    echo $file is a regular file
elif
    [ -d $file ]
then
    echo $file is a directory
else
    echo $file is not a regular file or a directory.
fi
```

This command first tests to see whether the file is a regular file; if it is not, it checks to see whether it is a directory; if it is neither, it gives the generic "not a regular file or directory" message. You can expand any if statement with an unlimited number of elif branches.

One nice thing is that you can indent your code to make things easier to understand, and you can also compress the statements themselves with the use of the semicolon, so the preceding listing could be more compactly written as:

```
if [ -f $file ] ; then
   echo $file is a regular file
elif [ -d $file ] ; then
   echo $file is a directory
```

```
else
  echo $file is not a regular file or a directory
fi
```

Note that the `then` should appear on a second line, so the semicolon after the expression is necessary. (Many shell programmers leave the `then` on its own line, even though it's not quite as space efficient.)

5. At some point, `if-then-else` code can become confusing. When you have many possible branches, you should use the `case` command. The syntax is a bit more complicated than the syntax for `if`:

```
case string in
pattern) command-block ;;
pattern) command-block ;;
...
esac
```

If you were looking for possible values for a variable, you could use `case`:

```
echo What do you want:
read var remainder
case $var in
house)    echo The price must be very high;;
car)      echo The price must be high;;
popsicle) echo The price must be low;;
*)        echo I do not know the price;;
esac
```

This `case` statement follows an input request and gives the user a rough idea of the price. A `case` list can contain any number of items. Note the special `;;` notation, which denotes the end of a `case` statement.

Here's another example, a mini `file` command:

```
case $filename in
  *.gif) echo Graphics Interchange Format ;;
  *.jpg) echo Joint Photographic Experts Group ;;
  *.png) echo Progressive Networking Group ;;
  *.tif) echo Tagged Interchange Format ;;
  *.scx) echo Screen Capture format ;;
  *)     echo unknown format ${filename#*.}
esac
```

In both of the previous examples, the pattern-matching algorithms used are for wildcards. Also note the `bash` variable trick to extract the filename suffix in the last conditional with the `#*.` modifier to the filename variable reference. To extract the other side (just the filename without the suffix), you could use:

```
${filename%.*}
```

6. Here's a simple shell script where the `read` command and `if` statements are useful together:

```
echo "Delete which file? "
read filename
if [ ! -f $filename ] ; then
  echo Can\'t delete $filename since it doesn\'t exist
else
  echo Deleting file $filename
  /bin/rm $filename
fi
```

This prompts for the filename and then tests to see whether the file exists before it tries to delete it with the `/bin/rm` invocation.

There are two basic conditional expressions, as well as a third shortcut, as explored in this task. You can test a condition and perform alternative actions by using `if` statements and their shortcuts. Or you can compare strings and perform any number of actions by using the `case` statement.

Task 16.5: Looping Expressions

If you want to run the same set of commands many times, instead of duplicating them in your script, you are better off using looping commands. There are two types of loops: determinate and indeterminate.

A *determinate* loop is one where you know exactly how many times you want to execute the commands before you enter the loop. Stepping through a list of files is a good example; you might not know the exact number of files when you're writing the script, but once invoked, you can start the loop for those files.

An *indeterminate* loop is one where you need to keep executing a command block until a condition is no longer true. You might be either waiting for something or performing a series of modifications to reach a goal.

1. The usual command for a determinate loop is the `for` command. It has the following syntax:

```
for var in list
do
    command-block
done
```

You can build any list you like. It could be a sequence of numbers or the output of a command. Earlier, I mentioned looping through a list of files. This is demonstrated with the following loop:

```
for var in `ls`
do
```

```
    if
        [ -f $var ]
    then
        echo $var is a regular file
    fi
done
```

This steps through all the files listed in the `` `ls` `` output, showing only regular files. Note that without the backquotes, the script would test for a file called `ls` in the current directory. A very different request!

A modification to the preceding code is that because you're in a shell script, you can use shell expansion to accomplish some things more efficiently. Instead of using `ls`, for example, how about the following?

```
for var in * ; do
 if [ -f $var ] ; then
    echo $var is a regular file
 fi
done
```

You can again also see in this example how reformatting the script can make it considerably more readable.

2. A nice trick that can be performed in a shell program is to step through the list of command-line arguments. The `for` loop provides a neat mechanism: If the in *list* part is omitted from the command, the `for` loop steps through the list of command-line arguments instead:

```
j=0
for i
do
    j=$(( $j + 1 ))
    echo $i is argument $j
done
```

This snippet steps through the command-line arguments and identifies where they are in the order of arguments.

In both cases, when you enter the `for` loop, you know how many times you need to run the loop. If you look at the case where you are waiting for something to happen, though, you need to use a different loop. The `while` loop is the solution for this problem.

NOTE

Another way to step through arguments in a script is to use the shell's `shift` command. We'll see that in the next hour.

---

3. In Task 16.3, I mentioned the case where you might want to wait on the arrival of a file. This echoes a real-world situation I recently faced. We were processing a program log file, but we did not know exactly when it would be placed in the shared server directory. We tried to set up the job to run after the file arrived, but this approach still ran into problems.

We solved the problem by using the `while` loop. At the end of the execution of our script, we created a checkpoint file. At the beginning, if the checkpoint file was newer than the log file, we would wait. Programmatically, that is:

```
while
    [ checkpoint -nt logfile ]
do
    sleep 60
done
```

This program would wait one minute between checks. If the new `log file` had not been written, the program would go back to sleep for 60 seconds and try again.

4. `while` loops can also be used in a determinate manner. In the case where you are not concerned with a variable's value but know a count of times to run a command block, you can use a counter to increment through the number:

```
i=0
while
    [ $i -lt 100 ]
do
    i=$(( $i + 1 ))
    commands
done
```

This is certainly easier than enumerating 100 items in a list!

The shell provides two convenient mechanisms for running a group of commands repeatedly. These loop commands are useful from both the command line and a program.

Task 16.6: bash Functions

Much of what's been covered in this lesson has been what I characterize as *flow control*: ways to specify what command to execute in what set of conditions. What's interesting about using bash as a programmatic shell is that you can actually create your own functions and use them throughout your scripting, as if you were in a more formal (powerful) programming environment.

The greatest value of functions is that they give you the ability to specify and access parameters.

Let's get our feet wet and see how they can significantly help you develop powerful shell scripts!

1. Functions are defined as follows:

```
function functionname
{
    shell commands
}
```

In some sense, all command aliases, as discussed earlier in the book, are really simple functions. Here's an example:

```
$ alias ls
alias ls='ls -F'
```

This can be rewritten as the function

```
function ls
{
    /bin/ls -F
}
```

and it would work in almost exactly the same way. The biggest difference is that there's no way to specify any other arguments to the `ls` command with the function, as written.

2. To add parameters, you simply add `$*` after the `-F` flag:

```
function ls {
  /bin/ls -F $*
}
```

Now a command like `ls /tmp` will work as desired!

3. Of course, the real value of using functions rather than aliases is that you can dramatically increase the level of sophistication of your new scripts.

As an example, I'd like to have a command that expands on the earlier snippet that indicated file type based on filename suffix. In the new version, I'd like to actually output some HTML fragments if the graphic can be viewed in a Web browser (that is, if it's a GIF or JPG image). The new version would also offer clickable links to HTML files found and would enable users to click to step into directories as they browse the system.

TIP

The first line of every shell script is special, specifying what program or shell should be used to interpret the commands in the file. It's denoted by `#!` and is pronounced "she-bang," for no obvious reason!

Here's my first stab at the problem, pre-functions:

```
#!/usr/local/bin/bash
# A Web-friendly directory browser that knows
```

```
# how to show graphic images:

directory=${QUERY_STRING:-$HOME}
iamcalled="browse.cgi"
webroot="/web"

echo "Content-type: text/html"
echo ""

echo "<h2>Directory $directory</h2><ul>"

cd $webroot/$directory

for filename in *
do
  case $filename in
    *.gif ) echo "<li><img src=$directory/$filename />"
            echo "<br /><tt>$filename</tt></li>" ;;
    *.jpg ) echo "<li><img src=$directory/$filename />"
            echo "<br /><tt>$filename</tt></li>" ;;
    *.htm ) echo "<li><a href=$filename>$filename</a></li>" ;;
    *.html) echo "<li><a href=$filename>$filename</a></li>" ;;
    *)      if [ -d $filename ] ; then
              echo "<li><tt><a "
              echo "href=$iamcalled?$directory/$filename>"
              echo "[$filename]</a></tt></li>"
            else
              echo "<li><tt>$filename</tt></li>"
            fi
            ;;
  esac
done

echo "</ul>"

exit 0
```

This works well, but there's much duplication of individual lines in the script, so this is a perfect case for a function. The first one I'll define is showname:

```
function showname
{
  echo "<tt><b>$1</b></tt></li>"
}
```

This is simple enough, and now I have the statement in one spot, rather than three, making it easier to maintain and expand the script.

4. One more refinement: Case conditionals can have multiple expressions if they're separated by the | or notation, which can make this considerably simpler:

```
#!/usr/local/bin/bash
# A Web-friendly directory browser that knows
# how to show graphic images:

directory=${QUERY_STRING:-$HOME}
iamcalled="browse.cgi"
webroot="/web"

function showname
{
  echo "<tt><b>$1</b></tt></li>"
}

echo "Content-type: text/html"
echo ""

echo "<h2>Directory $directory</h2><ul>"

cd $webroot/$directory

for filename in *
do
  case $filename in
    *.gif|*.jpg )
            echo "<li><img src=$directory/$filename /><br />"
            showname $filename
            ;;
    *.htm|*.html )
            echo "<li><a href=$filename>$filename</a></li>" ;;
    *)      if [ -d $filename ] ; then
              echo \
            "<li><tt><a href=$iamcalled?$directory/$filename>"
              echo "[$filename]</a></tt></li>"
            else
              echo "<li>"
              showname $filename
            fi
            ;;
  esac
done

echo "</ul>"

exit 0
```

5. Of course, the entire conditional and such could be poured into the function to make the code even cleaner. In fact, the main routine is just the following:

```
echo "Content-type: text/html"
echo ""

echo "<h2>Directory $directory</h2><ul>"

showdirectory $directory

echo "</ul>"
```

All the complex `case` statement conditionals are tucked neatly into the `showdirectory` function:

```
function showdirectory
{
  if [ ! -d $webroot/$1 ] ; then
    echo "Error: no directory $1 found"
    exit 0
  fi

  cd $webroot/$1

  for filename in *
  do
    case $filename in
      *.gif|*.jpg )
            echo "<li><img src=$directory/$filename><br />"
            showname $filename
            ;;
      *.htm|*.html )
            echo "<li><a href=$filename>$filename</a></li>" ;;
      *)     if [ -d $filename ] ; then
             echo \
           "<li><tt><a href=$iamcalled?$directory/$filename>"
             echo "[$filename]</a></tt></li>"
           else
             echo "<li>"
             showname $filename
           fi
           ;;
  esac
done
}
```

It's now easy to add error checking in the function (the `-d` test to see whether it's a directory before moving there with the `cd` command).

Functions can be quite complex, but even simple functions can help you get the most out of your shell interaction.

Summary

In this hour, you've just skimmed the basics of shell programming. You were introduced to the control structures of the shell and to two important commands. You can learn much more about shell programming; my popular book *Wicked Cool Shell Scripts* (No Starch Press, 2015) is one place you can dig much deeper into the subject.

Workshop

The Workshop summarizes the key terms you've learned and poses some questions about the topics presented in this lesson. It also provides you with a preview of what you will learn in the next hour.

Key Terms

command block   A list of one or more shell commands can be grouped in a conditional or looping statement, called a command block.

conditional expression   This is an expression that returns either `true` or `false`.

determinate loop   In this type of loop, the number of times the loop is run is known before the loop is started.

expression   This is a command that returns a value.

indeterminate loop   In this type of loop, the number of times the loop is run is not known before the loop is started.

loop   This is a sequence of commands that are repeatedly executed while a condition is true.

variables   These are names to label data that can change during the execution of a program.

zero-length variable   A variable that does not have a value assigned to it.

Exercises

1. How would you read in a street address in a shell program? How would you read in a name?

2. If you read in the number of people who read a newspaper and the number of people who subscribe to a particular paper, how would you determine the ratio of subscribers to readers?

3. How do you know whether a file has data?

4. How do you wait for data to be placed in a file?

Preview of the Next Hour

I'm really a big fan of shell script programming, I have to admit. In the next hour, I'll give you a guided tour of four simple shell scripts, scripts that will hopefully get you fired up about trying this lightweight programming environment yourself. Don't miss it!

Advanced Shell Programming

Goals for This Hour

In this hour, you will learn

- ▶ How to find files fast with `mylocate`
- ▶ How to count commands on your system with `cmdcnt`
- ▶ About finding your disk usage stats with `diskspace`
- ▶ How to waste time with the `hi-low` game

In the preceding hour, you learned about the basics of dropping a set of Unix commands into a file and turning them into a shell script. It turns out that shell scripts can be remarkably capable, and in just a few lines you can often produce sophisticated mini-programs that make your time at the command line more productive and even more fun. This hour expands on the shell script topic by presenting four shell scripts that should whet your appetite for scripting and demonstrate how Unix makes it simple to expand and customize your computing experience.

There are plenty of different shell scripts that you could use to explore more sophisticated scripting techniques, but I believe that the best approach is to study a few small, well-written scripts. You can always find shell scripts on your own system by using a command sequence like this:

```
cd /usr/bin
file * | grep -i shell\ script
```

On the latest Solaris system, this produces a list of 164 different shell scripts included with the operating system. There's lots to study when you want to learn more about shell scripting!

NOTE

The shell scripts presented in this hour are inspired by scripts included with my book *Wicked Cool Shell Scripts* (No Starch Press, 2015). If you find yourself really getting into scripting, pick up that book, which is an excellent follow-on to this hour, if I say so myself!

Searching a Database of Filenames with `mylocate`

Many versions of Unix and Linux include a terrific application called `locate`, which maintains a database of all file and directory names on your computer, letting you quickly and easily search for files and programs by name across all known file systems.

Locate can have a significant security flaw, however, in that it can end up running as root and index *everything on your system* rather than just the files and directories that you actually have permission to view.

There are also Unixes that just don't have `locate` and instead leave you having to work with the much slower (albeit more powerful) `find` command.

Let's sidestep both and create a version of `locate` that is actually a shell script. It's surprisingly easy!

Task 17.1: Building `mylocate`

There are two parts to the `mylocate` script—two different scripts. The first builds the database of every file and directory accessible to you, and the second utilizes the `grep` command to allow easy command-line searches of that database. You could almost write this as a pair of shell aliases, but a bit more sophistication will prove useful.

1. Use the `find` command to create a file that contains a list of absolutely every file and directory you can see on the file system. Be warned: This file will take rather a while to build. Here's the simple script that builds the `mylocate.db` file:

```
$ cat mkmylocatedb
#!/bin/sh

# mklocatedb - build the locate database using find. Must be root to run this

locatedb="$HOME/.locate.db"

find / -print > $locatedb

exit 0
```

Remember that once you've created this, and any other shell script, you need to use `chmod +x` filename to ensure that your script is directly executable.

When you run this program, you'll see thousands of permission errors streaming past your screen, which is harmless but quite annoying. Eliminating them requires a little more shell trickery:

```
$ ./mkmylocatedb 2> /dev/null
```

The 2> redirects only `stderr` (the error messages), ensuring that anything sent to *standard out* (that is, to `stdout`) will be displayed to the screen while hiding all warnings and error messages. The output file `/dev/null` is a "bit bucket," a digital hole in the ground. You can add as much as you want to `/dev/null`, and it all just vanishes, with the device never getting any bigger than zero bytes.

After some period of time (at least a few minutes), the script will be done, and the first half of the script is completed.

2. To see what's been added to the file, let's have a peek inside:

```
$ head -10 ~/.locate.db
/
/.nfs4
/var
/var/info
/var/inf/usr_share_info_dir.backlink
/var/info/usr_share_info_dir
/var/db
/var/db/ipf
/var/sadm
/var/sadm/pkg
```

How many lines does the file contain?

```
$ wc -l ~/.locate.db
  173251 /export/home/taylor/.locate.db
```

Your results might actually be even larger.

3. With the database built, it's simple, again, to create a script that uses `grep` to allow easy file searching:

```
#!/bin/sh

# locate - search the locate database for the specified pattern

locatedb="$HOME/.locate.db"

if [ $# -eq 0 ] ; then
  echo "Usage: locate pattern"
  exit 0
fi

exec grep -i "$@" $locatedb
```

That's all there is to it. The conditional checks the number of arguments given to the script to ensure that the user specified a pattern; `$#` is the number of arguments itself. The last line requires a bit of explanation, however. Shell scripts are run within copies of your login shell. (Well, technically, they're run in the shell specified on the very first line, hence the special #! notation.) This means that a shell script consumes memory, requires its own process, and so on. If the script invokes a program, that runs separately, too, so if the shell script invokes `grep`, there are then three processes running: the login shell, the subshell for the script, and `grep` itself.

To simplify things a bit, the special `exec` command replaces the subshell with the command specified rather than adding it. Basically, it saves a process, but the shell script effectively ends as soon as that `exec` is encountered since the shell that's running it is replaced by the specified command.

The special notation `$@` simply hands all the arguments specified to the script along to the `grep` command.

4. Enough explanation. Let's run our new script a few times! First off, how many C source files are there? The first attempt would be to simply use " .c" as the pattern, but that would be a mistake. You'll recall from earlier that `grep` works with regular expressions, and " .c" turns out to match any letter, followed by a *c*, anywhere in the line:

```
$ ./mylocate ".c" | wc -l
   134933
```

The first trick is to escape the period, so it's not considered a regular expression token. To do this, you simply preface the period character with a backslash:

```
$ ./mylocate "\.c" | wc -l
    3245
```

Much better! But it's still matching files like `sample.css` because it has the pattern " .c" embedded. To force the pattern to only match the end of lines, add the $ regular expression token:

```
$ ./mylocate "\.c$" | wc -l
     144
```

This makes sense! Now double-check that it's what you think it is:

```
$ ./mylocate "\.c$" | head -5
/usr/demo/net-snmp/demo_module_8/me1LoadGroup.c
/usr/demo/net-snmp/demo_module_8/demo_module_8.c
/usr/demo/net-snmp/demo_module_2/demo_module_2.c
/usr/demo/net-snmp/demo_module_5/demo_module_5.c
/usr/demo/net-snmp/demo_module_1/demo_module_1.c
```

5. To make this part of your overall environment, there's another step required: adding it to your PATH so that you can just type in the name of the command without any fuss. The

best long-term solution is to create a new `bin` directory in your home directory and then use that as a repository for new scripts and commands you create:

```
$ cd
$ mkdir bin
```

Now move your scripts into this new directory and mark them as executable:

```
$ cd bin
$ chmod +x *
```

Then modify your `PATH` so that the shell knows to look in this new directory for commands. This can be done on the command line. However, if you append it to your `.profile` instead, it'll be fixed forever instead of just until you log out:

```
$ echo 'export PATH="${PATH}:$HOME/bin"' >> ~/.profile
```

That's it. Now you can just type in command names (the exact names of your shell scripts), and they'll be run much the way that `ls` lists files and `ssh` connects securely to another Unix server.

This first script demonstrates a number of useful shell script programming techniques, including taking full advantage of all the power that Unix offers. Just as importantly, you now know how to add new directories to your `PATH` and turn shell scripts into new commands that are available on the command line—an invaluable skill!

Task 17.2: How Many Commands Do You Have?

As an example of how a shell script can use the `PATH` variable discussed in Task 17.1, let's have a look at `cmdcnt`, another simple script that adds up the executable files in every directory that's in your `PATH`. The key to this script is, again, a looping mechanism, though this time instead of using `while`, we'll use `for` because it's easier to step through a set of options until the end is reached.

1. To step through the `PATH` variable, a simple strategy is to replace every occurrence of a colon with a space:

```
$ echo $PATH
/bin:/sbin:/usr/bin:/usr/sbin:/sw/bin:/usr/X11R6/bin:/Users/taylor/bin
$ myPATH="$(echo $PATH | sed -e 's/:/ /g')"
$ echo $PATH
/bin /sbin /usr/bin /usr/sbin /sw/bin /usr/X11R6/bin /Users/taylor/bin /sw/bin
```

This is a reasonably simple transformation: `sed` substitutes a space for every colon found. You could do the same thing with the `tr` command, of course. Remember that with Unix, you always have more than one way to solve a problem!

2. For each directory, say that you want to count all the files that are executable, not just how many files there are. This can be accomplished by using the -x conditional to the test command, so for each file in each directory in the PATH, if the -x condition is true—that is, if the specified file is marked as executable—you want to add one to the counter. If the -x condition is false, you want to add one to nonex, the non-executable files counter. Here's a script to do this:

```sh
#!/bin/sh

# cmdcnt: a simple script to count how many executable commands
#   are in your current PATH.

myPATH="$(echo $PATH | sed -e 's/:/ /g')"
count=0 ; nonex=0

for directory in $myPATH ;   do
  if [ -d "$directory" ] ; then
    for command in $(ls "$directory") ; do
      if [ -x "$directory/$command" ] ; then
        count="$(( $count + 1 ))"
      else
        nonex="$(( $nonex + 1 ))"
      fi
    done
  fi
done

echo "$count commands, and $nonex entries that weren't marked executable"

exit 0
```

Notice that as a nice bonus, this script also keeps track of how many files it encounters in the collective set of all directories in the PATH and counts those, too.

3. Do you wonder what would happen if you ran the script on a few different systems? Watch and see. To identify a specific version of Unix, use the uname command:

```
$ uname
FreeBSD
$ cmdcnt
954 commands, and 44 entries that weren't marked executable
```

My FreeBSD server has slightly fewer less than 1,000 commands marked as executable. Run the same command on a different FreeBSD system, however, and the results are significantly different:

```
$ uname
FreeBSD
```

```
$ cmdcnt
1962 commands, and 22 entries that weren't marked executable
```

Amazing, isn't it?

4. Check out a few more command counts. Here's what I get on Mac OS X:

```
$ uname
Darwin
$ cmdcnt
1086 commands, and 16 entries that weren't marked executable
```

These results are for SuSE Enterprise Linux, Red Hat Enterprise 3 Linux, and Solaris, respectively:

```
$ uname
Linux
$ cmdcnt
2059 commands, and 22 entries that weren't marked executable
```

```
$ uname
Linux
$ cmdcnt
1665 commands, and 0 entries that weren't marked executable
```

Finally, here the command is running on the Solaris reference system:

```
$ uname
SunOS
$ cmdcnt
2049 commands, and 15 entries that weren't marked executable
```

Quite a surprising variation in command count, given that they're all theoretically running the same base Unix/Linux standard operating system!

This is an example of a short script that offers a useful and interesting capability—one that isn't part of the existing suite of Unix commands included with your own OS.

NOTE

The variation in command count should intrigue you. What commands are included in one version of Unix or Linux that aren't included in another? Why would different versions have such dramatically different command counts?

Task 17.3: Who Is Using All the Disk Space?

Another common question is about disk space utilization. There are commands like df that show you all the disk space used across your entire system, but even with the -h "human friendly" output format, the result is still rather puzzling. Instead, a shell script can add up all the individual disks and offer a neat summary of disk space by utilizing the df command and a small awk script.

1. The key command in this script is df -k, which, by itself, produces this rather complicated output:

```
$ df -k | head -11
Filesystem            1024-blocks       Used Available Capacity Mounted on
rpool/ROOT/solaris     31739904      4391256   21344377   18%    /
/devices                      0            0          0    0%    /devices
/dev                          0            0          0    0%    /dev
ctfs                          0            0          0    0%    /system/contract
proc                          0            0          0    0%    /proc
mnttab                        0            0          0    0%    /etc/mnttab
swap                    5330348         1620    5328728    1%    /system/volatile
objfs                         0            0          0    0%    /system/object
sharefs                       0            0          0    0%    /etc/dfs/sharetab
/usr/lib/libc/libc_hwcap1.so.1  25735629   4391256   21344373   18%   /lib/libc.
➥ so.1
$
```

2. The script that utilizes the df command actually has only one real command in it—awk— because all the work is done within the awk script:

```
#!/bin/sh

# diskspace - summarize available disk space and present in a logical
#     and readable fashion

tempfile="/tmp/available.$$"

trap "rm -f $tempfile" EXIT

cat << 'EOF' > $tempfile
    { sum += $4 }
END { mb = sum / 1024
      gb = mb / 1024
      printf "%.0f MB (%.2fGB) of available disk space\n", mb, gb
    }
EOF

df -k | awk -f $tempfile

exit 0
```

Isn't this cheating? How can you write a shell script if in fact it's actually an awk script? This is a fair question, and the answer I offer is that smart shell script programming is all about utilizing all the tools available in the Unix environment and putting them together in useful and novel ways. In this case, rather than puzzle through doing this as a "pure" shell script, the awk utility makes summing up the values in the fourth column of the df output and presenting the result in megabytes and gigabytes a breeze.

3. Let's run the script on a few systems. Here you see that there's not much space at all:

```
$ diskspace
263 MB (0.26GB) of available disk space
```

On the other hand, here's another system that has lots of disk space:

```
$ df -k
Filesystem             kbytes     used    avail capacity  Mounted on
/dev/md/dsk/d10      6050182 1288911 4700770     22%   /
/proc                      0        0        0      0%   /proc
mnttab                     0        0        0      0%   /etc/mnttab
fd                         0        0        0      0%   /dev/fd
swap                 5334352       32 5334320      1%   /var/run
/dev/md/dsk/d40      5289294 1800564 3435838     35%   /local
/dev/md/dsk/d90      8684395 4657949 3939603     55%   /home4
/dev/md/dsk/d60      8684395 4996601 3600951     59%   /home1
/dev/md/dsk/d80      8684395 5087755 3509797     60%   /home3
/dev/md/dsk/d70      8684395 4891352 3706200     57%   /home2
/dev/md/dsk/d30      1987399  143548 1784230      8%   /tmp
/dev/md/dsk/d100     8684395   40520 8557032      1%   /mqueue
/dev/md/dsk/d50     52104655 19815602 31768007    39%    /mail
bandit:/go          35009161 7821905 26837165     23%    /Net/bandit/go
cnssrc:/caus         8703856 6522112 1311359      84%    /Net/cnssrc/usr/caus
cnssrc:/cns         35006620 25965686 5540272     83%    /Net/cnssrc/usr/cns
$ diskspace
213623 MB (208.62GB) of available disk space
```

This output is much more interesting and a great example of how the summary really helps make sense of this dump of data.

Here's the Solaris system that's our reference system:

```
$ diskspace
239689 MB (234.07GB) of available disk space
```

That's not too bad: one-quarter of a terabyte of space!

4. Let's talk briefly about some of the elements of this script, now that you can see its utility. The sequence $$ is a shell script shorthand for the current process ID:

```
tempfile="/tmp/available.$$"
```

This is a simple way to guarantee that two simultaneous invocations of this script won't end up working with the same temporary filename (which could be a disaster!).

This line sets up a *signal trap*, a command that will be invoked when the specified signal, or error, is encountered:

```
trap "rm -f $tempfile" EXIT
```

In this case, it's the EXIT signal. (Technically, this should be referred to as SIGEXIT, but the trap command is forgiving of this simple shorthand.) This is an elegant way to ensure that when the script finishes running, it also removes the tempfile that was created. Remember, neatness counts.

5. The awk script is a bit complex, but when you learn that there are two blocks of code here, it'll seem a bit more straightforward. It's important to know that there are two primary blocks of code, surrounded by { and }, and the first block applies to each and every line matched, while the second is invoked only *after* the last line of the input is read:

```
    { sum += $4 }
END { mb = sum / 1024
      gb = mb / 1024
      printf "%.0f MB (%.2fGB) of available disk space\n", mb, gb
    }
```

For each line in the input (the output of df -k, remember), the first block simply adds the value of the fourth field to the variable sum. This sums up the available space, in kilobytes. When done, the block END { } is matched, both megabytes and gigabytes are calculated, and the results are shown on the screen with the printf command.

Not too confusing after all, is it?

One thing that the diskspace script example demonstrates is the importance of being knowledgeable about how to best use a wide range of different Unix commands. This is a good reason for spending some time every day reading man pages and every few weeks picking this book off the shelf and flipping through it again.

Task 17.4: Let's Play a (Shell Script) Game!

Enough serious scripting! We've spent almost a dozen pages being useful. Let's switch our attention to a simple guessing game, hi-low. This is the kind of game that engages my son as a simple programming project, but it's really a binary search masquerading as a game.

The basis of the game is that the computer is going to randomly pick a number between 1 and *n*, and then you have to figure out that number in the minimum number of guesses. The trick is to . . . Oh, wait. Let's try the game, and I'll tell you the trick *after* we've played it a few times!

1. The toughest part of this game is generating a random number, a task that turns out to be much more difficult than it initially seems. In fact, computer scientists have spent an

extraordinary amount of time trying to generate truly random numeric sequences for encryption algorithms and similar.

A typical Unix system has two or three different random number libraries for just this reason. You can see this for yourself: Just type `man -k random`, and you'll see just how many matches appear.

Of course, it's just a game, right, so if we're not perfectly random but *appear* random, that's actually sufficient for this particular script.

Fortunately, modern Unix—and Linux—systems recognize the need for convenient access to random numbers, and the shell supports a special variable `$RANDOM` that produces a different random number between 1 and `MAXINT` (2**16, or 32767) each time you reference it.

Here's a quick demonstration:

```
$ for i in 1 2 3 4 5 6 7 8 9 10 ; do
    echo $RANDOM
done
14335
1829
5301
32149
29112
4091
19813
11287
22004
16074
$
```

These 10 numbers appear random—certainly sufficiently random for our needs with this simple game!

So how do we constrain the value? We don't want to guess a number between 1 and 32,767. That turns out to be easily done with the shell's built-in math feature:

```
number=$(( $RANDOM % $biggest ))
```

The `%` notation is the *modulus* operator, which finds the remainder of the division. Remember learning long division? The modulus is the part that's left over after you ascertain how many times the denominator goes into the numerator. For example, 7 % 3 = 1. Can you see why? 7 / 3 = 2 with 1 left over, so the modulus is 1.

This is perfect for our needs because in the unlikely event that `$RANDOM` is smaller than the variable `biggest`, we can just use that value. If it's larger, we can throw away everything that's divisible by `bigger` and use the remainder. Either way, it's now 1 .. $biggest (that is, a range of numbers between the value 1 and the value of the variable $biggest).

2. The basic logic of this game is to pick a number and then ask for a value, compare it to the selected number, then output whether it's a match, too low, or too high. In the latter two cases, we'll increment a `guesses` counter so the script can also tell the users how many guesses they had.

Here's the script:

```
#!/bin/sh
# hi-low - a simple number guessing game

biggest=100                          # maximum number possible
guess=0                              # guessed by player
guesses=0                            # number of guesses made
number=$(( $RANDOM % $biggest ))     # random number, 1 .. $biggest
# NOTE: On Solaris, omit the "$$" above

echo "You're trying to guess a number between 1 and $biggest"

while [ $guess -ne $number ] ; do
  echo -n "Guess? " ; read guess    # NOTE: On Solaris, use: echo "Guess? \\c"
  read guess
  if [ "$guess" -lt $number ] ; then
    echo "... bigger!"
  elif [ "$guess" -gt $number ] ; then
    echo "... smaller!"
  fi
  guesses=$(( $guesses + 1 ))
done

echo "Right!! Guessed $number in $guesses guesses."

exit 0
```

The `while` loop runs until the number is guessed. Once matched, the script drops out of the loop entirely and shows the last `echo` statement, including how many guesses it took. Then it exits.

3. Let's play it a few times to see how it works:

```
$ hi-low
You're trying to guess a number between 1 and 100
Guess? 50
... bigger!
Guess? 75
... smaller!
```

```
Guess? 69
Right!! Guessed 69 in 3 guesses.

$ hi-low
You're trying to guess a number between 1 and 100
Guess? 50
... bigger!
Guess? 75
... smaller!
Guess? 68
... bigger!
Guess? 73
... smaller!
Guess? 71
Right!! Guessed 71 in 5 guesses.
```

Three guesses is lucky. Five guesses is good. More than seven guesses, and you're being inefficient in your playing strategy.

4. Remember that I said I'd tell you the secret strategy to games like this? Here's the trick: To solve the hi-low game, you need to split the set of possible numbers as evenly in half as possible on each and every guess. If you're choosing a number in the range 1 to 100, then the first guess should be right in the middle: 50.

With one guess, you'll then be able to eliminate over half of the possible numbers. (Think about that. In both cases when the game said that I needed to guess a number higher than 50, it told me that 1–49 weren't possible and that 50 wasn't a possibility. Therefore, the resultant number had to be in the set 51–100.)

Each time your guess should be right in the middle again.

This turns out to be a logarithmic problem, and the exact number of guesses it should take to solve a 1–100 hi-low game is actually log2(100), or 6.6. We can round up to 7 and then state unequivocally that if it takes you more than seven guesses, you're not playing smart.

This also means that if you wanted to try playing the game with a number between 1 and 1,000, then that should only add three guesses to the game, using an optimal strategy.

Next time some youngster asks you to play this game, you now know the winning strategy!

I wouldn't want to try to write *Call of Duty* or *Halo* as a shell script, but for rudimentary games, the shell offer a simple and straightforward programming environment. If you want a challenge, see if you can write the game hangman as a shell script. In my book *Wicked Cool Shell Scripts*, I present a full implementation of this game in 74 lines—including comments!

Summary

In this hour, you had a chance to delve further into the fun and interesting world of shell script programming, and you saw how knowledge of the commands available at the Unix command line also gives you the ability to write some remarkably sophisticated shell scripts. Even better, almost all shell scripts are portable across a wide range of Unix and Linux systems. All of the scripts presented in this hour work without modification on FreeBSD, Red Hat, Debian Linux, and even Mac OS X. (Solaris just requires a couple of tweaks in order for the hi-low game to work properly.)

Workshop

The Workshop summarizes the key terms you've learned and poses some questions about the topics presented in this lesson. It also provides you with a preview of what you will learn in the next hour.

Key Terms

modulus The modulus is the remainder value after a numerator is divided by a denominator.

signal trap A signal trap is a shell script command that lets you associate a specific set of tasks with a signal event. See the signal(2) man page for more information.

Exercises

1. What would happen if you ran the script mkmylocatedb by using the sudo capability in Unix? Why would that be a potential security hole?

2. The first line in a script starts with #!. What's that mean, and what important function does this line serve in shell script programming?

3. How would you modify the cmdcnt script to have it work in situations where one of the directories in the PATH has a space in its name?

4. Offer an explanation for why there's such a dramatic difference in the number of commands across different Unix installations.

5. If the optimal number of guesses in hi-low for a game ranging from 1 to 100 is 7, and the optimal number of guesses for a game ranging from 1 to 1,000 is 10, how many guesses should it take for you to guess the number if the values range from 1 to 10,000? (Hint: Try man bc.)

Preview of the Next Hour

In the next hour, you'll learn how to work with printers in the Unix environment. It's not easy, but with a good tour guide, you'll make it out of the jungle unscathed.

HOUR 18
Printing in the Unix Environment

Goals for This Hour

In this hour, you will learn

- ▶ How to find local printers with `lpstat`
- ▶ About CUPS
- ▶ How to send a print job to a printer with `lpr` or `lp`
- ▶ About formatting print jobs with `pr` and `col`
- ▶ How to work with the print queue by using `lpq` and `lprm`
- ▶ About working with cloud-based printing services

Printing is one of the greatest shortcomings of Unix. Generating printouts is a sufficiently common task that it should be fairly easy to accomplish. However, in this one area of Unix, continual conflict exists between the System V and BSD groups, to the detriment of all.

This hour focuses on some of the most common Unix commands for working with printers. It is a primer on learning what printers are hooked up to your system, how to send output to a printer, how to check that your print requests are in the queue for printing, and how to remove your print requests from the queue if you decide not to print.

Various techniques can minimize the complexity of printing in Unix. The best one is to create an alias called `print` that has all the default configuration information you want. If you define `PRINTER` as an environment variable (probably in your `.login` file or similar), most of the Unix print utilities will default to that device, for example, when searching print queues for jobs. The queue, or list, is where all print jobs are placed for processing by the specific printer.

NOTE

The differing "philosophies" of BSD and System V have caused problems in the area of printing. In a nutshell, because Unix systems are almost always networked (that is, hooked together with high-speed data-communications lines), the most valuable feature of a printing tool would be allowing the user to choose to print on any of the many printers attached to the network. For this to work, each machine with an attached printer must be listening for requests from other machines. The root of the BSD versus System V problem is that the two listen for different requests. A System V machine typically can't send a print job to a printer attached to a BSD machine and vice versa. And we haven't even started talking about Linux systems, Windows servers, and Mac systems yet. It's, well, complicated.

Making a Printed Copy

It's one thing to create wonderful material in your Unix account and another entirely to have it printed. That's what this lesson is all about.

Task 18.1: Finding Local Printers with `lpstat`

Of the many problems with printing in Unix, none is more frustrating than trying to figure out the names of all the different printers available, what kinds of printers they are, and where they're located.

Fortunately, all modern Unix and Linux systems—and even Mac OS X—include support for the `lp` family of printer commands, most notably the `lpstat` command, which lists printers available on the system, albeit with very user-unfriendly names.

1. Jump in and use `lpstat` to see if your system has any printers configured:

```
$ lpstat
$
```

Nothing. But you might actually have a printer configured on the system nonetheless because what `lpstat` shows is the current status of the printer queue, not a list of all printers on the system.

2. There are a number of different starting flags, but the one that you'll use with `lpstat` more often than anything else is `-a`. Here's why:

```
$ lpstat -a
Samsung_ML_191x_252x_Series___MiniMe accepting requests since Sat Jun 20
➥ 22:57:19 2015
$
```

There's a printer configured and accepting print requests after all. Of course, its name is more than a bit unfriendly:

```
Samsung_ML_191x_252x_Series___MiniMe
```

Still, this is how you ascertain what printers are configured and available with `lpstat`.

3. You can fix the name problem by creating a nickname for this particular printer. Doing so will require a judicious copy and paste to make sure that you get exactly the current complex name in use. This is accomplished with the helpful `lpadmin` command:

```
$ lpadmin -p "Samsung_ML_191x_252x_Series___MiniMe" -c "ml191"
$
```

Turns out you can't easily create nicknames, but you can create a new class of printers called ml191. That's what the -c flag does above.

One more step is required: You need to enable the destination and let it accept print jobs:

```
$ lpadmin -p "ml191" -E
$
```

Now, finally, you can work with a friendlier name:

```
$ lpstat -a ml191
ml191 accepting requests since Mon Jun 29 09:39:48 2015
```

Quite a relief!

The first, and perhaps biggest, hurdle for printing on Unix has been solved: figuring out what printers are available and, as needed, being able to configure a more command-line-friendly nickname through lpadmin.

Task 18.2: An Introduction to CUPS

Modern Unix and Linux systems—again including Mac OS X —are commonly built atop a different printing system, not the lp commands. The more powerful and flexible solution is the Common Unix Printing System (CUPS). It's an attempt at a unified solution to the chaos of printing and the fractured printer interaction on the various Unix systems that occurred as different vendors tried to innovate without sharing code or even matching each other's rudimentary features.

The philosophy behind CUPS is quite interesting, actually. It's based on layers of processing and filtering and meta-languages for the printouts themselves. It shows up in unlikely places, too, including within the 10.x Mac OS X printing subsystem.

The task of installing and configuring CUPS is beyond the scope of this introductory book, but let's at least have a brief glimpse at the system and the usual way to add a new printer to a CUPS-friendly Unix box.

1. In most cases, plugging in a USB-based printer to a Unix or Linux system is sufficient for it to be recognized and properly configured and then to show up as an available device for command-line and GUI-based usage. Check to see if your particular printer is known by CUPS by referring to the supported printer list at www.openprinting.org.

   Double-check the configuration of your particular printer by directing a Web browser to http://localhost:631/. (This is easiest through a GUI system like GNOME, as demonstrated in Hour 24, "GNOME and the GUI Environment.") Figure 18.1 shows the result.

FIGURE 18.1
Accessing CUPS through a Web browser: permission denied.

2. Oops! As you can see, you'll need to go back to the command line and invoke the following command:

```
$ cupsctl WebInterface=yes
$
```

Now try that browser access to `localhost:631` again, as shown in Figure 18.2.

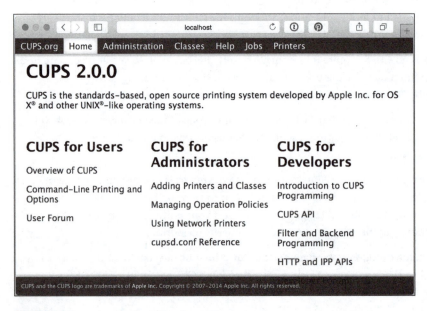

FIGURE 18.2
CUPS is easiest to work with via a Web browser.

3. Click on the Printers tab to see what printers, if any, you have configured (see Figure 18.3).

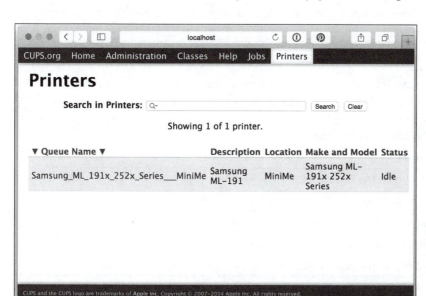

FIGURE 18.3
A Samsung printer ready to go in the CUPS interface.

4. Can't get things to work correctly with your printer? You might need to install a PostScript interpreter (GhostScript is the most popular) or similar. You can learn about how to troubleshoot your particular printer configuration by going to http://www.openprinting.org.

However hardcore your command-line zeal for Unix, there are still a few tasks that are more easily accomplished from a graphical interface like GNOME. And while CUPS is now extraordinarily powerful and flexible, I recommend that you try to get any new Unix printer configured and online through the Unix or Linux GUI tools, not the command line. Once you've done so, they become available for both command-line and graphical interface interaction, fortunately.

Task 18.3: Printing Files with `lpr` or `lp`

Now that you have identified the name of the printer to use, how do you send information to the printer? If you are on a BSD system, the command to do this is `lpr`. You can print the results of a pipe command by adding `lpr` at the end of the pipeline, or you can print files directly by specifying them to the program. You can even use < to redirect input.

NOTE

If you're using a System V version of Unix, you will need to use the `lp` command instead. As you read through this hour, you will see the differences between `lpr` and `lp` indicated. Note how the philosophies of the two vary.

Numerous flags are available for `lpr` and `lp`; the most valuable ones are listed in Table 18.1 and Table 18.2. Notice the different meanings of the `-P` flag with the two commands.

TABLE 18.1 Useful Flags for `lpr`

Flag	Meaning
`-h`	Do not print the header page.
`-i`	Indent the entire file eight spaces before printing.
`-L`	Print in landscape (sideways) mode, if the printer is capable of doing so.
`-P`*printer*	Send the print job to printer *printer*.
`-R`	Print pages in reverse order.

TABLE 18.2 Useful Flags for `lp`

Flag	Meaning
`-d`*printer*	Send the print job to the printer named *printer*.
`-P`*n*	Print only page *n*.
`-t`*title*	Use *title* as the cover page title, where *title* is any string.

1. Here's a demonstration of what happens if you try to use `lp` or `lpr` without specifying a printer and without having the PRINTER environment variable set. First, remove the environment variable definition for PRINTER by setting it to an empty string:

```
$ PRINTER=""
$ who | lpr
lpr: No printer specified
Broken pipe
```

Some systems default to a printer named `lp` in this situation, so if you don't get an error message, that's what happened. If you have `lpstat` (a command for checking the status of a printer), the `-d` flag will result in `lpstat` listing your default printer.

To specify a printer, use the `-P` flag with `lpr` or the `-d` flag with `lp`, followed immediately by the name of the printer:

```
$ who | lpr -Pattic3
```

Specifying a printer with the -P flag (or -d with lp) will always override the environment variable specified in PRINTER; therefore, you can specify the default printer with PRINTER and specify other printers as needed without any danger.

Notice that I printed the output of the who command but received absolutely no information from the lpr command regarding what printer it was sent to, the print job number, or any other information.

To make life easier, I'm going to redefine PRINTER:

```
$ PRINTER=attic3
```

2. To find out what's in the print queue, I can use lpstat -pprinter on System V or the lpq -Pprinter command:

```
$ lpq -Pattic3

attic3@intuitive.com:   driver not active
        Printing is disabled.

Pos  User      Bin    Size   Jobname
---  ----      ----   ----   -------
  1  KOSHIHWE  0104   008    KOSHIHWE0104a
  2  KOSHIHWE  0104   008    KOSHIHWE0104b
  3  KOSHIHWE  0104   008    KOSHIHWE0104c
  4  kleimanj  0317   032    kleimanj0317a
  5  zeta      0042   008    zeta0042a
  6  jharger   0167   008    jharger0167a
  7  jharger   0167   008    jharger0167b
  8  ssinfo    0353   000    ssinfo0353a
  9  fuelling  0216   024    fuelling0216a
 10  zeta      0042   152    zeta0042b
 11  tkjared   0142   012    tkjared0142a
 12  SUJATHA   0043   016    SUJATHA0043a
 13  SUJATHA   0043   024    SUJATHA0043b
 24  taylor    0889   000    taylor0889a

attic3: waiting to be transmitted to intuitive.com

The queue is empty.
```

Quite a few print jobs are waiting to be sent, but it's not obvious why the printer is disabled. (The output of the lpq and lpstat commands is explained in detail later in this hour.)

3. To print the file dickens.note in landscape mode, without a header page, indented eight spaces, and in reverse page order, I can use the following flags:

```
$ lpr -hiLR < dickens.note
```

If I did this often, a shell alias could be helpful:

```
$ alias lpr='lpr -hiLR'
```

On a System V machine, you also could create the alias `lpr='lp'`, though be careful because none of the particular options shown in the previous example are available with `lp`.

If you find yourself printing to a couple of different printers quite often, you easily can define a few shell aliases to create printer-specific `print` commands:

```
$ alias mathprint='lpr -Pmathlw'
$ alias libprint='lpr -Plibrary'
$ alias edprint='lpr -Pedlw'
```

On System V machines, the aliases would look like this:

```
$ alias mathprint='lp -dmathlw'
$ alias libprint='lp -dlibrary'
$ alias edprint='lp -dedlw'
```

4. Some systems have a command `lpinfo` that also offers information about printers:

```
$ lpinfo mathlw
mathlw: server.utech.edu; MATH 734; multiple HP LaserJet Pro
```

To find out more information about the printer, you can specify the `-v` flag:

```
$ lpinfo -v mathlw
mathlw description:
        driver: /usr/local/lib/lp/lpmq
        printer control group: cc
        graphic filter: /usr/local/bin/psplot
        log file: /usr/spool/lpr/mathlw/logfile
        lock file: /usr/spool/lpr/mathlw/lock
        hardware line: /dev/null
        maximum job count per user = 25
        subqueue list: mathlw1,mathlw2,mathlw3
        maximum print file blocks = 3000
        make unique via bin change
        network driver: /usr/local/lib/lp/lpnc
        ditroff filter: /usr/local/lib/devps/devps
        print formats: graphics, ditroff, use pr, troff
        queue ordering: age
        host attachment: server.utech.edu
        spooling directory: /usr/spool/lpr/mathlw
        location: MATH 734
        description: multiple HP LaserJet Pro
```

5. The `lpinfo` command also can show you a list of what printers are available, but I find the output format considerably more difficult to understand than the output of `lpstat`:

```
$ lpinfo -a | head -15
aglw:    server.utech.edu; AG 23; multiple HP LaserJet Pro
aglw1:         server.utech.edu; AG 23; HP LaserJet Pro
aglw2:         server.utech.edu; AG 23; HP LaserJet Pro
aglw3:         server.utech.edu; AG 23; HP LaserJet Pro
aglw4:         server.utech.edu; AG 23; HP LaserJet Pro
alpslw: sentinel.utech.edu; LIB 111; HP LaserJet ProX
bio:     ace.utech.edu; COM B117; DataPrinter (self-service)
cary:    franklin.utech.edu; CQuad (NE-B7); IBM 4019 Laser Printer
cslw: server.utech.edu; CS 2249; HP LaserJet Pro
cs115lw:       expert.utech.edu; CS 115; IBM 4019 LaserPrinter (for CS180)
cs115lw2:      expert.utech.edu; CS 115; IBM 4019 LaserPrinter (for CS180)
csg40lw:       franklin.utech.edu; CS G040; IBM 4019 LaserPrinter
csg50lw:       franklin.utech.edu; CS G050; IBM 4019 LaserPrinter
cslp1: expert.utech.edu; CS G73; C.Itoh, white paper (self-service)
eng130ci:      age.utech.edu; ENG 130; C.Itoh, white paper (self-service)
Broken pipe
```

If you find this output readable, you're undoubtedly becoming a real Unix expert!

In this instance, the output of the `printers` command specifies the physical location of the printer, showing that I need to go to another building to pick up my hard copy

Task 18.4: Formatting Print Jobs with `pr` and `col`

The printout I generated in Task 18.3 looked good but boring. I would like to have a running header on each page that specifies the name of the file and the page number. I'd also like to have a bit more control over some other formatting characteristics. This is where the `pr` command comes in handy. Not intended just for printing, `pr` is actually a general pagination and formatting command that can also be used to display information on the screen. Even better, `pr` is available on both BSD and System V Unix.

The `pr` program is loaded with options, most of which can be quite useful. For example, `-2` makes the output two columns, which is useful for printing results of the `who` command in landscape mode. The most useful options are presented in Table 18.3.

TABLE 18.3 Useful Flags in `pr`

Flag	Meaning
-n	Produce n-column output per page.
+n	Begin printing on the nth page.
-f	Don't print the page header and footer information.

Flag	Meaning
-h*header*	Use *header* as the head of each page.
-w*n*	Set the page width to *n* characters (for landscape mode).
-m	Print all files at once, one per column.

1. My printout of the who command showed me that my choice of paper was poor. In a 128-character-wide landscape printout, I actually used only the first 30 characters or so of each line. Instead, I can use pr to print in two-column mode:

NOTE

On some Unix systems, the -f flag to pr causes the program to put form feeds at the bottom of each printed page. To suppress the header and footer, use -t. I warned you that printing in Unix is chaotic, right?

```
$ who | pr -2 | more


May  9 13:48 2015    Page 1


root       console May 6 18:02    ab        ttypk  May 9 07:57  (nova)
princess   ttyaV   May 9 13:44    dutch     ttypl  May 8 13:36  (dov)
tempus     ttyaW   May 9 13:43    malman    ttypm  May 9 13:07  (dov)
enatsuex   ttyaY   May 9 13:41    bakasmg   ttypq  May 9 13:09  (age)
coxt       ttyaZ   May 9 13:35    dodsondt  ttyps  May 8 11:37  (age)
scfarley   ttyAa   May 9 13:36    md        ttypv  May 8 08:23  (kraft)
nancy      ttyAb   May 9 13:12    rothenba  ttypw  May 9 13:15  (trinetra)
rick       ttyAc   May 9 13:12    xuxiufan  ttypy  May 9 13:16  (ector)
fitzte     ttyAd   May 9 13:47    nashrm    ttyq3  May 9 13:04  (pc115)
maluong    ttyAe   May 9 13:46    dls       ttyq5  May 9 13:06  (dialup01)
af5        ttyAg   May 9 09:12    myounce   ttyq8  May 9 02:14  (limbo)
zjin       ttyAh   May 9 13:44    liyan     ttyq9  May 9 13:11  (volt)
herbert1   ttyAi   May 9 13:29    daffnelr  ttyqA  May 9 13:36  (localhost)
ebranson   ttyAj   May 9 13:44    mm        ttyqB  May 9 10:32  (mm)
billiam    ttyAk   May 9 13:36    jlapham   ttyqC  May 9 12:46  (mac18)
linet2     ttyAm   May 9 11:04    chuicc    ttyqE  May 9 13:38  (icarus)
--More--  _
```

Notice that the pr program not only made this a two-column listing but also added a page header that indicates the current date and page number.

2. The header still doesn't contain any information about the command name, and that would really be helpful. Fortunately, I easily can add the header information I want by using pr:

```
$ who | pr -h "(output of the who command)" -2 | more


May  9 13:50 2015  (output of the who command) Page 1


root      console May 6 18:02    ab        ttypk    May 9 07:57  (nova)
princess  ttyaV   May 9 13:44    dutch     ttypl    May 8 13:36  (dov)
tempus    ttyaW   May 9 13:43    malman    ttypm    May 9 13:07  (dov)
enatsuex  ttyaY   May 9 13:41    bakasmg   ttypq    May 9 13:09  (age)
coxt      ttyaZ   May 9 13:35    dodsondt  ttyps    May 8 11:37  (age)
scfarley  ttyAa   May 9 13:36    md        ttypv    May 8 08:23  (kraft)
nancy     ttyAb   May 9 13:12    rothenba  ttypw    May 9 13:15  (trinetra)
rick      ttyAc   May 9 13:12    xuxiufan  ttypy    May 9 13:16  (ector)
fitzte    ttyAd   May 9 13:47    dls       ttyq5    May 9 13:06  (dialup01)
maluong   ttyAe   May 9 13:46    myounce   ttyq8    May 9 02:14  (limbo)
maritanj  ttyAf   May 9 13:49    liyan     ttyq9    May 9 13:11  (volt)
af5       ttyAg   May 9 09:12    daffnelr  ttyqA    May 9 13:36 (localhost)
zjin      ttyAh   May 9 13:48    mm        ttyqB    May 9 10:32  (mm)
herbert1  ttyAi   May 9 13:29    jlapham   ttyqC    May 9 12:46  (mac18)
ebranson  ttyAj   May 9 13:44    chuicc    ttyqE    May 9 13:38  (icarus)
--More-- _
```

That's much better.

3. I might want to compare the contents of two different directories. The -1 flag to ls forces the ls program to list the output one filename per line, so I can create a couple of files in this format easily:

```
$ ls -1 src > src.listing
$ ls -1 /tmp > tmp.listing
```

These files look like this:

```
$ head src.listing tmp.listing
==> src.listing <==
calc-help
calc.c
fixit.c
info.c
info.o
```

```
==> tmp.listing <==
Erik/
GIri/
Garry/
MmIsAlive
Re01759
Re13201
Sting/
VR001187
VR002540
VR002678
```

Now I can use pr to build a two-column output:

```
$$ pr -m src.listing tmp.listing | head -15


May   9 13:53 2015    Page 1



calc-help                          Erik/
calc.c                             GIri/
fixit.c                            Garry/
info.c                             MmIsAlive
info.o                             Re01759
massage.c                          Re13201
                                   Sting/
                                   VR001187
                                   VR002540

Broken pipe
```

4. This would be more helpful if I could turn off the blank lines automatically included at the top of each listing page, which is a job for the -f flag (or -t, if your version of pr is -f for form feeds):

```
$ pr -f -m src.listing tmp.listing | head -15
May   9 13:56 2015    Page 1



calc-help                          Erik/
calc.c                             GIri/
fixit.c                            Garry/
info.c                             MmIsAlive
info.o                             Re01759
massage.c                          Re13201
                                   Sting/
                                   VR001187
                                   VR002540
                                   VR002678
```

```
                         VR002982
                         VR004477
Broken pipe
```

It looks good.

5. Now it's time to print by piping the output of the `pr` command to the `lpr` command:

```
$ !pr | lpr
pr -f -m src.listing tmp.listing | lpr
```

6. As you proceed with printing tasks in Unix, you might find sporadically that you get output of the form H^HH^HH^Hhe^He^He^Hel^Hl^Hl^Hll^Hl^Hl^Hlo^Ho^Ho^Ho. Many versions of the `man` command output bold text in just this fashion: What you're seeing is a letter followed by a backspace, the letter, a backspace, the letter, and a backspace, and the letter one last time. The above is "Hello" in this manner.

NOTE

The backspace-for-emphasis format is from old daisy-wheel and dot-matrix printers (remember those? I do!) and makes no sense with modern printers. If you see this, you'll want to know about using the helpful `col` command with its `-b` flag, which strips out all the backspace sequences. You simply add it to your pipe:

```
$ pr -f -m src.listing tmp.listing | col -b | lpr
```

The `pr` command can be used to ensure that your printouts are always clean and readable. Again, it's a perfect place to create an alias, such as `alias print='pr | lpr'` or `alias print='pr | lp'`. Even without any flags, `pr` automatically adds page numbers to the top of each page.

Task 18.5: Working with the Print Queue

On a personal computer, you might have your printer directly connected to your system, so anything you print using File -> Print (on Windows and the Mac) instantly prints. Larger networks tend toward shared printers with print queues to manage the order of jobs and pages coming out of the device, however. This is a model that underlies all Unix printing systems: When you send a file to a printer with `lpr` or `lp`, the request is added to a queue of files waiting to print. Your request goes to the bottom of the list, and any subsequent print requests are added below yours. Your print request gradually moves up to the top and prints when its turn has arrived.

Sometimes it can be frustrating to wait for a printout. However, a queuing system has advantages over simply allowing users to share a single printer. The biggest of these is that you can use the `lprm` command to change your mind and remove print requests from the queue before they waste paper.

The `lprm` command works with the print job name, which you can learn by checking the print queue using `lpq`. Both `lprm` and `lpq` can either use the default PRINTER setting or can have printers specified with `-Pprinter`. The `lpq` command also can limit output to just your jobs by adding your account name to the command.

If your system doesn't have `lprm`, use the `cancel` command to remove entries from the print queue. The `lpstat` command is also the System V replacement for the `lpq` command, though many sites alias `lpq = lpstat` to make life a bit easier.

To use `cancel`, you need to specify the name of the printer and the job ID, as listed in the `lpstat` output. For example, if I had print request ID 37 on printer `hardcopy`, I could cancel the print request with the command `cancel hardcopy -37`.

Let's have a look.

1. A glance at the `mathlw` queue shows that many files are waiting to print:

```
$ lpq
```

```
mathlw@server.utech.edu:   driver not active
          Printing is disabled.

    Pos   User      Bin    Size   Jobname
    ---   ----      ----   ----   -------
      1   KOSHIHWE  0104   008    KOSHIHWE0104a
      2   KOSHIHWE  0104   008    KOSHIHWE0104b
      3   KOSHIHWE  0104   008    KOSHIHWE0104c
      4   kleimanj  0317   032    kleimanj0317a
      5   zeta      0042   008    zeta0042a
      6   jharger   0167   008    jharger0167a
      7   jharger   0167   008    jharger0167b
      8   ssinfo    0353   000    ssinfo0353a
      9   fuelling  0216   024    fuelling0216a
     10   zeta      0042   152    zeta0042b
     11   tkjared   0142   012    tkjared0142a
     12   SUJATHA   0043   016    SUJATHA0043a
     13   SUJATHA   0043   024    SUJATHA0043b
     14   SUJATHA   0043   044    SUJATHA0043c
     15   bee       0785   012    bee0785a
     16   bee       0785   056    bee0785b
     17   bee       0785   028    bee0785c
     18   info      0353   004    info0353b
     19   info      0353   000    info0353c
     20   info      0353   000    info0353d
     21   info      0353   004    info0353e
     22   stacysm2  0321   000    stacysm20321a
     23   info      0353   000    info0353f
     24   taylor    0889   000    taylor0889a
```

```
mathlw: waiting to be transmitted to server.utech.edu
```

The queue is empty.

My print job, named `taylor0889a`, is job number 24 name.

The printer is also turned off. You can see at the top of the `lpq` output the telltale message `driver not active Printing is disabled`. Obviously, if the printer is disabled, it's rather futile to wait for a printout! Still, let's just proceed with the expectation that it'll resume printing momentarily.

2. To limit the output to just those print jobs that are mine, I specify my account name:

```
$ lpq taylor
mathlw@server.utech.edu:    driver not active
        Printing is disabled.

Pos  User      Bin   Size  Jobname
---  ----      ----  ----  -------
  1  taylor    0889  004   taylor0889a

mathlw: waiting to be transmitted to server.utech.edu
```

The queue is empty.

3. To check the status of another printer, I can specify the printer with the `-P` flag:

```
$ lpq -Pb280il

b280il@franklin.utech.edu:          driver not active

The queue is empty.

b280il:    waiting to be transmitted to franklin.utech.edu
```

The queue is empty.

This looks like a better printer to use; its queue is empty.

4. To remove my print job from the `mathlw` print queue, I specify the print job name from the `lpq` output:

```
$ lprm taylor0889a
```

Unix carries out my command without giving me confirmation that it has succeeded, but a quick check with `lpq` shows that it worked:

```
$ lpq taylor
mathlw@server.utech.edu:    driver not active
        Printing is disabled.
```

```
The queue is empty.

mathlw: waiting to be transmitted to server.utech.edu

The queue is empty.
```

NOTE

I wish that the default for the `lpq` command would show only print jobs that I have in the queue, and I could use the `-a` flag to show all print jobs queued. Furthermore, instead of incorrectly saying `The queue is empty`, `lpq` should report something more useful, such as `there are 23 other print jobs in the queue`. Such is the Unix life, though.

5. Now I resubmit the print job request, this time to the `b280il` printer:

```
$ !pr -Pb280il
pr -f -m src.listing tmp.listing | head -15 | lpr -Pb280il
```

Uh oh! I don't want that `head -15` cutting off the information in the printout. Here's the fix:

```
$ lpq -Pb280il
b280il@franklin.utech.edu:        driver active; no job printing

Pos  User      Bin   Size  Jobname
---  ----      ----  ----  -------
  1  nfsuser   0058  268   nfsuser0058a
  2  nfsuser   0054  012   nfsuser0054a
  3  taylor    0889  000   taylor0889a

b280il:     waiting to be transmitted to franklin.utech.edu

The queue is empty.
```

To remove my print request, I use `lprm`:

```
$ lprm taylor0889a
"taylor0889a" not located.
```

I've made a second mistake! I need to specify the printer:

```
$ lprm -Pb280il taylor0889a
```

Now I can fix the original command and print the files correctly:

```
$ pr -f -m src.listing tmp.listing | lpr -Pb280il
```

Unix offers some printing capabilities you might not be accustomed to working with, particularly the capability to change your mind and stop a print job before it touches paper. You can see that it's a good idea to set the PRINTER environment variable to your favorite printer so that you can save yourself from struggling to enter weird printer names each time you print a file.

Summary

A few judiciously defined aliases can save you a lot of frustration down the road. Get your printer of choice configured and set up with your Unix system's printer setup utility, adding it to CUPS if needed. Then choose your favorite printer, define the PRINTER environment variable to point to that printer, and give yourself an alias that includes all the options you like for your printouts. You might consider creating an alias pq to show your own print requests queued for your favorite printer. (This is easy to do. Use alias pq='lpq $LOGNAME' or alias pq='lpstat -u $LOGNAME'.) You also could show only your print requests, if any, by tucking a grep into the command: alias pq='lpq | grep $LOGNAME'.

Workshop

The Workshop summarizes the key terms you've learned and poses some questions about the topics presented in this lesson. It also provides you with a preview of what you will learn in the next hour.

Key Terms

PostScript This printout formatting language is designed to allow sophisticated page layout from various programs. GhostScript is an open source implementation of the PostScript language and is included as part of the CUPS distribution.

print job name This is the unique name assigned to a print job by the lpr or lp command.

print queue All print jobs are placed in a queue, or list, for processing by a specific printer.

Exercises

1. Use the lpinfo -a command or the printers command to find out what printers are available on your system. Which command is easier to use? How many printers are available?

2. Is your PRINTER variable already set to a printer? Is it the printer you would choose?

3. Use man -k to see what commands you have on your system that work with the printers and print queues. Use man to peruse them.

4. Show three ways to print the file dickens.note with lpr.

5. Add a print job to the queue and then remove it with lprm. What happened?

6. How would you use pr to add A Tale of Two Cities as a running title across each printout page of the file dickens.note? How would you start the printout on the second page of the file?

Preview of the Next Hour

In the next hour, you'll learn about the various ways you can archive backups and otherwise work with your file system as a whole. You'll also learn about how Unixes now work with package management systems to make the process of installing software considerably less work.

HOUR 19
Archives and Backups

Goals for This Hour

In this hour, you will learn

- ▶ About the `tar` tape archive utility
- ▶ About using zip to create PC-compatible ZIP archives
- ▶ How to use `compress` to shrink down large files, along with `gzip` and `bzip2`
- ▶ About `cpio` and `tcio`
- ▶ About a common personal backup scheme
- ▶ How to work with package management systems

It's your worst nightmare: You wake up, log in to your newly customized Unix account, and find that everything is gone. All your aliases, shell scripts, mail files, and HTML documents...missing. You email the administrator in a panic, and she responds, "Oh, yeah, sorry. Had to reformat the drive."

Now, granted, it would be a pretty poorly run system in which the administrator thought it would be acceptable to reformat the drive without restoring all users' data to the condition it was in immediately beforehand. But it does happen. Especially with hobbyist systems or university clusters, the policy will often be that they'll try to restore your data after a reinstall, but they'll make no guarantees. In any case, the techniques we're about to go over will stand you in good stead if you're ever running your own Unix system.

To avoid the sort of horrible situation just described, you need a solid archival and backup strategy for your own files, and that's the focus of this lesson. In particular, we will explore the `tar` command as a simple tool for making single-file backup images of large amounts of information, and we will examine the `compress`, `gzip`, and `bzip2` commands to shrink the resultant archives as small as possible.

There are a number of ways to write your backup data to a tape unit, CD-RW, or network backup device. Most of them work with the `cpio` or `tcio` commands, so they'll be examined this hour, too. I've used Unix and Linux systems for 25-plus years, and `tar` remains the cornerstone of my own backup strategy.

With the rise of cloud storage, however, many people are backing up files and archives directly to a cloud drive like Dropbox, Google Drive, or even iCloud. Some are easy to access from the command line, others not so much. Since the cloud systems were designed for graphical user interfaces, they all require complicated programs to be installed and verified before you can use them from a command line, however, and that's definitely beyond the scope of this book. If you'd like to learn more, do some Google searches for "google drive from linux command line" or similar. And be prepared for the complexity.

Finally, this hour wraps up with a brief discussion of modern Unix package management systems, notably Red Hat Linux's RPM system. If you're on a contemporary Unix system, it's a must-read.

Regardless of which of these backup strategies you choose, I highly recommend that you do *something* to ensure the survival of your data. Even if your administrator insists that she does regular backups and your files are safe, it's dangerous to rely on someone else to protect your precious data!

NOTE

Indeed, I have personal experience with the danger of relying on backups. It was way back in December 1999, when I noticed a hacker had broken into our Unix system and was destroying files. (I used `ps` to see what he was doing.) I tried to log him out and protect the system, but it was too late. We lost everything. Fortunately, we had backup tapes . . . until we tried to use them. Then we found the unpleasant truth: The backups hadn't been working for weeks, and the failed backups kept overwriting the tapes. As a result, we lost over a month of files, software development, and client documents—not a pretty sight.

The `tar` Tape Archive Utility

It's not glamorous, but `tar` has been around forever on Unix. It was originally written to work with tape devices, actually, and has helped create millions of backups. What most people don't realize is that `tar` can be really useful for regular folk who don't need to learn how to write to a tape device or otherwise administer the computer. It might not be the most efficient tool for every task, but it's definitely fast and easy to work with once you figure out all the flags.

Task 19.1: Learning to Use `tar`

Even though you can use about 20 different flags with `tar`, fundamentally the program has three modes of operating: building an archive, showing the contents of an archive, or extracting files from an archive. They are `tar -c` (for creation), `tar -t` (for a table of contents of an archive), and `tar -x` (to extract data). `tar` commands look like this:

```
tar [flags] file or directory names
```

Let's take a look at how `tar` works.

1. To start out, I'd like to create a quick archival snapshot of all the files and folders in my home directory. To do this, I create an output file in /tmp:

```
$ tar -cf /tmp/backup.tar *
$
```

There was no output, but it took about 10 seconds to execute, so I assume that something happened. The `-c` flag tells `tar` to create an archive, remember, and `-f file` indicates the name of the output file. `*`, of course, indicates that all files and folders in the current directory should be matched.

CAUTION

Be careful with `*` expansion and `tar`. In this first example, the backup didn't include any of my dot files or the dot directories created by various programs, including my `.profile` and `.bashrc` files. If you're backing up your home directory, use `.` for the archive to ensure that you get absolutely everything, as demonstrated below.

A quick peek with `ls` tells the surprising story:

```
$ ls -l /tmp/backup.tar
-rw-r--r--  1 taylor  wheel  15360000 Feb  8 02:52 /tmp/backup.tar
$
```

Wow! That's a big output file—15.3 megabytes.

2. To get more output and have a better idea of what's going on, I redo the archive command, but this time I add the `-v` (verbose) flag:

```
$ tar -cvf /tmp/backup.tar .
.
./.cshrc
./.login
./.mailrc
./.profile
./.rhosts
./.bash_history
./Talks
./Talks/Writeups
```

```
./Talks/Writeups/biz-and-the-net
./Talks/Writeups/html-half.1
./Talks/Writeups/html-half.2
./Talks/Writeups/instant-homepage
./Talks/Writeups/intro-to-the-net

lots and lots of output removed

./pict.pict
./browse.sh
./test.html
./Exchange
./Exchange/build-exchrate
./Exchange/exchange.pl
./Exchange/exchange.db
./etcpasswd
./badjoke
./badjoke.rot13
$
```

Pretty straightforward, isn't it?

3. To have a peek at what's inside a tar archive file, use the -t flag instead of -c for a *table of contents* instead of *creation* request:

```
$ tar -tf /tmp/backup.tar | head
.
./.cshrc
./.login
./.mailrc
./.profile
./.rhosts
./.bash_history
./Talks
./Talks/Writeups
./Talks/Writeups/biz-and-the-net
$
```

Notice that I piped the output to head so that I only see the top 10 lines.

I get more information about the archival files by combining -t with the -v verbose flag:

```
$ tar -tvf /tmp/backup.tar | head
drwxr-xr-x 2 taylor    taylor      0 Feb  7 14:41 .
-rw-r--r-- 1 taylor    taylor    817 Dec 14 16:09 ./.cshrc
-rw-r--r-- 1 taylor    taylor    581 Dec 14 16:09 ./.login
-rw-r--r-- 1 taylor    taylor    105 Dec 10 04:04 ./.mailrc
-rw-r--r-- 1 taylor    taylor    201 Dec 10 04:04 ./.profile
-rw------- 1 taylor    taylor     65 Dec 10 04:04 ./.rhosts
```

```
-rw-------  1 taylor   taylor   7545 Feb  7 15:30 ./.bash_history
drwxrwxr-x  2 taylor   taylor      0 Dec 14 16:09 ./Talks
drwxrwxr-x  2 taylor   taylor      0 Dec 14 16:09 ./Talks/Writeups
-rw-r--r--  1 taylor   taylor   1832 Dec 14 16:09 ./Talks/Writeups/biz-and-the-net
$
```

4. Now that I have a basic archival file, what can I do with it? Well, the easiest thing is to change the output from a file to a Unix archive device, so I can make a quick backup:

```
$ tar cf /dev/rst0 .
$
```

In the old days, it would have taken about 20 minutes to write to a backup tape, but newer media like a DVD burner work much faster—and a USB 3.0 flash drive is lightning fast. Regardless of the media onto which I copy the archive, now I have a copy of all my files that I can drop in my pocket, without worrying about whether the computer might crash or whether the admin is checking the validity of system backups.

5. In addition to writing backups and creating snapshots of files and folders for safety purposes, using tar turns out to be a great way to transfer clusters of files from one computer to another.

NOTE

ftp is a file transfer program (File Transfer Protocol) that lets you easily send files between two computers, basically a login/transfer file/logout system.

With the /tmp/backup.tar file created, all I'd have to do is use ftp to transfer it to another computer—or just email it to myself, if it's not insanely big—and then use tar on that computer to unpack it and replicate all of my files and folders on that system:

```
$ ftp intuitive.com
Connected to intuitive.com.
220 intuitive.com FTP server (Version wu-2.6.1(1) Sat May 2 14:46:30 PDT 2015)
ready.
Name (intuitive.com:taylor): taylor
331 Password required for taylor.
Password:
230 User taylor logged in.
Remote system type is UNIX.
Using binary mode to transfer files.
ftp> put /tmp/backup.tar
local: /tmp/backup.tar remote: backup.tar
227 Entering Passive Mode (206,184,139,134,121,43)
150 Opening BINARY mode data connection for backup.tar.
226 Transfer complete.
15800320 bytes sent in 171.45 seconds (90.00 KB/s)
```

```
ftp> quit
221-You have transferred 15800320 bytes in 1 files.
221-Total traffic for this session was 15800805 bytes in 1 transfers.
221-Thank you for using the FTP service.
221 Goodbye.
$
```

After the archive file has been transferred to the remote system, it's just a matter of unpacking things on the remote computer:

```
$ ls
$ tar -xf backup.tar
$ ls -F
CraigsList/      Shuttle/         buckaroo            pict.pict
Exchange/        Src/             etcpasswd           test.html
Gator/           Stuff/           getmodemdriver.sh*  test.sh*
Lists/           Talks/           getstocks.sh*       testfile
Lynx.trace       badjoke          gettermsheet.sh*    tif.tif
Mail/            badjoke.rot13    gif.gif
News/            bin/             jpg.jpg
Old/             browse.sh*       niftylister.tar
$
```

Quickly and easily done.

6. To get output from the tar extraction as it goes along, you could add the -v flag:

```
$ tar -xvf backup.tar
.
./.cshrc
./.login
./.mailrc
./.profile
./.rhosts
./.bash_history
./Talks
./Talks/Writeups
./Talks/Writeups/biz-and-the-net
./Talks/Writeups/html-half.1
./Talks/Writeups/html-half.2
./Talks/Writeups/instant-homepage
./Talks/Writeups/intro-to-the-net

lots and lots of output removed

./pict.pict
./browse.sh
./test.html
./Exchange
```

```
./Exchange/build-exchrate
./Exchange/exchange.pl
./Exchange/exchange.db
./etcpasswd
./badjoke
./badjoke.rot13
$
```

7. One important capability of tar worth showing here is that you can extract specific files and folders from an archive based on a pattern given to the program:

```
$ tar -xvf backup.tar Exchange
tar: WARNING! These patterns were not matched:
Exchange
$
```

8. Oops! Patterns have to be left-rooted (that is, they need to exactly match starting at the very first character of the file or directory name). Let's try again:

```
$ tar -xvf backup.tar ./Exchange
./Exchange
./Exchange/build-exchrate
./Exchange/exchange.pl
./Exchange/exchange.db
$
```

The tar command has a ton of options; the most useful of them are summarized in Table 19.1.

TABLE 19.1 Useful Options to tar

Option	Meaning
-c	Create an archive.
-f	Use the specified output filename.
-h	Follow symbolic links as if they were normal files or directories.
-H	Follow symbolic links on the command line only.
-j	Use bzip2 for compression.
-m	Do not preserve file modification times.
-p	Preserve user and group ID as well as file mode information.
-t	Show the table of contents of an archive.
-v	Enter verbose mode for more explanatory output.
-x	Extract files from an archive.
-Z	Compress an archive using compress.
-z	Compress an archive using gzip.

If you have a remote Unix account and a local PC or Macintosh, one great use of `tar` is to occasionally build an archival snapshot of all your files and then FTP them to your local computer. We'll talk about this in the latter part of this hour.

The `zip` Archive Utility

While `tar` is a popular archival utility for the Unix world—including Linux—when you get to the land of PCs and laptops, the ZIP archive format turns out to be far more common and far more popular. The good news is that there's a command-line ZIP interface available in modern Unixes like Solaris, so let's have a look!

Task 19.2: Learning to Use `zip`

If you thought that the `tar` command had a lot of command flags and options, wait until you get a look at `zip`. It's so complicated that just about every time I use it, I have to read the man page again to see some examples. And I've been working with Unix and command lines for a ridiculously long time.

Let's take a look.

1. To start out, I'll do the same thing I did in Task 19.1: Create a quick archival snapshot of all the files and folders in my home directory. But this time, I'll create an output file in `/tmp`:

```
$ zip /tmp/archive *
  adding: Desktop/ (stored 0%)
  adding: Documents/ (stored 0%)
  adding: Downloads/ (stored 0%)
  adding: Public/ (stored 0%)
  adding: cmdcnt.sh (deflated 45%)
  adding: diskspace.sh (deflated 24%)
  adding: hi-low.sh (deflated 44%)
  adding: test/ (stored 0%)
  adding: testme (stored 0%)
```

2. Here's what I've created:

```
$ ls -l /tmp/*zip
-rw-rw----   1 taylor    staff       2016 Apr 30 15:11 /tmp/archive.zip
```

This seems quite small, but a close examination reveals that most of my directories are empty (`Desktop`, `Documents`, `Downloads`, etc.), which is why the `zip` command reported `stored 0%` when it encountered them.

3. Creating an archive is easily done with no command flags needed. But, oh, there are plenty of command flags, which you can summarize with the `-h` help flag:

```
$ zip -h
Copyright (c) 1990-2008 Info-ZIP - Type 'zip "-L"' for software license.
```

```
Zip 3.0 (July 5th 2008). Usage:
zip [-options] [-b path] [-t mmddyyyy] [-n suffixes] [zipfile list] [-xi list]
The default action is to add or replace zipfile entries from list, which
can include the special name - to compress standard input.
If zipfile and list are omitted, zip compresses stdin to stdout.
  -f   freshen: only changed files      -u   update: only changed or new files
  -d   delete entries in zipfile        -m   move into zipfile (delete OS files)
  -r   recurse into directories         -j   junk (don't record) directory names
  -0   store only                       -l   convert LF to CR LF (-ll CR LF to LF)
  -1   compress faster                  -9   compress better
  -q   quiet operation                  -v   verbose operation/print version info
  -c   add one-line comments            -z   add zipfile comment
  -@   read names from stdin            -o   make zipfile as old as latest entry
  -x   exclude the following names      -i   include only the following names
  -F   fix zipfile (-FF try harder)     -D   do not add directory entries
  -A   adjust self-extracting exe       -J   junk zipfile prefix (unzipsfx)
  -T   test zipfile integrity           -X   eXclude eXtra file attributes
  -y   store symbolic links as the link instead of the referenced file
  -e   encrypt                          -n   don't compress these suffixes
  -h2  show more help
```

4. With those flags in mind, I want to get a table of contents listing of the archival ZIP file. You can do this and also actually unpack a ZIP archive through a different command called unzip, logically enough. Without any arguments, it offers up some help information:

```
$ unzip
UnZip 6.00 of 20 April 2009, by Info-ZIP.  Maintained by C. Spieler.
Sendbug reports using http://info-zip.org/zip-bug.html; see README for
details.

Usage: unzip [-Z] [-opts[modifiers]] file[.zip] [list] [-x xlist] [-d exdir]
Default action is to extract files in list, except those in xlist, to exdir;
file[.zip] may be a wildcard.  -Z => ZipInfo mode ("unzip -Z" for usage).

  -p  extract files to pipe, no messages    -l  list files (short format)
  -f  freshen existing files, create none   -t  test compressed archive data
  -u  update files, create if necessary     -z  display archive comment only
  -v  list verbosely/show version info      -T  timestamp archive to latest
  -x  exclude files that follow (in xlist)  -d  extract files into exdir
  -n  never overwrite existing files        modifiers:
  -o  overwrite files WITHOUT prompting     -q  quiet mode (-qq => quieter)
  -j  junk paths (do not make directories)  -a  auto-convert any text files
  -U  use escapes for all non-ASCII Unicode -aa treat ALL files as text
  -C  match filenames case-insensitively    -UU ignore any Unicode fields
  -X  restore UID/GID info                  -L  make (some) names lowercase
  -K  keep setuid/setgid/tacky permissions  -V  retain VMS version numbers
  -O  CHARSET  specify char encoding for DOS, Windows and OS/2 archives
                                            -M  pipe through "more" pager
  -I  CHARSET  specify a character encoding for UNIX and other archives
```

```
See "unzip -hh" or unzip.txt for more help.  Examples:
  unzip data1 -x joe   => extract all files except joe from zipfile data1.zip
  unzip -p foo | more  => send contents of foo.zip via pipe into program more
  unzip -fo foo ReadMe => quietly replace existing ReadMe if archive is newer
```

That's not complex, is it? Yikes. Nonetheless, the examples at the very bottom are a helpful reminder.

5. To simply get that table of contents, here's the command:

```
$ unzip -l /tmp/archive.zip
Archive:  /tmp/archive.zip
  Length      Date    Time    Name
---------  ---------- -----   ----
        0  10-27-2014 10:00   Desktop/
        0  10-27-2014 10:00   Documents/
        0  10-27-2014 10:00   Downloads/
        0  10-27-2014 10:00   Public/
      458  03-16-2015 07:42   cmdcnt.sh
      252  03-16-2015 08:02   diskspace.sh
      440  03-16-2015 08:28   hi-low.sh
        0  12-28-2014 11:42   test/
        0  01-29-2015 12:35   testme
---------                     -------
     1150                     9 files
```

Weird output format, very un-Unixlike.

6. Finally, here's how I actually extract files from a ZIP archive:

```
$ unzip archive.zip
   Archive: archive.zip
  creating: Desktop/
  creating: Documents/
  creating: Downloads/
  creating: Public/
 inflating: cmdcnt.sh
 inflating: diskspace.sh
 inflating: hi-low.sh
  creating: test/
extracting: testme
```

One thing that makes ZIP an interesting archival format—other than that it's compatible with every OS available, from Windows 10 to Mac OS X to built-in support in utilities like Google Drive—is that it gives you more control over the compression algorithms used.

Go back to the zip command and notice the -1 and -9 flags, for example, which tell the program to put more or less effort into compressing the individual files in the archive than normal.

But even the normal ZIP archive compressed the files in this particular archive an average of 30%. Across hundreds or thousands of files, that can be quite a meaningful amount of disk space!

Shrinking Your Files with compress

One thing you'll notice about the tar command is that it can generate remarkably large files. In fact, although disk space is relatively cheap nowadays, a single tar file can easily put you over quota on your system or at least make you unpopular with the other users.

You can use zip instead, which offers compression, or you can use the direct interface to the capability, using a solution called compress.

Action 19.3: Shrinking Large Files on Unix

The compress command is available on all versions of Unix, though sometimes zip is actually a better program in terms of how well it can compress files. The problem is, zip isn't universally available, particularly on older Unix systems. Both compress and zip fundamentally do the same thing: They use different compression algorithms to minimize the size of the file or files given.

1. First, let's see what compress can do with the backup.tar file created earlier:

```
$ ls -l backup.tar
-rw-r--r--  1 taylor  wheel  15800320 Feb  8 02:58 backup.tar
$ compress backup.tar
$ ls -l backup.tar
ls: backup.tar: No such file or directory
```

Uh oh! No need to panic, though: The compress program automatically renames the compressed file to have a .Z filename suffix, so you know it's compressed:

```
$ ls -l backup.tar.Z
-rw-r--r--  1 taylor  wheel  7807489 Feb  8 02:58 backup.tar.Z
```

Not too bad: It's gone down from 15.8MB to 7.8MB.

2. To reverse the file compression process and have it return to its original state, use uncompress:

```
$ uncompress backup.tar.Z
$ ls -l backup.tar
-rw-r--r--  1 taylor  wheel  15800320 Feb  8 02:58 backup.tar
```

3. It turns out that there's a useful flag to compress that lets you see how much it's compressed things:

```
$ compress -v backup.tar
backup.tar:     49.4% OK
```

A quick turn with a calculator will confirm that it's just about 50% smaller in size. Before finishing up, I want to uncompress it again:

```
$ uncompress -v backup.tar.Z
backup.tar.Z:   202.3% OK
```

4. For comparison, let's have a quick look at the zip command, which offers very similar capabilities:

```
$ ls -l backup.tar
-rw-r--r--  1 taylor  wheel  15800320 Feb  8 02:58 backup.tar
$ zip backup.tar.zip backup.tar
   adding: backup.tar (deflated 67%)
$ ls -l backup.tar.Z
ls: backup.tar.Z: No such file or directory
```

Whoops! I'm running on autopilot. In fact, when zip is invoked, it has two required parameters: the archive name and the name of the file or folder to place in the archive. So not .Z but .zip:

```
$ ls -l backup.tar.zip
-rw-r--r--  1 taylor  wheel  5214105 Feb  8 02:58 backup.tar.zip
$
```

You can see that it did a better job of compressing this particular file than compress did: It's only 5.5MB, instead of 7.8MB. Different files will have different compress/zip results, and some rare files won't be any smaller when compressed, for reasons known only to the folk who invented the compression algorithms.

5. To uncompress (expand) the file, use unzip, as shown earlier:

```
$ unzip backup.tar.zip
Archive:  backup.tar.zip
replace backup.tar? [y]es, [n]o, [A]ll, [N]one, [r]ename: y
   inflating: backup.tar
$
```

All back to normal!

NOTE
A number of different zip archive programs are available, depending on your flavor of Unix or Linux, including gzip, bzip2, and rzip. They differ in subtle ways but are all worth investigating if you send a lot of archival files or are tight on space with your Unix system.

Most of the files you have are likely too small to worry about compressing to save space. But if you are building large archival files or if you're planning on transferring large files through FTP, compress or zip can be your new best friend, saving you substantial transfer time.

Exploring the Unix Tape Command: cpio

It shouldn't surprise you that the Unix system has general-purpose backup programs that optionally can write to a tape device or other archival data storage unit. It's called cpio and is consistent in use with the overall philosophy of Unix.

Action 19.4: A Quick Exploration of cpio

To more fully understand how this command works, it's necessary to see it in action.

1. The most important difference between cpio and tar is that cpio expects to read the list of files needing backup from standard input rather than as a directory or set of filenames specified on the command line.

   This doesn't seem like a big deal, but it really is, particularly when you combine cpio with the find command. Here's a typical usage:

   ```
   $ find . -name "*.c" -print | cpio -oO sourcefiles.cpio
   $
   ```

   This invocation (-o indicates that I want to create an output archive, and -O lets me specify the output filename) makes an archive called sourcefiles.cpio that comprises all the *.c source files in the current directory and below. This would be quite tricky to accomplish with tar.

2. I can examine the contents of the archive:

   ```
   $ cpio -itI sourcefiles.cpio
   ./bin/fixit.c
   ./Src/Embot/embot.c
   ./Src/Embot/error.c
   ./Src/Embot/interact.c
   ./Src/Embot/log.c
   ./Src/Embot/mail_utils.c
   ./Src/Embot/savemsg.c
   ./Src/Embot/sendfile.c
   ./Src/Embot/utils.c
   ./Src/Misc/usage_summary.c
   ./Src/Misc/fixit.c
   ./Src/Misc/info.c
   ./Src/Misc/isnew.c
   ./Src/Misc/mydate.c
   ./Src/Misc/showmatches.c
   ./Src/Misc/change.c
   ./Src/change.c
   ./Src/cleanup.c
   ./Src/cribbage.c
   ./Src/expandurl.c
   ./Src/extract-mall.c
   ```

```
./Src/futuredate.c
./Src/import.c
./Src/assemble.c
./Src/make-html.c
./Src/old-import.c
./Src/process-data.c
./Src/showmatches.c
./Src/sum-up.c
./Src/text-counter.c
./Src/login.c
./Src/calc.c
$
```

In this case, the -i flag indicates that I want to have it read an existing archive, -t indicates that I only want a listing of the files, not to have them extracted, and -I lets me specify the input filename.

3. The easiest way to extract a file is to specify the pattern that should be compared. Notice in this case that I'm going to feed the archive into cpio as standard input. It's a common way to use the command:

```
$ cpio -i cribbage < sourcefile.cpio
cpio: WARNING! These patterns were not matched:
cribbage
$
```

Nope. The pattern cribbage didn't work. In fact, it wasn't a regular expression, so cpio helpfully indicated that there weren't any matches. Here's an improved attempt:

```
$ cpio -i '*cribbage*' < *cpio
cpio: Unable to create ./Src/cribbage.c <No such file or directory>
$
```

4. We're almost there, but there's still a problem, though the cpio error message isn't too helpful in explaining what's happening. The problem is that there is no Src directory, and the program can't create subdirectories without a new flag, -d, being added. The error message is more confusing than informative of that fact, however.

While I'm at it, I'll also add -v to ensure some verbose output as it unpacks:

```
$ cpio -ivd '*cribbage*' < *cpio
./Src/cribbage.c
30 blocks
$
```

Got it. Hurray!

Table 19.2 summarizes the most useful `cpio` flags.

TABLE 19.2   Useful `cpio` Starting Flags

Flag	Description
`-A`	Append specified files to an existing archive.
`-a`	Reset access times of input files after copying.
`-d`	Create directories as required.
`-E`	Specify a file containing all the filenames to be added to the archive.
`-i`	Extract files from a `cpio` archive.
`-I`	Specify an input archive file.
`-L`	Follow symbolic links.
`-o`	Create an output archive.
`-O`	Specify the output filename. (The default is to send the information to standard output.)
`-R`	Set the owner of the extracted files to a specified user ID.
`-t`	Print a table of contents (used with the `-i` flag).
`-v`	Provide verbose output format.

The flag examples listed in this table might not make the value of `cpio` obvious, but the reason that system administrators love this program is because it can read standard input for a list of files to add to an archive. As you'll see in the next section, this makes a very sophisticated level of archival behavior a breeze.

Personal Backup Solutions

Before we leave this discussion of backup and archive solutions, I'd like to talk a bit about a couple of ways that you can use these commands to improve the reliability and safety of your own interaction with Unix.

There are two basic ways that I use these tools myself: to create "snapshots"—automatically dated archives of the files I'm currently creating—and to create "last changed" files that I can write to an archival device.

Action 19.5: A Personal Backup Scheme

It's a good thing you paid attention during the shell scripting lesson (Hour 16, "Shell Programming Overview") because the solution shown here is a shell script that uses `tar` to build instant archives.

1. The first step in this script-building process is to figure out a solution for creating filenames that automatically have the date and time included. This is done with a backquote invocation of the `date` command but an invocation that utilizes the `+%` format string option:

```
$ date +%m.%d.%Y.%H:%M
11.08.2015.14:34
$
```

The date specified is *month.day.year.hour:minute*.

2. Now I create a snapshot filename with this suffix:

```
snapdir="$HOME/Snapshots"
thedate="$(date +%m.%d.%Y.%H:%M)"
outfile="$snapdir/snapshot.$thedate.tar.gz"
```

This saves the date/time format as variable `thedate` and then creates an `outfile` filename for use later in the script that is prefaced with the name of the snapshot directory. On my system, `outfile` ends up looking like this:

```
/home/taylor/Snapshots/snapshot.12.08.2015.14:40.tar.gz
```

This is just what I want.

3. There isn't much more to the script—just the actual invocation to the `tar` command itself. To make it a bit more sophisticated, the script will use the first argument, if present, as the directory to back up. Otherwise, it'll use the current directory as the default. Also notice the use of the `-z` flag to automatically `zip` the resultant output (which is why the `.gz` was added to the `outfile` variable above, too).

Here's the entire script, short and sweet:

```
$ cat snapshot.sh
#!/bin/bash

snapdir="$HOME/Snapshots"
thedate="$(date +%m.%d.%Y.%H:%M)"
outfile="$snapdir/snapshot.$thedate.tar.gz"

if [ $# -gt 0 ] ; then
  dirs=$1
else
  dirs="."
fi

echo "Backing up $dirs to $outfile"
```

```
tar -czf $outfile $dirs

echo "done."

exit 0
$
```

4. And here it is in use:

```
$ alias snapshot="$HOME/bin/snapshot.sh"
$ snapshot
Backing up . to /home/taylor/Snapshots/snapshot.11.08.2015.14:50.tar
done.
$
```

With this in your toolkit, you can easily save a current copy of your work at any time prior to major edits or at any historic time in the life of your project.

5. In a similar way, backup scripts usually use a *marker* file that saves the last-backed-up time and date for comparison purposes. It relies on the -cnewer *marker-file* option to find, which then compares the last-modified date of all files encountered against the marker file and lists only those that are newer. It can be used as part of a pipeline:

```
find $HOME -cnewer $HOME/.marker -print | cpio -o /dev/rst0
touch $HOME/.marker
```

Amazingly, this is all that is needed to have an incremental backup written to /dev/ rst0 (usually your tape or other archival device on your Unix system) where the only files added are those that you've changed more recently than the previous backup.

The combination of tar, cpio, the compress utilities, and a bit of imagination regarding how to put them all together can yield remarkably valuable results and expand your toolkit a great deal.

Perhaps just as importantly, the last action of the find pipe to cpio demonstrates the fundamental elegance of Unix: an entire backup regimen in two lines of script. Pretty cool, eh?

Working with Linux Package Managers

No discussion of tar and other archival systems would be complete without a brief discussion of Linux package managers, software suites that make it simple to install—or even remove— applications and software packages from your computer. Instead of you having to worry about "tarballs" or similar, package managers make working with software a breeze.

NOTE

You'll notice that I said "Linux" here, not "Unix". One of the biggest things that Linux brought to the Unix world is package management systems. So why include this topic in the book? For completeness. I realize that there's a good chance that while you're reading this book to learn Unix, you might well be using a Linux command line to test and learn everything. That's okay; I've been testing everything on Linux systems, too.

The premier package manager for modern Linux systems is Red Hat Package Manager, known more informally as RPM. Originally just available on the Red Hat (now Fedora) Linux system, it has become a common method of distributing software in the Unix community and certainly across most flavors of Linux systems.

There are some upstarts, though, notably the Debian Package Manager, DBM, which offers a simpler interface and a more flexible package creation environment. If you've bumped into the Fink package manager on Mac OS X, you might be surprised to know that it's based on DBM.

In case you'd like to learn more about the package management system on your own version of Unix or Linux (or Mac, for that matter), Table 19.3 provides a handy list.

TABLE 19.3 Package Management Systems

Distribution	Package Management System(s)
Debian Linux	dpkg
Red Hat Linux	RPM
Slackware Linux	tgz
GNU/Linux	Upkg
Mac OS X	Fink and MacPorts
Microsoft Windows	Cygwin
Solaris Unix	pkgadd
AIX Unix	install
HP-UX Unix	Software Distributor

Summary

Whether it's to assuage your anxiety about unstable servers, to avoid possible problems with poor backups and inattentive administrators, or simply to help you package up and move large sets of files around, tar and its partner programs are a great help. Every time I have to move from one system to another, I invariably use tar, compress, and ftp as a power trio.

Further, while you can download `tar` archives or similar from the Internet, the ability to use the RPM or a similar package management system makes it incredibly easy to browse through and install just about any open source application that's compatible with your version of Unix or Linux.

Workshop

The Workshop poses some questions about the topics presented in this hour.

Exercises

1. What's the key difference between `tar` and `cpio`?

2. What's wrong with this command?

   ```
   tar cvf OUTPUT.tar *
   ```

3. Try both `compress` and `zip` on a few large files to see which produces better results. Try `zip` on a very small file, too, and see what happens.

4. Build, move, and then unpack a directory tree using `zip`. Is it easier or harder to use than `tar` for this task?

5. Using your native package management system, find and install `bzip2` and then use that on the same large files you used for question 4 to see if it does a better job with compression.

Preview of the Next Hour

In the next hour you'll learn about the ability to communicate with other users on your computer through electronic mail.

HOUR 20
Using Email to Communicate

Goals for This Hour

In this hour, you will learn

- How to read email with `mailx`
- How to send email with `mailx`
- About sending mail to the rest of the digital universe

It's time to learn about what's arguably the lifeblood of any operating system in today's connected world: the ability to communicate with other users on your computer and elsewhere through electronically transmitted mail, or email. You've probably been using email for years through graphical interfaces—perhaps Gmail in a browser, or Microsoft Outlook or Apple Mail. Turns out that just as with so many other Internet tools, email got its start on the Unix command line, and that's still a place where it's very much at home—and what this lesson is all about.

Of all the places in Unix where there is variety, most of it surely is found in electronic mail, or *email*. At least 15 programs are available from various vendors to accomplish two tasks: to read mail from and send mail to other folks. In this hour, you'll learn about the standard electronic mail system, Berkeley Mail. As it happens, I wrote an email system of my own that you can often find on Linux and other Unix-like systems called the Elm Mail System. It's a full-screen alternative mail program that's widely distributed. We'll stick with Berkeley Mail for this hour, however, because like a number of different screen-oriented email programs (Mush, Pine), Elm works identically from the command line.

There are, of course, graphically oriented email programs, too, in the Unix world, most notably Thunderbird, a fully featured email application that's part of the Mozilla browser suite. We'll look at Thunderbird in Hour 24, "GNOME and the GUI Environment," when we peek at the X11 graphical interface atop Unix.

Interacting with the World

Much of what you've learned in this book has been about how you can exploit Unix to be more productive. Now it's time to learn how to communicate with others, to learn about what I consider the "killer app" of Unix and of the Internet overall: electronic mail.

Task 20.1: Reading Electronic Mail with `mailx`

Of all the capabilities of Unix, one of the most popular is undoubtedly the ability to send electronic mail to another user—even on another computer system—with a few keystrokes. In this section, you'll learn how to work with other users on your own computer, and later in this hour you'll learn how to send mail to folks who are on different computers, anywhere in the world.

Various programs for reading mail can be used on Unix systems, but the two most common are `mail` and `Mail`. (The latter is also often called `mailx` on SVR4 systems.) Because of the similarity of the names, the former is known as "mail" and the latter as either "cap mail" ("cap" for the uppercase, or capital, *M*) or "Berkeley Mail." I refer to "Mail" either as Berkeley Mail or using its AT&T name, `mailx`. You won't want to use `mail` to read or write mail if Berkeley Mail is available to you because Berkeley Mail is much easier to use. As a result, I will focus on using Berkeley Mail.

To send mail, you simply state on the command line the account name of the recipient, indicate a subject, enter the message itself, and poof! Your missive is sent through the system and arrives at the recipient's terminal posthaste. When mail arrives for you, the shell or one of various optional utilities, such as `biff` or `newmail`, can notify you. Each time you log in, the shell checks for email, and if you have any, will say `You have mail` or `You have new mail`. You can save mail in files called *mail folders*.

Berkeley Mail has many command options, both flags that you can specify when you invoke the program from the command line and commands used within the program. Fortunately, you can always request help while you're in the program to review these options. The most noteworthy flags are `-s subject`, which enables you to specify the subject of the message on the command line, and `-f mailfolder`, which enables you to specify a mail folder to read rather than the default (which is your incoming mailbox).

The most valuable commands to use within the program are summarized in Table 20.1.

TABLE 20.1 `mailx` Command Summary

Command	Meaning
delete *msgs*	Mark the specified messages for deletion.
headers	Display the current page of *headers* (the cryptic lines of information at the top of an *email* message; I explain them a bit later in this lesson). Add a + to see the next page or a - to see the preceding page.

Command	Meaning
help	Display a summary of Berkeley Mail commands.
mail *address*	Send mail to the specified address.
print *msgs*	Show the specified message or messages.
quit	Leave the Berkeley Mail program.
reply	Respond to the current message.
save *folder*	Save the current message to the specified mail folder.
undelete *msgs*	Undelete the messages you've specified for deletion using the delete command.

1. I have lots of electronic mail in my mailbox. When I logged in to the system today, the shell indicated that I had new mail. To find out what the new messages are, I use mailx (though I also could have typed Mail because they're synonymous on my machine):

```
$ mailx
mailx version 5.0.  Type ? for help.
"/var/mail/taylor": 9 messages 5 new
     1 disserli Mon Nov 22 19:40  54/2749 "Re: Are you out there"
>N   2 Laura.Ramsey Tue Nov 30 16:47  46/1705 "I've got an idea..."
 N   3 ljw      Fri Dec  3 22:57  130/2712 "Re: Attachments"
 N   4 sartin   Sun Dec  5 15:15  15/341 "I need your address"
 N   5 rustle   Tue Dec  7 15:43  29/955 "flash cards"
     6 harrism  Tue Dec  7 16:13  58/2756 "Re: Writing Lab OWL proj"
     7 CBUTCHER Tue Dec  7 17:00  19/575 "Smartphone Based GRE's"
     8 harrism  Tue Dec  7 21:46  210/10636 "writing  environments"
 N   9 v892127  Wed Dec  8 07:09  38/1558 "Re: Have you picked up"
& _
```

I have lots of information here. On the first line, the program identifies itself as Mail version 5.0. Somewhat tucked away in that top corner is the reminder that I can type ? at any point to get help on the commands.

The second line tells me what mailbox I'm reading. In this case, I'm looking at the default mailbox for my incoming mail, which is /var/mail/taylor. On your system, you might find your mailbox in this directory, or you might find it in a directory similarly named /usr/mail. Either way, you don't have to worry about where it's located because Berkeley Mail can find it automatically.

The 3rd through 11th lines list mail messages I have received from various people. The format is N in the first column if I haven't seen the piece of mail before, a unique index number (the first item in each listing is 1), the account that sent the message, the date and time the message was sent, the number of lines and characters in the message, and the subject of the message, if known. Figure 20.1 illustrates this more clearly.

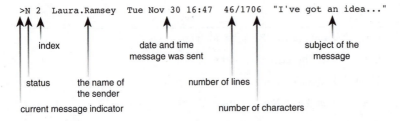

FIGURE 20.1
Understanding the message display in *mailx*.

2. To read a specific message, I need to enter only the index number of that message:

```
& 7
Message  7:
From: CBUTCHER Sun Dec  7 17:00:28 2014
From: Cheryl <CBUTCHER>
Subject:      Smartphone Based GRE's
To: Dave Taylor <TAYLOR>

I've scheduled to take the smartphone-based GRE's in Indy.
Call me crazy but someone's got to do it.  I'll let you know how it goes.

Do you know anyone else that has taken the GRE's this way?  I figure
there's a paper in it somewhere.......

If you have that handout from seminar in a file, could you please send it
to me?

Thanks.

& _
```

This message is from my friend Cheryl Butcher. Collectively, the first set of lines in the message—each a single word, a colon, and some information or other—is the *header* of the message, or the electronic equivalent of the postmark and envelope. The header always includes `From:`, `Subject:`, and `To:`, specifying the name and electronic address of the sender, the subject of the message, and the list of recipients.

3. To respond to this message, I enter `reply`:

```
& reply
To: CBUTCHER
Subject: RE: Smartphone Based GRE's

_
```

Anything I now enter will be sent back to Cheryl:

```
Hi. I am very interested in hearing about your reaction to the
smartphone-based GRE test. I'm sure you're correct that there
is a paper there, but wouldn't it be best to work with ETS on the
project?

I'll dig around and find those handouts soonest.

Happy holidays!

Dave
```

To end the message, I either press ^d on its own line or use the shorthand . by itself:

```
.
Cc: _
```

Berkeley Mail is now asking me to specify any other people I might like to have receive *carbon copies* of this message. Entering an account name or two here will allow the designated people to see a copy of this message to Cheryl. Because I don't want anyone else to read this message, I press Return, which sends the message and returns me to the prompt:

```
& _
```

4. I now can use the headers command to see what is the current message (the one I just read). It's the message indicated by the > (refer to Figure 20.1):

```
& headers
    1 disserli Mon Nov 22 19:40  54/2749 "Re: Are you out there"
    2 Laura.Ramsey Tue Nov 30 16:47  46/1705 "I've got an idea..."
N   3 ljw      Fri Dec  3 22:57  130/2712 "Re: Attachments"
N   4 sartin   Sun Dec  5 15:15  15/341 "I need your address"
N   5 rustle   Tue Dec  7 15:43  29/955 "flash cards"
    6 harrism  Tue Dec  7 16:13  58/2756 "Re: Writing Lab OWL proj"
>   7 CBUTCHER Tue Dec  7 17:00  19/575 "Smartphone Based GRE's"
    8 harrism  Tue Dec  7 21:46  210/10636 "writing environments"
N   9 v892127  Wed Dec  8 07:09  38/1558 "Re: Have you picked up"
& _
```

To save Cheryl's message in a folder called cherylmail, I use the save command:

```
& save cherylmail
"cherylmail" [New file] 19/575
& _
```

Naming conventions for folders are the same as for Unix filenames: Avoid punctuation and spaces to make your life easier, though dashes and underscores are fine.

5. Now that I'm done with this message, I can mark it for deletion with the `delete` command:

```
& delete 7
&
```

Notice that after I enter `headers`, Cheryl's message vanishes from the list:

```
& headers
      1 disserli Mon Nov 22 19:40  54/2749 "Re: Are you out there"
      2 Laura.Ramsey Tue Nov 30 16:47  46/1705 "I've got an idea..."
  N   3 ljw       Fri Dec  3 22:57  130/2712 "Re: Attachments"
  N   4 sartin    Sun Dec  5 15:15  15/341 "I need your address"
  N   5 rustle    Tue Dec  7 15:43  29/955 "flash cards"
      6 harrism   Tue Dec  7 16:13  58/2756 "Re: Writing Lab OWL proj"
  >   8 harrism   Tue Dec  7 21:46  210/10636 "writing environments"
  N   9 v892127   Wed Dec  8 07:09  38/1558 "Re: Have you picked up"
&
```

Look closely at the list, and you will see that it hasn't completely forgotten the message; the program hides message 7 from this list. I could still read the message by using `print 7`, and I could use `undelete 7` to pull it off the deletion list.

NOTE

Deleted messages in Berkeley Mail are actually marked for future deletion and aren't removed until you quit the program. When you quit, however, there's no going back. A deleted message is gone. While you're within the program, you can delete and undelete to your heart's content.

---

6. Now I want to delete both of the messages from `harrism` (numbers 6 and 8):

```
& delete 6 8
```

Now the list of messages in my mailbox is starting to look pretty short:

```
& h
      1 disserli Mon Nov 22 19:40  54/2749 "Re: Are you out there"
      2 Laura.Ramsey Tue Nov 30 16:47  46/1705 "I've got an idea..."
  N   3 ljw       Fri Dec  3 22:57  130/2712 "Re: Attachments"
  N   4 sartin    Sun Dec  5 15:15  15/341 "I need your address"
  N   5 rustle    Tue Dec  7 15:43  29/955 "flash cards"
 >N   9 v892127   Wed Dec  8 07:09  38/1558 "Re: Have you picked up"
&
```

TIP

Most commands in Berkeley Mail can be abbreviated to just their first letter—as you can see above with h being a shortcut for `headers`—which cuts down on typing.

---

7. You can save a group of messages to a file by specifying the numbers between the `save` command and the folder name:

```
& save 6 8 harris
6: Inappropriate message
```

Oops. I had deleted messages 6 and 8. I must undelete them before I can proceed:

```
& undelete 6 8
& save 6 8 harrismail
"harrismail" [New file] 268/13392
```

8. Now I use the `quit` command to get out of this program:

```
& quit
Saved 1 message in mbox
Held 6 messages in /var/mail/taylor
$
```

The messages that I viewed and didn't delete are moved out of my incoming mailbox to the file `mbox`. The messages I saved and the messages I marked for deletion are silently removed, and all remaining messages are retained in `/usr/spool/mail/taylor`.

NOTE

The biggest complaint I have with Berkeley Mail is that it does all this activity silently. I don't like the fact that saved messages are deleted automatically from the incoming mailbox when I quit and that—more importantly—messages I've read are tossed automatically into another folder. To ensure that messages you've read aren't moved into `mbox` when you quit, you can use the `preserve` command, which you can use with a list of numbers, the same way you can use other Berkeley Mail commands. Any message that you `preserve` will remain in your incoming mailbox.

You have to use it to get the hang of it, but it's worthwhile: Berkeley Mail offers quite a lot of power, enabling you to read through your electronic mail, save it, and respond as needed with ease, all without leaving the command line. The program has considerably more commands than are shown in this initial task, too, so further study is helpful.

Task 20.2: Sending Mail from the Command Line

Now you know how to read your electronic mail using Berkeley Mail (`mailx`), and you know how to send mail from within the program. How do you send messages and files to people from the command line? It's quite simple. You even can specify the message subject with the `-s` starting flag.

1. To send a message to someone, enter the name of the command followed by the recipient's account name:

```
$ mail marv
Subject: Interested in lunch tomorrow?
_
```

I now can enter as many lines of information as I want, ending, as within the Berkeley Mail program itself, with either ^d (call this "Control-D" to sound like a Unix old-timer) or . on a line by itself:

```
I'm going to be in town tomorrow and would like to
rustle up some Chinese food. What's your schedule
look like?

Dave
.
Cc: _
```

Again, I'm offered the option of copying someone else, but—again—I opt not to do so. Pressing Return sends the message.

2. To send a file to someone, combine file redirection with the use of the -s flag:

```
$ mail -s "here's the contents of sample.file" marv < sample.file
```

The file was sent without any fuss.

3. Even though mailx gives you no indication, several commands are available for use while you're entering the text of a message, and all can be listed with ~?:

```
$ mail dunlap
Subject: Good morning!
~?
-------------------- ~ ESCAPES ---------------------------
   ~~              Quote a single tilde
   ~a,~A           Autograph (insert 'sign','Sign' variable)
   ~b users        Add users to Bcc list
   ~c users        Add users to Cc list
   ~d              Read in dead.letter file
   ~e              Edit the message buffer
   ~f messages     Read in messages, do not right-shift
   ~h              Prompt for Subject and To, Cc and Bcc lists
   ~i variable     Insert variable into message (~a := ~i sign)
   ~m messages     Read in messages, right-shifted by a tab
   ~p              Print the message buffer
   ~q,~Q           Quit, save letter in $HOME/dead.letter
   ~r,~< file      Read a file into the message buffer
   ~r,~< !command  Read output from command into message
   ~R              Mark message for return receipt
   ~s subject      Set subject
   ~t users        Add users to To list
   ~v              Invoke display editor on message
   ~w file         Write message onto file (no header)
   ~x              Quit, do not save letter
   ~!command       Run a shell command
   ~|,~^ command   Pipe the message through the command
```

```
~:,~_ command    Execute regular mailx command
~.          end of input
~?          print this help message
------------------------------------------------------------
_
```

The most important ones to remember are ~v, to start vi with the message as entered to that point in the edit buffer; ~r, to include the contents of a file; ~h, to edit the message headers; ~!, to invoke a shell command; and ~p, to show the message that's been entered so far:

```
    I wanted to wish you a cheery good morning!  You asked about
the contents of that one file, so here it is:
~!ls
Archives/         bin/              deleteme          sample
InfoWorld/        buckaroo          dickens.note      sample2
Mail/             buckaroo.confused keylime.pie       src/
News/             cheryl            mbox              temp/
OWL/              csh.man           newsample
awkscript         dead.letter       owl.c
!
```

The output of the command isn't included in the message, but is shown on screen if you use the ~p command:

```
~p
-------
Message contains:
To: dunlap
Subject: Good morning!


    I wanted to wish you a cheery good morning!  You asked about
the contents of that one file, so here it is:
(continue)
_
```

4. To read in a file, use the ~r command:

```
~r dickens.note
"dickens.note" 28/1123
```

Here, the contents of the file are included in the note, but mailx didn't list the contents to the screen. Again, using ~p lists the current message:

```
-------
Message contains:
To: dunlap
Subject: Good morning!
```

```
    I wanted to wish you a cheery good morning!  You asked about
the contents of that one file, so here it is:

                    A Tale of Two Cities
                         Preface

When I was acting, with my children and friends, in Mr Wilkie Collins's
drama of The Frozen Deep, I first conceived the main idea of this
story.  A strong desire came upon me then, to
embody it in my own person;
and I traced out in my fancy, the state of mind of which it would
necessitate the presentation
to an observant spectator, with particular
care and interest.

As the idea became familiar to me, it gradually shaped itself into its
present form.  Throughout its execution, it has had complete possession
of me; I have so far verified what
is done and suffered in these pages,
as that I have certainly done and suffered it all myself.

Whenever any reference (however slight) is made here to the condition
of the Danish people before or during the Revolution, it is truly made,
on the faith of the most trustworthy
witnesses.  It has been one of my hopes to add
something to the popular and picturesque means of
understanding that terrible time, though no one can hope
to add anything to the philosophy of Mr Carlyle's wonderful book.

Tavistock House
November 1859
(continue)
```

5. I can fine-tune the headers by using the ~h command:

```
~h
To: dunlap_
```

Pressing Return leaves it as is, and pressing Backspace lets me change it as desired.

```
Subject: Good morning!
```

Pressing Return a few more times gives me the opportunity to change other headers in the message:

```
Cc:
Bcc:
(continue)
```

The `Cc:` header allows me to specify other people to receive this message. `Bcc:` is what's known as a *blind carbon copy*, an invisible copy of the message. If I send a message to `dunlap` and a carbon copy to `cbutcher`, each can see that the other received a copy because the message will have `To: dunlap` as a header and also will list the other's name after `Cc:`. If I want to send a copy to someone without any of the other parties knowing about it, that's where a blind carbon copy can be helpful. Specifying someone on the `Bcc:` list means that that person receives a copy of the message, but his or her name doesn't show up on any header in the message itself.

6. Finally, I use `^d` to end the message.

```
^d
Cc:
$
```

All so-called *tilde commands* (which all begin with the ~, or tilde, character) are available when you send mail from the command line. They also are available when you send mail while within the Berkeley Mail program.

Task 20.3: Sending Email to the Rest of the World

The most common use of the Internet is probably to send electronic mail between individuals and to mailing lists. What's really a boon is that everyone, from New York to Los Angeles, Japan to Germany, South Africa to India, has an address that's very similar, and you've already seen it a million times, and probably used it a dozen or more times today alone. You know, *user@host.domain*, where *user* is the account name or full name, *host* is the name of the user's machine, and *domain* is the user's top-level domain (TLD).

By reading the host and domain information from right to left (from the outside in, really), you can decode information about someone by looking at the person's email address. My address, for example, is `taylor@intuitive.com`, which, reading right to left, tells you that I'm at a commercial site (`com`) with a company by the name of Intuitive Systems (`intuitive`). My account name is `taylor`.

There are lots of top-level domains; the most common are shown in Table 20.2.

TABLE 20.2   Common Top-Level Internet Domains

Domain	Type of Site or Network
edu	Educational sites
com	Commercial businesses
mil	Military or defense systems
net	Alternative networks accessible via Internet
org	Nonprofit organizations
us	United States systems not otherwise classified

1. Sending mail to someone on the Internet is easy. If you'd like to send me a message, for example, you could use this:

```
$ mailx taylor@intuitive.com
Subject: _
```

Enter the message and end with a ^d as you would in any email message. It is immediately sent to me.

NOTE

I invite you to drop me a note, letting me know how you're enjoying this book, any problems you might have encountered, and any commands you were puzzled by that might be easier with a bit more explanation. If nothing else, just say hi!

---

2. Although electronic mail addresses always follow the same format, they can vary quite a bit. To give you an idea of the variation, here are a potpourri of addresses from some mail I've recently received (with details changed for privacy):

```
$ grep '^From:' /usr/spool/mail/taylor
From: Steve Frampton <frampton@vicuna.ocunix.on.ca>
From: Joanna Tsang <tsang@futon.SFSU.EDU>
From: "Debra Isserlis" <disserli@us.oracle.com>
From: ljw@ras.amdahl.com (Linda Wei)
From: Cheryl <CBUTCHER@VM.CC.PURDUE.EDU>
From: harrism@mace.utech.edu (Mickey Harris)
From: v892127@nooteboom.si.hhs.nl
From: harrism@mace.utech.edu (Mickey Harris)
From: "Barbara Maxwell" <maxwell@sales.synergy.com>
From: steve@xalt.com (Steve Mansour)
From: abhasin@itsmail1.hamilton.edu (Aditya Bhasin)
From: gopher@scorpio.kent.edu
From: marv@netcom.com (Marvin Raab)
```

The notational convention for the From: line in electronic mail clearly varies. You see three basic notations in this list: just an address, such as the one from gopher@scorpio.kent.edu; an address with the name in parentheses, such as the message from Linda Wei about one-third of the way down the list; and a line with the person's name followed by his or her email address in angle brackets, such as the first listed line.

Notice the various sites from which I've received electronic mail in the past few days: SFSU.EDU is San Francisco State University, oracle.com is Oracle Corporation in California, PURDUE.EDU is Purdue University, xalt.com is from XALT Corporation, and kent.edu is Kent State University. The message from v892127@nooteboom.si.hhs.nl is from an educational institution in the Netherlands!

3. How do you map a domain name to an organization? That's surprisingly easy on the command line too, with the whois command. Let's have a look, but first, a warning: There are so many disclaimers in the whois program that it produces about 75 lines of output, and the 10 lines we're interested in reading are often buried, so a bit of detective work is often required.

Here's how it looks for the domain ISIPP.COM:

```
$ whois isipp.com

Whois Server Version 2.0

Domain names in the .com and .net domains can now be registered
with many different competing registrars. Go to http://www.internic.net
for detailed information.

    Domain Name: ISIPP.COM
    Registrar: GODADDY.COM, LLC
    Sponsoring Registrar IANA ID: 146
    Whois Server: whois.godaddy.com
    Referral URL: http://registrar.godaddy.com
    Name Server: A.AUTH-NS.SONIC.NET
    Name Server: B.AUTH-NS.SONIC.NET
    Name Server: C.AUTH-NS.SONIC.NET
    Name Server: NS.ISIPP.COM
    Name Server: NS2.PRGMR.COM
    Name Server: NS3.PRGMR.COM
    Status: clientDeleteProhibited http://www.icann.org/
    ➥ epp#clientDeleteProhibited
    Status: clientRenewProhibited http://www.icann.org/
    ➥ epp#clientRenewProhibited
    Status: clientTransferProhibited http://www.icann.org/epp#Prohibited
    Status: clientUpdateProhibited http://www.icann.org/
    ➥ epp#clientUpdateProhibited
    Updated Date: 15-apr-2015
    Creation Date: 17-aug-2003
    Expiration Date: 17-aug-2023

>>> Last update of whois database: Mon, 18 May 2015 22:34:58 GMT <<<

NOTICE: The expiration date displayed in this record is the date the
registrar's sponsorship of the domain name registration in the registry is
currently set to expire. This date does not necessarily reflect the expiration
date of the domain name registrant's agreement with the sponsoring
registrar. Users may consult the sponsoring registrar's Whois database to
view the registrar's reported date of expiration for this registration.
```

TERMS OF USE: You are not authorized to access or query our Whois
database through the use of electronic processes that are high-volume and
automated except as reasonably necessary to register domain names or
modify existing registrations; the Data in VeriSign Global Registry
Services' ("VeriSign") Whois database is provided by VeriSign for
information purposes only, and to assist persons in obtaining information
about or related to a domain name registration record. VeriSign does not
guarantee its accuracy. By submitting a Whois query, you agree to abide
by the following terms of use: You agree that you may use this Data only
for lawful purposes and that under no circumstances will you use this Data
to: (1) allow, enable, or otherwise support the transmission of mass
unsolicited, commercial advertising or solicitations via e-mail, telephone,
or facsimile; or (2) enable high volume, automated, electronic processes
that apply to VeriSign (or its computer systems). The compilation,
repackaging, dissemination or other use of this Data is expressly
prohibited without the prior written consent of VeriSign. You agree not to
use electronic processes that are automated and high-volume to access or
query the Whois database except as reasonably necessary to register
domain names or modify existing registrations. VeriSign reserves the right
to restrict your access to the Whois database in its sole discretion to ensure
operational stability. VeriSign may restrict or terminate your access to the
Whois database for failure to abide by these terms of use. VeriSign
reserves the right to modify these terms at any time.

The Registry database contains ONLY .COM, .NET, .EDU domains and
Registrars.

For more information on Whois status codes, please visit
https://www.icann.org/resources/pages/epp-status-codes-2014-06-16-en.
Domain Name: ISIPP.COM
Registry Domain ID: 102188762_DOMAIN_COM-VRSN
Registrar WHOIS Server: whois.godaddy.com
Registrar URL: http://www.godaddy.com
Update Date: 2013-11-12T16:59:07Z
Creation Date: 2003-08-17T06:58:58Z
Registrar Registration Expiration Date: 2023-08-17T06:58:58Z
Registrar: GoDaddy.com, LLC
Registrar IANA ID: 146
Registrar Abuse Contact Email: abuse@godaddy.com
Registrar Abuse Contact Phone: +1.4806242505
Domain Status: clientTransferProhibited http://www.icann.org/epp#Prohibited
Domain Status: clientUpdateProhibited http://www.icann.org/epp#Prohibited
Domain Status: clientRenewProhibited http://www.icann.org/epp#Prohibited
Domain Status: clientDeleteProhibited http://www.icann.org/epp#Prohibited
Registry Registrant ID:
Registrant Name: Anne Mitchell
Registrant Organization:
Registrant Street: 2525 Arapahoe Ave.
Registrant Street: E4-302

```
Registrant City: Boulder
Registrant State/Province: Colorado
Registrant Postal Code: 80302
Registrant Country: United States
Registrant Phone: 8007593818
Registrant Phone Ext:
Registrant Fax:
Registrant Fax Ext:
Registrant Email: amitchell@isipp.com
Registry Admin ID:
Admin Name: Anne Mitchell
Admin Organization: Law Offices of Anne P. Mitchell
Admin Street: #282
Admin City: Sunnyvale
Admin State/Province: California
Admin Postal Code: 94086
Admin Country: United States
Admin Phone:
Admin Phone Ext:
Admin Fax:
Admin Fax Ext:
Admin Email: shedevil@apmlaw.com
Registry Tech ID:
Tech Name: Anne Mitchell
Tech Organization: Law Offices of Anne P. Mitchell
Tech Street: #282
Tech City: Sunnyvale
Tech State/Province: California
Tech Postal Code: 94086
Tech Country: United States
Tech Phone:
Tech Phone Ext:
Tech Fax:
Tech Fax Ext:
Tech Email: shedevil@apmlaw.com
Name Server: A.AUTH-NS.SONIC.NET
Name Server: B.AUTH-NS.SONIC.NET
Name Server: NS.ISIPP.COM
Name Server: NS2.PRGMR.COM
Name Server: NS3.PRGMR.COM
Name Server: C.AUTH-NS.SONIC.NET
DNSSEC: unsigned
URL of the ICANN WHOIS Data Problem Reporting System: http://wdprs.internic.net/
Last update of WHOIS database: 2015-05-18T22:00:00Z

For more information on Whois status codes, please visit
https://www.icann.org/resources/pages/epp-status-codes-2014-06-16-en
```

```
The data contained in GoDaddy.com, LLC's WhoIs database,
while believed by the company to be reliable, is provided "as is"
with no guarantee or warranties regarding its accuracy.  This
information is provided for the sole purpose of assisting you
in obtaining information about domain name registration records.
Any use of this data for any other purpose is expressly forbidden without the
prior
written permission of GoDaddy.com, LLC.  By submitting an inquiry,
you agree to these terms of usage and limitations of warranty.  In particular,
you agree not to use this data to allow, enable, or otherwise make possible,
dissemination or collection of this data, in part or in its entirety, for any
purpose, such as the transmission of unsolicited advertising and
and solicitations of any kind, including spam.  You further agree
not to use this data to enable high volume, automated or robotic electronic
processes designed to collect or compile this data for any purpose,
including mining this data for your own personal or commercial purposes.

Please note: the registrant of the domain name is specified
in the "registrant" section.  In most cases, GoDaddy.com, LLC
is not the registrant of domain names listed in this database.
```

The most important fields here are at the end. Notice that you can now see the name, address, and contact email address for the owner of this particular domain, based in Sunnyvale, California.

Try this for yourself: Use `whois intuitive.com` to find out if I really own the domain.

Sending email with users throughout the world is one of the coolest parts of learning Unix, or, indeed, of being on the Internet in general. Nowadays, just about every article in a magazine or newspaper includes an email address, every book author includes his or her email address, and every TV show has a Web site and Twitter account. It's a simple task to send a message or tweet if I have questions or kudos on something. Most magazines, from the *Utne Reader* to *MacWorld*, also list email addresses and social media handles for the entire editorial staff.

Summary

It can be frustrating and annoying to be pestered by waves of email from unknown folk, so I recommend that you practice your command-line email options by sending mail to yourself and then to just your immediate friends, who will hopefully be forgiving of your hiccups.

Workshop

The Workshop summarizes the key terms you've learned and poses some questions about the topics presented in this lesson. It also provides you with a preview of what you will learn in the next hour.

Key Terms

blind carbon copy   You can send an exact copy of a message without the awareness of the main recipient.

carbon copy   You can send an exact copy of a message to other people. Each recipient can see the names of all other recipients on the distribution list.

email   Email is electronically transmitted and received mail or messages.

mail folder   A mail folder is a file containing one or more email messages.

mail header   The To:, From:, Subject:, and other lines at the beginning of an email message—all the lines up to the first blank line—together are considered the header.

mailbox   A mailbox is a mail folder.

preserve   Preserving a message means ensuring that it doesn't move out of your incoming mailbox even though you've read it.

starting flag   You can specify parameters on the command line when you invoke a program.

tilde command   A tilde command begins with ~ in Berkeley Mail or the Elm Mail System.

undelete   Undeleting a message means restoring the deleted message to its original state.

Exercises

1. Send yourself a message using `mailx`.

2. Send me a message saying hi to `taylor@intuitive.com`.

3. Use Berkeley Mail to read your new message and then save it to a file, delete it, undelete it, and save it to a mail folder.

4. Start Berkeley Mail so that it reads in the newly created mail folder rather than in your default mailbox. What's different?

5. If Elm is available to you, try using it to read your mail. Do you like this mail program or Berkeley Mail better? Why?

Preview of the Next Hour

In the next hour, you'll learn about how to use the `ssh` and `sftp` programs to interact with computers throughout the Internet.

Connecting to Remote Systems Using SSH and SFTP

Goals for This Hour

In this hour, you will learn

▶ About connecting to remote Internet sites with SSH

▶ How to use SFTP to transfer files

▶ How to work with anonymous FTP archives

In the preceding hour, you learned how to use email to interact with other users both on your system and elsewhere on the Internet. In this hour, you'll see how to use common Unix tools to connect to remote systems and transfer files and programs back and forth at will.

This hour provides a quick overview of how to connect to other Unix systems on the Internet, both to transfer files and to interact directly.

Stepping Beyond Your Own System

You can do lots of things on a local Unix system, but your system is hooked up to the rest of the Internet, which gives you access to the world. Fortunately, Unix offers some powerful tools to let you exploit your network connectivity.

Task 21.1: Connecting to Remote Internet Sites with SSH

The really fun part of Unix is that it's the most connected operating system in the world. The variety of services available for users of a networked Unix machine can be staggering.

The Internet can help you with three main tasks: using remote systems, sending mail to remote users, and sending files back and forth with remote file systems.

Classic commands for interacting with a remote system are `telnet` and `ftp`. `telnet` opens up a command-line interface for interaction on the remote system; `ftp`, or File Transfer Protocol, allows you to upload and download files easily. The problem is, neither `telnet` nor `ftp` is encrypted, which makes them dangerous and makes having their respective ports open on a server doubly dangerous and a vulnerability for hacker attacks.

As a result, I can't recommend you ever use either `telnet` or `ftp`. This lesson shows you how to use ssh (the encrypted replacement for `telnet`) and sftp (the encrypted version of `ftp`). Once you get the hang of using these tools, you'll be ready to interact with remote systems safely and securely.

If you know that a remote site is a Unix system, the easiest way to log in to that site is to use the `ssh` command. SSH stands for *secure shell*, in case you're curious.

1. First, I'll use `ssh` to connect to a remote system on which I have a login account and see whether I have a certain file there:

```
$ ssh intuitive.com
The authenticity of host 'intuitive.com (104.131.46.171)' can't be
established. RSA key fingerprint is 34:ba:0e:84:e8:ef:82:59:7c:91:2e:8f:0b:
2e:50:08. Are you sure you want to continue connecting (yes/no)? yes
Warning: Permanently added 'intuitive.com,104.131.46.171' (RSA) to the list of
known hosts.
dtaylor@intuitive.com's password: _
```

If you've never connected to a particular remote host via SSH, you can see that it uses public key encryption and so needs to establish a shared encryption key. To do this, you need to indicate your trust that the remote system is the machine you think it is, which is what the prompt shows. You can also see that I have answered yes, which is needed only once per remote system.

By default, `ssh` assumes that your account on the remote system has the same name as your account on your home system. If you need to use a different account name, specify it with the `-l` *account* option:

```
$ ssh -l dave intuitive.com
dave@intuitive.com's password:_
```

After I enter my password, I'm logged in to the remote system:

```
Last failed login: Tue May 26 18:14:27 EDT 2015 from ip-64-134-29-252.public.
➥ wayport.net on ssh:notty
There was 1 failed login attempt since the last successful login.
Last login: Thu Apr 30 18:12:27 2015 from c-98-245-91-148.hsd1.co.comcast.net
[taylor@ado105 ~]$
```

Using `ls` tells me what I want to know:

```
[taylor@ado105 @]$ ls
Global.Software    News/            history.usenet.Z
Interactive.Unix   Src/             login
Mail/              bin/             testme
[taylor@ado105 @]$
```

2. The `ssh` command offers a shorthand notation for logging out of the remote system; instead of using `logout`, you can simply enter `~.` to do the job. To stop the `ssh` session, use `~^z`.

I choose to log out the normal way:

```
[taylor@ado105 @]$ exit
Connection to intuitive.com closed.
$
```

Now I'm back on the original computer system.

3. Turns out there are a number of the tilde commands available, which you can learn about by typing `~?` at any point during the SSH connection:

```
~?
    Supported escape sequences:
    ~.  - terminate connection
    ~B  - send break (SSH protocol 2 only)
    ~C  - open a command line
    ~R  - Request rekey (SSH protocol 2 only)
    ~^z - suspend ssh
    ~#  - list forwarded connections
    ~&  - background ssh (when waiting for connections to terminate)
    ~?  - this message
    ~~  - send the escape character by typing it twice
        (Note that escapes are only recognized immediately after newline.)
[taylor@ado105 @]$
```

The `ssh` command is fast and easy, offering a simple way to jump onto a remote system and use the command line, including screen-oriented programs like `emacs` or the `vi` editor. It's the functional equivalent of using VLC or RDP to get a remote GUI session to a Windows machine or Mac; but because Unix is command-line driven, a textual terminal gives you all the functionality of being on the machine locally with none of the need for heavyweight telepresence servers to be installed on the remote machine. I use it quite frequently.

Sure, you could still use `telnet` or its partner program `rlogin`, but both of those have security problems that make them poor choices in this modern era of widescale computer hacking and system break-ins. It's best to ensure that they're disabled on the server itself and just learn `ssh`!

Task 21.2: Third-Party SSH Connections

I've already pointed out the security problems with `telnet` and its ilk. There are important considerations, not the least of which is that the information between the client and the server is "in the clear." That is, if you could somehow interpose a network packet sniffer that could filter out just the `telnet` traffic, you could read the account/password pair and everything that's displayed on the remote user's display.

Although a number of possible solutions exist for this problem, Tatu Ylönen at Helsinki University of Technology in Finland came up with the best one: SSH. *SSH* is essentially a point-to-point encrypted `telnet` protocol. If your server supports SSH, and odds are excellent that it does, you should unquestionably use it. There are no downsides that I've found, and the additional security is a definite boon.

On the PC side, the SSH client of choice is unquestionably PuTTY, which includes SSH support and can be found at http://www.putty.org. Better yet, it's free. You can't go wrong with that price.

For Macintosh users, an SSH client is included with Mac OS X, so you need merely open up the Terminal (it's in Applications -> Utilities) and type `ssh` to get started.

If you're on a Unix or Linux system, you already have an SSH client. Just type `ssh` and see what happens. If it's not included, ask your sysadmin, or use Google to search for "ssh client" and the name of your flavor of Unix.

CAUTION
_____

Two incompatible versions of the SSH protocol, SSH 1 and SSH 2, can be installed on servers. If you try to connect to a secure server and it fails, try the other protocol. (All SSH clients give you a choice.) Start with the more modern SSH2 protocol if you have an option.

---

1. Connecting to a secure server with a command-line SSH application is a breeze: Just type `ssh` at the command line:

```
$ ssh taylor@intuitive.com
The authenticity of host 'intuitive.com (128.121.96.234)' can't be
established.
RSA1 key fingerprint is e0:41:23:6a:1d:e5:d0:d6:10:8c:fd:66:ac:9c:14:c0.
Are you sure you want to continue connecting (yes/no)? yes
Warning: Permanently added 'intuitive.com,128.121.96.234' (RSA1) to list of
known hosts.
taylor@intuitive.com's password:
```

2. After you're connected to an SSH server, the remote system appears almost exactly as though you've got a hardwire connection, including any screen-oriented programs like editors, without any performance issues or other downsides.

The Internet is a tremendously popular place, both for nice folk offering lots of cool and compelling information and for bad people trying nefarious schemes to break in and steal information. I don't think of myself as overly paranoid about things, but I like the security that I get from using SSH instead of `telnet`, and on my own servers, I run SSH software, and regular `telnet` clients cannot connect.

Task 21.3: Copying Files with SFTP

The main program used to copy files on the Internet used to be an ugly system called ftp, named after the protocol it implements: *File Transfer Protocol*. Like much of Unix, ftp can take a while to master, particularly because no effort has been made to make it at all user-friendly. The more modern—and strongly recommended—alternative is SFTP, Secure FTP, and that's what I'll explore in this portion of the lesson.

SFTP is easy to work with: You enter sftp along with the name of the remote system on the command line. You are prompted for the account password; then you are dropped into SFTP with the connection open and waiting.

Many sites have anonymous ftp capabilities (that is, allow access from the Internet without requiring a specific account on the machine), as we'll explore in the next task. For those, you can use the old-school FTP program since encryption isn't necessary to download white papers or source code.

Systems allowing anonymous connections are set up so that you don't need your own computer account to connect and copy files from their archives. To use these systems, enter ftp as the account name and then enter your own email address as the password. (For example, I'd enter ftp as the account and then taylor@intuitive.com as my password.) The most important commands available in sftp once you're connected to a remote server are summarized in Table 21.1. The most important one to remember is quit, which you use when you're done.

TABLE 21.1 Valuable sftp Commands

Command	Meaning
bye	Quit sftp.
cd *path*	Change remote directory to *path*.
chgrp *grp path*	Change group of file *path* to *grp*.
chmod *mode path*	Change permissions of file *path* to *mode*.
chown *own path*	Change owner of file *path* to *own*.
df [-hi] [*path*]	Display statistics for current directory or file system containing *path*.
exit	Quit sftp.
get [-Ppr] *remote* [*local*]	Download file.
reget *remote* [*local*]	Resume file download.
help	Display this help text.
lcd *path*	Change local directory to *path*.
lls [*ls-options* [*path*]]	Display local directory listing.

Command	Meaning
lmkdir *path*	Create local directory.
ln [-s] *oldpath newpath*	Link remote file (-s for symlink).
lpwd	Print local working directory.
ls [-1afhlnrSt] [*path*]	Display remote directory listing.
lumask *umask*	Set local umask to *umask*.
mkdir *path*	Create remote directory.
progress	Toggle display of progress meter.
put [-Ppr] *local* [*remote*]	Upload file.
pwd	Display remote working directory.
quit	Quit sftp.
rename *oldpath newpath*	Rename remote file.
rm *path*	Delete remote file.
rmdir *path*	Remove remote directory.
symlink *oldpath newpath*	Symlink remote file.
version	Show SFTP version.
!*command*	Execute *command* in local shell.
!	Escape to local shell.
?	Synonym for help.

1. I want to pick up a file from intuitive that I saw earlier, when I used ssh to look at the remote system. To start sftp, I specify the account and host at the command line:

```
$ sftp dtaylor@intuitive.com
The authenticity of host 'intuitive.com (104.131.46.171)' can't be
established. ECDSA key fingerprint is 9e:f5:53:3d:3f:41:e1:ee:19:9b:ee:0e:11:1
9:0c:df. Are you sure you want to continue connecting (yes/no)? yes
Warning: Permanently added 'intuitive.com,104.131.46.171' (ECDSA) to list of
known hosts.
dtaylor@intuitive.com's password: -
```

Since I haven't used sftp to connect to the remote system before, it asks about the RSA encryption key. I'm sure that's the right server, so yes gets me to the password prompt.

Once I've correctly entered the remote account password, I'm ready to go:

```
Connected to intuitive.com.
.
sftp> _
```

2. Now I'm at the `sftp` program prompt, and any of the commands shown in Table 21.1 will work here. I use `dir` and `ls` to list my files in different formats:

```
sftp> ls -l
-rwxr-xr-x  1 taylor    users0     4941 Oct  4  1991 .Pnews.header
-rw-r--r--  1 taylor    users0     2103 Sep 30 19:17 .article
-rw-r--r--  1 taylor    users0      752 Apr 17  1998 .cshrc
drwx------  2 taylor    daemon     4096 Dec  6 14:25 .elm
-rw-r--r--  1 taylor    users0       28 Nov  5 09:50 .forward
-rw-r--r--  1 taylor    users0     1237 Dec 13 09:40 .login
-rw-r--r--  1 taylor    users0        6 Aug  6  1991 .logout
-rw-r--r--  1 taylor    users0      538 Dec  6 14:32 .newsrc
-rw-r--r--  1 taylor    users0     1610 Feb 17  1992 .plan
-rw-r--r--  1 taylor    users0        0 Aug  6  1991 .pnewsexpert
-rw-r--r--  1 taylor    users0       45 Feb  2  1993 .rnlast
-rw-r--r--  1 taylor    users0        6 Feb  8  1993 .rnlock
-rw-r--r--  1 taylor    users0    16767 Jan 27  1993 .rnsoft
-rw-r--r--  1 taylor    users0      114 Apr  6  1998 .sig
drwxr-xr-x  4 taylor    users0     4096 Nov 13 11:09 .tin
-rw-r--r--  1 taylor    users0     1861 Jun  2  1997 Global.Software
-rw-------  1 taylor    users0    21194 Oct  1  1995 Interactive.Unix
drwx------  4 taylor    users0     4096 Nov 13 11:09 Mail
drwxr-xr-x  2 taylor    users0     4096 Nov 13 11:09 News
drwxr-xr-x  2 taylor    users0     4096 Nov 13 11:09 Src
drwxr-xr-x  2 taylor    users0     4096 Nov 13 11:09 bin
-rw-r--r--  1 taylor    users0    12445 Sep 17 14:56 history.usenet.Z
-rw-r--r--  1 taylor    users0     1237 Oct 18 20:55 login
-rw-r--r--  1 taylor    users0      174 Nov 20 19:21 testme
sftp> dir
Mail        News              bin       Global.Software    history.usenet.Z
Src         Interactive.Unix  testme    login
sftp>
```

As you can see, there's a surprising amount of difference between the `dir` command (which you use to get a directory listing in `ftp`) and the `ls -l` command. I definitely prefer the latter.

NOTE

One trick for using the `ls` command within `sftp` is that if you specify a set of command flags as a second word, it works fine as shown. Specify a third argument, however, and `sftp` saves the output of the command into a local file by that name; so `ls -l -C` would create a file called `-C` on your system with the output of the `ls -l` command. Awkward.

3. To transfer the file `login.txt` from the remote system, I can use the `get` command:

```
sftp> get login.txt
Fetching /home/taylor/login.txt to login.txt/home/taylor/login.txt 100%   46
➥ 0.0KB/s   00:00
sftp>
```

This can get a bit tricky. I've just copied the `login.txt` file from `intuitive.com` (where I SFTP'd) to the local Unix system where I'm running the `sftp` command itself. On the local system, SFTP gave the file the same name as it had on the remote system: `login.txt`.

4. Alternatively, I could use `get` and specify a wildcard pattern similar to one I'd give the shell:

```
sftp> get log*
Fetching /home/taylor/login.txt to login.txt
/home/taylor/login.txt                      100%   46      0.0KB/s   00:01     ftp>
```

There was only one match, so the transfer was easy. The wildcard forms of `get` and `put` are particularly useful if you want to transfer many files at once, so `get *.?` would get `*.c`, `*.h`, and any other source files that have a single-letter suffix to their filenames, for example.

That job was easily accomplished. In the next task I will look on another system that supports anonymous FTP to see what's available.

5. To disconnect, I enter `quit`:

```
sftp> quit
$
```

Though the interface is relatively crude, SFTP provides an easy and efficient method of transferring files quickly between two systems, regardless of operating system. It's worth learning, but if you'd prefer, you can always get a nice graphical front end, either within X11, Windows, or the Mac environment.

Task 21.4: Exploring Anonymous FTP Archives

FTP is a simple though insecure method of transferring files, but it turns out that you can work with many FTP archives even if you don't have an actual login account on the system. Known as *anonymous FTP archives*, these sites are typically massive archives of data and applications and a valuable alternative to the more common Web-based archival sites. Let's have a look!

1. There are hundreds of information servers on the Internet, offering an astounding variety of information, from weather service maps to the full text of the Bible and *Alice in Wonderland* to the source listings of thousands of programs. In this example, I want to look at the anonymous FTP archive at a software repository called The Armory. This time we'll use the FTP program, not SFTP, with a host called `ftp.armory.com`. It's easy to just open up a new archive site:

```
$ ftp ftp.armory.com
Connected to ftp.armory.com.
220 deeptht FTP server ready.
Name ftp.armory.com:taylor(ftp.armory.com:taylor): ftp
331 Guest login ok, send your complete e-mail address as password.
```

```
Password:
230-Welcome to the armory.com anonymous FTP archives.
230-All of the archives are under /pub.
230-Archives maintained by deepthought users are in /pub/user/<username>,
230-which you can also refer to by "~username", e.g.
230-cd ~rstevew
230-to change to the directory maintained by deepthought user "rstevew".
230-See the file /pub/index for one-line descriptions of all of the files
230-except the user-maintained archives.
230-If you have a web browser, see http://www.armory.com/~ftp/
230-for an HTML version of the same index.
230-
230-The file "index" contains one-line descriptions of the files below this
230-directory, except for the user-maintained files.
230-If you have a web browser, see http://www.armory.com/~ftp/
230-for an HTML version of the same index.
230-The files under "midnight_beach" are maintained by jon@armory.com.
230-The files under "electronics" are maintained by rstevew@armory.com.
230-Anonymous ftp directories maintained by other users are under the directory
230-"user".  You can also refer to user-maintained directories with "~username"
230-
230 Guest login ok, access restrictions apply. Remote system type is UNIX.
➥ Using binary mode to transfer files.ftp>
```

For the password, standard protocol is to enter your email address, but you can actually enter anything you'd like—hence the "anonymous" part of anonymous FTP.

Now I can use dir to look around:

```
ftp> dir
227 Entering Passive Mode (192,122,209,23,30,94)
150 Opening ASCII mode data connection for /bin/ls.
total 130
-rw-r--r--    1 other        1657 Oct 22  2002 .indexhead
-rw-r--r--    1 other         510 Jul 27  1996 .message
-rw-------    1 other        1153 Nov 12  2003 Makefile
dr-sr-xr-x    7 other        1120 Jul 24  2014 admin
drwsr-xr-x   10 sys           192 Jun 03  2009 dos
lrwxrwxrwx    1 sys            12 Apr 13  2012 electronics -> user/rstevew
-rw-r--r--    1 sys         40608 May 29 23:30 index
drwxr-xr-x    4 sys            64 Jun 03  2009 lib
dr-sr-xr-x    3 other         128 Jun 03  2009 linux
drwxrwxr-x    2 jons          176 Jun 03  2009 midnight_beach
drwsr-xr-x    2 other          96 Jun 03  2009 misc
dr-sr-xr-x    3 other          80 Jun 03  2009 osx
lrwxrwxrwx    1 sys             1 Apr 13  2012 pub -> .
drwsr-xr-x    5 other         976 Mar 22  2012 scobins
dr-sr-xr-x    6 other        2256 Jan 05  2012 scripts
dr-sr-xr-x    4 other         624 Jul 20  2011 source
```

```
drwsr-xr-x    3 other          112 Jun 03  2009 text
dr-sr-xr-x    3 other           96 Jun 03  2009 unixware
drwxr-xr-x   38 other          640 May 02  2014 user
dr-sr-xr-x    3 other          288 May 27  2011 www
226 Transfer complete.

ftp>
```

It looks as though there might be something of interest in the unixware directory, but before we explore that directory, I'll check out the index message.

2. To read a text file, I get it but copy it to /dev/tty. Or, if I'm worried that it's longer than a few lines, I get it and then use the ! shell escape to view it locally, as shown:

```
ftp> get index
local: index remote: index
227 Entering Passive Mode (192,122,209,23,43,229)
150 Opening BINARY mode data connection for index (40608 bytes).
100% |*********************************| 40608        39.73 KiB/s    00:00 ETA
226 Transfer complete.
40608 bytes received in 00:01 (37.32 KiB/s)
ftp> !head index
Having <a href=ftpserve.html>problems connecting to the FTP server</a>?

deepthought's archives are in the following directories:
#index
/*
admin ........ Administrative utilities (ksh and gawk programs)
dos .......... DOS utilities
misc ........ Miscellaneous archives
scobins ...... Binary executables for SCO UNIX 3.2v5
scripts ...... Interpreted programs, mostly ksh and gawk scripts
ftp>
```

Ah, not too exciting after all. I'll jump into unixware and see what's there instead.

3. I use cd to change to that directory and then dir to see what's available there:

```
ftp> cd unixware
250 CWD command successful.
ftp> dir
227 Entering Passive Mode (192,122,209,23,105,229)
150 Opening ASCII mode data connection for /bin/ls.
total 80
-rw-r--r--    1 1042         18724 Jan 16  2003 cwtmp
drwsr-xr-x    2 sys             64 Jun 03  2009 help_pages
-rw-r--r--    1 sys            357 Jan 16  2003 index
-rw-r--r--    1 source       17236 Mar 19  2002 pcmd
226 Transfer complete.
ftp>
```

This time, I look at the `index` file directly:

```
ftp> get index /dev/tty
local: /dev/tty remote: index
227 Entering Passive Mode (192,122,209,23,11,86)
150 Opening BINARY mode data connection for index (357 bytes).
unixware/
Binary executables for SCO UnixWare.  Tested only under UnixWare 7.
Source is in the source/ directory.
# HTML version at http://www.armory.com./~ftp/index.html#unixware/

Filename  Description
cwtmp     Remove useless entries from wtmp & fix wtmp & utmp corruption.
pcmd      Push characters into tty input buffer, as though typed at keyboard.


226 Transfer complete.
357 bytes received in 00:00 (4.20 KiB/s)
ftp>
```

There's a lot on this archive server, as you can see. I could explore further with `cd` and `dir`, until I found something of interest, but I'm going to instead drop the connection with `quit` and be done with this quick tour of anonymous FTP!

NOTE

With the rise of Web-based archives like SourceForge, FTP archives are dinosaurs that are becoming more obsolete each year. It's hard to find useful ones nowadays, and unless there's a compelling reason to work this way, I suggest that exploring archives, grabbing source files, and copying documents are all better done through Firefox or another graphically oriented utility.

Using FTP is still a legit way to obtain information from the Internet if you're careful about how you use it, however. Thousands of systems offer various services via anonymous FTP: Table 21.2 lists a few of the most interesting ones.

TABLE 21.2   Some Interesting `ftp` Archives

Site	Institution and Available Information
`ftp.sfu.ca ftp.sfu.ca`	San Francisco University. Files: MS-DOS, Mac
`apotheca.hpl.hp.com`	Hewlett-Packard Research Labs, Palo Alto, California. Files: X11, recipes, `cron`, `map`, Modula-3
`ftp.sri.com`	SRI International. Files: Improving the security of your Unix system
`ftp.columbia.edu`	Columbia University. Files: `kermit`

Summary

There's no question that the interface to `sftp` is awkward. The good news is that most people have a Windows or Macintosh system as their actual desktop, and there are a ton of great FTP and SFTP clients for both systems.

Most modern FTP clients also support SFTP and, as I said in the beginning of the hour, you really should be using the Secure FTP system for file transfers unless there's a compelling reason not to do so. It's just smart.

Workshop

The Workshop summarizes the key terms you've learned and poses some questions about the topics presented in this lesson. It also provides you with a preview of what you will learn in the next hour.

Key Terms

anonymous FTP   This system responds to `ftp` queries that does not require you to have an account on the system. Used largely by public code repositories and university file servers.

search string   A search string is the pattern specified in a search.

Exercises

1. Use `telnet` to try to log in to one of the FTP server sites shown in Table 21.2. You won't have an account, so drop the connection once you see a `login:` prompt.

2. Use `ftp` to connect to `ftp.columbia.edu` and see what files the university has made available to anonymous FTP users. Copy one onto your system and read through it to see if it transferred correctly.

3. What's the main difference between `telnet` and `ssh`? `ftp` and `sftp`? Which ones are better choices, and why?

Preview of the Next Hour

This lesson offered you a tour of the basic tools of the Internet. In the next hour, you will learn how to search on your Unix system—and elsewhere on the Internet—for specific files and how to work with them.

Searching for Information and Files

Goals for This Hour

In this hour, you will learn

- ▶ How to use the `find` command and its weird options
- ▶ How to use `find` with `xargs`
- ▶ About working with files on the Internet

One of the greatest challenges in Unix is finding the files you want, when you want them. Even the best organization in the world, with mnemonic subdirectories and carefully named files, can break down and leave you saying to yourself, "I know it's somewhere, and I remember that it contains a bid for Acme Acres Construction to get that contract; but for the life of me, I just can't remember where it is!"

In this hour, you'll learn sophisticated ways to find specific information on a Unix system. The powerful `find` command and its partner, `xargs`, are the primary focus of this hour, but you'll also learn some additional commands that are quite useful to know.

Finding What's Where

The more you use Unix, the more likely you'll end up losing track of where some of your files are. In Unix, however, there's a cool tool to help you find them again.

Task 22.1: The `find` Command and Its Weird Options

The `grep` family can help you find files by their content. There are many other ways to look for things in Unix, and that's where the `find` command can help. This command has a notation that is completely different from all other Unix commands: It has full-word options rather than single-letter flags. Instead of using `-n pattern` to match filenames, for example, `find` uses `-name pattern`.

The general format for this command is to specify the starting point for a search through the file system, followed by any actions desired. The list of the most useful of the many, many options, or flags, is shown in Table 22.1.

TABLE 22.1 Useful Options for the `find` Command

Option	Meaning
`-atime` *n*	True if the file was accessed *n* days ago.
`-ctime` *n*	True if the file was created *n* days ago.
`-exec` *command*	Execute *command*.
`-mtime` *n*	True if the file was modified *n* days ago.
`-name` *pattern*	True if the filename matches *pattern*.
`-print`	Print names of the files matched.
`-type` *c*	True if the file is of type *c* (as shown in Table 22.2).
`-user` *name*	True if the file is owned by user *name*.

The `find` command checks the specified options, going from left to right, once for each file or directory encountered. Further, `find` with any of the time-oriented commands can search for files more recent than, older than, or exactly the same age as a specified date, with the specifications -*n*, +*n*, and *n*, respectively. Some examples will make this clear.

1. At its simplest, `find` can be used to create a list of all files and directories below the current directory:

```
$ find . -print
.
./OWL
./OWL/owl.h
./OWL/owl
./OWL/owl.c
./OWL/simple.editor.c
./OWL/ask.c
./OWL/simple.editor.o
./OWL/owl.o

lots and lots of output removed

./dead.letter
./who.is.who
./src.listing
./tmp.listing
././.wrongwords
./papert.article
```

2. To limit the output to just those files that are C source files (those that have a `.c` suffix), I can use the `-name` option before the `-print` option:

```
$ find . -name "*.c" -print
./OWL/owl.c
```

```
./OWL/simple.editor.c
./OWL/ask.c
./OWL/handout.c
./OWL/WordMap/msw-to-txt.c
./OWL/WordMap/newtest.c
./OWL/feedback.c
./OWL/define.c
./OWL/spell.c
./OWL/submit.c
./OWL/utils.c
./OWL/parse.c
./OWL/sendmail.c
./owl.c
./src/calc.c
./src/info.c
./src/fixit.c
./src/massage.c
```

Using the -name option before the -print option can be very handy.

3. To find just files that have been modified in the past seven days, I can use -mtime with the argument -7 (including the hyphen):

```
$ find . -mtime -7 -name "*.c" -print
./OWL/owl.c
./OWL/simple.editor.c
./OWL/ask.c
./OWL/utils.c
./OWL/sendmail.c
```

If I use just the number 7 (without a hyphen), I will match only files that were modified exactly seven days ago:

```
$ find . -mtime 7 -name "*.c" -print
$
```

To find C source files that I haven't touched for more than 30 days, I use +30:

```
$ find . -mtime +30 -name "*.c" -print
./OWL/WordMap/msw-to-txt.c
./OWL/WordMap/newtest.c
./src/calc.c
./src/info.c
./src/fixit.c
./src/massage.c
```

4. With find, I now have a tool for looking across vast portions of the file system for specific file types, filenames, and other attributes.

To look across the /bin and /usr directory trees for filenames that contain the pattern cp, I can use the following command:

```
$ find /bin /usr -name "*cp*" -print
/bin/cp
/bin/rcp
/usr/bin/cpan
/usr/bin/cpio
/usr/bin/cpp
/usr/bin/cpp-3.3
/usr/bin/cpp-4.0
/usr/bin/escputil
/usr/bin/scp
/usr/include/architecture/i386/cpu.h
/usr/include/cpio.h
/usr/include/gcc/darwin/3.3/c++/bits/cpp_type_traits.h
/usr/include/gcc/darwin/4.0/c++/bits/cpp_type_traits.h
/usr/include/netinet/tcp.h
/usr/include/netinet/tcp_fsm.h
/usr/include/netinet/tcp_seq.h
/usr/include/netinet/tcp_timer.h
/usr/include/netinet/tcp_var.h
/usr/include/netinet/tcpip.h
/usr/include/tcpd.h

lots of output omitted

/usr/X11R6/lib/X11/fonts/encodings/microsoft-cp1258.enc
/usr/X11R6/lib/X11/locale/ibm-cp1133
/usr/X11R6/lib/X11/locale/microsoft-cp1251
/usr/X11R6/lib/X11/locale/microsoft-cp1255
/usr/X11R6/lib/X11/locale/microsoft-cp1256
```

NOTE

This type of search can take a long time on a busy system. When I ran this command on a loaded server, it took almost 5 minutes to complete!

5. To find a list of the directories I've created in my home directory, I can use the -type specifier with one of the values shown in Table 22.2. Here's one example:

```
$ find . -type d -print
.
./OWL
./OWL/Doc
./OWL/WordMap
./.elm
./Archives
```

```
./InfoWorld
./InfoWorld/PIMS
./Mail
./News
./bin
./src
./temp
$
```

TABLE 22.2   Helpful **find** **-type** File Types

Letter	Meaning
d	Directory
f	File
l	Link

6. To find more information about each of these directories, I can use the -exec option to find, which specifies a subcommand to execute against each file in the result set. Unfortunately, I cannot simply enter the command; the exec option must be used with {}, which will be replaced by the matched filename, and \; at the end of the command. (If the \ is left out, the shell will interpret the ; as the end of the find command.) You also must ensure that there is a space between the {} and the \; characters:

```
$ find . -type d -exec ls -ld {} \;
drwx------ 11 taylor      1024 Dec 10 14:13 .
drwx------  4 taylor       532 Dec  6 18:31 ./OWL
drwxrwx---  2 taylor       512 Dec  2 21:18 ./OWL/Doc
drwxrwx---  2 taylor       512 Nov  7 11:52 ./OWL/WordMap
drwx------  2 taylor       512 Dec 10 13:30 ./.elm
drwx------  2 taylor       512 Nov 21 10:39 ./Archives
drwx------  3 taylor       512 Dec  3 02:03 ./InfoWorld
drwx------  2 taylor       512 Sep 30 10:38 ./InfoWorld/PIMS
drwx------  2 taylor      1024 Dec  9 11:42 ./Mail
drwx------  2 taylor       512 Oct  6 09:36 ./News
drwx------  2 taylor       512 Dec 10 13:58 ./bin
drwx------  2 taylor       512 Oct 13 10:45 ./src
drwxrwx---  2 taylor       512 Nov  8 22:20 ./temp
```

7. The find command is commonly used to remove core files that are more than a few days old. These core files are copies of the actual memory image of a running program when the program dies unexpectedly:

```
$ find . -name core -ctime +4 -print
./Archives/core
./bin/core
$
```

The core files can be huge, so occasionally trimming them is wise. It's just a small step from the preceding `find` command, which shows matching core files:

```
$ find . -name core -ctime +4 -exec /bin/rm -f {} \;
$
```

There's no output from this command because I didn't use the `-print` at the end of the command. What it does is find all files called `core` that have a creation time that's more than four days ago and removes them.

The `find` command is a powerful command in Unix and one of my favorites. It helps you find files by owner, type, filename, and just about any other attribute. The most awkward part of the command is the required elements of the `-exec` option, and that's where the `xargs` command helps immensely.

Task 22.2: Using `find` with `xargs`

You can use `find` to search for files, and you can use `grep` to search within files, but what if you want to search a combination? That's where `xargs` is helpful.

1. A few days ago, I was working on a file that was computing character mappings of files. I'd like to find it again, but I don't remember either the filename or where the file is located.

What happens if I use `find` and have the `-exec` argument call `grep` to find files containing a specific pattern?

```
$ find . -type f -exec grep -i mapping {} \;
typedef struct mappings {
map-entry character-mapping[] = {
int         long-mappings = FALSE;
        case 'l': long-mappings = TRUE;
            if (long-mappings)
        /** do a short mapping **/
        /** do a long mapping **/
        /** Look up the specified character in the mapping database **/
        while ((character-mapping[pointer].key < ch) &&
            (character-mapping[pointer].key > 0))
        if (character-mapping[pointer].key == ch)
          return ( (map-entry *) &character-mapping[pointer]);
# map,uucp-map   = The UUCP Mapping Project = nca-maps@apple.com
grep -i "character*mapping" * */* */*/*
to print PostScript files produced by a mapping application that runs on the
bionet.genome.chromosomes      Mapping and sequencing of eucaryote chromosomes.
./bin/my.new.cmd: Permission denied
typedef struct mappings {
map-entry character-mapping[] = {
int         long-mappings = FALSE;
```

```
        case 'l': long-mappings = TRUE;
            if (long-mappings)
        /** do a short mapping **/
        /** do a long mapping **/
        /** Look up the specified character in the mapping database **/
        while ((character-mapping[pointer].key < ch) &&
               (character-mapping[pointer].key > 0))
        if (character-mapping[pointer].key == ch)
            return ( (map-entry *) &character-mapping[pointer]);
or lower case values. The table mapping upper to
```

The output is interesting, but it doesn't contain any filenames, so there's no way to know from which files these lines were extracted.

2. A second, smarter strategy would be to use the -l flag to grep so that grep specifies only the matched filename:

```
$ find . -type f -exec grep -l -i mapping {} \;
./OWL/WordMap/msw-to-txt.c
./.elm/aliases.text
./Mail/mark
./News/usenet.alt
./bin/my.new.cmd: Permission denied
./src/fixit.c
./temp/attach.msg
$
```

This is a step in the right direction, but the problem with this approach is that each time find matches a file, it invokes grep, which is a very resource-intensive strategy.

3. You can use xargs to read the output of find and build calls to grep that specify a lot of files at once. (Remember that each time a file is seen, the grep program will check through it.) This way, grep is called only four or five times, even though it might check through 200 or 300 files. By default, xargs always tacks the list of filenames to the end of the specified command, so using it is easy:

```
$ find . -type f -print | xargs grep -l -i mapping
./OWL/WordMap/msw-to-txt.c
./.elm/aliases.text
./Mail/mark
./News/usenet.alt
./bin/my.new.cmd: Permission denied
./src/fixit.c
./temp/attach.msg
```

This gives the same output as the command in step 3 but is quite a bit faster.

4. What's nice about this approach to working with find is that because grep is getting multiple filenames, it automatically includes the filename of any file that contains a match when grep shows the matching line. Removing the -l flag results in exactly what I want:

```
$ find . -type f -print | xargs grep -i mapping
./OWL/WordMap/msw-to-txt.c:typedef struct mappings {
./OWL/WordMap/msw-to-txt.c:map-entry character-mapping[] = {
./OWL/WordMap/msw-to-txt.c:int          long-mappings = FALSE;
./OWL/WordMap/msw-to-txt.c:          case 'l': long-mappings = TRUE;
./OWL/WordMap/msw-to-txt.c:           if (long-mappings)
./OWL/WordMap/msw-to-txt.c:      /** do a short mapping **/
./OWL/WordMap/msw-to-txt.c:      /** do a long mapping **/
./OWL/WordMap/msw-to-txt.c:      /** Look up the specified character in the
➥ mapping database **/
./OWL/WordMap/msw-to-txt.c:        while ((character-mapping[pointer].key
./src/fixit.c:  /** do a long mapping **/
./src/fixit.c:  /** Look up the specified character in the mapping database **/
./src/fixit.c:  while ((character-mapping[pointer].key < ch) &&
./src/fixit.c:           (character-mapping[pointer].key > 0))
./src/fixit.c:  if (character-mapping[pointer].key == ch)
./src/fixit.c:    return ( (map-entry *) &character-mapping[pointer]);
./temp/attach.msg:or lower case values. The table mapping upper to
```

When used in combination, find, grep, and xargs are a potent team to help find files lost or misplaced anywhere in the Unix file system. I encourage you to experiment further with these important commands to find ways they can help you work with Unix.

Task 22.3: Getting Files from the Internet

The find command makes it pretty easy to find files on your own Unix system, but I actually find myself getting files more often from the Internet than directly from another place on my own system. It turns out that there are a remarkable number of different ways that you can download files from a remote system, approaches that are far easier than using the clunky ftp or sftp programs discussed in the previous hour.

Which tool you use depends on what you have available in your Unix system, too: The three I'm going to consider are GET, curl, and lynx. lynx is especially noteworthy, actually, because it is a text-based Web browser, and it's quite a bit more powerful than will be suggested in this hour.

1. You might not know it, but books written more than about 80 years ago are no longer protected by copyright laws. This is good for those of us who like to read, and it also means that there are organizations that have put in the effort to scan and produce digital versions of some of the most popular works from the last few hundred years. Chief among them is Project Gutenberg—www.gutenberg.org—where you can download literally thousands of different books in plain-text format.

Rather than wind through their directory structure, though, let's say that you emailed me and mentioned that you were really a fan of Lewis Carrol's brilliant *Alice in Wonderland* (well, its more formal title is *The Adventures of Alice in Wonderland*, but for our purposes that's not important). I responded by saying Good news! I have a plain-text version of this great book available for download from my Web site. Here's the URL: http://www.intuitive.com/tyu24/alice.tgz.

The question now is, using the command line, how do you retrieve this document? That's the realm of GET, curl, and lynx. But let's look at these in reverse order, shall we?

2. It's probable that you have the text-mode Web browser lynx installed on your computer. The easiest way to know for sure is just to try it:

```
$ lynx -dump http://www.intuitive.com/tyu24/alice.tgz > alice.tgz
```

Did it work? If you didn't see any sort of error message, you should now have a gzip'd tar archive of the full text to *Alice in Wonderland*. Unpack it with the commands gunzip then tar, as explained in Hour 19, "Archives and Backups."

If you received a command not found error, perhaps lynx is installed but not in your PATH. Use locate to try to find it:

```
$ locate lynx
```

If that fails too, you might need to try one of the other utilities.

3. The next possibility is a great command-line utility called curl, which also accepts URLs and makes it a breeze to download and save things, but *it's critical to remember that down-loaded data is dumped to the screen by default, unless you specify the -O option (that's a capital letter O).*

Here's how you could use curl to save the Alice archive file:

```
$ curl -O http://www.intuitive.com/tyu24/alice.tgz
```

It's even easier than using lynx because you don't need a command parameter!

The curl command has quite a bit more power, including support for grabbing a range of files at once. With this notation, the command would get you file1.txt, file2.txt, and so on:

```
$ curl 'http://test.domain/folder/file[1-10].txt'
```

Note that this command expands the square brackets *on the remote system*, not locally.

You can also use curl to get ftp: and even https: files because it speaks about a dozen different transfer protocols. In fact, curl can even *upload* files via FTP.

The curl command also has a ton of different options, and if you're interested in learning how to use it, man curl is a critical first stop.

4. The third possible command you could use is GET, which is actually part of a Perl communications package. Type in the command without any arguments, and it'll tell you exactly
how it can be used:

```
$ GET
Usage: GET [-options] <url>...
    -m <method>    use method for the request (default is 'GET')
    -f             make request even if GET believes method is illegal
    -b <base>      Use the specified URL as base
    -t <timeout>   Set timeout value
    -i <time>      Set the If-Modified-Since header on the request
    -c <conttype>  use this content-type for POST, PUT, CHECKIN
    -a             Use text mode for content I/O
    -p <proxyurl>  use this as a proxy
    -P             don't load proxy settings from environment
    -H <header>    send this HTTP header (you can specify several)

    -u             Display method and URL before any response
    -U             Display request headers (implies -u)
    -s             Display response status code
    -S             Display response status chain
    -e             Display response headers
    -d             Do not display content
    -o <format>    Process HTML content in various ways

    -v             Show program version
    -h             Print this message

    -x             Extra debugging output
```

Just like curl and lynx, GET allows you to work with Web-based content on the
command line. This means that if you happened to know that I keep a copy of the
uncompressed Alice file on my server, too, you could search it for occurrences of the word
walrus, say, without ever having to save a copy on your own disk:

```
$ GET http://www.intuitive.com/tyu24/alice.txt | grep -i walrus
Just then she heard something splashing about in the pool a little way off, and
she swam nearer to make out what it was: at first she thought it must be a walrus
or hippopotamus, but then she remembered how small she was now, and she soon made
out that it was only a mouse that had slipped in like herself.
$
```

Pretty cool trick, isn't it?

Oh! To get the compressed archive, the command looks pretty darn similar to the previous
invocations (but note that you need to redirect the downloaded data into a file):

```
$ GET http://www.intuitive.com/tyu24/alice.tgz > alice.tgz
```

Once you start thinking about ways that you can work with Web content on a command line, you'll realize that this capability truly is one reason Unix is a fabulous working environment. Think about it: Any file, any data, any HTML you can obtain from the Web you can incorporate into a shell script or otherwise `grep` through to find key salient data. From stock quotes to weather, dictionary lookups to RSS feed parsing, the combinations of `lynx`, `curl`, or `GET` plus the thousands of Unix commands are unbeatable!

Summary

This hour started by exploring the powerful `find` command, one of the more potent commands in Unix. It has many esoteric options, and to get the full power from `find`, `xargs`, and `grep`, you need to experiment. Then you moved to learning how to work with Unix commands to access Internet data, whether accessible on an FTP server, a Web site, or even a secure Web site.

Workshop

This Workshop poses some questions about the topics presented in this hour. It also provides you with a preview of what you will learn in the next hour.

Exercises

1. Use `find` and `wc -l` to count how many files you have. Be sure to include the `-type f` option so that you don't include directories in the count.

2. Use the necessary commands to list the following:

   ▶ All filenames that contain `abc`

   ▶ All files that contain `abc`

3. How many times does the word *hookah* appear in *Alice in Wonderland*?

Preview of the Next Hour

The next hour introduces you to the powerful Swiss Army knife of Unix: the Perl programming language. From simple one-liners to thousand-line programs, it's a must-know for all modern Unix users.

Perl Programming in Unix

Goals for This Hour

In this hour, you will learn

▶ About `Exchange`, a demonstration currency translator written in Perl

▶ How to check code quality with `-w`

▶ About online Perl documentation and information

▶ About other useful Perl commands

In this hour, I introduce you to the Perl scripting and programming language. Perl is an *interpreted* language, so it doesn't require you to use a compiler as an intermediate step in getting it to work, as C and Java do. Perl works much more like shell scripts, which makes it an easier-to-use development tool.

Whether or not you plan on getting involved with Unix programming, I definitely encourage you to read more about Perl. In addition to being an elegant and powerful Unix tool builder, Perl is also one of the classic programming languages of choice for Web professionals. Want to delve deeper into Web development, though? Then you'd be smart to learn PHP and Python. Both are definitely Unix friendly, and more and more code is being written in those languages, along with Ruby.

In this hour, you'll learn what tools are available with the standard Perl distribution to help you develop smart, fast programs. This lesson describes a program that enables you to do easy currency translation to prepare for travel overseas.

NOTE

Surprisingly, Perl isn't included with every Unix implementation. If you don't have it, or if your version of Perl is earlier than 5.0 (try `perl -v` to find out what version you have), then go to http://www.perl.org to find out about downloading a newer version.

Flexible and Powerful: Perl

Programming in C, the language developed alongside the Unix operating system, offers considerable flexibility. C is the core language of the Unix operating system itself, but it was originally designed for system-level programming tasks. Perl, by contrast, was designed to be a powerful language for string or word processing. You can most easily see the difference by exploring a programming task, so that's what we'll do in this hour of the book.

Task 23.1: Exchange, a Demonstration Currency Translator Written in Perl

When some friends of mine returned from traveling throughout the world on an extended trip they commented that they were baffled by the sheer variety of currencies. They're not the first to observe this, of course, but I thought "what a great Perl program to write!"

Translating currencies is simple once you get the formula and exchange rates. Here in the United States, currency values are usually presented relative to a single U.S. dollar, so the euro might be valued at 0.9100, which means that every dollar you exchange is worth just a bit less than €1. Exchange $20, and it will net you 20×0.9100, or €18.2.

The Exchange program started out life by reading in the current exchange rates for six major world currencies (U.S. dollar, Japanese yen, euro, Swiss franc, Indian rupee and British pound), prompting for an amount in U.S. dollars, and then showing the equivalent value in these other currencies. Much more useful, however, is the capability to translate from any one of these currencies to the other five. Further, sites exist on the Internet that show the daily currency exchange rate, so ensuring up-to-date rates is another desirable program feature.

And thus Exchange was born. It's a program that lets you quickly convert between any of the six major world currencies, using a separate shell script to ensure that the conversion rates are up-to-date. This task shows how I built it out with Perl and Unix.

1. The basic logic flow (or *algorithm*, if you want to be technical about it) for the Exchange program is this:

   ```
   Read current exchange rates
   Repeat
     Ask user for an amount and currency
     Translate that into US dollars
     Show the equivalent value in the other five currencies
   Until done
   ```

2. Perl supports subroutines to help develop clean, readable programs, so let's have a peek at the main code in the program:

   ```
   #!/usr/bin/perl

   &read_exchange_rate;      # read the exchange rate table into memory
   ```

```
# now let's cycle, asking the user for input...

print "Please enter the amount, appending the first ";
print "letter of the name of\nthe currency that you're ";
print "using (Euro, Franc, Yen, Rupee, Pound) - \n";
print "the default value is US dollars.\n\n";
print "Amount: ";

while (<>) {

  ($amnt,$curr) = &breakdown(chop($_));

  $baseval = $amnt * (1/$rateof{$curr});    # translate into USD

  printf("%2.2f USD, ", $baseval * $rateof{'U'});
  printf("%2.2f Euro, ", $baseval * $rateof{'E'});
  printf("%2.2f Rupee, ", $baseval * $rateof{'R'});
  printf("%2.2f Swiss Franc, ", $baseval * $rateof{'F'});
  printf("%2.2f Yen, and ", $baseval * $rateof{'Y'});
  printf("%2.2f Pounds.\n\nAmount: ", $baseval * $rateof{'P'});
}
```

The first line needs to point to your Perl interpreter; an easy way to find it is to use which perl on the command line.

I've added some fancy output formatting with the print statement, but otherwise this code is quite similar to the algorithm you've already seen. Notice that the array rateof uses the first letter of the currency as an index and returns the current exchange rate relative to the U.S. dollar (that is, $rateof{'E'} is actually 0.9100).

One slick thing about Perl is that a subroutine can return a list of variables, as you see demonstrated in the call to the breakdown subroutine, which returns both $amnt and $curr.

3. Two subroutines are included in this program, read_exchange_rate and breakdown. Let's consider them in reverse order.

The breakdown subroutine receives the user-entered currency amount and splits it into two parts: the numeric value and the first letter of the currency indicator, if any (the default currency is U.S. dollars):

```
sub breakdown {
  @line = split("", $_);       # split at space

  $amnt = $line[0];
  if ($#line == 1) {
    $curr = $line[1];
    $curr =~ tr/a-z/A-Z/;          # normalize to uppercase
    $curr = substr($curr, 0, 1);   # extract first char only
```

```
    } else { $curr = "U"; }
    return ($amnt, $curr);
}
```

I won't go into too much detail here—Perl can be somewhat overwhelming when you first start working with it—but if the subroutine is given a value such as 34.5 yen, it will return $amnt = 34.5 and $curr = 'Y'.

4. The current exchange rate is read in from an associated data file, exchange.txt, which contains the exchange rate for the six currencies (although the exchange rate for U.S. dollars is always 1, of course!):

```
sub read_exchange_rate {
  open(EXCHRATES, "exchange.txt") ||
    die "Can't find current exchange rates.\n";

  while ( <EXCHRATES> ) {
    chomp; my @fields = split;  # remove control chars, break up into words
    $curr = @fields[0];
    $val  = @fields[1];
    $rateof{$curr} = $val;
  }
  close(EXCHRATE);
}
```

By default, Perl opens files for reading when the open command is used. Here on lines 2 and 3 you can see that the exchange.db file is being opened for reading. || die is a shorthand way of saying "if the open fails, output the error message and quit immediately."

The exchange.txt data file looks like this:

```
U:1
F:0.940270
E:0.909735
P:0.653988
R:63.747500
Y:124.159500
```

5. Here's the cool part about this program: The exchange rates can be lifted off a handy Web page automatically, to ensure that they're always current and accurate. I accomplish this task by using the curl utility, as demonstrated in the previous hour, to grab a page from x-rates.com that has the exchange rates, then a few simple Unix commands in a pipeline to strip out the information I don't want and reformat it as needed.

It's all dropped into a shell script, `build-exchrate`:

```
#!/bin/sh

# Build a new exchange rate database by using the data on x-rates.com

src=http://www.x-rates.com/table/?from=USD&amount=1
srcUrl=http://www.x-rates.com/

curl="/usr/bin/curl -s"          # -s enables silent mode

currencies="(EUR|GBP|INR|CHF|JPY)"     # ISO symbols for currencies

echo "U:1"          # make sure we get this into the output file

$curl "$src" | grep '/graph/?from=USD' | grep -E "$currencies" | \
  sort | uniq | \
  sed 's/EUR/E/;s/GBP/P/;s/INR/R/;s/CHF/F/;s/JPY/Y/' | \
  cut -d'<' -f2,3 | \
  sed "s/'//g;s/>/:/g" | \
  cut -d= -f5

echo "# extracted from $srcUrl on $(date)"
exit 0
```

To learn more about the useful `lynx` command, use `man lynx` on your system. It's a good addition to your bag of Unix tricks, particularly within scripts and programs.

The output of the `build-exchrate` command is exactly the database file format, but it's sent to the screen rather than the data file:

```
$ build-exchrate
U       1
Y       124.065
E       0.9100
P       0.6537
F       0.9401
```

Creating the data file for the program is easy:

```
$ sh build-exchrate.sh > exchange.db
$
```

6. Let's now try out the `exchange` program and see how it works:

```
$ perl exchange.pl
Please enter the amount, appending the first letter of the name of
the currency that you're using (Euro, Franc, Yen, Rupee, Pound) -
the default value is US dollars.
```

```
Amount: 20
20.00 USD, 18.19 Euro, 1274.95 Rupee, 18.81 Swiss Franc, 2483.19 Yen, and
➥ 13.08 Pounds.

Amount: 20 pounds
30.58 USD, 27.82 Euro, 1949.50 Rupee, 28.75 Swiss Franc, 3797.00 Yen, and
➥ 20.00 Pounds.

Amount: 20 yen
0.16 USD, 0.15 Euro, 10.27 Rupee, 0.15 Swiss Franc, 20.00 Yen, and 0.11 Pounds.

Amount: 20 euro
21.98 USD, 20.00 Euro, 1401.45 Rupee, 20.67 Swiss Franc, 2729.58 Yen, and
➥ 14.38 Pounds.

Amount: 20 francs
21.27 USD, 19.35 Euro, 1355.94 Rupee, 20.00 Swiss Franc, 2640.93 Yen, and
➥ 13.91 Pounds.

Amount: 20 rupee
0.31 USD, 0.29 Euro, 20.00 Rupee, 0.29 Swiss Franc, 38.95 Yen, and 0.21 Pounds.
16.21 USD, 12.91 Euro, 20.00 Swiss Franc, 1753.20 Yen, and 8.87 Pounds.
```

Finally, one last query: In the United States the dynamite Red Hat Linux Enterprise Server client package (a great, inexpensive Unix for PC-based computers) costs $349. It's easy to use Exchange to compute the equivalent price for this product overseas:

```
Amount: 349 USD
349.00 USD, 317.50 Euro, 22247.88 Rupee, 328.15 Swiss Franc, 43331.67 Yen, and
➥ 228.24 Pounds.

Amount:
```

To quit the program, I use ^d to send an end-of-file signal.

TIP

You can get an online copy of the Exchange program and its companion build-exchrate shell script by visiting http://www.intuitive.com/tyu24/.

The Exchange program demonstrates how you can write succinct and sophisticated programs in Perl. It also demonstrates that Perl can be a bit confusing if you're uninitiated! That's why your best bet for learning Perl, or any other programming language, is to spend the time to find and read a good tutorial. An excellent place to start is at www.perl.org.

More importantly, the program demonstrates that it's the combination of tools—Unix commands and Perl— that enables you to really create some terrific applications.

Task 23.2: Checking Code Quality with -w

There are two main ways to run Perl programs: by typing `perl` followed by the name of your program (as shown previously) or by specifying program names directly on the command line. For the latter approach to work, you need to include `#!/usr/bin/perl` as the first line of your program (you can use `which perl` to ensure that's the correct path on your system, of course) and use `chmod` to make your program executable.

Whichever way you choose to invoke your Perl program, the Perl interpreter will scan the program to see whether it all makes syntactic sense and then actually begin executing the instructions specified.

The scan performed is rudimentary, though, and catches only the most grievous of mistakes. Add a simple -w flag, however, and the interpreter looks much more closely at the program, emitting various warnings (-w = warnings) for odd constructs and more.

Even Perl programs that work fine can generate quite a variety of warnings! In fact, `perl -w` is the Perl version of `lint`, a popular C programming language syntax-checking utility.

1. I start by making the `exchange.pl` program executable, to save a little bit of typing:

```
$ chmod +x exchange.pl
$
```

This is not much output, but no output is good news: It means everything worked fine.

2. I'm going to delete the semicolon after the call to `read_exchange_rate` in the `exchange.pl` file so that you can see what happens when the Perl interpreter finds the mistake.

Done. (We'll call that an "edit between the lines," okay?)

```
$ exchange.pl
Scalar found where operator expected at ./exchange.pl line 49, near "$rateof"
    (Missing semicolon on previous line?)
syntax error at ./exchange.pl line 49, near "$rateof"
syntax error at ./exchange.pl line 53, near "}"
Execution of ./exchange.pl aborted due to compilation errors.
```

Hmm . . . line 49, or line 53? Let's use the -n flag to the `cat` command to get line numbers, then `sed` to show only lines 48–53:

```
$ cat -n exchange.pl | sed -n '48,53p'
    48      $val  = @fields[1]
    49      $rateof{$curr} = $val;
    50      print "rateof: $curr = $rateof{$curr}\n";
    51    }
    52    close(EXCHRATE);
    53  }
```

Look closely: Neither line 49 nor line 53 is where the problem occurs (it's on line 48; the semicolon on the end of the line is missing), but this is a great opportunity to point out that you should never entirely trust the line numbers in compiler or interpreter error messages.

3. Now I invoke Perl with the -w flag to see whether it offers more advice on what's wrong with the program:

```
$ perl -w exchange.pl
Scalar value @fields[0] better written as $fields[0] at exchange.pl line 47.
Scalar value @fields[1] better written as $fields[1] at exchange.pl line 48.
Scalar found where operator expected at exchange.pl line 49, near "$rateof"
    (Missing semicolon on previous line?)
syntax error at exchange.pl line 49, near "$rateof"
syntax error at exchange.pl line 53, near "}"
Execution of exchange.pl aborted due to compilation errors.
$
```

There's help offered here, but it's a bit hidden. Look at output line 4. It knows that there's a semicolon missing but asks it in the form of a question. A bit weird, but it's the clue needed to get the script working again!

4. I'm going to restore the semicolon (though I won't show that here; just use vi to add it) and run the -w flag one more time to see whether there are any additional useful suggestions:

```
$ perl -w exchange.pl
Scalar value @_[0] better written as $_[0] at exchange.pl line 46.
Scalar value @_[1] better written as $_[1] at exchange.pl line 47.
Use of implicit split to @_ is deprecated at exchange.pl line 45.
Name "main::EXCHRATE" used only once: possible typo at exchange.pl line 50.
""Please enter the amount, appending the first letter of the name of
the currency that you're using (franc, yen, deutschmark, pound) -
the default value is US dollars.

Amount:
```

Wow! Lots of output, most of which is telling me that there are new, fancier ways to specify things (for example, use $_[1] instead of @_[1]).

5. Buried in all this output, however, is a bug in the program I surreptitiously added during the writing of this hour that the Perl interpreter found:

```
Name "main::EXCHRATE" used only once: possible typo at exchange.pl
line 50.
```

A closer look at the read_exchange_rate subroutine shows what's wrong:

```
$ cat -n exchange.pl | tail -12
    42  open(EXCHRATES, "exchange.txt") ||
```

```
43    die "Can't find current exchange rates.\n";
44
45  while ( <EXCHRATES> ) {
46    chomp; my @fields = split(":");
47    $curr = @fields[0];
48    $val  = @fields[1];
49    $rateof{$curr} = $val;
50  }
51  close(EXCHRATE);
52  }
```

Can you see the problem it has found? The open statement on line 42 creates a *file handle* called EXCHRATES, which is then used in the while statement (line 45), but when I went to close the file handle, I forgot the trailing *s* and called it EXCHRATE on line 51. An easy fix, fortunately!

Even the most carefully written Perl programs can have problems lurking. The -w flag isn't ideal, but you should become familiar with its use and learn how to distinguish important warnings from unimportant ones.

In this case, the bug identified wouldn't have broken anything or generated any incorrect results, but if I had continued to work on Exchange, not closing the file handle could have become a significant problem down the road.

Task 23.3: Online Perl Documentation and Information

Earlier I recommended that you buy a good Perl tutorial book to learn more about the language. Actually, though, the standard Perl installation includes a ton of online documentation, so you should start there, as described in this task.

1. If you've been trying all the examples as you've been reading the lessons, you're already familiar with the standard Unix man page format and how to find the information you see there. Man pages are good for summaries of how to work with individual commands, but they're much less useful for explaining large, complex programs such as bash, the Elm Mail System, or the Perl interpreter. That's why the Perl documentation is broken into a crazy number of man pages. Here are just the first 25:

```
$ man -k perl | grep '(1)' | head -25
piconv(1pm)          - -- iconv(1), reinvented in perl
a2p(1)               - Awk to Perl translator
config_data(1)       - Query or change configuration of Perl modules
enc2xs(1)            - -- Perl Encode Module Generator
eyapp(1)             - A Perl front-end to the Parse::Eyapp module
find2perl(1)         - translate find command lines to Perl code
h2ph(1)              - convert .h C header files to .ph Perl header files
h2xs(1)              - convert .h C header files to Perl extensions
```

```
par.pl(1)                    - Make and run Perl Archives
perl(1)                      - The Perl 5 language interpreter
perl(1), a2p(1)              - Practical Extraction and Report Language
perlaix(1)                   - Perl version 5 on IBM AIX (UNIX) systems
perlamiga(1)                 - Perl under Amiga OS
perlapi(1)                   - autogenerated documentation for the perl public API
perlapio(1)                  - perl's IO abstraction interface
perlartistic(1)              - the Perl Artistic License
perlbeos(1)                  - Perl version 5.8+ on BeOS
perlaix(1)                   - Perl version 5 on IBM AIX (UNIX) systems
perlamiga(1)                 - Perl under Amiga OS
perlapi(1)                   - autogenerated documentation for the perl public API
perlapio(1)                  - perl's IO abstraction interface
perlartistic(1)              - the Perl Artistic License
perlbeos(1)                  - Perl version 5.8+ on BeOS
perlbook(1)                  - Books about and related to Perl
perlboot(1)                  - This document has been deleted
POSIX (3)                    - Perl interface to IEEE Std 1003.1
```

Quite a few man pages, eh? Turns out that when you include all the "delta" pages that detail what's changed in each version and subversion, there are a staggering 403 Perl-related man pages just in section 1, user commands.

2. The good news (I think) is that the standard Perl man page offers a suggested order for reading the man pages that can help overcome some of the gasping, drowning feeling you probably have right now!

For ease of access, the Perl manual has been divided into a number of sections:

```
perl         Perl overview (this section)
perldelta    Perl changes since previous version
perlfaq      Perl frequently asked questions

perldata     Perl data structures
perlsyn      Perl syntax
perlop       Perl operators and precedence
perlre       Perl regular expressions
perlrun      Perl execution and options
perlfunc     Perl builtin functions
perlvar      Perl predefined variables
perlsub      Perl subroutines
perlmod      Perl modules: how they work
perlmodlib   Perl modules: how to write and use
perlform     Perl formats
perllocale   Perl locale support
```

```
perlref      Perl references
perldsc      Perl data structures intro
perllol      Perl data structures: lists of lists
perltoot     Perl OO tutorial
perlobj      Perl objects
perltie      Perl objects hidden behind simple variables
perlbot      Perl OO tricks and examples
perlipc      Perl interprocess communication

perldebug    Perl debugging
perldiag     Perl diagnostic messages
perlsec      Perl security
perltrap     Perl traps for the unwary
perlstyle    Perl style guide

perlpod      Perl plain old documentation
perlbook     Perl book information
perlembed    Perl ways to embed perl in your C or C++ application
perlapio     Perl internal IO abstraction interface
perlxs       Perl XS application programming interface
perlxstut    Perl XS tutorial
perlguts     Perl internal functions for those doing extensions
perlcall     Perl calling conventions from C
```

> (If you're intending to read these straight through for
> the first time, the suggested order will tend to reduce
> the number of forward references.)

I find the Perl man pages overwhelming, too, so don't worry if this doesn't make you want to leap online and read it all.

3. The smarter way to learn more about Perl is to read the online documentation. You can start at http://www.perl.org or jump straight to the terrific Perl reference material in HTML form at http://search.cpan.org/dist/perl/pod/perl.pod.

Start with the FAQs and the basic Perl man page, and then graduate to a book on the subject (or even a course)—and you'll be a Perl expert.

NOTE
_____

There are tons of books on Perl, ranging from the basics of the language to sophisticated database and enterprise programming references. A good starting point is *Sams Teach Yourself Perl in 24 Hours*.

_____

Task 23.4: Other Useful Perl Commands

There are useful pieces to the Perl environment other than just the -w flag to the interpreter! In this section I'll highlight some special command flags worth knowing to help you get the most out of Perl.

1. The first new flag to learn about is the -d (debug) flag. It's documented (in detail) in perldebug, the info page you'll want to read to learn about the various debugging commands.

2. An interesting variation in debugging requires another flag, the -e (execute the following command) flag. It lets you actually use the Perl interpreter interactively:

   ```
   $ perl -de 1

   Loading DB routines from perl5db.pl version 1.33
   Emacs support available.

   Enter h or 'h h' for help, or `man perldebug' for more help.
   main::(-e:1):   1
     DB<1> print "Hi!";
   Hi!
     DB<2> q
   $
   ```

   The 1 was actually a command to the Perl interpreter, and because I specified -d for debugging, the interpreter executed the command and then stopped for input.

3. If you'll be using Perl to write Common Gateway Interface (CGI) scripts for a Web server, you'll want to explore the -T (taint) flag, which keeps close track of the flow of user input for security. See perlsec for more information.

4. Finally, no discussion of Perl can be complete without highlighting the terrific Perl developer community and its Comprehensive Perl Archive Network (CPAN). The best place to learn about it is http://www.cpan.org.

NOTE

You can also use Perl interactively to learn about the CPAN modules available, though I've never had any luck with it myself. Try entering perl -MCPAN -e shell.

Spending some time learning the Perl language is very worthwhile. The Unix shell offers various capabilities, but you'll undoubtedly hit the edge as you become more sophisticated; that's where Perl can really help you go further.

Summary

The C programming language is the concrete foundation of the Unix operating system, but although it's powerful, it's also rigid and somewhat of a hassle for simple tasks. Perl is a great alternative and the next step up for programmers who are trying to bend Unix (or Linux) to their needs but finding the shell underpowered. I recommend that if you want to become a Unix genius, learn C first, but if you want to become a power user, Perl is the way to go.

Workshop

The Workshop summarizes the key terms you've learned and poses some questions about the topics presented in this lesson.

Key Terms

algorithm   An algorithm is a logical sequence of steps taken by a program.

file handle   This is an internal program variable that's used to refer to a specific file. In Perl, you use an `open` command to associate a file handle with a file.

Exercises

Go to http://www.intuitive.com/tyu24/ and download the files for this hour.

1. Congratulations! You just won £50! Use `Exchange` to see how much that's worth in U.S. dollars.

2. Find and fix the bug highlighted in the `exchange.pl` program earlier in this lesson. Run `perl -w` to confirm that it's fixed.

3. Read through the Perl FAQ man pages. What do the Perl FAQ authors recommend as the forum for free Perl advice?

4. What's a JAPH?

GNOME and the GUI Environment

Goals for This Hour

In this hour, you will learn

▶ How to tweak the GNOME configuration

▶ About working with the GNOME file manager

▶ How to surf the Web with Firefox

▶ About working with Thunderbird Email

If you've been working with a Unix or Linux system as you've gone through this book—and I dearly hope that you have—then you might have been curious about why you have icons, menus, and all sorts of other neat whiz-bang interface features on your display but we've been focused exclusively on the command line. The answer is simple: Many more Unix users work through an ssh connection than have a Unix or Linux system on their desktop. I haven't had a full-blown Unix system (other than a Mac) on my desk for at least 10 years, but I work with three different Unix and Linux servers every single day through the Internet.

It wouldn't be fair or reasonable to completely ignore the graphical world of Unix, however, particularly since it's improved so much in the past few years. I remember 20+ years ago when the folks at the Massachusetts Institute of Technology created a system called Project Athena and built a networked graphical interface layer on Unix called the X Window System. It was a huge evolutionary step, but X still had to go through many iterations and evolutionary hops before it got to the smooth, well-integrated and flexible graphical user interface (GUI) we know today as X11.

One interesting feature of the X architecture is that it separates out the fundamental requirements of a graphical windowing system from the bells and whistles of the interface particulars (color, typeface, icon pictures, etc.). As a result, dozens of different *window managers* have come and gone as the interface has become more sophisticated, more powerful, and more flexible. The two contenders for most popular window manager on X11 nowadays are the K Desktop Environment, known more informally as KDE, and the GNU Network Object Model Environment, thankfully known more informally as GNOME.

The trends are clear, however, and GNOME is going to emerge as the winner, the de facto standard window manager and, really, the user's experience of the X11 windowing environment, so that's what I'm going to focus on in this last hour.

GNOME and its partner X11 are distributed with a wide variety of Unix and Linux operating systems, and almost all flavors of Unix now have GNOME as the default window manager, too, notably including Oracle's Solaris and Red Hat's Fedora. Our reference OS for this book, Solaris 11, also ships with GNOME (version 2.30.2) as the default window manager.

In this hour, you'll take a quick visual tour of the GNOME environment, during which you'll see how to change the display configuration and how to work with the menu system. You'll even take a peek at a few really slick GNOME applications.

There's quite a lot you can do within the X11 and GNOME environment, as you might expect, so the focus of this last hour is on fundamental operations rather than exhaustive details. In previous hours, I've emphasized the two or three most important command flags for specific programs, and I'll be using the same philosophy herein to determine what should or shouldn't be shown. For just about every GNOME application, you can press F1 and get help. Do so, and you'll learn a lot more about how things work.

Tweaking Your Inner GNOME

Since the GUI isn't always a core part of Unix distributions, sometimes it's necessary to fiddle and prod to get the configuration you want on your computer. While the X11 side of things can be a bit arcane, GNOME is easy to fine-tune once you have it running.

Task 24.1: Fine-tuning Your GNOME Configuration

As in any other graphical environment, half the fun of working with GNOME is in fiddling and tuning its user environment to meet your own needs and desires. In the old days, altering the appearance or default programs included with GNOME was a complete nightmare that involved editing confusing configuration files that would break X11 entirely if you had a single missed punctuation mark or stray space. Fortunately, those days are long gone, and GNOME has just as many graphical configuration tools as your favorite Windows or Mac environment.

Of course, you won't need to make dozens of adjustments to get it to work just right, but it's useful (and fun) to know some of the capabilities, so let's take a brief tour.

1. The GNOME internal configuration tools are surprisingly friendly and helpful, and they can be reached by choosing Desktop -> Preferences (or System -> Preferences), as shown in Figure 24.1.

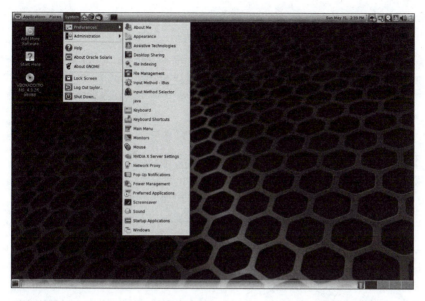

FIGURE 24.1
GNOME offers many different configuration options.

I'll choose Appearance so you can see how easy it is to configure your GNOME desktop. The Appearance Preferences window shown in Figure 24.2 appears.

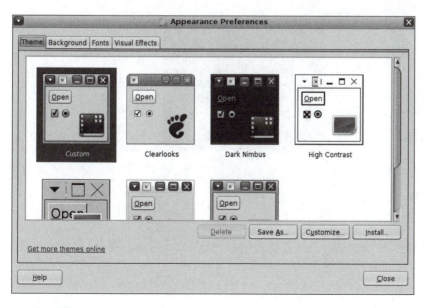

FIGURE 24.2
Fine-tuning the GNOME Theme preferences.

I'll select Sunrise, Beauty of Nature from Google's license-free wallpaper archive, and you'll see that in the screenshots later in this hour.

2. Another preference worth adjusting is the screensaver, and GNOME includes lots and lots of fun screensavers, I'm glad to report. Of course, you probably don't actually *need* a screensaver with modern screen and monitor design, but with so many choices, why not?

TIP

You might be presented with a window that says "The XScreenSaver daemon doesn't seem to be running on display :0.0. Launch it now?" when you try to adjust your screensaver settings. If you get this dialog, click OK: This daemon is a small application that launches the screensaver when necessary.

Whether or not you choose a graphical screensaver, one very important option to notice in the configuration screen shown in Figure 24.3 is "Lock Screen After X minutes," which is a very helpful security tool, particularly if you're in a public environment. With this setting enabled, after the specified number of idle minutes, the screensaver launches and requires your account password to return to the desktop environment.

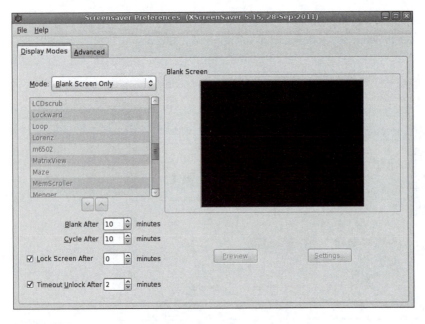

FIGURE 24.3
Check your Screensaver Preferences settings to ensure that the system locks after a few minutes. You'll thank me later, especially if you work in a computer lab.

The Advanced tab of the Screensaver Preferences dialog also offers a number of useful options, particularly for laptop Unix or Linux users, as shown in Figure 24.4.

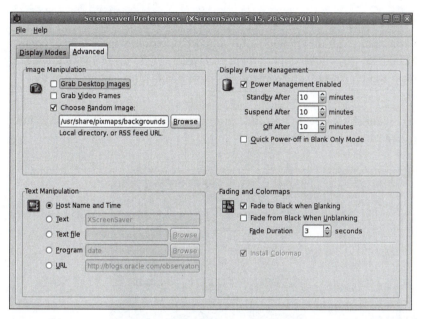

FIGURE 24.4
Advanced Screensaver Preferences settings help you save power and more!

I only enable power management when I'm using a mobile system, but there's really no reason not to have your system standby after an hour or more of inactivity, just to save power if nothing else. Here Standby is the time until the monitor goes black, Suspend is the time until the monitor itself goes into a power-saving mode (if supported), and Off is the time until the monitor is shut down completely.

There's no better demonstration of the power and professionalism of the GNOME interface than the fact that everything you could seek to customize can be easily modified through a friendly, logical, and intuitive graphical window. Whether you need to fine-tune your screen resolution, adjust your mouse controls, or enable a fun new screensaver, GNOME lets you make the changes you need without fuss or hassle.

Working with GNOME Applications

Adjusting the GNOME interface itself is fun and interesting, but just as Windows isn't much use without some applications, GNOME isn't going to get you very far just on its own. The key applications for productivity in this realm are a file system browser, a Web browser, and an email application.

Task 24.2: Working with the GNOME File Browser

In Unix you can do everything with the command line, and we've certainly spent a lot of pages in this book talking about cd, ls, and so on, but there's an easier way to interact with the file system, manage folders, rename things, and generally work with your Unix system. Enter the GNOME File Browser.

   1. The fastest way to launch the File Browser in a known place is to click on the Places menu, as shown in Figure 24.5.

FIGURE 24.5
Where would you like to start exploring your file system today?

   2. Choose File System as your starting point, and a grid of tiny folder icons appears, along with one or two system files, as shown in Figure 24.6.

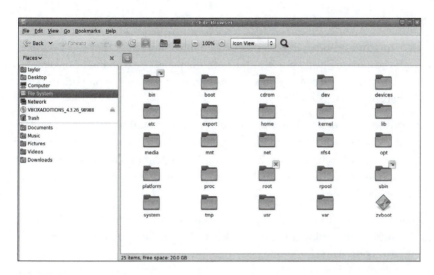

FIGURE 24.6
The easy way to explore your file system is with the GNOME File Browser.

Notice at the top of Figure 24.6 the menu that says Icon View. Click on it and choose List View instead. This gives you a big change in screen, as shown in Figure 24.7, and it's probably easier to work with if you're becoming a hard-core Unix expert.

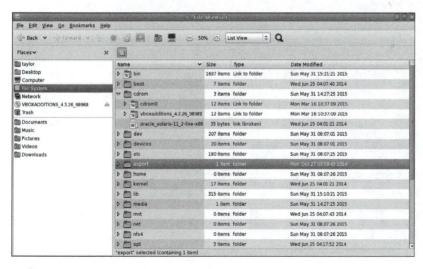

FIGURE 24.7
Super-helpful list view in the GNOME File Browser.

There's a lot you can do to customize and make changes to the file system through the GNOME File Browser. Experiment and click on the various menus to see what options are available. You'll be impressed!

Task 24.3: The Firefox Web Browser

If I were to keep track of my time on a per-application basis, I'm willing to bet that I spend more time in my Web browser than in any other application, with the possible exception of my email program. Even as I write this book and spend hours fine-tuning my prose and explanations, I still notice that I spend lots of time surfing the Web.

Since much of the modern Internet grew out of the Unix platform, it should be no surprise that Unix, and particularly the GNOME and X11 environment, offers support for a number of power-ful and capable Web browsers. It doesn't support Internet Explorer or Apple Safari, but that's okay because Firefox is a top-notch browser, available for all modern operating systems, and a good fit for the GNOME environment.

1. I don't know about how you surf the Web, but as a prolific blogger, I spend a lot of time reading news sites and other weblog sites. My favorite tool for reading online news is Google News, at news.google.com.

TIP

I don't have space to explain blogging here, but I write about it in depth at www.askdavetaylor. com. Also, if you're curious about my weblogs, Ask Dave Taylor is one of 'em, and I also have a film review site at http://www.DaveOnFilm.com and a parenting blog at http://GoFatherhood.com. You're invited to check them all out.

You can see the latest news according to Google News in Figure 24.8.

FIGURE 24.8
Firefox offers a powerful Web browser. Here I'm viewing the latest news on Google News.

2. You can also customize your Firefox experience, including setting a new home page and changing fonts, colors, languages, and much, much more. Choose Edit -> Preferences and you too can be a mad scientist!

    One of the most powerful capabilities of Firefox is its extensible plug-in architecture. There are dozens of different add-on utilities that you can download and install to expand the capabilities of your Web browser—capabilities that'll make you shake your head with sympathy for any poor Windows user who is trapped having to use Microsoft Internet Explorer.

You can learn a lot about Firefox—and download a version of Firefox for Windows or Mac systems—at the informative website www.getfirefox.com. If you haven't yet experienced this alternative browser, you need to head to this site and download the application for your computer today. You won't regret it.

Task 24.4: Using Thunderbird for Email

Earlier I talked about the amount of time I spend in different applications, and I commented that I spend lots of time in my Web browser. That's certainly true, but the majority of my computer time goes to email, actually, and I spend countless hours—heck, probably weeks each year—sending and answering email messages. If we include the ceaseless flow of spam, I get more than 1,000 messages each day. (Thank goodness for some good spam-filtering technologies!)

In the Unix world, there's no program more important to me than a good email program, and while I wrote my own email program many years ago (the Elm Mail System, as discussed in Hour 20, "Using Email to Communicate"), my needs for an email app have increased significantly since that was in development, and today I find that there are only a handful of applications that have the support I need for multiple accounts, multiple signatures, HTML format email, attachment decoding, IMAP, and so much more.

Fortunately, two of the best applications are available for the Unix/Linux/GNOME environment: Thunderbird (which is from the same group that produces Mozilla Firefox) and Evolution. For this very quick tour, let's just have a brief look at Thunderbird.

1. The first and most important task with an email program is configuring it to work with your Internet service provider, including incoming and outbound email servers, your own account name and email address, and so on.

    Thunderbird includes a configuration wizard that makes this first step easy to accomplish, so it shouldn't be more than a minute or two before you're ready to go, with your mailbox incorporated into the program, too, if there's anything in your server mailbox.

I just used my Google Gmail account. I easily entered the address and password and had Thunderbird automatically pick up all my pending mail and a list of my folders and my contacts list. It was remarkably fast and easy.

Once you have everything configured and have a few messages in your mailbox, you'll see a mailbox view similar to that shown in Figure 24.9.

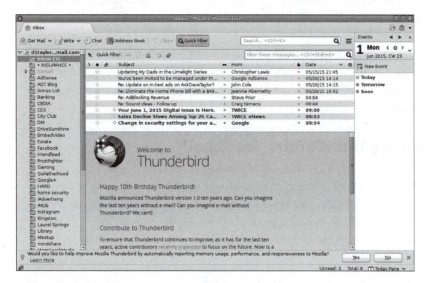

FIGURE 24.9
Thunderbird is an attractive and powerful email application.

2. Composing email is straightforward, too, with a sophisticated address book (Thunderbird can automatically pull in configuration and addresses information from a variety of different programs, including an IMAP-based system like Gmail or Yahoo Mail) and a composition window that's identical to its Windows and Mac email brethren, as illustrated in Figure 24.10.

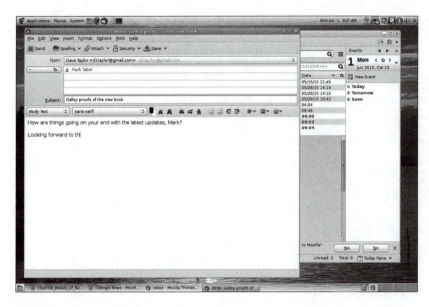

FIGURE 24.10
Composing a new email message in Thunderbird.

3. Just like Firefox, Thunderbird also has a zillion configuration and preference settings that you'll want to explore and tweak to meet your own preferred way of interacting with the program and your email, as shown in Figure 24.11.

And here's a bonus productivity tip: Change the settings to have Thunderbird check for new email less frequently than you prefer. Having fewer interruptions directly translates to greater efficiency and productivity in your work day.

Thunderbird demonstrates again the power of the open source community. This freely downloaded email application has many of the most important capabilities of commercial applications like Microsoft Outlook and an interface just as slick as Apple Mail. It might take a few hours to really master the program and configure it exactly as you need, but Thunderbird and the other popular open source Unix alternative, Evolution, are both excellent choices for your day-to-day electronic mail and communications.

TIP

You can learn more about Evolution at the OpenOffice website—www.openoffice.org—and you can learn more about Thunderbird at the Mozilla site—www.mozilla.org.

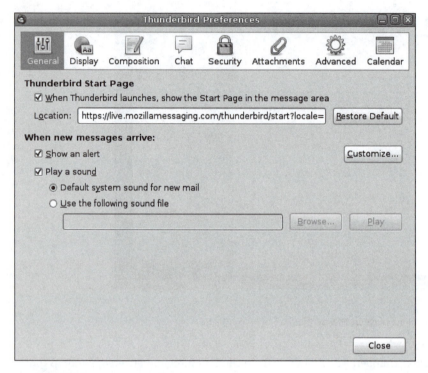

FIGURE 24.11
Lots and lots of preferences to tweak and tune in Thunderbird.

Summary

GNOME and the X11 system form the foundation of the twenty-first-century Unix experience, offering a graphical interface that's comparable in both features and ease of use to the best that Microsoft's Windows and Apple's Macintosh can offer. You can't go to the local computer store to get GNOME applications, but that's because they're probably already included on your system or available for the cost of a free download.

Congratulations!

You've gotten through the entire book, all 24 hours, and you're now a bona fide Unix expert. If you follow up by using the system as much as possible for a few weeks, you'll find that the commands, option flags, and pipes all begin to come naturally. Having used Unix in various flavors for over 30 years (it's hard for me to believe, but I first logged in as a freshman in college, back in 1980!), I can assure you that the reason Unix hasn't changed dramatically is that it's just so darn powerful, comprehensive, and useful.

The time you spend learning to become a Unix power user will be time very well spent, whether you're aiming at becoming an OS kernel hacker or simply want to be able to make the shared Web server on which you have an account jump through hoops.

Thanks for spending your time learning Unix with me! Feel free to pop over to Ask Dave Taylor (www.AskDaveTaylor.com) if you have any questions about Unix. And don't forget to stop by the official book website for scripts you can download and any errata reported by eagle-eyed readers like yourself (www.intuitive.com/tyu24). Please always feel free to drop me a note if want to let me know if you found this book helpful. You can reach me at d1taylor@gmail.com.

Workshop

The Workshop summarizes the key terms you've learned and poses some questions about the topics presented in this lesson.

Key Terms

blog   A blog (short for weblog) is a type of website that's built around a software tool that allows the user to easily add frequent, date-stamped entries and keep the website up-to-date.

blogger   A blogger is someone who writes entries on a weblog, or blog.

skin   *Skin* is jargon for the necessary graphics, icons, fonts, and similar needed to change the appearance, but not the functionality, of a graphical software application.

window manager   A window manager is a program that controls the windows within a graphical user interface environment. In the X11 world, GNOME is a popular window manager.

Exercises

1. Launch GNOME and get it working on your computer if you haven't already done so. Now, change the screensaver so that after 15 minutes of inactivity, it will prompt you for a password before you can use the system again.

2. Using Firefox, head over to Google's News service and give this way to keep track of breaking news a whirl. While you're at it, go through all the different Firefox preferences screens and see what you might want to tweak for your own tastes.

3. Configure and run an email program within GNOME. Send me a test message from the Thunderbird (or Evolution) program to confirm that you have everything working well. Don't forget to say "hi," too, while you're at it!

Common Unix Questions and Answers

There are hundreds of questions and answers buried in this book, ranging from "What's the right combination of flags to get a specific command to do something useful?" to "What commands work best in a given situation?" Further, learning Linux or Unix in only 24 one-hour lessons is a difficult task to accomplish, so you wouldn't be alone if you're a bit overwhelmed and are hitting the occasional speedbump on your road to becoming a true Unix guru.

That's why we included this appendix: so you would have quick answers to some of the most common Unix questions. These questions are compiled both from my experience working with Unix neophytes and the many Unix- and Linux-related questions that have been submitted to my Ask Dave Taylor website, online at www.askdavetaylor.com.

Without further ado...

How do I use `find|xargs` with filenames that contain spaces?

It's incredibly puzzling trying to figure out why you're seeing weird "file not found" errors when you're using the `find` command. Here's a typical example:

```
$ find ./test -print
./test
./test/Sample One
./test/Sample Three too
./test/Sample-Two
```

There's nothing unusual or confusing in this output, but notice that two of the files have spaces in their names, so when the `find` output is fed to `xargs`, bad things happen:

```
$ find ./test -print | xargs ls -l
ls: ./test/Sample: No such file or directory
ls: ./test/Sample: No such file or directory
ls: One: No such file or directory
ls: Three: No such file or directory
ls: too: No such file or directory
-rw-r--r--  1 taylor  staff  0 31 May 23:03 ./test/Sample-Two

./test:
```

```
total 0
-rw-r--r--  1 taylor   staff   0 31 May 23:03 Sample One
-rw-r--r--  1 taylor   staff   0 31 May 23:03 Sample Three too
-rw-r--r--  1 taylor   staff   0 31 May 23:03 Sample-Two
```

The problem is that `xargs` is blindly using spaces as field delimiters, meaning that `./test/Sample One` is actually being seen as `./test/Sample` and `One`, neither of which actually exist in the file system, as shown in the error message output.

Fortunately, the fix is easy: Use the `find` predicate `-print0` instead of `-print` to instruct `find` to expect spaces in the filenames and then make sure you also use the `-0` (zero) flag to `xargs`, which tells it that filenames aren't separated by spaces but rather by a special control character:

```
$ find ./test -print0 | xargs -0 ls -l
-rw-r--r--  1 taylor   staff   0 31 May 23:03 ./test/Sample One
-rw-r--r--  1 taylor   staff   0 31 May 23:03 ./test/Sample Three too
-rw-r--r--  1 taylor   staff   0 31 May 23:03 ./test/Sample-Two

./test:
total 0
-rw-r--r--  1 taylor   staff   0 31 May 23:03 Sample One
-rw-r--r--  1 taylor   staff   0 31 May 23:03 Sample Three too
-rw-r--r--  1 taylor   staff   0 31 May 23:03 Sample-Two
```

How do I find large files on my system?

Your file system is starting to fill up, and you really want to quickly identify the 10 or 20 largest files on the system so you can trim them, delete them, or whatever. This is a job for the `find` command again, this time using a slight variation of what's shown in the previous question.

You can search the entire file system by using / as the file argument, or you can search your own home directory by using `cd` to move into your home directory and then using the following:

```
$ find . -type f -print0 | xargs -0 ls -s | sort -rn | head -5
227064 ./Audio/TheE-MythRevisitedUn_mp332.aa
217056 ./Audio/Parent Night.aif
163488 ./Audio/Older Parent Night.aif
114384 ./Audio/Rahima Keynote.aif
104608 ./Audio/African Singing.aif
```

Notice that we've constrained the `find` to only match files, not directories, by using the `-type f` predicate, and then notice that instead of `ls -l` we use the more succinct (and more easily sorted numerically) `ls -s` instead.

Finding the five largest files on the entire file system would require this invocation:

```
find / -type f -print0 | xargs -0 ls -s | sort -rn | head -5
```

Remember that this'll take rather a while to run: It's probably going to list and sort more than 100,000 files on a typical Unix or Linux system.

How do I run a program on a schedule?

There are two different utilities in Unix that let you schedule execution of a program some time in the future.

The `at` Command

If you only want to do it *once* in the future, then use the `at` command:

```
$ at
usage: at [-q x] [-f file] [-m] time
       at -c job [job ...]
       at [-f file] -t [[CC]YY]MMDDhhmm[.SS]
       at -r job [job ...]
       at -l -q queuename
       at -l [job ...]
       atq [-q x] [-v]
       atrm job [job ...]
       batch [-f file] [-m]
```

For example, to run a script called `fixperms` tomorrow at 3 a.m., you can use the command

```
at 3am tomorrow fixperms
```

The man page has more information about this slick command.

cron

The other possibility, and the scheduling program that's used quite a bit more often on Unix systems, is `cron`, known also as `crontab` for the name of the file it executes. Every 60 seconds on your Unix system, the OS has the `cron` daemon check to see if any new commands need to be invoked.

Unfortunately, writing `crontab` entries can be a wee bit tricky, but here's a prototypical entry in a user's crontab, added by invoking the command `crontab -e`:

```
51 7 * * 1-5            $TRIVIAHOME/mailit -h -i -a
```

The fields in a `crontab` entry are, in order, minute, hour, day of month, month, day of week, command with optional flags or parameters. Asterisks in fields indicate that all possible values of that field are matched, so this `crontab` entry should be read as "at 7:15 a.m. on Monday through Friday (1-5 in field 5) of any day of the month or month of the year, run the `mailit` program with the -h, -i, and -a flags."

After having worked with Unix for many years, I find the `crontab` facility invaluable and typically have dozens of different scripts, programs, and utilities scheduled to run at different times of the day, week, month, or year. Heck, you can even use it for critical birthday reminders if you need to!

TIP

Mac systems and all Linux systems also have `cron`, which means you can easily have recurring programs or scripts on those systems, too.

Learn more at `man crontab`.

How do I fix file permission problems?

If you're seeing file permission problems, almost always the `chmod` command will fix the issue, but remember that sometimes it can be the permission of the directory *above the current directory* that's causing trouble. Use `ls -l` to ensure that your permissions are as you think and then use `id` to ensure that you're logged in to the account you think you are logged into. If needed, use `chmod` to change permissions so you have read, write, or execute permission, as needed.

How do I list files that don't match a given pattern?

This is an interesting question because it's easy to list files that match a given pattern by using `grep`, right? To match all files that contain the pattern `"Bill Gates"`, for example, you'd use the following, which would list the filenames that match the specified pattern:

```
grep -li "Bill Gates" *
```

To reverse the logic of this search, use the `-v` flag to `grep`:

```
grep -vli "Bill Gates" *
```

This will list the names of all files that *do not* contain the specified pattern. Sorry, Bill!

How do I view lines *X–Y* in a text file?

There are a bunch of ways you can pull out a snippet of content from a text file. The most common, though not the most efficient, is to use a combination of `head` and `tail` to chop out the desired piece. If you wanted lines 170–180, for example, use this:

```
cat -n infile | head -180 | tail -10
```

If you don't care about line numbers, though, there's a much more efficient solution, using the handy sed command:

```
cat -n infile | sed -n '170,180p'
```

This is quickly and easily done. In fact, if you don't want the line numbers, you can be even more succinct:

```
sed -n '170,180p' infile
```

By the way, the -n flag to sed stops its default behavior of echoing every line it sees to standard output (for example, the screen).

How do I add a new directory to my PATH?

If you're running bash, sh, or a variant shell, then you can add a new directory to your PATH, where directories are colon separated, by doing this:

```
export PATH="${PATH}:newdir"
```

For example, to add /usr /X11/bin to your path, use this:

```
export PATH="${PATH}:/usr/X11/bin"
```

You can also put the new directory in the front of the PATH by changing the order of the fields:

```
export PATH="/usr/X11/bin:${PATH}"
```

If you're in C shell or a variant, then your syntax is slightly different:

```
setenv PATH "${PATH}:/usr/X11/bin"
```

In either case, if you want the change to be permanent, go into your ~/.login or ~/.profile (csh and bash, respectively) and either tweak the existing PATH specification or add the appropriate line, as shown above.

For example, here's what's in my own ~/.profile:

```
export PATH="${PATH}:/sw/bin:/usr/X11R6/bin:/Users/taylor/bin";
```

How do I recover deleted files?

Ah, well, you can't recover deleted files. Unix doesn't have that sort of useful capability. That's why you have to take *extra care when deleting files*!

Also make sure that you're using at least a rudimentary backup strategy and saving everything on your system once a week, if not more frequently.

How can I set my shell to protect me from accidental deletions?

The key to having some protection from accidentally overwriting files is to use the `noclobber` setting to your shell when you log in. This is typically done by including `set noclobber` in your `.profile` or `.login`.

Here's what can happen if you don't have it set:

```
$ touch Bcareful
$ ls > Bcareful
$
```

Without `noclobber` set, I've just overwritten an existing file! Once it's specified, however, things work a bit better:

```
$ ls > Bcareful
bash: Bcareful: cannot overwrite existing file
```

It's still not perfect, but it's helpful nonetheless.

What do the shell errors `arg list too long` and `broken pipe` mean?

With a `broken pipe` error, you have lots and lots of data being sent from one command to the next, but the latter command stops accepting information after a certain amount of time. A typical example would be piping thousands of lines of output to a command like `tail -5`, which stops reading its input after five lines are displayed. It's typically nothing to worry about.

The other error, `arg list too long`, happens when you have lots of files in a directory, for example, and using * as a generic wildcard produces an expanded command line that's longer than the shell can deal with.

This is an error to be concerned about. If you see `arg list too long`, you need to figure out what's gone wrong and fix it to ensure that the commands or scripts are working as you expect. A typical solution would be to use the patterns `[a-m]*` and `[n-z]*` to split the wildcard match into two different sets of filenames.

Why use `ssh` instead of `telnet`? Or `sftp` instead of `ftp`?

How much would it bother you if someone else broke into your account and rummaged around, copied and decoded your password file, or perhaps defaced your website? Probably a lot. So do yourself a favor and make sure to always use the secure, encrypted remote login program `ssh` rather than `telnet` whenever possible, and if you need to transfer files between two systems, always try to use `sftp` rather than `ftp` for exactly the same reasons.

Oh, and don't forget, this goes *double* with public networks, like an open Wi-Fi hotspot!

Summary

There ya go. Frequently asked Unix questions. Are they the right questions and answers based on your own experience learning Unix? Send me a message and let me know!

Index

Learning Labs!

Learn online with videos, live code editing, and quizzes

SPECIAL 50% OFF – Introductory Offer
Discount Code: STYLL50

FOR A LIMITED TIME, we are offering readers of **Sams Teach Yourself** books a **50% OFF** discount to **ANY online Learning Lab** through Dec 15, 2015.

Visit informit.com/learninglabs to see available labs, try out full samples, and order today.

- **Read** the complete text of the book online in your web browser

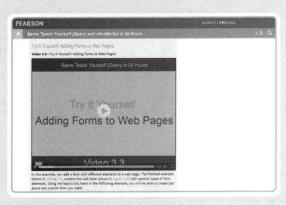

- **Watch** an expert instructor show you how to perform tasks in easy-to-follow videos

- **Try** your hand at coding in an interactive code-editing sandbox in select products

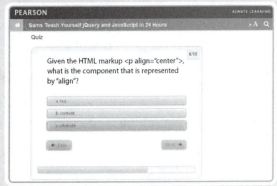

- **Test** yourself with interactive quizzes

33164100014799